11-09

The
Soldier of
Fortune
Murders

The Soldier of Fortune Murders

A TRUE STORY OF OBSESSIVE LOVE AND MURDER-FOR-HIRE

BEN GREEN

Delacorte
Press

Published by
Delacorte Press
Bantam Doubleday Dell Publishing Group, Inc.
666 Fifth Avenue
New York, New York 10103

Library of Congress Cataloging in Publication Data

Green, Ben, 1951–
    The *Soldier of fortune* murders: a true story of obsessive love and murder-for-hire/by Ben Green.
        p.   cm.
    ISBN 0-385-29940-0 (hc): $20.00
    1. Hearn, John Wayne. 2. Murderers—United States—Biography. I. Title.
HV6248.H37G74   1992
364.1'523'092—dc20
    [B]   91-17623
                                                                                                    CIP

Manufactured in the United States of America

Published simultaneously in Canada

January 1992

10 9 8 7 6 5 4 3 2 1

RRH

For the children who survived.
May they yet prevail.

ACKNOWLEDGMENTS

I owe a debt of gratitude to the many people who shared their stories with me. For many of them, I know that those interviews brought back painful memories.

I am equally grateful to the people who gave me access to vast quantities of court documents, investigative records and research materials, without which this story would have not been nearly so interesting or detailed. In particular, I wish to thank the following: David Menconi of the Boulder *Daily Camera;* Wiley Clark of the Florida State Attorney's office; Farnell Cole and Charlie Sanders of the Alachua County Sheriff's Department; Johnny Kearns; Judge Tom Elwell; Sheriff Ronnie Miller of the Brazos County Sheriff's Department; Bill Turner; Karen Heck; Laurie Bessinger and Frances X. Archibald of the South Carolina Department of Corrections; John Cason; former U.S. Congressman Bill Grant; and Dan Linder.

I also want to thank Joy Ellen Peace, Kelly Hoover, and my sister, Carol Green, for their help in completing the manuscript; Kim Maddox, for her valuable editorial suggestions; John Leach, for his fatherly advice; Harvey Kahn, who approached me about this project in the first place; my agent, Elizabeth Grossman, who steered me safely through it; my editor, Brian DeFiore; and Suzanne Telsey, Delacorte's attorney. Finally, I want to thank my wife, Tracie Schneider, who endured my compulsive behavior in finishing this book, and bought me a time clock to use on future ones.

AUTHOR'S NOTE

This is a true story. All of the events and conversations in this book have been reconstructed from court testimony, sworn depositions, investigative records, and my own extensive interviews with over 125 participants in the story.

As in any such story, there are sometimes conflicting accounts of a particular event. In those cases, I have chosen the version that, in my opinion, appeared to be most reliable and verifiable.

In a few instances, I have used aliases to protect innocent people, particularly children, whose lives would be needlessly disrupted by the publication of this book.

INTRODUCTION

Frankly, this story scares me to death.

It is a gruesome tale of three murders-for-hire—two in Florida, and one in Texas—that were as senseless as they were brutal. These were not crimes of passion, but of greed.

It is also a story about a magazine, *Soldier of Fortune*, that—incredible as it may seem—actually published classified ads for hit men. Whether it was done knowingly or not is still being debated in court, but what is undisputed is that these hit men advertised their services in a national publication, in some cases even listing their real names and phone numbers, and committed over two dozen felonies, including five murders. These are the *known* crimes —the ones that were discovered. How many others *may* have been committed, and remain undetected, will never be known.

Even more alarming, perhaps, this is a story about the people who responded by the *hundreds* to those ads (one ad alone generated ten to twenty phone calls per day). Who were these people? Some were kooks, obviously. Some may have been spooks (there are allegations of CIA and FBI involvement). But most, unfortunately, were "regular folks"—husbands and wives and neighbors of yours and mine—who rang the phone off the hook, calling at all hours of the day or night, requesting *every* imaginable crime: murder, kidnapping, political assassination, buying and selling illegal weapons, smuggling guns to the Nicaraguan *contras,* bombing the Baghwan Shree Rajneesh camp in Oregon, overthrowing foreign governments, to name just a few.

This story takes place in a world I've tried to isolate myself from in every way I can: I'm not a crime writer, I don't read murder mysteries, I avoid scary movies. It took weeks for me to decide to write the book, and months to finally reconcile that decision in my own mind. If the going price was $10,000 for killing a spouse and $5,000 for a mother-in-law, I wondered how much would it be for a writer. Two dollars and change?

Eight years ago, when I began writing my first book, I went out and bought a new ream of typing paper. Four years later, when I started my second book, I bought a new box of floppy disks. In 1989, when I started *this* book, I took my name out of the phone book and rented a post office box.

I haven't pretended to be a hardened police-beat reporter who's "seen this kind of thing a hundred times before." This was the *first* time I had seen "this kind of thing"—8-by-10 glossy crime-scene photos and autopsy reports about brain tissue with the "consistency of freshly ground meat"—and my own reactions have undoubtedly colored the writing of the book.

I care much less about bullet trajectories and the caliber of murder weapons than I do about the motivations and personalities of the characters in this story, and my approach reflects that. Police investigators and prosecutors look for a motive to explain *whodunit* —but this book is not a *whodunit,* it's a *how-could-they-have-done-it.*

Despite its gruesomeness, this is also an incredible love story —a love story that reminds us of what people are capable of, both for evil *and* for good. There are examples of sick, obsessive, deadly love—the kind of love that makes a person kill another human being. But more than that, it's a story about the love of two mothers for their children, and how these two women have dealt with the greatest tragedies that any mothers could ever face: the murder of a child, and a child who murders.

And ultimately, isn't tragedy a part of all the great love stories? If the gruesomeness of the story initially repelled me, it was the personalities that brought me back to it, and the love of these two mothers that inspired me.

Finally, this is a story with broad social and political implications. Most of those advertising their services in *Soldier of Fortune* magazine were Vietnam vets—and so were many of those who called them—which raises disturbing questions about this nation's continuing struggle to come to grips with that war and the men who fought it.

There are striking examples of how the ritual of war has been passed down from father to son in this culture: men whose childhoods were defined by their fathers' experiences in World War II and whose adult lives were framed by their own experiences in Vietnam. Their lives are testaments to the American infatuation with the warrior—from John Wayne to GI Joe to Rambo—and its effect on male conditioning.

The scope and richness of the story are enormous. It encompasses three murders, a criminal investigation spanning four states, and a multimillion dollar lawsuit against *Soldier of Fortune* magazine that generated profound First Amendment questions and political repercussions reaching all the way to the Reagan White House.

Luckily, much of it took place in my own backyard, culturally —in small towns in north Florida and east central Texas—where being a "local boy" rather than a big-city journalist, or worse still, a big-city *Yankee* journalist, proved helpful in gaining access to people and understanding the nuances of their lives.

The benchmark of whether I do justice to the story will be whether I avoid reducing it to a black-and-white morality play. This book cannot be a repeat of *In Cold Blood,* which was a portrait of murder in the American heartland in a much simpler time. Instead, it must embrace the ironies and paradoxes that, more than ever, now define the American spirit.

Part One

STEEP HOLLOW

February 21, 1985

1

"I LOVE YOU very much, Mother" are the last words Sandra Black says before driving home.

"I love you too, Sandra," Marjorie Eimann calls back from her front porch, where she is observing the last few moments of daylight on a dreary winter day on the prairies of east central Texas.

At the time, Marjorie thinks nothing of Sandra's farewell. It is the way her daughter says good-bye every afternoon before leaving Happy Face Nursery, the day-care center they started together in 1976, in the house next door to Marjorie's. It will only be later this evening—when Marjorie hears the commotion outside, hears her dog barking, and opens the door to find her son, Larry Eimann, and eight of her nine brothers and sisters there on the porch—that Sandra's "I love you very much, Mother" will be etched forever in her mind.

At this point, as Marjorie Eimann watches her only daughter start up the new Chevy van that her husband, Bob Black, leased for her two months before—another extravagant proffer of Bob's reborn love and commitment—all she notices is that Sandra is in a big rush to get home.

In fact, Sandra is running very late. Bob called her at five o'clock this afternoon to ask sweetly, "Honey, when are you coming home?" It was another sign of the "new Bob" who had first appeared at Christmas—or, more accurately, the "old Bob": the charming, dashing marine whom Sandra had married on Christmas Eve, 1967—before Vietnam, before the fits of anger and depression, before all the times he'd left her, and before his woman-

3

izing. This was the Bob that Sandra had fallen in love with, and perhaps *still* loved—or at least still wanted to believe when he promised her that *this* time he had really changed. Four months earlier, when her best friend had encouraged her to finally go through with her divorce, Sandra had said, "I just wish you'd known Bob before Vietnam."

When Bob called, Sandra told him that she'd be home by six o'clock; but it is nearly six now, and she still has a twenty-minute drive to Bark-n-Holler, their country home in Steep Hollow.

Marjorie Eimann isn't surprised to see her daughter rushing. Sandra is always in a hurry, trying to balance the demands of the day-care center with full-time mothering of Gary Wayne, her fifteen-year-old son, whom she is always rushing to drop off or pick up from somewhere—track practice in the spring, football practice in the fall, Boy Scout events all year long—before hurrying home to try to salvage her marriage and squeeze in time for her animals, the one great love she's had since childhood. Sandra raises purebred German shepherds and owns two horses.

This evening Sandra is rushing more than usual because Thursday is "dog night," when she attends a dog training class at Action Dogs USA. On top of that, Gary Wayne is sick with bronchitis. When Sandra arrived at Happy Face at seven-thirty this morning, she told Marjorie that Gary Wayne had spiked a fever and that she was keeping him home from school; and she asked Marjorie to look after him. Of course, Marjorie agreed, although Bob isn't working and could have easily looked after him. But Marjorie is accustomed to keeping Gary Wayne whenever he is sick or out of school, or when Bob has taken off again.

Today, the boy was in rough shape, with a terrible hacking cough and a 104-degree fever. At lunch-time, Sandra took him to see Dr. O.C. Cooper, who X-rayed his chest to make sure the bronchitis wasn't turning into pneumonia and prescribed two antibiotics.

Gary Wayne spent the afternoon sleeping in Marjorie's back bedroom. He was still in bed when Bob showed up unannounced at five-thirty and told Marjorie that he was taking Gary Wayne with him to buy a clutch cable for the boy's three-wheel motorcycle. Bob already had the three-wheeler loaded in the back of his El Camino pickup, parked out front.

Marjorie Eimann is accustomed to Bob Black doing unusual things, but this seemed strange even for him. The three-wheeler, which Bob made for Gary Wayne on his twelfth birthday, masterfully welding the frame out of a Yamaha motorcycle, has been broken for *months,* even before Bob ran off to California last summer, returning home only two weeks before Sandra's divorce was to become final. Why Bob suddenly has to fix the three-wheeler *this* afternoon, dragging Gary Wayne around town when the boy is running a fever, is beyond her.

Marjorie begged Bob to leave Gary Wayne with her, to even let him spend the night, but Bob insisted, saying, "I want the kid." So Marjorie backed down. Bob is the boy's father, after all, and Marjorie tries not to interfere in Sandra's marriage.

She followed Bob and Gary Wayne outside, still urging Bob to get Gary Wayne home to bed, then sat down on her porch. Normally, she would be next door at the day-care, greeting Happy Face parents as they come to pick up their kids, but it is late and most of the parents have already come. Marjorie sat down on the front step of her tiny concrete stoop, to wait for Sandra.

It is not a pleasant afternoon to sit outside. Although temperatures were in the mid-seventies earlier in the week—a harbinger of spring—this afternoon it is damp and overcast. Still, Marjorie always says good-bye to Sandra, so she sits . . . and waits.

Marjorie Eimann is sixty-two years old, short and plump, with a girlish titter of a laugh and a lilting Texas drawl that invites you right in. Her brown hair is flecked with gray. In the next six months it will turn completely white and start falling out in clumps.

This is home to Marjorie Eimann. She's lived in College Station since she was six years old, and here on Winding Road since 1965. It is a quiet neighborhood, with modest brick or asbestos-siding houses nestled in the shadows of Texas A&M University, which is only three blocks away. From her front stoop, Marjorie waves to neighbors returning home from work and to children passing by on their bikes. Over the years, she has kept many of the neighborhood children at Happy Face, including those of Larry Watson, the Brazos County deputy sheriff who lives across the street.

Finally, the last Happy Face parent arrives: Martha Lee, a twenty-one-year-old single mother whose eleven-month-old daughter Kristen is one of five babies in the "infant room." Although Martha is fifteen years younger than Sandra Black, the two women have become best friends, having discovered their common love of dogs and horses. In recent months, they have traveled together to dog shows in Houston and have gone horseback riding around Steep Hollow, where Martha lives too. She also attends dog class on Thursday nights, and sometimes she and Sandra drive out together to Action Dogs USA. But Martha called Sandra earlier this afternoon to say that she was feeling sick and would be late picking up Kristen, and that she wouldn't be going to class. Sandra offered to take Kristen home with *her* for the night, to give Martha a break, but the younger woman demurred. It is a decision that will haunt Martha Lee for years, wondering what might have happened to Kristen if she hadn't.

With Martha so late, Sandra is doubly rushed. Normally, she would have brought Chauncy, the young male shepherd that she is training as an attack dog (for a competition sport called *Schundzend*) with her to Happy Face and would have kept him in Marjorie's backyard so that she could leave straight from work. But this morning Bob asked her to leave Chauncy at home and to come home for supper. It was another example of Bob's new attentiveness—he could be so charming and persuasive when he wanted to be—and Sandra agreed. Now she will really have to fly to get out to Steep Hollow, feed Gary Wayne and Bob, and make it back to Action Dogs USA, ten miles south of College Station on Highway 6.

Marjorie watches Sandra hurry out of the day-care with a bag of groceries. At thirty-six, Sandra looks unnervingly like her mother: She is two inches taller than Marjorie but has the same round face, deep-set brown eyes, and olive complexion. She's wearing designer jeans; a favorite blouse with pink, mauve, and lavender stripes; and New Balance running shoes (which are maroon and white, the colors of Texas A&M University). She and Marjorie have started walking together every day, making a five-mile loop around the exercise trail on the A&M campus, as Sandra is once again trying to lose weight. She is big-boned like her father, Glen Eimann, and has fought a losing battle with her weight ever since she got married, when she weighed 112 pounds—a fact that Bob has never let her forget.

Sandra's weight has been one of the major problems in their marriage, which gets played out in an ugly, self-defeating cycle: Bob ridicules her when she puts on extra pounds, but also ridicules her when she starts dieting. A few sarcastic remarks from him—"You'll always be a fat slob and no one else would ever have you"—had been enough to discourage Sandra in the past, but now she's trying again, and succeeding.

Sandra opens the back door of the van and places the bag of groceries on the top shelf of the rear storage compartment. Inside it are four half-gallon tubs of Blue Bell ice cream (two chocolate chip and two French vanilla) that she bought on sale this morning at Piggly Wiggly after filling Gary Wayne's prescriptions at the K mart next door. Blue Bell ice cream, made in nearby Brenham, her father's hometown, is the pride of Texas and a great favorite of Bob's. Sandra bought the ice cream for him as a special treat, and stored it in the Happy Face deep freeze until now.

Marjorie watches Sandra make another trip inside and return carrying an electric skillet and a smaller pot, in which she has cooked supper for Bob and Gary Wayne: a pot roast, potatoes and gravy, and cream peas from Bob's garden (his specialty, grown from seeds his grandfather gave him). Sandra places the skillet on the bottom shelf of the storage compartment, squeezing it in beside her spare purse and two extra pairs of flats.

The new van is so plush that it hardly seems practical for Sandra, who is always lugging around Chauncy's dog carrier or bags of feed. It's a fully equipped 1985 Chevy van—brown with gold trim, outfitted with ceiling-to-floor carpeting, swiveling captain's chairs, a bar and a television set.

Marjorie thought it odd for Bob to lease it for Sandra when he didn't have a job, but the van is only *one* of *many* things since Bob's return that she doesn't understand. Marjorie and Sandra have always had a close relationship, but many things have happened in the past six months—unbelievable, ungodly, scandalous things—that Sandra hasn't shared with her mother. For instance, Marjorie is only vaguely aware of Bob's torrid love affair with his twenty-eight-year-old first cousin from California, Teresa Heatherington. She doesn't know about Bob's announcement to Sandra last fall that he intended to marry Teresa, or about Teresa's eventual decision to stay with her husband, which sent Bob reeling into a deep depression, culminating in a halfhearted suicide attempt.

All Marjorie Eimann knows is the obvious: that Bob came home in late August and slept at the day-care until October, when Sandra let him move back into the house; that he quit his electrician's job in October and is now studying to become an insurance salesman; and that since Christmas he has apparently been transformed with love for Sandra. The van, the huge diamond he bought her for Christmas, and the beautiful new barn he is building for her horses are proof of that.

Whatever doubts Marjorie still has about Bob, the important thing is that *Sandra* is happy, and there is *no* doubt about that. Sandra seems happier than she has been in years. Marjorie only has to think back to three weeks earlier, when Bob brought a bunch of papers to the day-care for Sandra to sign, and afterward, she bounded into the Happy Face kitchen and said giddily, "Mother, you cannot believe what I just did."

"What in the world did you do now?" Marjorie asked, laughing.

"I just did one of the best things I've ever done in my life," Sandra said. "I just bought a $100,000 life-insurance policy, and it's so much cheaper than my two small policies I'm going to cancel them."

"Well, Sandra, it sounds like you got a good deal," Marjorie said. What else could she say? What better indication could there be of Sandra's confidence in Bob and of their future together than her agreeing to the new insurance policy, which doubled her coverage from $50,000 to $100,000, and even paying for it herself?

At last, Sandra is ready to go. She calls out to three-year-old Aaron Watson, who is playing in his front yard, teasing him about his daddy shooting at blackbirds, then looks up at Marjorie. "I'll see you at seven-thirty in the morning," she calls out.

"I'll be here," Marjorie replies casually.

Then, as Sandra climbs into the van, she says the words that Marjorie will always remember: "I love you very much, Mother."

"I love you too, Sandra," Marjorie says. She watches as Sandra backs out of the driveway, pulls up to the stop sign, turns left onto Holleman Drive, and disappears out of view.

•   •   •

Marjorie Eimann is alone now. Twilight is settling quickly over Winding Road, and the winter sky glows pale red in the west, behind Texas A&M. Marjorie's house is built on the highest point in College Station—not really a hill, but a gentle rise—which catches the cool evening breeze in the summer and the fierce Texas blue northers in the winter. A hundred years ago, this was a staging area for great cattle drives. Here, thousands of Texas longhorns, a wild breed that was rangy and mean enough to survive weeks of hardship on the prairie where domestic breeds could not, had milled together in one last rebellious throng before setting out on their journey to the slaughterhouse. But on this night the ghosts of that wild legacy are nowhere around. There is a chill in the air—it is still winter, after all—and a misty rain has begun to fall. Marjorie Eimann gets up and goes inside, on the last night she will ever enjoy such peace.

2

JOHN WAYNE HEARN sits alone in the living room of Sandra Black's house. Outside, darkness is falling quickly over the barren pastures and fields. Here on Steep Hollow Circle, lights are already on in the other houses. Suppers are on the stove, children are setting the tables, families are sitting down to dinner.

But no lights are on in Sandra Black's house. No supper is on the table. The house, in fact, has been ransacked: furniture overturned, drawers opened and rifled, clothing and papers scattered across the beds and floors. It looks like the work of a common burglar.

But John Wayne Hearn is no burglar. The burly, thirty-eight-year-old Vietnam vet sitting in the darkened living room is a hired assassin, waiting to kill Sandra Black. He was contacted by Bob Black through an ad in *Soldier of Fortune* magazine and offered $10,000 to kill Sandra, to be paid out of her new life insurance policy.

Hearn has been expecting her for nearly an hour. Earlier, after helping Bob Black ransack the house, he stood by glumly while Bob called Sandra at Happy Face to find out when she would be home. Then Bob went into the master bedroom and came out carrying a Ruger .22 pistol, which he handed to Hearn, saying, "Use this one; it's my wife's." Bob Black owns fourteen other guns, including many that are more powerful, but Hearn knows that a .22 is a deadly weapon at close range. A larger-caliber bullet will sometimes blow right through a person so quickly that, if it doesn't hit any vital organs, the victim may survive. But a .22 bullet fired into the head will rattle around the brain cavity, bouncing off bone and tissue and inflicting fatal damage. Sandra Black's .22 now lies on the coffee table in front of him.

If this were a typical gun-for-hire story, we might expect John Wayne Hearn to pass the time until Sandra arrives by checking out this unfamiliar gun: sighting down the barrel, hefting it to get used to the feel and weight, testing the action on the hammer. After all, Hearn, a seven-year Marine Corps veteran who served three tours of duty in Vietnam, is a trained weapons specialist and an expert with exotic weapons like the Winchester 1200, a clip-fed 12-gauge shotgun with a pistol grip, and the AR-7, a compact .22-caliber survival rifle that can be broken down to fit into its own stock. Hearn has committed two other murders in the past forty-five days; one with a Winchester 1200, the other with an AR-7.

Or perhaps, while he waits, he might be reviewing techniques from books he's recently read—*How To Kill, Volume 1* and *Get Even: The Complete Book of Dirty Tricks,* which he ordered out of *Soldier of Fortune* magazine.

Even more cynically, perhaps he might be spending the time flipping idly through today's edition of the Bryan-College Station *Eagle,* which lies open to the funny pages on the dining room table —nonchalantly reading the comics while waiting for the woman he is supposed to kill.

That's what one might expect from a professional hit man, a two-time murderer with no heart, no feelings, with only a job to do. But this is not a typical gun-for-hire story, and John Wayne Hearn is not a typical assassin. He does not fit the image of the one-dimensional, cold-blooded killers we see in television movies and fear in our dreams. And, in fact, what Hearn is actually doing in the darkened living room on Steep Hollow Circle is suffering a terrible case of the jitters.

He's been having second thoughts about this job for two days, and got cold feet so badly last night that he actually left Bryan and drove all the way to Houston, a hundred miles away, intending to leave.

Instead, he ended up, of all places, sitting around the landing field of the Goodyear blimp, located near the Houston airport on Interstate 45. The image sticks unalterably in the mind: why the

Goodyear blimp? Why stop there on the most decisive night of his life? Was Hearn drawn to the blimp in a subconscious act of propitiation for what he was about to do? He had already committed two murders, but the killing of Sandra Black would be his first pure murder-for-hire. The other two he could rationalize—one to win the woman he loves, and one to keep her—but this one will be strictly a business deal.

Perhaps Hearn was seeking a blessing from the Goodyear blimp—the purest icon of the American entrepreneurial spirit— for the terrible new business venture that he is about to launch: an entrepreneur of death.

It seems like such a bizarre place to contemplate a murder, yet, somehow, it fits. Compared to the shrines of other famous Texas murders—Lee Harvey Oswald barricaded behind boxes of textbooks on the sixth floor of the Texas School Book Depository, or Charles Whitman peering down from the twenty-seventh floor of the Tower at the University of Texas—the image of John Wayne Hearn (even his name screams out for caricature!) sitting in front of the Goodyear blimp, trying to work up his nerve, is the perfect metaphor for murder in the shallow world of the 1980s.

In truth, to Hearn, the blimp was something far more pragmatic and, ultimately, more tragic.

To him, it was a reminder of a failed dream. The one great dream of his life: to fly. As a boy, Hearn thrilled at the adventures of Sky King on television. As a twenty-one-year-old marine, home from Vietnam on thirty-day-leave, he soloed to earn his pilot's license, then volunteered to go back to Vietnam—not once, but twice—with the hope of becoming a Marine pilot. When that never materialized, he still hoped to become a commercial pilot.

At age thirty-eight he knows that will never happen, yet he still spends all of his extra money and spare time flying on weekends. In recent months, the dream has been rekindled by his ad in *Soldier of Fortune,* not as a legitimate pilot, as he had hoped, but as a pawn in a clandestine network supplying guns to the Nicaraguan *contras,* a campaign orchestrated from the basement of the White House by Lt. Col. Oliver North.

So for John Wayne Hearn, the Goodyear blimp was a reminder of the magic of flying, and an escape, for a few minutes, from what he has become. Sitting on the viewing stand, watching as the big dirigible slowly descended out of the brightly lit Houston sky and the attendants tied it down, he was transported back to the innocence of his youth: to Sky King and Penny, flying to the rescue every Saturday morning in the nick of time; to the ebullient spirit of his letters home from Vietnam, proudly announcing his long-awaited transfer to the First Marine Air Wing; and to the excitement that he still feels every time he takes up a plane, which brings a sense of power and freedom that he has not experienced anywhere else in his life.

Eventually, Hearn left the blimp and drove to a pay phone, where he placed a call to Gainesville, Florida, to the woman with whom he is recklessly head-over-heels in love: Debbie Banister. Once again, Hearn shared his doubts about this job with her, but Debbie was not sympathetic. Why should she be? Hearn has already killed two people for her: her husband and her ex-brother-in-law.

Debbie Banister was growing tired of Hearn's whining. Twenty-four hours earlier, when she dropped him off at the airport for the flight to Houston, Hearn had started wavering again, and Debbie reminded him of his two previous murders, and told him bluntly: "You shouldn't have a conscience." But this time, she was softer, gentler—telling him to keep up his nerve, that he could do it. Encouraged, Hearn drove back to Bryan to complete his task.

So here he sits, waiting, in Sandra Black's living room. He is not checking out the gun; he is not reviewing assassination techniques; he is not reading the funny papers. Instead, he is trying desperately to figure a way out of the house. Despite Debbie Banister's urgings, Hearn has made up his mind to get the hell out of the house and not go through with it. An hour earlier, he opened the back door, intending to leave, but the German shepherds started barking wildly. Hearn thought that Bob Black had put all of the dogs in the kennel, but one dog seemed to be loose. He could hear it running around and barking in the front yard. He also saw two neighborhood kids riding horses in the adjoining pasture. Even if he could get away from the dog, the kids would surely see him.

And where would he go? Bob Black brought him out to Steep Hollow this afternoon in his El Camino, pulling up next to the back porch so that Hearn could dash inside without being seen or riling the dogs. It is a seven-mile walk back to Bryan, to the Safeway parking lot where he left his rental car. What was he going to do, walk all the way back to town? With people coming home from work, he would obviously attract suspicion. So, feeling trapped, John Wayne Hearn closed the door.

Now he stands up and walks to the front window, too nervous to sit. His mind is racing wildly. Bob Black's whole schedule has turned to crap. Sandra was supposed to have been home a half-hour ago, but where is she? It's almost six-thirty, the time that Bob said *he* would be returning home with his son. What if Bob and the boy drive up at the same time that Sandra does? Will he have to shoot all of them?

Hearn is starting to panic. His hands are trembling, his breath is coming in short gasps. This is a man who faced death many times in the twenty-seven months that he spent in Vietnam—as a tank commander, an infantry grunt, and a door gunner on a Huey gunship. Once, his helicopter was shot down behind enemy lines, and the Vietcong were so close that he could hear their voices all around him in the jungle.

He is hearing voices now, too, but they are not the Vietcong; they are in his own mind. He hears Debbie Banister's silky voice again, telling him "You shouldn't have a conscience." It is power-ful, hypnotic, captivating. Hearn has been married four times and had many girlfriends, but no woman has ever affected him like Debbie Banister. Emotionally and sexually—*that* most of all—Deb-bie has overwhelmed him like no woman he has ever known. He feels that she understands him like none of his wives ever did. She appreciates him, buys things for him, wants to know about Vietnam and his flashbacks. He knows they need the $10,000 for the down payment on the beautiful log home they are planning to build, to start their new life together. Debbie's voice is soothing, confident, sensual: "Keep up your nerve. . . . You can do it. . . . You shouldn't have a conscience."

There is another voice in his head though, which is telling him to get out of the house while he still can. To run away, despite the dogs and the kids on horses and the seven miles back to town. It may be the voice of his own conscience—the one that Debbie Banister told him not to have—but if the voice has a familiar ring, it sounds like his mother, Mary Watson. For in truth, John Wayne

Hearn, professional gun-for-hire, self-styled mercenary, two-time murderer, is more than anything else a big mama's boy.

The love of a mother for her child is a powerful thing, but the depth and passion of Mary Watson's love for her son have seldom been matched. There have been few things in Hearn's life that his mother hasn't directed, encouraged, or controlled . . . until now.

In fact, Debbie Banister's greatest accomplishment isn't that she has convinced Hearn to kill people for money, but that she has won him away from his mother. Where four wives have tried and failed, Debbie has succeeded in dominating him more than Mary Watson. For the past four months, a monumental tug-of-war has been waged between two iron-willed women for Hearn's loyalty and allegiance—and far more than American troops ever succeeded at winning "the hearts and minds" of the Vietnamese people, this is a war that Debbie Banister has been winning . . . so far.

While Hearn waits in Sandra Black's living room, Mary Watson is back home in Columbia, South Carolina, worried to death. All she knows is that her "Johnny" has gone to Texas, supposedly to repossess an airplane for Sun Bank, Debbie Banister's employer in Gainesville. Nonetheless, Mary Watson is frightened. She's seen her son in love many times before (he has a history of falling hard and quickly), but never like this.

Too many strange things have happened since Debbie Banister came into his life: Debbie's ex-brother-in-law getting shot in January, followed by Debbie's husband, Joe, on February 2; then the visit from the Florida investigators just last week, who grilled Mary about Hearn's whereabouts the weekend of Joe Banister's death.

And then, there were the phone calls. Mary Watson's phone has been ringing off the hook with strange calls for Hearn that he wouldn't explain. For the first time since he came home from Vietnam, Mary Watson fears that her son is pulling away from her, that she is losing touch.

So there is a voice urging John Wayne Hearn to run out of the house and keep running all the way back to his mama in South Carolina, who will love him no matter what he's done.

But now it's too late. Hearn sees the headlights of Sandra's van turn into the long driveway. Now he has no choice. He reaches for the gun. His hands are shaking worse than before, and he's hyperventilating, unable to catch his breath. He picks up the Ruger off the coffee table, and hides behind the partition that divides the living and dining rooms. There is a two-foot space between the couch and the opening to the dining room; Hearn ducks in there, where he is hidden by the partition. He fights to control his breathing . . . and waits.

At times like this in Vietnam he could put his mind on automatic—"Don't think about what you're doing; just carry out the mission." Only later, when he got back to base, would the fear hit. But this is different. His mind won't go on automatic, even after two murders. The first one, Cecil Batie, had been the worst. He had driven around Gainesville all night long, driving by Batie's house again and again, unable to do it. At one point he even drove to Debbie Banister's house in Starke, thirty miles away, knowing that he couldn't go in because Joe Banister was home, but just to be near her, to feel her strength, to remind himself that her love was true. Finally, at five o'clock in the morning, when it was starting to get light, and he had to do it if he was ever going to, he stood in front of the plate-glass window with the Winchester 1200 in his hand, staring down at Cecil Batie asleep on the couch, and it was Debbie whom he thought of again, repeating a somber catechism over and over: "If I don't do it I can't have Debbie, if I don't do it I can't have Debbie, if I don't do it I can't have Debbie."

After that, killing Joe Banister three weeks later hadn't been as bad. He had just numbed out and done it, rationalizing it because Debbie had told him that Joe was beating on her.

But there is no way to rationalize this one. No way to numb out. Sandra Black hasn't done anything to anyone. It's a money deal all the way around—for him, for Debbie, for Bob Black. Bob has told Hearn about his girlfriend Teresa, but Hearn knows that he could have Teresa without killing his wife. It's the insurance money, pure and simple. Which is why Hearn refused Bob's offer of an additional $5,000 to kill Marjorie Eimann too, so that Bob could have the day-care center uncontested. Marjorie Eimann is a grandmother, and there are some things that John Wayne Hearn won't do.

Apparently, though, killing Sandra Black isn't one of them, for despite his second thoughts and cold feet, despite his shaking hands and hyperventilating lungs, Hearn has agreed to kill her—he even has some of Sandra's jewelry in his pocket, as collateral, until the insurance money comes through—and now he is preparing to do just that. When she walks in the kitchen, he intends to step out from behind the partition and shoot her in the head. She'll die instantly, painlessly—at least that's the plan, although, like all the other plans in John Wayne Hearn's life, it won't work out that way, leaving him to face the most agonizing moments of his life.

He hears the van door open and close, hears the dogs barking, welcoming Sandra home. Hanging on the wall directly across from him is a painting of Romal, Sandra's favorite shepherd. It is another reminder of the horror of what he is there to do. This is a woman who loves animals, loves children, loves her family. Everything around him in the house testifies to that. It is an elegant, well-kept home, with Sandra Black's loving touch visible throughout: the beautiful antique furniture that she has collected over the years; the lacy white curtains in the dining room, with a matching tablecloth on the round oak table; the basket of philodendron hanging across from him, spilling out of its planter with fecundity and life.

He hears the back door open, hears Sandra's footsteps on the kitchen floor. She doesn't see him, but he can see her, walking in with an electric skillet in her hands. When she puts the skillet down on the counter, he steps out from behind the partition—to do the job he was hired to do.

3

THE MARCH, 1985, ISSUE of *Soldier of Fortune* magazine, the "Journal of Professional Adventurers," is already on the newsstands in Bryan, Texas. It's a typical issue for SOF, the top-selling military adventure magazine in the world. The cover story is on the emotion-filled dedication of a new statue —three bronze soldiers standing arm in arm—at the Vietnam War Memorial in Washington, D.C. Included is a sidebar article on the burning in effigy of one of SOF's favorite targets, Jane Fonda. The article is entitled "Burn the Bitch."

Other articles include an on-location report on the fledgling El Salvador air force; a feature on combat knives, subtitled "A Shopping List for the Perfect Fighting Knife"; advice on the right choice for a police sidearm; a photo-essay on ice-climbing in the Colorado Rockies; a review of the Belgian-made FN MAG 58 machine gun; and a long piece on the 1978 assassination of Pedro Chamorro, the editor of Nicaragua's *La Prensa* newspaper, which helped spark the overthrow of the Somoza regime. This month, as usual, there's a full-page "Wanted" poster offering $100,000 to any pilot who flies a Soviet Mi-24 "Hind D" attack helicopter out of Nicaragua (SOF also has an outstanding bounty of $10,000 for information leading to the capture of Idi Amin).

This issue is being read in all fifty states and two dozen foreign countries, in the Pentagon (where SOF is sold on the newsstand), at CIA headquarters in Langley, Virginia, and on U.S. military bases around the world. With a monthly circulation of 175,000, *Soldier of Fortune* is the flagship of what its controversial publisher, Robert K. Brown, likes to call "hairy-chested journalism."

At SOF's headquarters in Boulder, Colorado, a liberal burg that Brown refers to derisively as "the People's Republic of Boulder," staff morale is running high. The magazine is celebrating its tenth anniversary year, and doing so with great fanfare: a special Tenth Anniversary logo adorns every article, congratulatory letters are pouring in from well-known politicians and military figures, and Col. Oliver North has secretly offered to up SOF's bounty for a Soviet Mi-24 helicopter to $1 million. The June, 1985, issue, featuring a cover photo of Sylvester Stallone as Rambo (which will become SOF's best-selling issue) is being put to bed.

Bob Brown, a gruff, shrapnel-scarred, fifty-three-year-old Army Reserve colonel with thinning hair, thick glasses, and two hearing aids, is proud of SOF's reputation as the best combat-news magazine in the world. His writers go where the action is—be it in Central America, Afghanistan, Lebanon, or Grenada—and don't just write about it, but *experience* it, sometimes *make it happen*!

SOF's combat-tested reporters brought back the first samples of Soviet 5.45mm assault-rifle ammunition from Afghanistan; scooped the U.S. Army in Grenada by uncovering secret New Jewel Movement documents; trekked through Laos in search of American MIAs; parachuted into Guatemala and El Salvador to aid earthquake victims; and traveled by bush plane, balloon, or motorcycle to report on brushfire wars in Suriname, Burma, Morocco, the Philippines, Angola, and Mozambique.

Soldier of Fortune has even been receiving kudos from the media establishment: *Newsweek* reported that the CIA and the Pentagon "rely on *Soldier of Fortune*" for information on Soviet operations in Afghanistan; *Time* credited SOF with uncovering valuable secret documents in Grenada; and the prestigious *Columbia Journalism Review* applauded SOF's "vivid, firsthand reporting from the world's current hot spots."

Politically, the whole country seems to be swinging Bob Brown's way. With Ronald Reagan's triumphant second inauguration party only a month old, Brown, the perpetual misfit and renegade, the unrepentant bullyboy who brags about getting kicked out of the Special Forces—not once, but twice—and thumbs his nose at politicians and generals alike, has become almost Establishment.

His unflinching positions on aid to the Nicaraguan *contras,* for years labeled extremist by the Establishment press, are now accepted Administration policies. His old Colorado drinking buddy Maj. Gen. John K. Singlaub is the front man for a worldwide *contra* supply-network with deep pockets in the Reagan White House. Clearly, Bob Brown is on a roll.

It hasn't always been this way. Brown started *Soldier of Fortune* in July, 1975, in the wake of the U.S.'s humiliating defeat in Vietnam and after the demise of *Stag* and *Argosy,* which had catered to the "hairy-chested" market in men's magazines. He raised $5,000 in seed money, put the first issue together in a friend's basement, and printed 8,500 copies, which one former SOF writer described as "looking as if [they] had been mimeographed in his bathroom by poorly trained gibbons."

The magazine was *immediately* controversial. Brown wrote an article entitled "American Mercenaries in Africa: How to Become One," and ran a grotesque photograph of a terrorist victim with the top of his head shot off.

Sales took off.

Brown had found his niche, walking a line between grisly sensationalism and the realities of war. He built his own persona—*and* magazine sales, which were intrinsically connected—by glorifying the professional mercenary ("merc," in SOF jargon) as the last, best, and only true defender of freedom and the American Way. Unfettered by lily-livered politicians or stuffed-shirt generals, the *Soldier of Fortune* merc—whether fighting in Rhodesia, Oman, or Uganda—was the embodiment of the twentieth-century warrior. It was hairy-chested, freedom-loving maleness at its best. It was an approach that sold magazines (nearly 200,000 per month by 1980) and also got Brown investigated by the Justice Department in 1979 for possible violations of the Neutrality Act. (Congresswoman Pat Schroeder accused him of recruiting mercenaries for Rhodesia, but the investigation was eventually dropped.)

To loyal readers, Brown was a staunch patriot leading the charge under SOF's "Death to Tyrants" banner. To mainstream conservatives, he was a saber-rattling anachronism. To liberals, he was a third-rate, sensationalist publisher who glorified war and hawked books on garrote-techniques, poisons, and silent death. As Fred Reed, a former SOF writer, described Brown's appeal: "The intriguing thing is the glorification of unprincipled ruthlessness, not of killing per se but of sordid, anonymous killing. The readers . . . want to shoot the bad guy in the back of the head with a silenced Beretta."

To still others, Bob Brown was almost a buffoon. Horribly absentminded, half-deaf, and an egregious self-promoter, Brown was a cross between Rambo and the Absentminded Professor— what Fred Reed called an "anti-Communist Peter Pan" in "Colonel Kangaroo's Paramilitary Theme Park."

Bob Brown never changed, but the Reagan Administration caught up with him. In February, 1985, *Soldier of Fortune* is still running the requisite stories on merc adventures worldwide, but Brown's staff has tried to tone down the magazine's renegade Spooks "R" Us image in an effort to become a serious combat-news magazine. The staff is more professional, the stories better written, the photos and layout top-notch.

Yet Bob Brown hasn't forgotten the audience that got him where he is today. From readership surveys, he knows that *Soldier of Fortune*'s readers are predominately young, single males, 60 percent of whom are military veterans (40 percent are Vietnam vets), who appreciate SOF's guts-and-glory editorial stance, its on-scene reports from military hot spots, monthly gun reviews (the average subscriber owns 13.1 guns), and sympathetic first-person reminiscences about Vietnam.

From the oddball letters and crank phone calls that come into the Boulder office, some of Brown's staff also suspect that some readers take the magazine a little too seriously. These wanna-be's, who periodically show up at the Boulder office in their camouflage fatigues looking to kill Commies with "Uncle Bob," seem to live vicariously through the pages of *Soldier of Fortune,* fantasizing themselves as glorious mercenaries taking on a hostile world. Bob Brown dismisses them as harmless Walter Mittys, and the SOF staff pins their nutty letters to the office bulletin board for comic relief.

Soldier of Fortune's sensationalist reputation still haunts the magazine in one major area: advertising. Brown's staff has tried for years to attract major national advertisers. "Vertical advertising," as it's known in the trade—beer, auto, cigarette companies. As part of that effort, at a staff meeting in February, 1984, SOF began developing its first formal ad policy, which spelled out what kind of ads would no longer be carried in the magazine: ads for fake diplomas or ID's, offers to "go anywhere" or "do anything," ads of questionable taste, "cookbooks" for poisons or illegal drugs, lock-picking manuals, ads that "may encourage our readers to engage in illegal activities," and finally the catchall, ads "found to be incompatible with the desired perception of our publication."

Despite the new policy, despite the magazine's improved image, despite the efforts of the advertising staff, the "vertical advertising" campaign has been a failure. The March, 1985, issue carries a few display ads from gun and knife manufacturers (Heckler & Koch, Springfield Armory, Buck Knives), mail-order companies such as Brigade Quartermasters, and offers for Dell Publishing's paperback edition of Col. Charlie A. Beckwith's best-selling *Delta Force.* But no beer, car, or cigarette ads. No "vertical advertisers."

So the display ads in the March issue are also typical for *Soldier of Fortune.* As usual, there is a full-page ad from Paladin Press, which Bob Brown cofounded in 1970, and which is still owned by his friend Peder Lund. The Paladin Press ad is missing some of the company's more provocative titles, such as *How To Kill, Vols. 1–5, Assassination Theory and Practice,* and *The Anarchist Cookbook,* which SOF, in keeping with its new ad policy, will no longer run.

And there are classified ads for many unusual products: World War I trench knives, .22-caliber tear-gas bullets, samurai swords, push daggers, Gurkha knives, electronic-bug detectors, night scopes, bionic ears, telephone scramblers ("FIGHT BIG BROTHER, 1985 IS HERE!"), six-foot-long blowguns, a BB sub-machine gun, silver-headed sword canes, stun guns, and a "ballistic" knife ("THE COMMIES HAD IT. WE STOLE IT. NOW YOU CAN BUY IT!!").

Is it any wonder that Budweiser, Ford, and Marlboro have stayed away? In fact, SOF's ads have turned off entire countries: New Zealand considered banning its sale in 1984, claiming that some ads were "indecent."

However, the display and classified ads are the least of Bob Brown's problems. At the back of the magazine, intermixed with the classifieds, are the "personal-services ads." Brown's senior editors—Dale Dye and Bill Guthrie—have been urging him to do away with these ads altogether, to once and for all clean up the image of the magazine. But Bob Brown likes the mystique of the personal-services ads, likes the sensational aura they lend his publication. And it is *his* publication. As founder, publisher, and sole owner, he knows what's best for the magazine, knows what his readers want, and so he overrules his staff. The personal-service ads will stay. His editors can clean them up a bit, in line with the new policy, but Brown wants the personal-services ads run. A sampling from the March, 1985, issue is instructive:

> Ex-Marine, Vietnam Vet seeks dirty work. Will Travel, all jobs considered. Discretion assured and expected

> For Hire. Short Term, High Risk Preferred, have passport, will travel. No job too dangerous.

> Investigator, Special Operative, all jobs considered.

> WE DO IT ALL AND WE DO IT BETTER, U.S.M.C. Vet Team, Pilot available.

> ADJUSTOR. Selective, effective. BILL STRINGFELLOW.

> EX-MARINES—'Nam Vets, Weapons Specialists, Jungle Warfare, Pilot M.E.. High risk assignments in U.S. or overseas. WORLD SECURITY GROUP,

The last ad, which also included two phone numbers, was submitted in May, 1984. It has been running in *Soldier of Fortune* since the September, 1984, issue. The wording meets all the requirements of the new ad policy. Senior editor Bill Guthrie, who urged Bob Brown to drop *all* personal-service ads from the magazine, has personally approved it. The ad was submitted by a thirty-eight-year-old Marine Corps veteran from Atlanta, Georgia. His name is John Wayne Hearn.

Part Two

THE MUDDY BRAZOS

Texas is heaven for men and dogs,
but hell on women and oxen.

—*a nineteenth-century
pioneer woman*

1

THE BRAZOS RIVER runs wide and muddy to the Gulf of Mexico. One of three major rivers partitioning the state's vast central plains, the Brazos has been at the heart of the glorious history of Texas.

Since 1540, when Francisco Vásquez de Coronado forded the Rio Grande with an army of 300 Spanish conquistadores, searching for the fabled Seven Cities of Cibola, this immense land has been a symbol of swaggering opportunity and adventure. And although Cibola proved to be only a barren Zuni pueblo, the mythic inheritance of Texas remains intact, four hundred and fifty years later: the Alamo, Davy Crockett, Sam Houston, Texas Rangers, cattle drives and range wars, Comanches and Apaches, oil gushers, millionaire wildcatters in snakeskin boots, barbecue, LBJ, JFK, and J.R. Ewing.

The Brazos River has carried its share of that legacy on its winding 840-mile journey to the Gulf, along with the silt and runoff from a 41,000-square-mile watershed, which turn it into a muddy torrent after a hard rain. The river is high banked and majestic at points, bordered by thick stands of willows and cottonwoods, although many of its shallow bends are unnavigable.

The Caddo Indians called it the Tokonohono, but legend has it that Coronado's bedraggled expedition, near death from lack of water, was led to the muddy river by Indian guides, and promptly named it *Rio de los Brazos de Dios*. It was an impressive name that reflected the Spaniards' gratitude to the guiding force that went, sword-in-hand, with their quest for gold: River of the Arms of God.

For three centuries, Texas was fought over by explorers, missionaries, trappers, pirates, freebooters, squatters, and opportunists of every ilk; and the Brazos River, with its fertile bottomlands and abundant game, was in the thick of the action.

In 1684, the French explorer LaSalle led an expedition to America to challenge Spanish hegemony, but he missed the mouth of the Mississippi, landed instead at Matagorda Bay, and after losing two of his four supply ships, was murdered by his own disgruntled men on the banks of the Brazos.

In 1691, Spain blazed *El Camino Real,* the King's Highway, across the northern boundary of present-day Brazos County, which became the major thoroughfare through Spanish *Tejas* for the next 150 years. *El Camino Real* also brought the first Americans. In December, 1821, Stephen F. Austin established the first colony of American settlers at San Felipe de Austin, on the Brazos.

Most of Austin's "Old Three-Hundred" were well-to-do Southern planters looking for fertile land at cheap prices, and they quickly established a cotton-based society that paralleled the one they had left behind. By 1825, there were 1,347 white settlers in Austin's colony, and 443 black slaves.

The American invasion of Texas was on. By 1830, the population had swelled to 15,000, with Anglos outnumbering Mexicans four to one. Cultural, political, and religious differences between Anglo-Texans and the newly independent Mexican government might have made war inevitable, but when it finally came, in 1836, history was once again played out on the Brazos.

On March 2, 1836, the Texas Declaration of Independence was adopted at an emergency convention at Washington-on-the-Brazos. The declaration was of no help to William Travis and Davy Crockett and the 180 men besieged by Santa Anna's 4,000 elite troops inside the ruins of an old Spanish fort, the Alamo, who were martyred four days later. However, after Sam Houston's ragtag volunteers decimated Santa Anna's army at the Battle of San Jacinto on April 21, it was at Washington-on-the-Brazos that the new Texas Republic adopted its first constitution and established the capital.

Since then, the course of Texas history has largely bypassed the Brazos. The capital was moved to Austin, the state's population centers to Houston and Dallas-Fort Worth, the oil boom to east

Texas. All that's left of Washington-on-the-Brazos, which was skipped over by the railroad in 1858, is a state park commemorating its past. And, of course, the old Brazos River, as dark and muddy as ever, which still rolls on, and still remembers.

2

IT IS HERE, in the Brazos River valley, that Marjorie Eimann has spent her entire life. She was born on a family farm in Millican on July 31, 1923, the second child of Henry and Liddie Bell Arnold (known as Liddie B.).

When Marjorie was born, cotton was still king in Texas, but its hundred-year reign was tottering as a result of one tremendous oil gusher, Spindletop, that blew in on January 10, 1901, near Beaumont, and catapulted Texas into the industrial age.

Except along the Brazos. Here, small farmers like Henry Arnold were caught in the downward-spiraling poverty of the feudal South, and the boll weevil and shrinking European markets soon forced thousands into bankruptcy. Even more foreboding, much of the land was played out and exhausted, a result of erosion, overplanting, and ignorance. Stories of picking "bumblebee cotton," which grew so puny and low to the ground that "a bumblebee could sit on his ass and reach the flowers," are still told, bitterly, by oldtimers in the Brazos Valley. The exhausted land, in combination with sustained drought, would give rise to the horror of the dust bowl in less than a decade.

Henry and Liddie B. struggled to hold on to their little farm. Henry planted corn, raised hogs and cows, and fed the family with the vegetables he raised in his truck patch. When times got hard, he would go south to Seguin, and hire on to pick cotton in the remaining plantations.

Liddie B.'s rock-ribbed faith in God also sustained them. This was the heart of the Bible Belt, where the highest compliment a woman could receive was to be known as "a good Christian mother"—and Liddie B. earned that designation.

Basic survival occupied more of their attention than the political currents raging across Texas in the 1920s. The Ku Klux Klan, riding a crest of postwar antiforeign sentiments and longstanding racism, was experiencing a major resurgence, and Texas was the greatest Klan stronghold in the nation: in 1923 the Klan-dominated state legislature passed a "white primary law" that barred blacks from voting in Democratic primaries (it was eventually overturned by the U.S. Supreme Court in 1927); by 1924 the Klan controlled *every* public office in Dallas; and that same year hooded Klansmen mounted a serious campaign for the governorship.

By 1929 Henry and Liddie B. could no longer make a go of it in Millican. It wasn't the stock market crash on October 23, 1929, but the moribund farm economy that finally drove them off the land. So, like thousands of other Texans, they sold their farm. Then they packed up their growing young family and headed fifteen miles up the road to College Station.

Which wasn't a town at all, but a campus. College Station was created in 1876 to house the Texas Agricultural & Mechanical College. Business leaders in Bryan, a raw frontier town and cotton-trading center, raised $50,000 and donated 2,416 acres of land four miles south of town—far enough away from its saloons and bawdy houses that "the morals of the students would be protected."

The college was built on the summit of a vast prairie, and the wild mustangs, longhorns, rattlesnakes, and scorpions gave way grudgingly. One student was reportedly attacked by wolves outside the main building, and a mathematics professor complained that the howling of wolves furnished an "all night serenade."

By the time the Arnold family arrived in 1929, A&M's enrollment had surpassed two thousand, in four major schools: agriculture, engineering, veterinary medicine, and arts and sciences. The school was all male, and military training was compulsory.

The A&M Corps of Cadets has been the inspiration for the school's rituals and traditions, which are more numerous—and are perhaps observed more rabidly—than at any college in the country: "Aggie Muster," when Aggies pay homage to dead alumni; "the Twelfth Man," begun in 1922, when an Aggie reserve football

player came out of the stands and suited up after injuries had
decimated Coach Dana X. Bible's regulars (since then, the entire
A&M student body has stood during every football game, to show
its readiness to do the same); "Midnight Yell Practice," a pep rally
held before every home football game; and "the Aggie Bonfire," a
four-story-high bonfire lit the night before the annual Thanksgiving Day football game with A&M's hated rival, the University of
Texas.

By 1929 another A&M tradition was also firmly established:
the ubiquitous "Aggie joke." The school's "ag" curriculum and
hayseed reputation generated thousands of jokes about bumbling,
oafish, unmannered Aggies—a tradition that still flourishes today.
Example: how many Aggies does it take to eat an armadillo? Three;
one to eat the armadillo and two to look out for cars.

No doubt, many of the jokes originated in Austin, home of the
University of Texas, whose law school has supplied the bulk of the
state's political leaders. It was a rivalry grounded in class struggle:
rich city boys versus poor country boys, teasips (as Aggies disdain-
fully call UT students) versus hayseeds. Not surprisingly, the ava-
lanche of jokes made Aggies even more fanatical in their loyalty to
their school—and their hatred of UT.

When Henry and Liddie B. moved into a little farmhouse on
Old County Road, south of campus, College Station was still more
country than town, with crumbling roads, a handful of stores, and
open prairies surrounding the A&M campus. But to Marjorie Arnold, a six-year-old farm girl from Millican, it was a new world of
wonder and excitement. The campus was most impressive: three
dozen stoic sandstone buildings marshalled around the tree-lined
entrance to Old Main, with its stately Greek Revival portico and
massive rotunda.

Henry Arnold got a job at the A&M power plant, pushing
wheelbarrow-loads of coal up a big ramp to the boiler. When he
arrived home in the evenings, trudging across the fields because he
couldn't afford a car, his face would be black with coal dust. He
worked twelve hours a day, seven days a week, for eleven dollars a
week.

Their rent was ten dollars a month, and the remaining money
went for staples: flour, salt, sugar, coffee, red beans (called "Texas
strawberries"), and rice. Henry's truck patch still supplied the bulk

of their vegetables, but Liddie B. and the children also canned vegetables "on halves" for local farmers. One year, they put up 1,800 cans of vegetables, of which 900 were theirs. To supplement their regular diet, the Arnold boys hunted rabbits and squirrels in the fields surrounding the A&M campus, and pulled twenty-pound "yellow cats" barehanded out of hollow logs in the Brazos.

It took every bit of it to survive. The Arnold family was growing quickly, with new children born almost every year. There would be ten altogether: six boys and four girls. The younger ones referred to Milton, the oldest boy, as "Brother" and called Marjorie "Sister," a practice that continues today—Marjorie is "Aunt Sister" to her nieces and nephews.

It was the closeness of their large family—and a lot of backbreaking labor—that enabled the Arnolds to survive the Great Depression, which arrived, full-blown and wind-driven, in the Brazos Valley in 1931, when cotton prices plummeted to five cents a pound (down from eighteen cents in 1928). But at least Henry Arnold had a steady job—even with its paltry salary—and his abundant truck patch; many other families had neither.

During the summers the Arnold children earned money for school clothes by picking cotton for local farmers. Dragging thirty-foot-long cotton sacks down scraggly rows in the hot sun taught them all they ever wanted to know about bumblebee cotton. Marjorie, built low-to-the-ground like the cotton, was the fastest picker in the lot. "I never could outpick her," Milton admits grudgingly. They were paid ten dollars per hundred pounds—the standard rate—and Marjorie's brothers Bill and Aubrey devised a secret method to reach that goal. "We never would have made a hundred pounds if we hadn't followed behind Sister, picking cotton out of a hole in her bag," Aubrey says with a laugh.

If there was money left over on Saturday night, Henry would take the family to Opersteny's Cafe in downtown Bryan, where he would buy each child a Big Red soda and a hamburger.

For fifteen years, the family rented small houses that they could afford, until Henry and Liddie B. had finally scrimped together enough money to buy their own place: a wooded fifty-acre homestead northeast of campus. It had only a small farmhouse with no electricity or indoor plumbing, but it was *theirs,* which was the important thing, and they named it "the Homeplace."

•   •   •

One day, Henry Arnold brought home for dinner a strapping sixteen-year-old German boy who worked with him at the power plant. Glen Eimann was from Brenham, thirty miles south of College Station, one of two dozen Texas towns settled by German immigrants.

Glen was born on his family's hundred-acre homestead on July 30, 1923. His immigrant grandfather kept to the old ways—speaking only German—but Glen's father quit the farm in 1928, when the Sun Oil Company struck oil right across the road. Charles and Lydia Eimann moved into company housing on the Sun Oil field, where Glen lived until he was sixteen.

It was a shallow field that paled in comparison to the giant strikes in east Texas, and therefore lacked the hysteria—and the squalor—of the larger boomtowns. There, oily muck pervaded everything; salt water turned the streets into rivers of mud; lack of plumbing and potable water led to terrible outbreaks of flu, dysentery, and typhoid; and the constant stench of gas caused inflamed eyes, nausea, and gas poisoning. One boomtown wife, accused of murdering her husband, was acquitted after jurors decided that the dead man deserved his fate—for subjecting his wife to such a miserable life.

Glen left home at age sixteen, ready to see the world. He moved first to Houston, then to College Station, where he found a job at the A&M power plant, got invited to dinner, and met Henry Arnold's diminutive, brown-haired daughter.

He and Marjorie went to a movie that night and were soon going steady. When she graduated from high school in 1941, Glen gave her an engagement ring. However, their wedding plans were postponed by the Japanese bombing of Pearl Harbor on December 7, 1941. Glen joined the Navy in February, 1942, and shipped out for the South Pacific on the U.S.S. *Portland,* a heavy cruiser. He saw action at Tarawa, the Marshall Islands, Leyte Gulf, and Okinawa, among other battles.

Marjorie spent the war years working in the A&M faculty post-office, a tiny cubbyhole in the administration building, where she stamped outgoing mail, sorted incoming mail, and kept the books.

When the war ended, Glen returned to College Station and

stopped by the A&M power plant to say hello to his friends. The manager asked him about his plans for the future.

"I guess I'll do the same thing I always do—chase girls and drink a little beer," Glen replied. As a favor to the manager, he agreed to work for a few days; he ended up staying forty-one years.

Glen and Marjorie resumed their courtship and were married on April 4, 1946. They moved into a little house on campus—at 2 Norton Street in an area called "the Hill"—a cluster of houses rented to the A&M Volunteer Fire Department. Glen joined the fire department to qualify for the house, which rented for seven dollars a month.

While he worked seven days a week at the power plant, Marjorie worked in the campus laundry for forty-one cents an hour. Yet neither one minded the hard work because they had a goal they were working toward, a dream they were pursuing. It was the dream shared by an entire generation of postwar newlyweds: they wanted to have a baby.

3

SHEPHERD, TEXAS, lies in the heart of the east Texas timber belt. The town was not named for its founder, as one might expect, but for B.A. Shepherd, a Houston banker who laid out the Houston, East and West Texas Railroad in 1875.

It was symbolic of the era. B.A. Shepherd built his railroad to haul trees, not people. The legacy of Texas is one of both opportunity and plunder, in equal portions, and by 1875 the virgin pine forests of east Texas were being ravaged with the same ferocity as were the buffalo and the Comanche on the open range. A dozen sawmills were already operating in Houston, and Shepherd, fifty-seven miles to the north, was a convenient way station between the piney woods and the mills.

This is where Mary Watson (née Hawthorne) was born, on October 9, 1927. By then, east Texas was sprouting forests of oil derricks instead of pine, but the products—and the profits—were still being shipped to Houston. Shepherd was once again a point of passage, this time between Houston's refineries and the boom-towns of Kilgore, Longview, and Henderson.

Tragically, Mary's mother died from pneumonia soon after her birth. Today, we know about the critical bonding that takes place between mother and infant, but what kind of pall is cast upon the child whose life begins in the shadow of her mother's funeral?

Her father, Nathaniel Hawthorne, was a truckdriver who hauled drilling equipment to and from the oil fields. With two motherless children to take care of—Mary and her older brother—

he remarried a few years later, but Mary and her stepmother were never close. Despite a forlorn childhood, she tapped a reservoir of inner strength and fierce determination that has motivated her ever since. "I had one of the poorest childhoods anyone ever had," Mary says, "but I think it made a stronger person of me."

In high school, she had her heart set on becoming a nurse, but her father refused to give his permission. Bitterly disappointed, Mary considered other options: World War II had broken out, and there were new opportunities for women in the military. She asked her father if she could join the service, but once again he refused. It was the last time she would ask his permission for anything. "From then on, I started *doing* instead of *asking*," she says.

She left home and moved to Houston, where she got a job with Trailways bus services, driving a local route between Houston and outlying towns. One weekend, Mary and a girlfriend, who also worked for Trailways, went to Corpus Christi on holiday. On the way, they passed the terminal of the Texas Transport Company, where gleaming tractor-trailers were lined up in the yard. "Boy, I'd like to drive one of those," her girlfriend remarked. She was joking, but Mary took her up on it: "Let's go ask for a job."

The supervisor at Texas Transport laughed in their faces. The idea of two teenage girls working as over-the-road drivers was outlandish, even with a war on. "I'll make you a deal, girls," he said with a smirk. "You see that rig parked over there? Back it out and drive it over here and I'll give you a job." He was taunting them; the semi was jammed between two other trucks, and even an experienced driver would have had trouble backing it out.

But he hadn't counted on Mary's determination. "God must have been with us," she says, "because we climbed up in that cab and backed it out of there without a bit of trouble." The stunned supervisor had no choice but to hire them. Ironically, the man eventually became their biggest booster, and bragged that the two girls were the safest drivers he had.

They worked as a team, hauling high octane fuel to some of the fifteen army air force bases located in a triangle between Corpus Christi, San Antonio, and Harlingen. They would pick up a handful of bills of lading in Corpus and head out on the road, sometimes being away for a week or more. At night, they would pull into small roadside parks, stretch out in the seat, prop their feet out the window, and go to sleep. For a rebellious teenage girl from Shepherd, it was liberating. "I thoroughly enjoyed it," Mary says. "We were free, we could do what we wanted to do, and nobody was breathing down our necks."

In 1943 she moved to Freeport, a thriving chemical center at the mouth of the Brazos River. Her father and stepmother were living there, and he was working for Dow Chemical. Mary got a job with Camp Chemical, working in a laundry. She was working the counter one day when a young soldier came in to pick up his clothes. She noticed him staring at her, but he didn't speak.

Two weeks later, they met again, by chance, and began dating. The young soldier's name was Joe Pickett. He was from Mississippi, and he was soon smitten by the robust, strong-willed young woman. On October 13, 1943—one week after Mary's sixteenth birthday—they were married in Freeport.

In a fairy tale they would have lived happily ever after, but this was real life. According to family sources, Mary and Joe Pickett had an argument, he got mad, and reportedly asked for a transfer overseas. True, the war was winding down—Hitler was retreating before the pincer thrusts of U.S., British, and Soviet troops; and the Japanese, while still formidable, were steadily giving ground in the Pacific—but some of the fiercest fighting still remained.

Pickett shipped out for the European theater in early 1945. He and Mary might have been able to resume their life together when he returned—after all they were young and still in love—but then tragedy struck with blinding, unrelenting finality. Joe Pickett was gone. In an instant. In a flash. In a terse telegram from the War Department saying that he had been "killed in action"—the most brutal words in the language of war. *How could it be?* In another few weeks, the war in Europe would be over. The whole country would erupt in V-E day celebrations—with ticker-tape parades down Broadway and spontaneous dancing in the streets.

To the rest of the world, it was as if their love had never existed. All Mary had were his medals, his commendations, his Purple Heart. She had briefly met his family, but there were no supportive in-laws to share her grief, no loving family of her own to fall back on, no visible proof of their love.

Except for one thing. The one thing that would still be there after the medals had been locked away in a box, still too painful to look at. The one thing that would always remind her of Joe Pickett, and would carry the full blessing and burden of her immense grieving love: his son, born October 10, 1945. The son of a dead war hero and an eighteen-year-old girl.

She named him John Wayne.

4

MARJORIE EIMANN started vomiting in September, 1947, and didn't stop for nine months. She was ecstatic—at least as much as she could be with her head in the toilet, which is where it was most of the time. Dr. S.C. Richardson enrolled her in the sixty-nine-dollar "flat-rate" obstetric plan (no wonder there was a baby boom!) and estimated her due date as June 1, 1948.

She was so nauseated that she had to quit her job at the campus laundry, and she spent most of her time in bed. Dr. Richardson gave her B_6 shots to build up her hemoglobin count, but nothing stopped the nausea.

She went into labor on June seventh—one week late—and Glen drove her to the hospital. The old Bryan Hospital had no air-conditioning, and Marjorie—in the throes of hard labor and still vomiting—suffered terribly in the sweltering summer heat.

Hour after hour went by, yet Marjorie's cervix wasn't dilating. As the afternoon wore on, the heat and tension began to affect everyone. Dr. Richardson wore cowboy boots, and every time he came to check on her, Liddie B. could hear him clomping up the hospital stairs. "Lord have mercy!" she would say irritably, "there's no way I'd let a man with cowboy boots be my doctor." After fourteen hours of labor, Marjorie still hadn't dilated, so Dr. Richardson performed a cesarean section. Marjorie vomited right up until they put her to sleep.

Sandra Kay Eimann was born at 9:40 P.M. on June 7, 1948. She weighed eight pounds and one and one-half ounces, and the entire Arnold family remarked on her beauty. Marjorie, who was unconscious for most of the first three days, hardly noticed. Dr. Richardson took Glen aside and told him, "Whatever you do, don't let her get pregnant again. It'll kill her."

Marjorie spent ten days in the hospital and another six weeks recuperating in bed. Henry Arnold stopped by #2 Norton Street every morning on his way to work and dropped off Liddie B., who looked after Marjorie until Glen got off work. There would be a stack of dirty diapers waiting for him every night when he got home. "Glen didn't mind hanging out diapers, but he didn't want any of his friends to see him," Marjorie says with a laugh. "If he saw a car coming he'd go sit on the back porch until it passed."

With the C-section and Marjorie's extended hospital stay, Sandra's birth cost much more than Dr. Richardson's sixty-nine-dollar flat rate. Glen and Marjorie had no health insurance; so Glen sold pints of blood to pay off the bill and took a second job at a local service station. Marjorie's long convalescence prevented her from going back to work full time, but she started keeping children at home when Sandra was a few months old—a job she would hold for thirty-five years.

As she grew up, Sandra was cute, curly-headed, outgoing, and *always* busy. She was the first Arnold grandchild in Brazos County (although two older cousins lived in Sinton) and had the full attention of two adoring grandparents and seven aunts and uncles.

Early on, she developed a passionate love for animals, which would continue throughout her life. Her uncles kept her supplied with puppies—much to Marjorie and Glen's consternation. "One would get killed and we'd have a funeral and they'd bring her another," says Glen.

Of all her relatives, she was closest to her grandfather Henry Arnold, whom she called "Pa-Paw" (Liddie B. was "Me-Maw"). Sandra and Henry had a natural affinity: she loved animals, and Henry had a passel of them at the Homeplace—cows, dogs, chickens, turkeys, and ducks. The very first photograph taken of Sandra, at three weeks old, was on the porch of the Homeplace, with one of Henry's chickens standing behind her.

The Homeplace was a wonderful playground for a child, and it quickly became Sandra's favorite haunt. Henry had dredged out a large pond—a "tank," as it's called in Texas—where the kids fished and swam in the summer. And Henry's truck patch was bigger and more bountiful than ever; he grew enough sweet corn, tomatoes, black-eyed peas, watermelons, and cantaloupes to feed the whole family and still have surplus to sell in town.

It was country living, and little Sandra loved it. Henry would stop by the Hill every day after work in his old pickup truck, blow the horn, and call out: "Sandra, you want to go home with me?" Before he had finished, Sandra would be racing for the door. If Marjorie protested, saying, "Now, Daddy, she needs to stay home tonight," Henry would drive off, leaving Sandra wailing on the front porch. She'd cry so loudly that he could hear her a block away, and he'd turn around and come back—knowing that by then Marjorie would have inevitably given in. Sandra would jump in the truck and off they'd go.

Henry and Sandra were already close, but they became inseparable when he bought a horse. From then on, Marjorie could forget about trying to keep Sandra at home. "She'll be all right; she's got her horse," Henry would say, and they were gone again.

Of course, it was really *Henry's* horse, but Sandra quickly appropriated it. She was so young that she was still half-scared of the animal, but she would chase it around and around the pasture, trying futilely to catch it. The horse would finally grow tired of the game and bolt away or, as it did once, turn and chase Sandra up a tree.

•   •   •

It was the "quiet fifties," and College Station fit right in with the mood of the country. The 1950 Census listed the town with a population of 7,268, including a grand total of *two* policemen: one patrolled during the day and one at night.

Elsewhere, Ike was in the White House, blacks were still in the back of the bus, Elvis Presley was just learning to shake his pelvis, and mothers and fathers had a few more years of peace.

Sandra Eimann's childhood took a dramatic turn in 1953, when Henry Arnold suffered a massive heart attack. He was only fifty-three, but the years of hard physical labor had taken their toll. The attack was so severe that the doctors didn't expect him to live through the night, and were afraid to even move him to the hospital. Deacons from Rock Prairie Baptist Church maintained an all-night prayer vigil by his bed; the next morning, Henry was still alive, but he looked as if he'd aged twenty years.

He was almost totally incapacitated and had to retire from the power plant. He was only a few months shy of having twenty-five years of service, which would have qualified him for full retirement benefits; instead, he drew a measly $70 a month.

Henry's retirement gave him more time for his rapidly growing horde of grandchildren, who—along with fishing—became his primary vocation. Every afternoon, he'd drive into town to make his rounds: the first stop was Martin's Place, to play dominoes and nurse a beer with his old cronies; then Central Texas Hardware for fishing supplies or seeds; and finally the Piggly Wiggly, where he'd buy the meat for supper and a sack of bananas, oranges, or fruit pies for treats. Then he made the rounds of the grandkids: he'd pull up in the driveway of each house and blow the horn, and the children would come running to get their daily treat from Pa-Paw.

Sandra's life changed even more dramatically in 1956, when her brother Larry was born. After Dr. Richardson's warning, Marjorie had tried to accept not having other children, but when Sandra started going to school, her yearning for another child—particularly a son—returned.

"One more time, Glen, and then I'll have my tubes clipped and tied," she pleaded. Glen wanted a son as much as she did, and so, against doctor's orders, they started trying to get pregnant. When Marjorie began vomiting in January, 1954, they knew they had succeeded.

If anything, her second pregnancy was worse than her first. Once again, she vomited from the first day to the last, and had to take almost-daily liver shots. Her new obstetrician, Dr. J.W. Geppert—who was bootless, to Liddie B.'s delight—scheduled a C-section two weeks early, for fear that Marjorie couldn't last the full term. Larry was born on October 12, 1954, and Glen shouted for joy when he heard it was a boy.

Sandra, on the other hand, pitched an absolute fit. She had enjoyed six years as an only child, and this new baby was an unwanted intrusion in her world. Eventually, though, she did a complete turnaround, and became rabidly protective. "That was her little brother, and she'd fight for him in a minute," Glen remembers.

It was a period of great flourishing for Sandra, who had her baby brother, her dogs, "her" horse, and Pa-Paw, as always. But Marjorie was not doing so well. Her nerves had been strained by her difficult pregnancy, and she would sit in Dr. Geppert's office and cry inconsolably. He told her, "Marjorie, if you don't get better we may have to send you to Austin."

Marjorie knew that "Austin" meant the state mental hospital. "You're not sending *me* to Austin," she said stubbornly. "I'm not leaving my kids." When she got home she called her father and told him what the doctor had said.

"You're not going anywhere," Henry declared.

"Well, Daddy, what am I going to do?" she asked.

"I'll tell you what *we* are going to do," he said. "I'm going down to Central Texas Hardware and buy you a rod and reel, and you're coming down here every day and going fishing with me."

Marjorie didn't take him seriously, but Henry called the next morning at eight o'clock sharp. "You ready?" he asked.

"Well, I guess so," she replied. Feeling ridiculous, she drove to the Homeplace; and while Liddie B. watched the baby, Henry walked Marjorie down to the tank, rigged up her new rod and reel, sat her down on the bank, and told her: "Watch the cork."

She didn't catch anything that first day, but Henry called again the next morning, and the next, and the next, until Marjorie was hearing "Watch the cork" in her sleep. Day by day, sitting peacefully in the shade of the willows with her old heartsick daddy, Marjorie began to get better. Her nerves calmed, her spirits lifted, and before too long she was well.

You won't find "watch the cork" in any psychology textbooks, but Henry Arnold was its master practitioner. "I guarantee you'll feel better," Marjorie says, laughing. "*I* made it."

• • •

As the decade ended, College Station nosed gently into the 1960s with no fire department, police station, or water tower, and with a street system in desperate need of repair. There were no hints of the explosive growth that would envelop Texas A&M in the next ten years, or of the political explosions that would rock the rest of the country.

But Sandra Eimann's life was rocked in its own right on September 19, 1961, when her beloved Pa-Paw stopped by the Hill as usual, distributing frozen fruit pies for treats, then rode to Hearne, thirty miles away, with his son Charles to check out a used car. When Charles came back from a test drive, the car salesman asked him, "Sir, was this fellow with you?" Henry Arnold had fallen over in the parking lot, broken his head open on the pavement, and died of a massive coronary.

An age of innocence had ended.

5

HOUSTON *isn't* on the banks of the Brazos River, but it could have been. About 1840, several enterprising Houston businessmen lobbied the fledgling congress of the Texas Republic to finance a rerouting of the Brazos to Houston, landlocked fifty miles from the Gulf. The Texas Congress rejected the bizarre scheme, but it typifies the history of Houston, which willed itself into existence, erupting out of a mosquito-infested swamp as a glittering monument to enterprise, determination, and greed.

Throughout its tumultuous history, Houston has had no time for afternoon *siestas,* no tolerance for limits, and no patience for restraint. Like God's message to Moses from the burning bush, Houston proclaimed itself "I Am That I Am," and heaven help anything—man, beast, or nature—that has stood in its way.

During one brief period in the late 1830s, Houston served as the capital of the Texas Republic. One newcomer to the city called it "the greatest sink of disipation [sic] and vice that modern times have known," and the representative from San Augustine County decried Houston as "that abominable place—that wretched mudhole—that graveyard of men." Shortly afterward, the capital was moved to Austin.

But the opening of the Spindletop oil field in 1901 and the dredging of the Houston Ship Channel in 1908 began Houston's rise from "wretched mudhole" to the largest city in the South. By the end of World War II, the demand for Texas crude oil, and a host of other petrochemicals, had made Houston the second largest port in the country, behind only New York, and the city's population was racing toward half a million.

• • •

It was into this frenzied environment that Mary Watson returned in late 1945 with her infant son. It was a formidable place to start a new life.

She had given birth to him in Center, Texas, near the Louisiana border, where her father was working for an oil pipeline company. But when he got transferred a few weeks later, Mary had her tiny trailer towed back to Houston. "I wanted to get on with my life," she says.

With typical determination, she decided that her son needed a father, and chose a cabinetmaker named John Paul Hearn (they were actually married on May 18, 1945, *prior* to her delivery). It was not a heart-stopping romance. John Hearn was thirty years older than Mary; but at least he provided a roof over her head, and gave her son—whom he adopted—the name he would carry through life: John Wayne Hearn.

They moved into a tiny frame house at 4409 Cedar Hill Street, on the north side of Houston. The neighborhood is just off U.S. 59, a major expressway, and only a few miles from the skyscrapers of downtown Houston, but it looks more like the outskirts of Tijuana than the fourth largest city in the U.S. Pawnshops, junkyards, rundown motels, and "goats for sale" signs border the highway. Incredibly, Houston has *no* zoning codes, as voters twice rejected zoning proposals—in 1948 and 1962—in the most bitter political battles in the city's history. Elsewhere, zoning is about as revolutionary as indoor plumbing, but this is Texas, Bubba, where romantic tales of the open range still run deep in the culture, and zoning has the prickly feel of barbed wire.

It wasn't much of a house, especially compared to the River Oaks mansions of Houston's millionaire oilmen, but Mary fixed it up and turned it into a home; she even built a sidewalk fr r their front door to the road herself. On September 15, 1947, she gave birth to a beautiful baby girl, Margaret Ann Hearn.

Mary had worked for a while as a bookkeeper for a dentist; but she decided after Ann was born that she needed a more profitable trade, and she enrolled in the Josephine Hodge Beauty School.

Postwar prosperity had created a big demand for beauticians, as middle-class women could now afford to have their hair done. Mary got her license and worked for another beautician until she had saved enough money to open her own shop: Mary's Beauty Parlor.

In her own resolute fashion, she had achieved more security than she'd ever had in her life: she had her house, her beauty parlor, a husband, and, most importantly, her two children. She took roll after roll of black-and-white photographs of the two of them: John and Ann sitting in toy cars, playing together in the yard, holding hands on the porch. The Kodak Company was building a financial empire on the enthusiasm of baby-boom parents, and Mary did her part.

But it didn't last. Her marriage to John Paul Hearn collapsed in 1951. Given the thirty-year age difference, it wasn't surprising. Reflecting the curious nature of the relationship, Mary still refers to him as Mister Hearn.

She filed for divorce on May 21, 1951, claiming that Hearn had come home drunk "on numerous occasions, too numerous to enunciate here," and had beaten her and the children and threatened her life. Her attorney summoned several of her neighbors to testify against Hearn, but one of them, Ila Mae Penny, disputes the charges against him. "When you get a divorce you can say anything, but I never saw any problems," says eighty-one-year-old Penny, who still lives in the same house. "Mr. Hearn was a nice man."

Whatever the case, Hearn didn't contest the divorce *or* show up for the hearing, and the judge awarded Mary thirty dollars per week in child support (in 1959, she filed charges against Hearn for failure to pay it).

With her children so young, Mary decided it was best not to talk to them about her marital problems. "The children never knew any problems I had with Mr. Hearn," she says. "I never put anybody down." Symbolically, in her photo collection there is one shot of John Hearn, Mary, and the two children standing in front of their home—and Hearn's face has been crudely ripped out.

On July 27, 1951, eighteen days after her divorce was final, Mary got married again, to Earl Springer, a thirty-two-year-old assistant manager at a grocery store. Springer was from Covington, Tennessee—forty miles north of Memphis—and painted a rosy picture of it as a wholesome place to raise kids. At his suggestion, Mary sold her beauty shop, loaded up the kids, and moved to Covington in the fall of 1951.

They rented a farmhouse on the edge of town, and Mary used the money from her beauty shop to buy a closed-down restaurant in Covington. She ran an ad in the local newspaper:

> We would like to announce that we have assumed management of "the Courtesy Cafe." We appreciate the patronage of past customers and wish to extend everyone a cordial invitation to visit with us. Breakfasts, lunches, dinners, and short orders will be served as well as special dinners on Sundays and holidays. Let us give you a chance to prove the superiority of our menu and service.

John Wayne Hearn, who was five, started school in Covington, and would stop by the restaurant every morning to eat a hamburger and a malt for breakfast. The restaurant did well, but the rest of Earl Springer's rosy picture did not pan out: the farmhouse they rented was just a rundown shack, with no running water, no indoor plumbing, only a drop cord and a bare bulb hanging from the ceiling in each room, and cracks in the walls that the wind whipped through in winter.

Springer had a bad temper, as did Mary, and the children sometimes got caught in the crossfire. "My mother had a very bad temper," Ann says. "My brother and I had to share a bed in Tennessee, and I remember her waking us up in the middle of the night with a belt, because she claimed we were playing. But we were dead asleep. I can remember going to school with the whole side of my face black-and-blue."

After three years, Mary had had enough of Covington, and the family moved back to Houston in 1954. The city was growing faster than ever. That year, the metro population topped one million, and residents sported "I'm One in a Million" bumper stickers.

Houston had become the "new Jerusalem" for legions of oil-rich millionaires, and their holiest shrine was the opulent bar of the Shamrock Hotel, opened in 1949 by wildcatter Glen McCarthy.

McCarthy's "Emerald Folly" boasted sixty-three shades of green, a thousand-car garage, the world's biggest beds, and refrigerated garbage. When Frank Lloyd Wright first saw it he remarked, "I always wondered what the inside of a jukebox looked like."

Mary and Earl Springer moved first to 10½ Street, in the Heights area, but soon moved to Pasadena, south of Houston.

Pasadena, which means "land of flowers," got its name from the meadows of wildflowers that bloomed along Vince's Bayou, and was also famous as the site of Santa Anna's capture after the Battle of San Jacinto. However, by 1954, the meadows of wild-flowers had long since been bulldozed for the Ship Channel, and the historic site of Santa Anna's capture was enveloped in the stinking haze of oil refineries and chemical plants.

Pasadena is the "other side of the tracks" in Houston, both literally and figuratively. The Port Terminal Railway, the Southern Pacific, and the Ship Channel form its northern border; and while the big oil companies had their headquarters in gleaming skyscrapers in downtown Houston, they built their oft-exploding storage tanks and sulphur-spewing refineries in Pasadena. Indeed, Houstonians joked that you could always recognize people from Pasadena because they smelled like sulphur.

Pasadena had one brief moment of glory, in the 1970s, as the home of Gilley's Saloon, the Mecca for "urban cowboys," who flocked there to drink long-neck Lone Star beers, dance the Texas two-step, and ride the mechanical bull made famous by John Travolta in the movie *Urban Cowboy.* But Gilley's is now closed, and Pasadena's only national renown is for the Phillips Petroleum explosion in October 1989, which killed 22 people and injured 124.

There is no way to underestimate the town's ugliness: storage tanks, chemical plants, and belching smokestacks stretch as far as the eye can see, on a scale comparable only, perhaps, to the chemical belt of New Jersey. Like the yellow smog that hovers above it, industry completely envelops the town: oil storage tanks sit right next to neighborhood playgrounds, only thirty feet from the swing sets and teeter-totters.

Mary rented a house at 5454 Firefly Street, one block from the Houston city limits. The tiny frame houses are jammed together, with almost nonexistent side yards. One mile away is a huge Mobil plant, and beyond it, a dismal sea of tanks and smokestacks.

This is where John Wayne Hearn spent the formative years from ages ten to fourteen. Although he knew nothing about his real father, he was unknowingly carrying Joe Pickett's legacy on his young shoulders: the older he got, the more he looked like Joe, and Mary felt a pang of sadness whenever she looked at him. According to his sister Ann, it also made him Mary Watson's favorite.

"Growing up, my brother was always number one and I had to take a backseat," Ann says, more with resignation than bitterness. "He was always Mama's boy, and I was on the outside looking in."

Mary Watson denies any favoritism toward Hearn, but even her denial is telling: "Ann was a little devil. She would do devious things that no one would see her do, that John would get blamed for."

•　•　•

It was a long way from the Shamrock Hotel to Firefly Street, but Mary tried to make a decent life for her children: she sewed most of their clothes, took them to the beach at Galveston on Saturdays, and to the Heights United Methodist Church on Sundays. Hearn, who had joined the Cub Scouts in Tennessee, joined the Boy Scouts when he turned twelve.

But, once again, Mary's relationship foundered: she divorced Earl Springer in 1957. Soon, she began dating Tom Watson, a friend of Springer's from Tennessee, who had been renting a room in their house. Watson was a low-key, happy-go-lucky fellow who adored Mary *and* her kids, and was soon asking her to marry him. But already twice burned, Mary wasn't ready to risk another failure.

In 1959 Watson joined the Army and went to Fort Chaffee, Arkansas, for boot camp. One weekend in May, Mary and the kids drove up to see him. It was a grueling drive—five hundred miles on two-lane roads—and when they arrived, Watson again asked her to marry him. This time, surprisingly, she agreed. "I really wasn't ready to get married again, but the kids wanted me to because they liked Tom," she explains.

They had to drive across the state line to Poteau, Oklahoma, to get a blood test on a Saturday, and then went looking for the justice of the peace. They stopped at a gas station near the courthouse.

"Do you know where we can find the justice of the peace?" Tom asked the attendant.

"*I'm* the justice of the peace," the man replied dourly.

"Well, we want to get married," Tom said.

"When?"

"Right now."

"Where?"

"Right here is fine with me," Tom said, joking.

"I'm game," said Mary, who was exhausted after the long drive.

"You don't really want to get married in a service station, do you?" Tom asked.

"Why not?" she replied. "I'm tired."

But Tom thought better of it; so while the kids waited in the car, Tom and Mary walked to the courthouse and were married.

When they returned, Ann nudged Hearn and said, "Ask him."

"*You* ask him," he retorted.

"No, *you* ask him," Ann insisted.

Mary turned around. "Ask him what?"

Ann giggled and said, "Can we call you Dad?"

Tom Watson laughed and said yes, and he's been "Dad" ever since. After two false starts, Mary had finally found a father for her children and a loving husband for herself.

•   •   •

When he finished boot camp, Tom Watson was assigned to Fort Benning, Georgia, and Mary and the kids moved with him. On a private's salary, they could only afford to rent an eighteen-foot-long mobile home that had one bed for Tom and Mary and bunk beds for the kids. They stored their belongings outside in cardboard boxes, stacked under an awning and covered with plastic: clothes in one box, dishes and kitchenware in another.

Mary earned extra money by spit-shining servicemen's boots, and washing and ironing their fatigues. On months they ran short of cash, she secretly dipped into her meager savings, which were soon gone.

Materially, they had very little, but their two years in Fort Benning were the most idyllic they had. "That was really where our life began," Mary says. "We didn't have anything but each other, but here is love, here is security, here is someone who cares for your children. . . . I was happier than I had ever been in my entire life."

Fort Benning is the first place that holds vivid memories for John Wayne Hearn. The years before are a blur of foggy images of Houston and Covington. At fourteen, Hearn had grown into a tall, gangly boy with a big shock of hair that he oiled and combed into a wave, Elvis style. Now in junior high, he was a mediocre student, and fairly shy. But he did have a good sense of humor and liked to clown around. His big interests were music and dancing, and Mary took home-movies of him and Ann dancing in the front yard.

It was the first time that he or Ann had ever had a normal family life. Tom and Mary took them to the movies, to the Skyline drive-in for a hamburger and a milk shake, and to the Ice Capades when it came to town. A friendly pastor at St. Mary's Road Methodist Church enrolled them in the Methodist Youth Fellowship, which sponsored softball games, dances at the church, and various youth outings. According to Mary Watson, the pastor nicknamed Hearn "the Little Crusader" because he invited so many children to church with him.

Fort Benning was also where Hearn first learned about his real father. It happened by accident. The family returned to Houston on leave, and Mary asked their landlady to keep an eye on their trailer. Being nosy, the landlady snooped around and discovered the locked box with Joe Pickett's medals and commendations, found the key, and opened it. When Mary came home, the woman asked her about Joe Pickett, and Mary admitted the truth. Being nosy *and* a meddler, the woman then blabbed the news to Hearn.

"I guess that was just about the saddest thing that ever happened to me," Mary says. "Up to that point I didn't feel like I should tell him anything—just let everything go, and one day, when he wanted to know, I'd tell him in the right manner."

Learning the truth about his father had two effects on Hearn. First, it deepened the bond with his mother. It became *their* secret. "After this happened we would talk about his father when no one was around—just mother and son talk," Mary says. "I would tell him how special his dad was, and that one day he would meet someone just as special."

The other effect was that for the first time Hearn had a direction in life. Fort Benning had given him a new beginning, but Joe Pickett gave him a past. And not just *any* past, but a *heroic* one that gave meaning to his life, beyond the foggy memories of Houston and Covington, and the years not worth remembering.

Because the truth is, not only are Hearn's *memories* of his early years fuzzy, but so was *he*. In his mother's eyes, of course, he had always been wonderfully funny, superbly intelligent, a model Boy Scout, and a dedicated evangelist; but in reality he was at most a mediocre student, a middling Boy Scout, and an inconsistent Christian. Yes, he liked to clown around and loved to dance, but those were hardly qualities on which to build a life. There had been nothing that really motivated him, nothing that made him stand out from the crowd—until Joe Pickett.

•   •   •

The family's peaceful interlude in Fort Benning ended in December, 1960, when Tom Watson was shipped overseas to Germany, where Cold War tensions were building to a head in Berlin.

Mary and the kids moved back to Houston, and rented a duplex at 924 Fugate Street, in the Heights. It was a step up from Firefly Street or Cedar Hill Street. The houses are small and modest, but it was a decent working-class neighborhood, with no "goats for sale" signs in the front yards or oil-storage tanks behind the house.

On January 5, 1961, Hearn enrolled in the eighth grade at Hogg Junior High. With Tom Watson overseas, he became the man of the house, and tinkered constantly with Mary's 1960 Pontiac Bonneville, even though he was still too young to drive.

Music remained his biggest interest. He and Ann were excellent dancers, and spent their Friday and Saturday nights at a skating rink near Playland Park—where they won several dance contests, both on skates and off. They danced the jitterbug and the twist, the latest craze, popularized by Chubby Checker.

That fall, he entered the ninth grade at San Jacinto High School and there discovered an outlet for the new sense of purpose in his life: reserve officer training corps (ROTC).

He threw himself into the ROTC program with great fervor: he made the ROTC drill team (which competed all over the state) and was promoted to staff sergeant his first year. "ROTC was his life," says Mary Watson. "It made him feel closer to his natural father and to Tom, who was in the Army." He had finally found something at which he excelled, and his self-confidence soared: he liked the way he looked in his starched khaki uniform with the gold braid on his shoulder, and he started dating a member of the Golden Gauchos, San Jacinto's girls' drill team.

At sixteen, Hearn was coming into manhood, propelled forward by a magnificent new inheritance from his dead father. He had a heroic role model to live up to. *Two* role models, in fact: Joe Pickett and Tom Watson. And so, armed with the knowledge of Joe Pickett's sacrifice, and bolstered by Tom Watson's love, John Wayne Hearn marched into the 1960s with new confidence and purpose, at last knowing what to do with his life: he wanted to be a soldier.

Part Three

SEMPER FIDELIS

1

. . . as the Hueys came in—very fast and very low, maybe twelve feet off the ground—he saw Francis giving the helicopters a big thumbs-up sign and thought: What a jerk. We're getting creamed and this guy's pretending it's The Sands of Iwo Jima. *Then he saw one of the door gunners, leaning precariously out the side of his helicopter, returning Francis' gesture—it seemed half the people in the war were playing John Wayne. . . .*

—Joe Klein
Payback

The South China Sea glistened in the afternoon sun as the giant C-141 Starlifter descended toward a sprawling airfield at the tip of a dog-eared harbor. Peering down, Pfc. John Wayne Hearn saw bat-winged fishing boats, looking like tiny water bugs, nimbly picking their way among the huge freighters and cargo ships. Brilliant snow-white beaches stretched south along the curving shoreline, framing a narrow delta of rice paddies and marshes; while in the distance, lush green foothills kowtowed before the lonesome, jagged peaks of the Annamite mountain range. "It don't look like a war's going on to me," Hearn thought to himself. Da Nang looked like a beach resort, the way he pictured Acapulco or Rio de Janeiro, which he had never seen.

When the C-141's huge cargo door dropped open, he marched out of the air-conditioned plane into a force field of muggy, searing heat that sucked the air out of his lungs. He had been warned about the heat, but nothing had prepared him for *that* kind of heat.

At a staging area, he was assigned to 1st Battalion, 9th Marines, issued an M-14 service rifle and two magazines of ammunition, and loaded into a truck for the ride to battalion headquarters on Hill 55, eight miles south of Da Nang.

Da Nang air base was a mammoth complex. The first American combat troops in Vietnam—the 9th Marine Expeditionary Brigade, 3,500 strong—had been sent on a "limited mission" in March, 1965, to defend the Da Nang base. When Hearn arrived one year later, U.S. troop strength was at 215,000 and increasing every day (it would reach 385,000 by the end of the year), but the primary mission of the 55,000 Marines "in-country" was still to protect the Da Nang area.

Da Nang was command headquarters for I Corps Tactical Zone, a narrow 225-mile long strip of mountainous jungle that stretched north to the demilitarized zone, south to Binh Dinh province, and west across the Annamite range to the Laotian border. I Corps was inhabited by 2.6 million Vietnamese, 98 percent of whom lived in coastal villages such as Con Thien, Quang Tri, My Lai, and the old Imperial City of Hue—names not yet known to the American public. Farther inland, in the intractable wildness of the Annamites, lay a remote basecamp called Khe Sanh.

I Corps would be the setting for the most brutal fighting of the war (over half of the American soldiers killed in Vietnam after 1967 died there), but on the day Hearn arrived in April, 1966, Da Nang looked like any air base in the States: Air Force F-100's, F-105's, and B-57's lined the east side of the airfield, Marine F-4 Phantoms and helicopters lined the west side, and a maze of maintenance shops and hangars surrounded the field. Farther back were a giant PX, administration buildings, and rows of barracks. The barracks were left over from the French, but at least they had hot and cold running water and flush toilets. "Damn, this is Vietnam?" Hearn joked with his three buddies from tank school, who had all volunteered for Vietnam together. "These guys are living nice."

He saw no sign of Operation Rolling Thunder, the daily bombing of North Vietnam that had been going on since February, 1965, and heard no artillery or mortar fire in the nearby mountains. Nor was there any sign of the near-civil war that was raging between the South Vietnamese government and militant Buddhist priests in their saffron robes, whose self-immolations had inspired general strikes and armed insurrections in Hue and Da Nang. Both the Vietcong and the Buddhists would soon make their presence felt within the fortified compound of Da Nang air base, but on this day the illusion of American invincibility remained.

John Wayne Hearn had seen the war on television, and he was eager for his first action. His opportunity came quickly. On the way out to Hill 55, his truck came upon an infantry squad pinned down by sniper fire from a nearby village. The squad leader had called up a tank for assistance, which was sitting in the road, waiting for the sniper to fire again—so it could blast him with its powerful guns. But the sniper was coyly refusing to fire; so both sides were playing a waiting game.

Hearn hustled out of the truck with the other "cherries" and took cover behind the tank, his heart pumping with adrenaline. The tank commander explained the situation, and Hearn, eager to prove himself, volunteered to run down the road to a little bridge and shoot into the village, trying to draw the sniper's fire. "I pulled a real 'John Wayne'—something stupid like you see in the movies," he recalls. "I was actually stupid enough to run two hundred feet down the road to that bridge, stand up with nothing in front of me, and empty twenty rounds into that village, and thank God nobody shot at me."

A few minutes later, the Vietcong started firing at the tank with a recoilless rifle, and a big red ball of fire came hurtling over the top of the tank and exploded in the field behind Hearn. That's when the reality hit: He could have been killed on his first day, on the way out to his unit.

When the infantry squad finally swept through the village, the VC were gone. It was a frustrating encounter that would be repeated many times during Hearn's twenty-seven months in Vietnam.

He had been trained as a crewman on a light-duty tank called an Ontos, a fearsome killing-machine equipped with six 106 mm recoilless rifles plus two .50-caliber machine guns. The Ontos was designed as a tank hunter, but in the jungles of Vietnam it was used primarily as a mobile artillery unit, or for escorting convoys. It had a three-man crew—a loader, a driver, and the tank commander, who operated the guns. Hearn started out as a loader, the most vulnerable of the three because he had to go outside to reload the big guns.

After two months in Vietnam, John Wayne Hearn had been under fire many times, had seen good friends killed, and understood the reality of the war in all its horror. As a dutiful son, he wrote home nearly every day, letting his mom know he was all right. Sometimes he enclosed photographs his buddies had taken: shots of John Wayne Hearn the warrior, leaning against his tank or squatting behind an M-60 machine gun; or John Wayne Hearn the clown, flexing his biceps or fussily combing his hair. Even 12,000 miles from home, fighting a war in a distant jungle, he was still playing the clown, mugging for the camera with a boyish grin.

But his grin couldn't disguise the fact that he was fighting the most confusing war in U.S. history, and the first person he killed drove home the point: it was a woman with a baby. Hearn's commanding officer claimed that the woman, who worked in a nearby village, was a merchant by day and a VC at night, and ordered him to shoot her. When Hearn refused, the officer threatened to shoot *him;* so he fired, and the woman literally exploded (she had been booby-trapped), killing the baby too. It was a traumatic experience that Hearn wrote home about, telling his mom that he could imagine *her* holding the baby.

The letter would have dramatic repercussions. Just a few weeks later, when Hearn came in off a sweep, his commanding officer called him in. "Pack your stuff, Hearn, you're leaving," he said.

"Whaddya mean, I'm leaving?" Hearn asked.

"You're a sole surviving son, aren't you?"

Hearn was taken aback. "Well, yeah. . . . How'd you know?"

"All I know is I've got an order transferring you *today.* They want you out of the country in twenty-four hours."

Five hours later he was on a plane to Okinawa. When he reported in, he told the CO, "I want to go back to Vietnam."

"You can't go back to Vietnam," the officer replied. "You're a sole surviving son."

"What started all this?" Hearn asked, dumbfounded. "I didn't ask to leave Vietnam."

"Well, son, evidently your mom got in touch with a congress-man and the congressman got in touch with the Defense Depart-ment and the Defense Department said to get your ass out of Vietnam."

"My mom?" Hearn said in disbelief.

Yes, exactly—his mom. That explained everything.

• • •

There was a joke going around that went like this: "What's the difference between the Marine Corps and the Boy Scouts?" "The Boy Scouts have adult leadership." "Dig it," the grunts would say. . . . The Corps came to be called by many the finest instrument ever devised for the killing of young Americans.

—Michael Herr
Dispatches

Mary Watson had been terrified about Hearn going to Viet-nam, although she tried to hide her feelings. She still cries remem-bering how he broke the news. "He said 'Mom, I have volunteered for Vietnam—so Dad won't have to go,' " she recalls, her eyes filling with tears.

At some level, though, she must have been preparing herself for that announcement since the day Hearn first learned about his real father. Every step he had taken since—beginning with ROTC classes at San Jacinto High—had moved him closer to following in Joe Pickett's footsteps.

In 1962 the family left Houston after Mary was robbed at gunpoint while working at a local drugstore. They moved to Stevensville, Michigan, where Tom Watson's sister lived.

When Hearn enrolled in the tenth grade at Lakeshore High School, he learned, to his great dismay, that the school didn't offer ROTC. As a substitute outlet for his energies, he went out for junior varsity football, and lettered as a defensive tackle.*

---

* Many people consider Hearn a compulsive liar, which may or may not be true, but he is definitely a compulsive *embellisher* who exaggerates the facts to make himself look good. His description of his JV football career is a good example: "My mom used to film some of the football games, and I used to really enjoy watching those. It was like I was everywhere. Every time a tackle was made, it was made by John Hearn, number 72, and I just enjoyed hearing my name announced in front of this huge stadium slap full of people."

He barely maintained the C average he needed to play sports, and was more interested in cars than girls. Tom Watson helped him buy his first car—a 1955 Chevrolet Belair—and got him a part-time job at the Phillips 66 gas station where he worked. Music was still his favorite hobby. At Christmas, Hearn and a friend bought matching sweaters and slacks, combed their hair in wavy ducktails —à la the Everly Brothers—and made the rounds of local parties pretending to be a singing duo. Mary Watson took pictures of them singing into an unconnected microphone, and doing the twist. A year later, when the Beatles took the U.S. by storm, Hearn and three friends bought Beatle wigs and began imitating the Fab Four. He was never in a band himself, but at least he could pretend.

In April, 1963, Hearn found something to fill the void of ROTC: he joined the Navy Reserve. He went to reserve meetings on weekends, and to Great Lakes, Illinois, that summer for six weeks of Navy boot camp.

When school started that fall, he had more going for him than ever before: good friends, a car, a job, the Navy Reserve, and football. However, it all quickly unraveled. He made the varsity football team, but injured his knee before the first game and had to quit. Then, in October, 1963, Ann dropped out of school at age sixteen and got married—setting off a holy war between her and her mother. "When she quit school on top of getting married, I almost lost my mind," says Mary Watson. "It was like I was losing her, because she had to be with her husband and I had to take a backseat . . . and it's hard for me to do that."

When Hearn started dating a girl whom Mary disapproved of, she actually moved the family out of Michigan to keep from "losing" him too. "We felt like if we could just separate John from this girl everything would be okay—and it worked out good," she says. "We didn't like the cold weather anyway; so Tom and I decided to get John out of there."

They moved to Sarasota, Florida, where Mary had an old friend. The separation might have worked, but the move didn't. Uprooted from his friends, his job, and his reserve unit, Hearn floundered at Sarasota High School. He was ready to quit school, and made the rounds of the local recruiting offices one afternoon.

A fat Marine Corps sergeant told him: "You'll never make a marine."

The man was baiting him, but Hearn swallowed the hook: "I tell you what, Sarge, if I wasn't already in the Navy Reserve I'd join the Marines just to show you."

"That's no problem," the sergeant replied. "I can transfer you into the Marines right now."

"Do it," Hearn retorted. So the sergeant did: he wrote out an interservice transfer, and arranged for a "deferred enlistment" after Hearn's senior year of high school.

Hearn was afraid to tell his mother what he'd done, and she didn't find out until the fat sergeant showed up at their front door one day and told Hearn that he had to catch a bus to Jacksonville to take the Marine Corps entrance test. "I want you to know I followed that bus down the Tamiami Trail as far as I could go, just a-waving," Mary says. "Lord, I hated to see that boy go."

He was supposed to come home and finish high school, but when he got to Jacksonville he decided to waive his deferment and go on to boot camp. At least partly, he was rebelling against his mother. "I was ready to get out on my own and do what *I* wanted to do," he says. So on April 24, 1964, John Wayne Hearn was sworn into the United States Marine Corps for a four-year term. He called his mother that day and told her that he was leaving for Parris Island, South Carolina, the next morning.

• • •

Marine boot camp at Parris Island in the 1960s was legendary for its brutality, but it wasn't tough enough to keep Mary Watson away from her son. Several weeks into basic training, Hearn wrote home and said that he was in the hospital, without explaining why. In a panic, Mary called the hospital.

"Your son is blind," a sergeant told her.

"What do you mean he's blind?" she exclaimed. "I am coming up there to see him."

"You can't, ma'am," the sergeant replied.

"Can't" is the wrong word to use with Mary Watson when her son is involved. "Don't tell me I *can't,*" she said fiercely, and hung up.

She and Tom Watson drove straight through to Parris Island —a thirteen-hour drive. A guard stopped them at the front gate. "I'm sorry, ma'am," he said, "but you can't see your son."

Mary's anger had been building for thirteen hours, and now it erupted at the unsuspecting guard. "Don't tell me I can't see him!" she bellowed. "This place will not hold me and you and hell too!"

She demanded to know where the hospital was, but the guard refused to tell her. "Well, I'll find it myself," she snapped. She stomped back to the car, told Tom, "Move over, I'm driving," and barreled past the gate.

She was stopped again at the front desk of the hospital. "I'm sorry, ma'am, but you can't come in," a clerk told her.

"I'm *in*," she declared. "Now I want to see my son."

And see him she did. The Marine Corps boasted that it was looking for "a few good men," but it needed more than that to stand up to Mary Watson on a rampage.

The problem was that Hearn had become temporarily sun-blinded after a long march on the beach. The condition cleared up in a few days, and Mary and Tom made the long trek back to Sarasota. But after several similar trips in the next month, they *moved* to Parris Island. "We were coming up almost every other weekend, and I finally said, 'Tom, I think we better just move up there. I don't think we can keep doing this,' " she says.

They moved to Beaufort, right outside of the base. Mary would sneak out and watch Hearn's platoon march and drill, which, according to Ann, resulted in Hearn being called a "baby" by the other men.

After his graduation, Mary and Tom moved to Columbia, South Carolina, and have been there ever since. Ann, who was pregnant at the time, and whose husband was stationed overseas with the Marines, moved with them. "We moved to Columbia with twenty-one dollars, a pregnant girl, and a U-Haul trailer with everything we owned," Mary says. Tom Watson got hired at a gas station four hours after they hit Columbia, and Mary got a job in the K mart drug department.

After boot camp, Hearn went to Sea Duty Indoctrination School at Norfolk, Virginia. There, he met a high school senior named Donna Graves, fell in love—it was the first of his many whirlwind courtships—and married her in October, 1964. They spent their honeymoon night on a broken-down Greyhound bus on their way to Columbia. Hearn was taking his bride home to stay with Mama while he reported to the aircraft carrier U.S.S. *Saratoga* for a nine-month Mediterranean cruise.

It was his first chance to see the world: France, Spain, Greece, Gibraltar, Crete, and Italy. He was one of sixty Marines who provided security for the ship's nuclear weapons, and he also competed on the Armed Forces judo and karate squad. At six feet one inch and 190 pounds, he had the size and strength to be a formidable heavyweight.

But two events ruined his *Saratoga* tour: He started having marital problems one month after coming on board; then he severely twisted his left knee (the same one he'd hurt playing football) in a judo exhibition. The knee swelled up and had to be drained several times, and eventually required surgery. However, his problems with Donna were inoperable: she apparently decided that being married to an absentee husband whom she hardly knew was not for her, and returned home to Virginia.

Upset about his marriage, Hearn got into a series of minor difficulties on the ship—arguments, indebtedness, two unauthorized absences—and on December 1, 1965, was sent in for a psychological evaluation. The psychologist's report noted Hearn's marital problems; cited "numerous occasions" that he had "blatantly lied"; and described him as immature, extremely manipulative, impulsive, insecure, with much underlying hostility and predominant "sociopathic features." The psychologist recommended that Hearn be removed from the ship as a reliability risk, and concluded: "His manipulations and lies must be taken for what they are and treated accordingly."

Hearn was booted off the *Saratoga* and transferred to tank school at Camp Lejeune, North Carolina. With the Vietnam War heating up, he and three buddies decided to volunteer. "Everybody else was getting *sent* over there, but these four idiots walk in and say, 'We want to go to Vietnam,' " Hearn recalls. After his stint on the *Saratoga,* there was a year-long waiting period before Hearn could be sent overseas again, but he signed a waiver—and was soon on his way to Vietnam.

•   •   •

When he ended up in Okinawa three months later, he couldn't have been too surprised: he knew his mother. Getting a son pulled out of Vietnam might have been an impossibility for most mothers, but not for Mary Watson. Once her protective instincts kicked in, neither the United States Marine Corps nor the Defense Department (nor any other government agency since, for that matter) was able to withstand the relentless barrage of letters and phone calls emanating from Columbia, South Carolina.

It was Hearn's letter about shooting the Vietnamese woman that did it. "When I read that letter, I just went ape," Mary says. "I started making phone calls. When you love your child you do what you have to do, believe me. And it's not *who* you know, it's not *what* you know, it's the determination that you have."

She kept calling until she found out about the policy that sole surviving sons didn't have to serve in combat, then made an appointment with her congressman. A few days later, John Wayne Hearn was on a plane to Okinawa.

However, Mary Watson's heartaches were not over. After three months in Okinawa, where he was assigned to the Armed Forces police, Hearn wrote her and said that he was volunteering to go back to Vietnam. It was the specter of his dead father that motivated him. "The main reason I wanted to go back was because my father had died in the war, and I felt like this was what I was supposed to do," he says.

He signed a waiver of his rights as a sole surviving son; flew back to Da Nang in August, 1966; was reassigned to the 2nd Battalion, 9th Marine Division (as a tank driver); and wound up back on Hill 55, the same place he had left three months before.

• • •

When he came home at the end of his first tour in April, 1967, he had one thing on his mind: flying. He had been enamored with flying since childhood, when *Sky King* had been his favorite TV show. One Saturday morning while watching it, he told his mother: "Someday, Mom, I'm going to do that." After returning home on thirty-day leave, he started taking flying lessons at Owens Field in Columbia.

He wanted to fly so badly that, unbeknownst to his mother, he had already signed a six-month extension to go back to Vietnam— on the condition that he be transferred to the Marine Air Wing. His dream was to become a helicopter crewman, eventually qualify for officer candidate school, and become a marine pilot. It wasn't totally farfetched: combat promotions came quickly in Vietnam (Hearn had already been promoted to sergeant in January, 1967), and there was a growing demand for pilots.

In what had become his usual pattern, he didn't tell his mother about the extension until a few days before he had to leave. When he arrived back in Da Nang, he got a rude introduction to what marines call sarcastically "the Big Green Weenie": the Marine Corps transferred him to the 1st Marine Air Wing, as promised, but to an *infantry* unit protecting a Hawk missile battery outside of Da Nang. Not only would he have no chance to fly, but he would be a grunt (his secondary training specialty, or MOS) with a far greater chance of being killed than when he'd been in tanks.

Hearn's six months at the Light Anti-Aircraft Missile (LAAM) battery were his worst in Vietnam. In the Ontos company he had seen death at a distance, but now he was a platoon sergeant responsible for forty-two men, and death was all around him. His squads might stay out on reconnaissance patrols for two days or ten days, sometimes without ever making enemy contact, and sometimes with skirmishes every day. Whether experiencing mind-numbing boredom or the terror of a firefight, the men lived on the edge of uncertainty. They were fighting an invisible enemy in a mapless war, and every step they took could be their last: any path could be mined, any bush booby-trapped, any open field a perfect ambush.

For those who survived, it was easier to go numb than face the anguish over their comrades' death. They channeled their grief into anger at the Vietcong, whom they depersonalized as "gooks," "zips" or "dinks." Yet sometimes the reality of who they were actually shooting at broke through. Hearn once killed a nine- or ten-year-old boy with an AK-47—and the memory still haunts him. "I hollered at him at least a dozen times to drop it," he says, "but when he raised it to his shoulder I killed him. And it bothers me a lot. He was about the same age as *my* little boy, and everytime I see my boy I think about it. But it was a case where if I didn't shoot him, he was going to kill me. It wasn't no toy he was playing with. There weren't no toy guns in Vietnam."

Besides the Vietcong, there were the constant hazards from the land itself: incessant heat, flies, malaria-carrying mosquitoes, vipers, leeches, and from October to May, the depressing north-east monsoon—a cold steady drizzle, called the *crachin,* that brought an inch of rain each day, temperatures in the forties at night, and impenetrable fog that hampered artillery and air support. Hearn's letters to his mother reflect the monsoon's toll:

> 7 October '67: I wish this weather would go one way or the other. One day it rains and then it stops and gets hot again. At times it rains for five or six days straight and then the sun shines for a couple hours and then it starts raining again. It does tend to get to you after awhile. . . .

> 9 October '67: The rain is starting to get to us all right now. . . . No matter what we wear we still get wet. I have a set of rain gear and I still get wet. If you don't get wet from the rain you get wet from sweating in it.

As his six months at the LAAM battery counted down, Hearn checked off the remaining days on a calendar. But when his tour dwindled to the last few days, he decided to extend for *another* six months—this time with a written proviso that he be assigned to a helicopter squadron.

He was still determined to fly, plus he was in love with a girl from Singapore named Loy Chin, whom he had met on R&R. In typically quick fashion, Hearn proposed; and Loy Chin accepted. He wrote home joyfully, telling Mary Watson of his plans to marry Loy Chin and bring her home to the States. When Mary didn't reply right away, Hearn—fearful of her disapproval—wrote a more beseeching letter:

> 6 October '67

> Dear Mom Dad & Family,

> Well hello their again. I hope you are not to mad at me to write to me. if you are I'm sorry. Mom its like you and dad. You and dad love each other very much. Its the same with Loy Chin and myself. I know you understand. You have to. I haven't recieved an answer to my letter telling you that I was going to get married. When I do I can just about see whats going to be in it. . . . Mom, Loy Chin

means all the world to me. I know you understand this. I'm
sure that you do. Mom does dad understand also. I hope
he does. . . .

When his second tour ended in November, 1967, he went to
Singapore on thirty-day leave, instead of going home. It was probably just as well. He would have had to face not only his mother's
concerns about Loy Chin but an American public that was bitterly
divided over the war. For a twenty-two-year-old marine who had
just volunteered for his *third* tour, it would have been a disillusioning homecoming.

On October 21, 1967, fifty thousand antiwar demonstrators
marched on the Pentagon, chanting "Hey, hey, LBJ, how many
kids did you kill today?"

By November, 1967, dissension over the war had reached
even the White House. Defense Secretary Robert McNamara, once
the war's staunchest proponent, had grown disillusioned and resigned to head the World Bank. Although a majority of the American public still supported the war, forty-four percent favored with-
drawal (up from eighteen percent).

Vietnam had become a military and political quagmire for
Lyndon Johnson, threatening to scuttle his Great Society domestic
programs and his 1968 reelection bid. In November, 1967, Senator Eugene McCarthy of Minnesota announced that he would challenge Johnson in the Democratic primaries as an antiwar candidate, and LBJ was even more paranoid about presidential
preference polls that showed Robert Kennedy (still an unannounced candidate, who had recently turned against the war) leading him by 20 percentage points.

Only Gen. William Westmoreland remained the eternal opti-
mist. Westmoreland was still convinced that his "war of attrition"
would eventually break the will of the North Vietnamese people.
As proof, he pointed to the ever-increasing weekly body counts of
North Vietnamese and Vietcong casualties, and promised that the
magic turning point was drawing nigh.

However, the American public seemed to be paying more
attention to the body count of *American* dead, which was also increasing steadily. By December, 1967, U.S. troop strength was at
486,000, yet Westmoreland was asking for additional combat bat-

talions and pressing Johnson to activate the reserves—a political
gauntlet that LBJ was unwilling to run.

But if the American people were losing faith, John Wayne
Hearn was not, and he returned to Vietnam for his final tour of
duty with great optimism: he was in love, he had his transfer papers
to the helicopter squadron, and he believed in the war as fervently
as ever. He wrote to his parents on December 12, 1967:

> Mom, theirs one thing that I want to tell you and dad. I
> want you both to understand this. If something does
> happen to me over here, I don't want you, dad or anyone
> to cry. I want you to hold your heads up and say, "that's
> my son, he died for something that he believed in." . . .
> Love, Johnny.

Mary Watson, brimming with pride, had the letter reprinted in
the Columbia newspaper.

•   •   •

*[Tet was] a huge collective nervous breakdown. . . . Vietnam was a
dark room full of deadly objects, the VC were everywhere all at once like
spider cancer, and instead of losing the war in little pieces over years we
lost it fast in under a week. After that, we were like the character in pop
grunt mythology, dead but too dumb to lie down.*

—Michael Herr
Dispatches

The Tet Offensive began in I Corps on the evening of January
29, 1968, with a rocket attack on MAG-16's helicopter squadrons at
Marble Mountain. John Wayne Hearn was checking the "Jesus
nut" on his Huey gunship's rotor assembly when a spin-stabilized
122-mm rocket roared over the top of his hangar, sounding like a
freight train right above his head. He started running for a bunker,
but a second rocket blew off the top of the hangar and the concus-
sion knocked him to the ground. Dazed, Hearn picked himself up
and stumbled on toward the bunker, where a dozen other men
were scrambling to get inside. Another rocket landed nearby, and
Hearn dove onto the pile of men, crawling over their backs to
safety. Sitting in darkness, he felt a dull throbbing in his right leg,

reached down to touch his pant leg, which was soaking wet, and realized he was bleeding. A finger-sized piece of shrapnel had buried itself five inches in his upper leg.

Although the wound was painful, it was not serious, and Hearn was only a minor casualty of the Tet Offensive. The American war effort, however, was fatally wounded. The surprise offensive by nearly seventy thousand NVA and Vietcong soldiers was launched simultaneously against a hundred villages and towns, including thirty-six of the forty-four provincial capitals, ten of which were overrun. Rocket and mortar attacks were launched, in broad daylight, against twenty-three airfields, including Da Nang, Marble Mountain, Cam Rahn Bay, and other presumably "secure" American bases.

After Tet, Westmoreland's daily briefings—already known derisively as the "five o'clock follies" or "jive at five" by war correspondents—were received with outright disbelief; while back home, Lyndon Johnson's credibility gap became a vast bottomless chasm. His popularity rating dropped from forty-eight to thirty-six percent, and approval of his handling of the war from forty to twenty-six percent.

On the heels of the Tet Offensive came the seemingly fruitless seventy-seven-day "siege" of Khe Sanh, and on March 16, 1968, the My Lai massacre, which wouldn't become public for another year. In *A Bright Shining Lie*, Neil Sheehan described the massacre, directed by Lt. William Calley, Jr., in which 347 unarmed villagers were killed:

> The American soldiers and junior officers shot old men, women, boys, girls, and babies. . . . The soldiers beat women with rifle butts and raped some and sodomized others before shooting them. They shot the water buffalos, the pigs, and the chickens. They threw the dead animals in the wells to poison the water. They tossed satchel charges into the bomb shelters under the houses. . . . All of the houses were put to the torch.

At Marble Mountain, John Wayne Hearn read the newspaper and magazine accounts of atrocities committed by U.S. soldiers, but after nearly two years in Vietnam—and after seeing mutilated

American soldiers with their penises cut off and stuck in their mouths or bamboo stakes rammed up their butts—he understood the revenge mentality that could lead to a My Lai.

Once, while his Huey gunship was ferrying a U.S. chaplain to outlying base camps to conduct services, they overheard a radio transmission calling for a medevac helicopter to pick up a wounded Vietnamese baby. Since Hearn's helicopter was close to the village, which was supposedly in a nonhostile zone, his pilot volunteered to fly in and pick up the child. When they landed, a Vietnamese woman holding a baby came running toward the chopper. The chaplain, sitting by the door, offered to go get the baby. He hopped out of the Huey and walked toward the woman. When he got within about five feet, she tossed the baby into his arms, and started running away. Hearn screamed at the chaplain to drop the baby and run, but he couldn't hear him over the noise of the turned-up chopper. A second later, the baby and the chaplain were both blown apart by a grenade tied to the child's back. Enraged, Hearn jumped behind his M-60 machine gun and shot the escaping woman, then continued pumping rounds into her lifeless body until his ammunition ran out.

•   •   •

By March, 1968, Lyndon Johnson's political disintegration was complete: two weeks after Westmoreland's request for an additional 206,000 troops, Senator Eugene McCarthy came within three hundred votes of beating Johnson in the New Hampshire primary, and four days later, Robert Kennedy announced his candidacy for president.

On March 31, Johnson announced his shocking decision to not run for reelection. Four days later, Martin Luther King, Jr. was gunned down in Memphis. Two months later, Robert Kennedy met the same fate in Los Angeles. The nation was in political upheaval.

2

1. *Syllogistic Reasoning:*   *All men are beasts.*
                              Bob's a man.
                              Therefore, Bob's a beast.
2. *Hasty Generalization:*
      *When we first met I knew we were meant for
      each other.*

> *Eimann, Sandra*
> *English 131-4*
> *January 13, 1967*
> *Homework*

At a spring picnic in 1966, Sandra Kay Eimann met a short, muscular, ruggedly handsome Texas A&M freshman named Bob Black. She had gone to the picnic with another A&M student, but that didn't stop Bob Black from going after her. And when Bob Black went after something, he usually got it.

Although Sandra had just graduated from A&M Consolidated High School in May, she was not naive about boys: she had gone steady several times in high school, and was dating an A&M band member. But she had never met anyone like Bob Black. He was a mature, witty, smooth-talking college freshman with a billboard smile and a booming laugh that could halt conversations across a crowded room. He looked so sharp in his A&M Corps of Cadets uniform, it was almost as if he had been born to wear one.

In many respects, he had.

Robert Vannoy Black, Jr. was born January 31, 1947, in Mexia,

Texas, a prototypical Texas boomtown.* His father, Robert V. Black, Sr. (who went by Vannoy or R.V.), grew up in Mexia and enlisted in the Army Air Corps in October, 1942, at age eighteen. A tail gunner on a B-24 Liberator, he was shot down over Austria in April, 1944, and spent the remaining thirteen months of the war in Stalag XVII-B, a German prisoner-of-war camp in Gneixendorf, Austria, near the Czechoslovakian border.

When Vannoy Black returned to Mexia after the war, he married Ivonne LaFoy, from nearby Groesbeck, and started working as a pipe fitter for Stanolind Pipe Company, owned by Standard Oil of Indiana. He was transferred three times in four years, and eventually settled in Haskell, Texas, in 1953. Bob was six years old at the time. His younger brother Gary was born later that year.

•   •   •

Located fifty miles north of Abilene, Haskell had a population of approximately four thousand. It was once the heart of the old Comanche territory, and the home for millions of head of buffalo. By 1953, however, the surrounding prairies of buffalo grass and mesquite had been plowed under and planted in cotton—the town's major economic base. Oil had also been discovered prior to World War II, and Stanolind's Canyon Reef and Sojourner fields brought many oil field workers to town.

Vannoy Black was one of them. He worked for Service Pipeline, a Stanolind subsidiary that employed about twenty families in town. The company pumped the crude oil from Haskell's fields to Texas City and Whiting, Indiana, where it was refined. Vannoy was the crew clerk: He kept the time cards, figured the payroll, kept track of the inventory of pipeline fittings, and manned the office. The pipeline men would drop by every afternoon to make their reports, and they would sit and shoot the bull with Vannoy. "He was real outgoing, real friendly—just a heckuva nice fellow," says Lee McLure, a retired Service Pipeline worker.

Many of the old Service Pipeline employees still live in town, and Haskell itself has changed little since the 1950s. It's actually

* In August, 1921, after a huge gusher blew in and Mexia's population zoomed from 4,000 to 40,000 in one week, martial law had to be declared.

smaller than it was then—with a population of 3,782—as the Texas oil industry fell on hard times in the 1980s.

This is small-town America at its best. The town square has a quaint old courthouse, and most of the town's businesses are laid out around it: Perry's 5 and 10, Radio Shack, the Personality Shop, Southside Barber, Western Auto, the Sears Catalog store, and the Haskell *Free Press.* The town has no movie theater (the only one has closed), one motel, two banks, two liquor stores, three restaurants (chicken-fried steak sandwiches are the house specialties at all three, but only the Dairy Queen is open after 9 P.M.), four car dealerships, five attorneys, six pages of oil-field listings in the Yellow Pages, and *twelve* beauty shops.

Three blocks north of the square, on Avenue E—the main drag—is Haskell High School, and behind it is the football stadium: "the Reservation, Home of the Haskell Indians." As you drive out of town in any direction, cotton fields stretch to the horizon, and at night you can see the lights of Stamford, Throckmorton, and Breckenridge flickering across the open prairie.

Haskell is the all-American town, and Bob Black, at least on the surface, was the all-American boy. The Blacks lived at 1109 6th Street, just three blocks off Avenue E. The houses were plain but comfortable, and many of the Blacks' neighbors still live there. Bob started first grade in Haskell the year they arrived and graduated from Haskell High in 1965. There were fewer than fifty people in his graduating class.

He was an excellent student: intelligent, studious, well-behaved in class. In 1964 he was one of five junior boys chosen to represent Haskell County at Boys' State—an American Legion-sponsored program in Austin, where students set up a mock state government for a week.

He was a physical fitness buff—he lifted weights and worked out constantly—and wore sleeveless T-shirts to show off his biceps. But he was also short and slow and ungainly, and although he played on the football team through his junior year, he never started. "He was the most uncoordinated kid that ever came into Haskell County," says Tim Burson, a former teammate. "But if he ever got ahold of you, you weren't going anywhere."

To his teachers, he seemed as clean-cut and straitlaced as you could get. "He was really gung ho," says Bill Blakley, his math teacher. "It was always 'Yes, sir' and 'No, sir'—almost *too* much so."

He got it from his old man. Vannoy Black was very demanding, and he ran the household with military discipline. He had a volatile temper and wouldn't hesitate to discipline Bob or Gary if they fell short of his standards. "[Vannoy] had a temper, and he was loud," one neighbor recalls.

The major watershed in Vannoy's life—and perhaps the biggest influence on Bob's upbringing—was the thirteen months that he spent as a prisoner of war. Although American and British POW's in German camps suffered many hardships—chronic food shortages, freezing barracks, infestations of fleas and body lice, and at the end of the war, forced marches across the German countryside that caused many casualties—they were relatively well treated compared to Russian POW's, and were treated far better than Allied POW's in *Japanese* camps. Only four percent of U.S. and British POW's died in German camps, while twenty-eight percent died in Japanese camps, and fifty percent of Soviet prisoners perished. It wasn't *Hogan's Heroes* by any stretch of the imagination, but neither was it *The Bridge over the River Kwai* or the "Hanoi Hilton."

Their greatest hardships were not physical, but mental: boredom, futility, depression, tedium, and guilt. To combat the numbing boredom, the more industrious POW's took Red Cross study courses, organized theater troupes and makeshift symphony orchestras, published in-house newspapers, and at night, gathered around illegal wireless sets or plotted largely unsuccessful escape attempts.

Guilt was more difficult to deal with, however. As Richard Garrett, author of *P.O.W.: The Uncivil Face of War* and a British POW himself, puts it:

> There was, perhaps, a feeling of guilt at having fallen into the enemy's hands. Should one have fought it out to the last round and died gloriously? War has an insatiable appetite for heroics and there was nothing heroic about surrender.

That "insatiable appetite for heroics" might define Vannoy Black's life—and his son's—better than anything else. Vannoy had only flown on *eleven* missions when he was shot down over Austria. "For you the war is over," his German captors told him in halting English. In truth, for him the war had hardly begun. Half of the crewmen on his plane evaded the Germans and made it back to the American lines to fight again, but Vannoy's parachute got caught in a tree, he injured his back in the fall, and he rode out the rest of the war as an inglorious hostage.

After the war, Vannoy loved to recount the hardships of his POW days to his sons and their young friends. James Walls, who lived two doors down, remembers: "Most men who had served in the war didn't really talk about it, but every time we went into the storm cellar during a tornado Black would tell us about being a POW."

In the microcosm of the stalag, discipline and duty were the two highest virtues, and Vannoy drilled those values into his sons. When President Kennedy suggested that American youths were out of shape and should make a fifty-mile hike, most people ignored the call. Not Vannoy Black: he woke up Bob at four o'clock one morning and marched him all the way to Abilene—fifty miles away. Sammy Baker, Bob's best friend, went with them. "I only made it to Anson (thirty-two miles), but they made it all the way," he says. "They were tough."

In an era of postwar permissiveness, Vannoy Black found the perfect vehicle to inculcate the values of the stalag in his sons: the Boy Scouts of America. Vannoy had been an Eagle Scout himself, and it was almost foreordained that Bob and Gary would follow in his footsteps. While other fathers placed a baseball bat and glove in their infant son's crib, hoping for a future major leaguer, Vannoy Black placed, figuratively, the Boy Scout handbook in Bob's.

Scouting was *the* all-consuming passion in Bob Black's adolescent years; nothing else was even close. He became a Cub Scout at age eight (his mother, Ivonne Black, was his den mother), and at eleven, he joined Boy Scout Troop 36, sponsored by the First United Methodist Church. The scoutmaster, Ed Smart, also worked for Service Pipeline, and Vannoy Black became very involved with the troop. Even here, military discipline prevailed. "They ran it more like a military operation than a Boy Scout troop," recalls one former member. "We marched and did all that stuff."

With his father's encouragement, Bob progressed quickly through the ranks: tenderfoot, second class, first class, star, life, and in 1963, he attained the coveted Eagle. For most boys, the Eagle badge is the pinnacle of their scouting careers, but Bob Black wasn't satisfied with that: He added a silver and a bronze palm (each represents five additional merit badges) and earned the God and Country award (for service work with his church) and the Order of the Arrow (for honor campers). He also served as a den chief for a Cub Scout den, and when he got too old for Boy Scouts, he joined the local Explorer post.

In the Black home, the tenets of the Boy Scout creed—*trustworthy, loyal, helpful, friendly, courteous, kind, obedient, cheerful, thrifty, brave, clean, and reverent*—were living concepts. And to his teachers, his neighbors, and his parents, Bob Black was the model Scout.

There was another side to Bob Black, however, that the adults didn't see. In a home where *appearances* were critically important, Bob apparently learned how to maintain the appearance of propriety—how to flash his big grin and shuck his way out of trouble—to get around his father's strict code of conduct and pursue baser desires that an Eagle Scout was not supposed to have.

His classmates saw a different Bob Black. He had a hair-trigger temper, and when it went off there was no telling what he might do: According to people in the neighborhood, he beat up younger boys, chased after one boy with a baseball bat, and allegedly chased another one down the street with a bayonet.

This disturbing side of his personality was most evident with small animals. Bob hated cats and bragged to classmates about electrocuting them, pouring gasoline on them and setting them on fire, or tying their tails together and watching them claw themselves to death. He told his biology teacher, Gerald McCoy (now the high school principal), that he liked to nail frogs in the middle of the road and watch cars run over them or put them in milk bottles, pour gasoline on them, and light it.

At Haskell High he was a cutup and was generally well liked, but he didn't really fit in with any particular group. There were the football players, the hotrodders, the student government types. Bob was on the fringes of all of those, but never really belonged. "He couldn't ever really fit in with *anybody*," says Tim Burson.

"He'd come over to a group of people and say something, trying to be funny, but it would be totally off the wall."

To get attention, Bob resorted to macho displays of strength and bravura: in science class, after studying muscles, he once pounded a safety pin into his arm and strutted around the classroom, showing off; another time, he held his hand over a Bunsen burner and laughed about it. "We talked about Bobby putting that safety pin in his arm for years," recalls another classmate. "He was always different—maybe a quarter of a bubble off."

Unable to fit in with the "regular" crowd, Bob began hanging out with other boys who were also on the fringes, and when juvenile pranks started occurring around town—teachers' houses egged, watermelons thrown in their yards, obscenities painted on school walls, and rival schools' playing fields burned—some classmates suspected that Bob was to blame. "We couldn't prove it, but we all knew—from his actions and what he said—that he was doing it," says one. But while his buddies were often hauled into the principal's office, Bob was smart enough not to get caught. "I remember his friends being in trouble at school all the time," says Gary Druesdow, "but I don't ever remember Bobby being in trouble."

Bob didn't date much until his senior year of high school, but it wasn't from lack of trying: he begged Margaret Ann Walls, who lived two houses away, to go out with him, and when she turned him down, asked her mother to intervene on his behalf. But Walls still refused. "If you went for a Coke with him, it was, to put it bluntly, a hand up your skirt," she explains. "He was so overly forward, I felt like I had to be very cautious." Gerre Colbert remembers that Bob would wait for her after school (while her boyfriend was at basketball practice) and try to walk her home. She refused, and always felt uneasy around Bob because of the "slanteyed looks" he gave her. Bob finally got a steady girlfriend in his senior year and dated her until he left Haskell.

In addition to his other interests, Bob was an avid hunter. Hunting is a rite of passage for young boys on the Texas plains, and Vannoy taught Bob well. On birthdays and at Christmas, he was given his own shotguns and deer rifle, which were the beginnings of a prized gun collection. Stalking deer on the prairie evoked romantic images of Comanche braves, and when Bob heard rumors of distant Indian blood in the family, he created an imaginary persona for himself—a proud Indian warrior with advanced hunting instincts and sensory perceptions—and even fashioned a secret Indian name for himself, which he continued to use as an adult.

When Bob graduated from high school, his choice of a college reflected the family's military bent: he enrolled at Texas A&M in the fall of 1965, and swapped his Boy Scout uniform for the pressed khakis of the A&M Corps of Cadets. It seemed like a natural fit. He had been "a quarter of a bubble off" in Haskell, but at A&M he quickly found his niche in the Corps.

He had been rehearsing for a military life since childhood, and he flourished in the ceremonial rituals of the Corps: there were daily drills, overnight marches, and weekend boot camps. A&M freshmen, known as "fish," were put through a rigorous hazing process: They had to take tiny "fish bites" in the cafeteria, so that they'd be ready to answer impromptu questions, and had to explain their whereabouts and actions at any time to demanding upperclassmen. Bob's skills of deception had been finely honed in Haskell, and he excelled at making up such "good bull" that he fooled the upperclassmen.

With his infectious laugh, cocksure attitude, and charming familiarity—he was almost *too* familiar, the kind of guy who acted like your best friend when he hardly knew you—Bob knew how to put on a good show for people. But the problem with always putting on a show is that you sometimes confuse ceremony with sincerity, appearance with substance, and manipulation with love.

•   •   •

When Sandra Eimann met Bob Black at the 1966 spring picnic, it was as if there were two different Bobs: one was the all-American boy and jaunty A&M corpsman and the other was an immature nineteen-year-old with a streak of phoniness running through his personality. Apparently, Sandra was impressed with the former, but when Bob first showed up at the Eimanns' house on Winding Road (they had moved there in July, 1965), Marjorie and Glen Eimann got a strong whiff of the latter.

Glen Eimann is a man of few words, but his gut told him that something was not quite right about Bob Black. "I draw conclusions about people fast, and he wasn't one of my fondest," he recalls. "He'd come on real nice, but you could see through it."

Sandra and Bob met at several other picnics over the next few months. There weren't a lot of eligible young women to choose from in College Station, so A&M boys often sponsored picnics and parties for high school girls. Texas A&M had only started admitting women in 1963, and there were still less than 200 out of a total student body of 9,500.*

Bob went to dinner at Winding Road a few times; met Sandra's family, including her grandmother Liddie B., and that was the extent of their relationship. Sandra was dating another A&M student, and eventually became engaged to him. But when the boy suddenly broke off the engagement, Bob made his move.

Emotionally, Sandra was at rock bottom after the breakup. Crying and depressed, she was spending most of her time in her bedroom. Bob phoned her several times, but Marjorie told him emphatically, "Sandra doesn't want to see you. She doesn't want to see anybody."

Marjorie assumed that was the end of it, but Bob quickly devised a scheme to circumvent her edict: He went to see Liddie B., whom he knew liked him, and offered to drive her over to Winding Road for a visit (Liddie B. had never learned to drive). He called Marjorie from her house. "Grandmother wants to come visit Sandy," he said.

"Bob, *don't* come over here!" Marjorie insisted. "We do not want you here—and please don't bring Mother over here."

"We're coming to visit Sandy," he replied cheerfully.

A few minutes later, Bob showed up at the Eimanns' front door with Liddie B. in tow, grinning his big grin like nothing was wrong.

Glen and Marjorie were both furious, but what could they do? "There was no way we couldn't let *Mother* in," Marjorie says. So Bob and Liddie B. went into the bedroom and talked to Sandra, and before long Bob and Sandra were dating.

Besides the broken engagement, Sandra was vulnerable for

* In keeping with tradition, A&M's status as a coed institution inspired a whole new genre of Aggie jokes—called "Maggie jokes." For example: How many Maggies does it take to operate a dishwasher? Four; three to shake the dishwasher and one to lick the plates.

other reasons. Although she was sweet and outgoing, she was no raving beauty, no homecoming queen. Her 1966 high school graduation picture shows a very ordinary girl with teased hair, black horn-rimmed glasses, and a tight-lipped smile, as if she were embarrassed about her teeth.

She was also a very old-fashioned girl. The popular battle cry of the sixties—sex, drugs, and rock and roll—was completely foreign to her, as were antiwar protests, flower power, hippies, yippies, and the summer of love. She got up every morning and went to school, went to work (she was the head bookkeeper at Briarcrest Country Club), came home and walked her dogs. She loved her mother and father, loved her younger brother, and loved her grandmother Liddie B. She went to Sunday School every week at Rock Prairie Baptist Church. Although she was taking college courses at Allen Academy, she had no great plans for a career. She wanted what most old-fashioned, traditional girls in College Station, Texas, wanted in 1966: a husband and a family.

And when Bob Black strutted into her very ordinary life, showering her with romance and sappy love poems, Sandra Kay Eimann was swept away. By January, 1967, she was already doodling "Sandra Kay Black" in her English notebook, trying the name on for size.

Glen and Marjorie swallowed their objections and accepted Bob as a fixture at the Eimann dinner table, but their concerns about him didn't go away. "Glen was a daddy that didn't interfere," Marjorie says, "but he hated Bob with a purple passion, because he had a way of getting what he wanted, no matter what. We just didn't think he was good for her."

They were also worried about Bob's attitude toward school. At Haskell High, Bob had been a big fish in a small pond, but at A&M he was just another fish, and a struggling one at that. He had signed up as an electrical engineering major, but wasn't prepared for the tough core curriculum: physics, chemistry, analytic geometry, engineering mechanics, electric circuit theory, and differential equations. He foundered badly in Calculus I, where a big smile and a line of good bull were of no help with integrals, functions, and derivatives, and was placed on scholastic probation at the end of his sophomore year.

"I think Bobby really loved the Corps more than he did

school," says Charlesie Henry, a friend of his at the time. "He thought he was pretty big stuff—but that goes along with the Corps. In the Corps you have a certain image of yourself, and Bobby was impressed with that. He spent a great deal of time with Corps activities, and it's hard to do that and make good grades at A&M."

Bob went to summer school in 1967 and managed to pull up his grades enough to get off probation by the fall semester, but with the meat of his electrical engineering courses still ahead of him, the celebrated Eagle Scout was facing the humiliating prospect of flunking out of school.

Which might explain what happened next. On September 28, 1967, Bob Black suddenly enlisted in the Marine Corps. "Bob stopped by the house one afternoon and he had this silly grin on his face, so I knew he was up to something," Marjorie Eimann recalls. "He said, 'Guess what I've done?' and I said, 'What in the world have you done now?' He said, 'I've just joined the Marines.' I couldn't believe it. I made him go call his mother and tell her, and I'm sure she just about fainted when she heard."

Not surprisingly, Bob's explanation of his sudden enlistment invoked the hallowed principles of the Boy Scout creed—the big buildup in Vietnam was under way, and he wanted to do his part to serve his country—but the fact was that if he had flunked out of school he would have lost his student deferment and been drafted anyway. Enlisting not only got him off the hot seat at A&M, it also boosted his sagging self-image: Instead of a mediocre student on the verge of failure, he was a gallant hero going off to war to defend his country against the forces of evil.

He shipped out in October, 1967, for basic training at Camp Pendleton, California, which is located, ironically, just down the road from San Clemente, the home of Richard Milhous Nixon, the penultimate master at remaking one's self-image, who at that very time was preparing to unveil the latest "new Nixon" for the 1968 presidential race.

Bob phoned Sandra often from Camp Pendleton, they corresponded regularly, and when he returned to College Station for Christmas he convinced her to marry him. Right *then.* It was a Saturday, but Bob called the county clerk at home and convinced him to open up the courthouse and issue the marriage license; he persuaded a Baptist preacher who lived across the street from the Eimanns to delay his family's vacation long enough to perform the ceremony; and his parents rushed down from Haskell.

The wedding was held on Christmas Eve, 1967, in the home of Mary McCulloch, Marjorie's sister. It was a beautiful ceremony: Sandra descended a winding staircase in a gown of white Aleskin silk (left over from her broken engagement), and Glen Eimann gave her away to the beaming groom, dressed magnificently in formal Marine blues.

After a honeymoon trip to New Orleans, and an elaborate wedding shower in Haskell, hosted by Vannoy and Ivonne Black, Bob flew back to San Clemente and Sandra went home to pack. On Valentine's Day, 1968, she left Winding Road and drove cross-country to San Clemente, carrying her poodle Tramp and her dreams of a storybook future.

3

"I've been having the dream again," a solid, tough-looking man said abruptly.

"What's the dream, Jim?" the facilitator asked.

"The truck blowing up. The bodies . . . it was my fault. I don't know how I missed that mine. . . . John Wayne wouldn't have missed that mine."

"Fuck John Wayne," said a large man wearing coveralls, devouring a hero sandwich.

—Joe Klein
Payback

John Wayne Hearn left Vietnam in July, 1968, the same way he came in, flying out of Da Nang in a C-141 Starlifter. From the air, Da Nang still looked like a beach resort, the way it had when he arrived. In fact, Hearn now recognized the shoreline of China Beach, where he had spent his best moments in Vietnam, relaxing with "doughnut dollies" from the Red Cross center and talking wistfully about home. Finally, he was going home for good.

Although Da Nang looked the same from the air, Hearn was very different from the naive, gung-ho Marine who had arrived twenty-seven months before. He knew that just beyond the magnificent beaches, in the jungles and mountains west of Da Nang, friends of his were fighting and dying.

By all past measures, he would have been returning home a war hero—even more of a hero than the dead father whose legacy he had tried to live up to. He had earned a Purple Heart, a Good

Conduct Medal, a Presidential Unit Citation, a Combat Action Medal, the Combat Aircrew Insignia, and an Air Medal with seven strikes (each strike designated ten combat missions in which his helicopter had received and returned fire).

But this was a different war from the one his father had fought, and when Hearn arrived at Travis Air Force Base in California, he was quickly shuttled onto a bus for Los Angeles International Airport and whisked off the base, passing antiwar protesters demonstrating outside the gates.

Hearn's reentry to "the World" was difficult. During his thirty-day leave, he tore his mother's screen door off its hinges when a neighbor's car backfired and Hearn raced outside looking for a bunker.

In September, 1968, he reported to Quantico, Virginia, where he was assigned as battalion armorer (he had acquired a third MOS, weapons specialist) for H&S Company, Schools Demonstration Troop. In October, when his four-year enlistment was up, he immediately reenlisted for six more years. He still dreamed of becoming a marine pilot; and on June 23, 1969, his commanding officer recommended him for the warrant officer program—the first step toward officer candidate school (OCS) and, hopefully, flight school. The CO wrote a glowing letter, describing Hearn as an "exceptional NCO with unlimited growth potential."

But six months later, he was out of the Marine Corps for good. While awaiting word on the warrant officer program, Hearn had been accepted at Quantico's physical fitness academy, an elite school where the toughest NCO's in the Corps were schooled as physical training instructors. Hearn went there as a fallback option: If he didn't make the warrant officer program, he could try for Parris Island as a PT instructor—one of the class duty assignments in the Corps.

But he twisted his left knee on one of the long endurance runs, reaggravating his old knee injury, then twisted it again, and again. On November 18, 1969, he was admitted to Bethesda Naval Hospital, where Navy doctors concluded that even with surgery, the knee had suffered so much permanent damage that he would never be fit for active duty. So, on January 31, 1970, he was permanently retired from the Marine Corps with a thirty percent disability.

Overnight, the only two things he had ever wanted to be in life —a soldier and a pilot—were taken away. He could try to go to a civilian flight school, but with only a high school GED (which he had earned in the Marines) and no military flight experience, his chances of being hired by a commercial airline were minuscule. His seven years in the Marine Corps had left him no useful job skills in the outside world, where there was no call for tank commanders, infantry grunts, door gunners, or weapons specialists.

And so, at age twenty-five, with a bum knee, a broken dream, a box of medals from a war no one cared about, and a head full of bad memories, John Wayne Hearn was starting over.

4

In the war that I had known, men often lied about the nature of their wounding. Not at first; but later. I'd lied a little myself in my time. Especially late in the evening.

—Ernest Hemingway
Madrid, April, 1937

Bob Black took to the discipline and protocol of the Marine Corps as if he'd been preparing for it all his life, which, in some ways, he had. He completed basic training as the top marine in his platoon, which earned him a preference on his next assignment: officer candidate school at Quantico, Virginia.

Bob and Sandra moved to Quantico in June, 1968, and rented a trailer in Stafford, Virginia. It was a happy time for them. In August, Sandra bought her first purebred German shepherd, a silver and black male named Major. At Christmas, both sets of in-laws—the Eimanns and the Blacks—came from Texas for a two-week visit, and they toured Gettysburg and Washington, D.C.

In October, 1968, Bob completed OCS near the top of his class, and was commissioned as a second lieutenant. Once again, he was given a preference on his next assignment, and requested flight school. Twenty/thirty vision in his right eye disqualified him from being a pilot (20/20 was required), but on March 22, 1969, Bob and Sandra (who was two months pregnant) arrived at the naval air station in Pensacola, Florida, to begin Bob's training as a naval flight officer (NFO).

It had been a spectacular ride, so far. In eighteen months, Bob had advanced from a raw recruit—a buck private—to a second lieutenant starting flight training. He was on the verge of fulfilling his promise as an Eagle Scout, and living up to his father's greatest hopes. Whatever doubts he had about himself at Texas A&M, his glittering achievements in the Marine Corps had obliterated them.

True, not becoming a pilot was a major disappointment. Naval flight officers, while they filled important roles as bombardier/navigators (BN's) and radar intercept operators (RIO's), were still perceived as second-class citizens—sometimes even by themselves. A former navy fighter pilot told me that when he transferred to a new squadron, the NFO's in his *old* squadron gave him a going-away plaque that read: "If you ain't a pilot, you ain't shit." It was a common attitude. There was a perception of pilots as gallant flyboys who "pushed the envelope," while NFO's were merely "backseaters" along for the ride.

Even though he didn't make the grade as a pilot, Bob *was* pipelined into the sexiest track for marine flight officers: F-4 Phantoms, the newest jets in the Corps. He was going to be a radar intercept operator (RIO), who operated the F-4's radar screen, relaying targeting information to the pilot.

While Bob was in ground school at Pensacola, Sandra was carrying on family tradition by having a difficult pregnancy; she was sick often that summer. In late August, Glen and Marjorie drove Sandra—along with Tramp, Major, and a new baby crib all crammed into her 1960 VW bus—back home to Texas to have the baby.

Gary Wayne Black was born October 7, 1969. He got stuck in the birth canal, and the doctors said they were lucky to get him out alive. Bob, who was home on leave, had taken off for Haskell the day before Sandra went into labor, and barely made it back in time. Always a showman, Bob sneaked into her hospital room that night and slept *under* the bed—then bragged about it afterward.

In the excitement over her new baby, Sandra paid little attention to the antiwar protests that were going on around the country. That was easy to do in the sheltered backwater of Bryan-College Station. One week after Gary Wayne's birth, 250,000 antiwar protesters assembled in Washington, D.C., for the first Moratorium

Day, and a second moratorium rally on November 15 drew even larger crowds.

They were hardly noticed in College Station. The day after the second rally, the front page photo in the Bryan-College Station *Eagle* was of four local high school girls wearing football helmets and applying makeup. They were not preparing to storm the Pentagon but to play in a Powder Puff football game. "Stop the game while I powder my nose," the cutline read.

Texas A&M was one of the most conservative colleges in the country, and its lone "radical" group, the Campus Committee of Concern, decided not to participate in the moratorium, but passed out 1,500 voter registration cards instead. "Several of us are against the war," the group's leader explained meekly, "but we aren't trying to influence people in any way. We just want to get them out to vote." A&M president Earl Rudder had already promised "a hell of a fight" to any campus troublemakers and had also declared that any professor who wore a beard was "just trying to substitute a beard for knowledge."

What *did* matter to Sandra about the Vietnam War was whether Bob would have to go. President Richard Nixon had announced the first U.S. troop withdrawals in June, 1969 (by the end of the year 69,000 troops had come home), and his "Vietnamization" policy was reducing the need for marine aviators. If the war kept winding down, Bob might not be sent to Vietnam.

Bob completed his RIO training at Glencoe, Georgia, in January, 1970; received his "wings"; and was sent to El Toro, California, for a two-week training course. When he arrived, he wrote a letter to Sandra (who had stayed in College Station with the baby) filled with mundane details about per diem pay and his nagging cough, but threw in some typically flowery sentiments at the end: He promised to dream "sweet and loving dreams" of her that night and signed it, "With all of me—your lover." Sandra's return letter, while also expressing her love, was far more practical:

Dear Bobby,

Honey it was so great to hear your voice. But gee it made me awfully lonesome for you. And I can not wait till you get here. . . .

Bobby go to the comissary and pick up a case of Iso-mil by Similac. That is the formula Gary Wayne is on and it is 45 cents a can here.

I did some figuring and we just may come out ahead for once. But *don't* waste too much money in Calif.

Grandmother's birthday supper was really nice. I got a pretty good picture of her and Gary Wayne together. Everyone sure thinks he is pretty. And he was so sweet tonight, never whimpered and smiled continuously. . . .

On March 17, 1970, Sandra and four-month-old Gary Wayne flew to meet Bob at their new permanent duty-station: the Marine Corps air station at Kaneohe, Hawaii. Sandra was ecstatic. Kaneohe was the most exotic post in the Corps, and the twenty months they spent in Hawaii would prove to be the happiest time in their marriage. Bob was training in F-4 Phantoms, but still had time to go scuba diving nearly every day, and brought home fresh lobster and fish that they grilled for supper. Sandra's letters to her folks were filled with anecdotes about Gary Wayne and glorious picnics on the beach. For the first time, Sandra put on a lot of extra weight, but Bob didn't seem to mind.

• • •

On Thanksgiving Day, 1971, Sandra and Gary Wayne flew back home to Texas, and Bob flew with his squadron—VMFA-232, nicknamed the "Red Devils"—to Iwakuni, Japan. They were *not* on their way to Vietnam. In fact, for the Marine Corps, the Vietnam War was essentially over. There were still 140,000 U.S. troops in Vietnam, but all of the marines had gone home: the last marine F-4 squadron had been withdrawn in April, 1971, and the remaining marine ground troops had gone home a month later.

The Red Devils were being sent to Japan on a routine overseas tour (every squadron was periodically rotated overseas). For the first four months, it was a relaxing peacetime tour of duty: the squadron's fifteen F-4J Phantoms flew routine training exercises over Japan and the Philippines, squadron pranksters printed up bogus daily flight schedules (Date: 69 Jan 1972; Sunrise: When it's light; Sunset: When it's dark) and took gag photos for the Red Devils' annual yearbook (including one of a smiling Bob Black sitting in his F-4 cockpit reading *Playboy* magazine, with his scuba gear and a huge bag of popcorn draped around him). Bob sent Gary Wayne a miniature flight suit with his name stitched above the pocket, just like his own. He wrote Sandra almost every day, and sent Gary Wayne cassette tapes with recorded "letters."

The Red Devils were the oldest, and one of the most decorated, squadrons in naval aviation. The pilots and RIO's all had colorful nicknames: Groovy Chuck, Woodstock, Felonius Monk, Glass Man, Bottle Butt, and Hungry Joe. Bob was dubbed Blackie, naturally enough, and his pilot, a tobacco-chewing Iowan, was Capt. John "Streak" Blackman.

But everything changed on March 30, 1972, when 200,000 North Vietnamese troops poured across the DMZ and the Laotian border in the 1972 Easter Offensive. The South Vietnamese Army (ARVN) was thrown into a full-scale retreat, and in response, two marine F-4 Phantom squadrons—VMFA-232 and VMFA-115— were rushed into action.

In April, 1972, 1st Lt. Bob Black arrived in Da Nang in time for the fiercest air war since the 1968 Tet Offensive. President Nixon resumed the bombing of Hanoi and Haiphong on April 15, and launched Operation Linebacker on May 8, which authorized the mining of Haiphong Harbor. Air force, navy and marine planes made daily bombing runs, and averaged 15,000 attack sorties per month.

Between April and November, 1972, Bob and John Blackman flew over a hundred missions together. They provided air-to-ground support for ARVN troops and bombed NVA ammunition dumps, SAM missile sites, and artillery positions. After the squadron was transferred to Nam Phong, Thailand, in late May, they also flew air-to-air cover for B-52's bombing North Vietnam. The F-4, the workhorse of the Vietnam War, typically carried 5,000 pounds of bombs for air-to-ground assaults, or Sidewinder and Sparrow missiles when it flew cover for heavy bombers.

Bob and Blackman shared a "hootch" with two other flyers, and became close friends. "Bob was an *outstanding* RIO," says Blackman, now a vice-president of an Iowa manufacturing firm. "I always had great confidence in him in the cockpit." Apparently, the Marine Corps did, too, and promoted him to captain on July 1, 1972.

According to Blackman, Bob was deeply affected by the casualties of war. The Red Devils only lost one flyer over North Vietnam—Lt. Sam Cordova—but that loss hit close to home for Bob and Blackman: Cordova was one of their hootch-mates. Bob was also shaken when several friends from his old squadron in Hawaii —VMFA-212—were killed back-to-back.

Blackman says that Bob was "extremely compassionate" toward the South Vietnamese "nationals." He complained bitterly about one mission they flew over the DMZ, when they were not given a hard target for their 500-pound bombs and rockets, but were told to find a "target of opportunity." They flew down a river valley until they saw some unmanned fishing boats anchored in a cove, and dropped their ordnance on them. "Bob was concerned whether they were 'bad guys' boats, or just fishermen," says Blackman. "And in all honesty, they could have been people's fishing boats."

•   •   •

On October 23, 1972, President Nixon once again halted the bombing of North Vietnam, as the Paris peace talks appeared to be moving toward an agreement. On November 16, Bob Black and John Blackman flew out of Nam Phong on the same C-130, heading back home. Bob had earned the Air Medal with an Oak Leaf Cluster, the Vietnam Service Medal, the Vietnam Campaign Medal, and the National Defense Service Medal.

On January 23, 1973, U.S. and North Vietnamese negotiators in Paris signed a nine point cease-fire agreement, which took effect one week later.

That same month, Bob Black was "involuntarily separated" from the Marine Corps. The Marines (and every other branch of the service) were inundated with thousands of officers that it no longer needed. Only the cream of the crop survived. Bob had been an outstanding *RIO*, but he was not an outstanding Marine Corps *officer*, according to John Blackman. The Marines' officer evaluation sheet had only one block for "airmanship," and the rest of it focused on "officer qualities." "If you didn't go exactly by the book, you didn't get the highest evaluations," says Blackman. "That's what hurt Bob, if anything."

So he was let go. "Riffed," as it's called. Some officers were allowed to stay in at a lower rank, but Bob wasn't given that chance. He was given $10,000, placed on reserve status, and told to go home. For a man whose entire life had been aimed toward a military career, and who had achieved tremendous success in Vietnam, it was a crushing blow. Marjorie Eimann was sitting on the porch swing with him when he got the letter telling him that he had been let go. "He just sank, like everything had been pulled out of him," she recalls.

One day, he was a Marine Corps captain flying in F-4's—a war hero with medals hanging on his chest and a cock-of-the-walk strut —and the next day he was a twenty-five-year-old college dropout wondering what to do with the rest of his life.

• • •

On March 29, 1973, the last U.S. troops left Vietnam. The war was over.

Part Four

DEADLY LOVE

I remember riding in the car one day with my
mother and my sisters, when we saw two dogs
screwing in the middle of the road. They were
going at it hot and heavy, and wouldn't move,
so the cars were having to go around them.
My mother shook her head, and said, "You see
that, girls? Just remember, *pussy* is a powerful
thing."

—*Carucha Alexander*

1

JOHN WAYNE HEARN was bored.

Fourteen years had passed since his medical discharge from the Marine Corps. Fourteen very unremarkable, forgettable years —almost as forgettable as the first fourteen years of his life, before Fort Benning.

Since 1971, he had made his living as an over-the-road truck driver. During his peak years in the mid-seventies, when he had owned his own truck, he had grossed $3,000 a month and had been living the good life: he owned a $50,000 Peterbilt semi, a new car, a pickup truck, a speed boat, a share of a single-engine Cessna, and a new split-level home in Columbia, which he had bought for his young bride, a sixteen-year-old, raven-haired beauty named Debra McLamb. But then he lost the truck in bankruptcy proceedings; lost his young wife in divorce court; and sold the house, the boat, and the plane.

By April, 1984, all he had to show for those fourteen years was a string of eight moves, fourteen different jobs, and four failed marriages. Each marriage was a result of a whirlwind courtship— initiated by Hearn, of course—and ended almost as quickly. His wives had married him for security, or to get away from home, or because he was persistent—but not for love. His fourth wife, Elaine Hearn, had left him for good on February 7, 1984, after another futile attempt at reconciliation.

When Elaine moved back to Columbia, Hearn moved into the bunk room at Old Dominion Truck Lines in Atlanta, where he worked as a company driver. But after a few weeks there his boss kicked him out, so Hearn and another Old Dominion driver, Paul Englett (who was also separated from his wife), rented a $245 a month one-bedroom apartment in Riverdale, an Atlanta suburb.

At age thirty-seven, John Wayne Hearn was sleeping on a hideaway bed he'd borrowed from his mother, driving a 1973 GMC pickup with almost 100,000 miles on the odometer, and had $31.54 in his savings account. He still made good money—$500 to $600 a week from Old Dominion, plus his $317 monthly disability check from the Marine Corps—but it stampeded through his checking account every month like a herd of drought-stricken cattle. He owed $1,500 on his Visa card, plus monthly installment payments to J.C. Penney, Sears, Zales Jewelers, Allstate insurance, and Beneficial Finance. To make matters worse, the Internal Revenue Service was demanding $200 a month in back taxes, which he had to start paying in June, 1984.

He no longer owned an airplane, but nearly every weekend he would rent a plane at Charlie Brown Airport in Atlanta, or Owens Field in Columbia. If he had a layover on the road, in Memphis or Birmingham or Cincinnati, he would find the nearest airstrip, take a check-out flight, and rent a plane for an hour. At seventy-five to a hundred dollars per hour, the bills ran up quickly.

He didn't drink and didn't go to bars, so he poured all of his extra money into flying—or into his newest hobby, photography. Hearn was hoping that photography might develop into a career. He had bought two 35mm cameras, along with a half-dozen lenses, a large-format Yashica portrait camera, studio backdrops and floodlights, and had set up a makeshift studio in his Riverdale apartment. He was building up his collection of "stock photos," hoping to sell them to magazines and newspapers, and even had business cards printed listing his specialties: "Insurance photography, weddings, sporting events, and aerial photography."

All in all, he was a hapless, sad-sack kind of guy, with no close friends and little social life. Living on the road, eating truck-stop food, he had ballooned up to 270 pounds after Elaine left him (his weight fluctuated wildly with his marital problems), and he was a bloated reminder of the hard-muscled 190-pound Marine Corps sergeant he had once been.

His knees were also giving him fits. He injured his right knee —the good one—on a fair ride and had to have surgery, and degenerative arthritis was now attacking both knees. One doctor had predicted that he wouldn't be able to walk by the time he was forty; and although that seemed unlikely, he did have to wear knee braces to combat the numbing pain he experienced behind the wheel of his truck, sitting immobilized for hours at a time.

Emotionally, there were still lingering side-effects from Vietnam. He had not been debilitated by post-traumatic stress disorder (PTSD) the way some Vietnam vets had, but he had experienced periodic flashbacks. Studies indicated that it sometimes took ten years for the symptoms of PTSD to appear, and, indeed, Hearn's first flashback occurred in 1979, almost exactly ten years after his return from Vietnam.

One afternoon, he had suddenly flipped out, picked up a rifle, and started screaming at Debra (his wife at the time) as if she were the Vietcong. Terrified, Debra phoned Mary Watson, who rushed over and found Hearn barricaded in a back bedroom. Mary forced her way in and kept talking to him until she worked her way close enough to grab the gun. Afterward, Hearn remembered nothing about the incident.

There had been other incidents since then: Hearn would go into a rage and beat a frying pan on the kitchen floor or smash his fists through a wall. Eventually, Mary Watson had to put up wood paneling in her living room to cover the holes. When he got mad, he would completely lose control: According to Debra, he hit her, knocked her around, once even allegedly pointed a gun at his infant son. Another time, he started choking his sister, Ann, and punched Mary Watson when she tried to pry him off.

Always loyal to her son, Mary blamed the outbursts on Vietnam, but Ann and his wives attributed them to Hearn's bad temper. Around the country, the experts were similarly divided. In the early 1970s, when the first studies hinted at a post-Vietnam syndrome, the American psychiatric establishment and the Veterans Administration rejected the notion outright, and blamed the problems of Vietnam vets on "long-standing characterological difficulties" and "unresolved family and marital problems."

The American public was even more confused. Each week, on *Kojak, Streets of San Francisco,* and *Hawaii Five-O,* Vietnam vets were going berserk and killing people in drug-crazed frenzies. And there was some reality behind the stereotype. According to Joe Klein,

> By 1980, more Vietnam veterans had died since they came home than had been killed in the war. They comprised thirty percent of the nation's prison population (about 70,000). *Time* magazine estimated that ". . . something like a quarter of those who served may still be suffering from substantial psychological problems."

By 1982, the situation had improved dramatically: the American Psychiatric Association had listed PTSD as a recognized disorder in its revised *Diagnostic and Statistical Manual III;* the VA had accepted PTSD as a service-related ailment; the federal government had opened "vet centers" in most major cities; and the Vietnam Veterans of America, in the wake of a vet backlash over the 1981 homecoming of the American hostages from Iran, had become a powerful voice for the survivors of America's first military defeat.

When John Wayne Hearn started having flashbacks again, in 1982, he went to see a psychologist at Tinker Air Force Base in Oklahoma (Hearn was driving a truck in the oil fields). He was referred to the local vet center, attended a few group counseling sessions, but soon quit.

•   •   •

Mary Watson remained the only constant in his life, and she was as dominant as ever. She had talked a friend into giving Hearn his first truck-driving job in 1971, had kept his financial books at various times, held his permanent power-of-attorney, and spearheaded the bitter custody battle with Debra McLamb over his son Wayne—which Hearn won—and was now raising Wayne herself.

When the citizens-band-radio craze began in the mid-seventies, Mary hired a crane to install a huge antenna in her backyard, converted her spare bedroom into a radio room, and set up a powerful base station. It became an all-consuming hobby—she became an officer in a local CB club, organized a citizen-alert team to assist local law enforcement, even sold CB radios out of her house—but the underlying motivation for her was to be able to talk to Hearn when he was on the road. Many nights, "Yellowbird" would be calling over the airwaves for "Barefoot Cowboy," and depending on the atmospheric conditions, she could sometimes talk to him all the way to California.

According to Hearn's ex-wives, his relationship with his mother had been a major factor in the collapse of his last two marriages. "His mother could do no wrong," says Elaine, who complained that Hearn called his mother more than he did her when he was on the road, and always took his mother's side in every dispute. "If his mama had just stayed out of our lives, we might have been able to make a go of it," she says. Not surprisingly, it was Elaine who eventually left, and Mary Watson remained.

• • •

And so, in April, 1984, after fourteen years of driving a truck, John Wayne Hearn was ready for a change. He had been to forty-eight states and Canada, gone everywhere he wanted to go, seen everything he wanted to see. He was ready for something different—if not photography, then something *new* . . . something *exciting*.

He got a lot more than he bargained for.

2

In October, 1984, Bob Black made up his mind to kill his wife. It wasn't the first time he had made that decision: in 1982, he had offered a local biker, Mark Andrew Huber, $5,000 to kill Sandra. Huber had served time in the Texas state penitentiary for strong armed robbery; he rode a Harley-Davidson, belonged to the Los Vagabonds motorcycle gang, hung out at the Starting Gate and the Watering Hole, the local biker bars, and worked part-time as a tattoo artist, creating multicolored full-body fantasy scapes of Harley icons, super-hero bikers and big-breasted women. All of that qualified him, at least in Bob Black's mind, as a potential gun-for-hire. If you went out looking for a hit man in Bryan, Texas, the biker crowd was the likely place to start.

According to Huber, Bob approached him on three or four different occasions, suggesting various schemes of how the job could be done. In one scenario, Huber was supposed to follow Sandra home on FM 1179, pull up beside her, and shoot her in the head with one of Bob's shotguns. In another, he would steal a semi from work and run her off the road. The planning went so far that Bob drove Sandra's car to Huber's house so he would know what it looked like, and gave him $500 as a down payment on the deal, promising the remainder when Sandra's life insurance policy paid off.

Huber would claim later that he never had any intention of killing Sandra and was just playing Bob for a sucker—ripping off his money—but he was serious enough about the offer to ask *another* biker, John-Boy Gorris, if he wanted to help him kill Bob Black's old lady and split the $5,000.

Gorris is an imposing figure: a short, enormously fat Haystack Calhoun look-alike with tattoos (two of which are Mark Huber creations) covering both arms and his immense back and chest. He looks like a "bad boy," and has two felony theft convictions (one for stealing Harley parts from a friend), but otherwise has a mild-mannered reputation. "He's a wimp," says Charlie Owen, a Brazos County deputy sheriff. "You've seen drugstore cowboys? He's a drugstore biker—just a big old fat boy who likes to ride Harleys."

Gorris told Huber that he wasn't interested in the job and that Huber was stupid for thinking about doing it himself. But Bob Black wanted to make sure: several days later, he went to see Gorris himself and asked if Huber had talked to him about "his problem" and if Gorris was going to take care of it for him. Gorris told him no, that he didn't want to get involved.

A few days later, Bob went back to Huber and asked for his $500 back, saying that he had changed his mind about killing Sandra. By that time, however, Huber had already spent all but seventy-five dollars of the money partying at the Harley races in Porter, Texas, where he had been flashing a big wad of money and buying beer for his friends. Huber gave Bob the seventy-five and told him that he could beat the hell out of him if he wanted to, but the rest of the money was gone. Bob was bigger and stronger than Huber and probably could have, but he left without doing anything. Huber and his friends would be laughing about the incident for weeks. It was just another "crazy Bob" story to add to the list.

It seemed like everybody had one. Bob Black hung out on the fringes of the biker crowd, tried to *act* like a biker—particularly if he thought it would help him pick up women—but really wasn't one. He rode a big-twin Harley all right, but it was a weekend-warrior FXR Touring bike with ABS plastic saddlebags, a custom fairing, and a rear-mounted Touring Pak—not a real street hawg. On weekends, Bob would put on his black Harley T-shirt and his blue denim vest—decorated with his Marine Corps wings, his Pistol Expert medal, and a giant Harley eagle sewn on the back—and cruise the biker swap meets, always carrying his camera, trying to add to his prized collection of "tittie shots." (A biker tradition:

Men yell "Show us your tits!" to passing women, and the willing ones yank up their T-shirts and flash the admiring onlookers.)

Bob Black acted like a biker on the weekends, but then every Wednesday night he would put on a nice shirt and a Windbreaker and attend the weekly meeting of the Cavaliers, a husband-and-wife motorcycle club whose members rode those despicable Honda Gold Wings. *Riding with a bunch of damn rice-burners, for Chrissakes!* It was a Harley rider's worst nightmare (a popular biker T-shirt reads: "God made Hondas to keep niggers off Harleys"). But Crazy Bob seemed to fit right in. The Cavaliers would ride to nearby towns—Dime Box or Hearne or Conroe—eat dinner in a nice restaurant, then ride back to their comfortable homes, middle-class jobs, and happy families. It was enough to make a real biker puke.

Which was why they all had a Crazy Bob story: the guy was such a phony. He tried to come on like Billy Badass: always bragging about how many women he'd laid, always telling stupid jokes and laughing too loud—with that *weird* laugh of his—and trying to convince girls to ride out to the Highway 6 rest area and let him take tittie shots to send to *Easy Rider* magazine.

But every time he'd leave, inevitably, someone would mutter, "What an asshole." That was his signature. Every time his name was mentioned, somebody always said it: "That asshole." The real bikers saw right through him, and were laughing at him behind his back. Even when he tried to get Mark Huber to kill his old lady, they were playing him for a fool. When Huber told his sister what Crazy Bob had asked him to do, he laughed and said, "I just wanted to take the motherfucker's money."

So *this* time, in October, 1984, when Bob once again decided to kill Sandra, he would not go looking for a hit man in the biker crowd. He wouldn't approach Mark Huber or John-Boy Gorris or any of the other biker trash. No, *this* time he would look for a higher-class person—someone who wouldn't take his money and blow it on beer at the Harley races and then laugh behind his back. No, *this* time he would find someone who understood the importance of loyalty and allegiance, someone who shared the values that had defined his life. And *this* time, *he* would have the last laugh. *Semper fi, motherfucker!* This time he'd find a marine.

3

IT WAS A LONG FALL for an Eagle
Scout. A long fall for an A&M corpsman in his starched khakis. A
long fall indeed for a jaunty Marine Corps flight officer hitting
Mach 2.4 at 48,000 feet in his F-4J Phantom. It was a long, twisted
fall from grace.

Bob Black's personality traits were all in place *before* he ever
went to Vietnam, but there is no doubt that his downhill slide
began at the moment he was involuntarily separated from the
Marine Corps. Until then, he had always had a uniform to fall back
on: the Boy Scouts, the A&M Corps of Cadets, the Marines. The
uniform had given him ready-made answers, prepackaged values
and beliefs. *"Yessir! Nossir!"*—the roles had all been defined for him
in advance. The uniform also disguised the other Bob Black: the
teenage boy who mutilated frogs and undressed girls with his
"slant-eyed" looks, the floundering Aggie on the verge of flunking
out, the flight officer that the Marine Corps had let go. And
stripped of the shiny brass and starched khakis, with nothing but
his own character to fall back on, Bob Black was a very immature,
unstable individual.

•   •   •

When Bob returned to College Station in January, 1973, he and
Sandra used the $10,000 separation pay he had received from the
Marines to buy a cute brick home at 1400 Gunsmith, just two
blocks from Winding Road. It was their first real home.

Gary Wayne was three years old, and he absolutely worshiped

his father. A Marine Corps flight officer was easy to idolize. Gary Wayne loved to wear the miniature flight suit that Bob had sent him from Japan and loved to play with his toy aircraft carrier, which had tiny jet planes that could be launched across the room. Bob and Gary Wayne would sit in his bedroom and play with it for hours. For Gary Wayne, the toy planes were a connection to his father's glorious career. For Bob, they were all he had left.

·   ·   ·

After moving to Gunsmith, Sandra took a job as the local distributor for the Houston *Post,* in charge of all the newspaper carriers in Bryan-College Station. She would meet the carriers every morning at three o'clock at a nearby warehouse where they rolled their papers. Bob rented the back half of the warehouse and started Old Gritty Sandblasting. He sandblasted and painted trucks for Bryco, Inc., a local concrete supplier. It was a huge comedown from F-4 Phantoms, but Bob didn't mind hard physical labor and could do anything he set his mind to do.

Which was the problem. He was often moody and depressed, and his temper, which had always been bad, was worse than ever: He would get mad at work and hurl tools across the warehouse, leaving big dents in the steel walls. At home, he once smashed a child-sized rocking chair that Sandra's grandparents had given her into little pieces; another time, he got mad and drove his truck into the side of the house, as if trying to knock it down.

After one such fit, he left home (it was the first of many times), went to Houston, and got a job at a service station. Sandra suspected that he was with another woman, and filed for divorce. The divorce became final on January 7, 1974, but Sandra didn't tell anyone in her family about it—not even her mother (she didn't want to burden Marjorie, who had gone through a divorce herself in February, 1972).

The divorce didn't put a stop to Sandra's problems. On November 30, 1974, she filed a complaint with the College Station police, alleging that Bob had been drinking and driving slowly by the house, trying to frighten her. The strain showed physically, too: By the end of 1974 Sandra was up to 157 pounds.

In 1975 Bob returned to Haskell for his tenth high school reunion, ran into his old neighborhood friend, Sammy Baker, and told him that he was desperate for a job. Baker lived in Midland, the hub of the west Texas oil industry, and encouraged Bob to move there. In fact, when Baker returned home he found Bob a job with a local oil company, then called him and told him to come out.

Bob spent the first two months in Baker's backyard, living out of his pickup truck with a camper top. The two men would sit in the backyard at night and talk. Baker was alarmed by Bob's state of depression: he was still bitter about his involuntary separation from the Marines and couldn't seem to get over it. "Bobby wasn't the same person I knew growing up," Baker recalls. "I mean, he was all starch and brass, and when he latched on to the Marines he was as proud as he could be. After they let him go, he wasn't the same."

Baker tried to get Bob to talk about Vietnam, hoping that would lift his depression. Bob was reluctant at first but gradually opened up and shared some of his more disturbing experiences: he told Baker about accidentally dropping napalm on his own troops and on Vietnamese civilians and watching his friends get shot down. He recounted one horrifying incident on a low-level bombing run where he looked over and saw blood splattered all over the canopy of the F-4 flying beside him. According to Bob, a young Vietnamese boy had shot through the underbelly of the plane and killed the pilot, and the remaining planes turned around and dumped all of their napalm on the boy. "Bobby had a lot of guilt trips about Vietnam," Baker says.

The intriguing thing about Bob's stories is that most of them *never happened,* according to John Blackman, the pilot that he flew with nearly every day. "The story about killing the boy is absolute bullshit," Blackman says emphatically. He says that he can document in his log book that they only carried napalm three or four times during their entire tour in Vietnam, and *never* dropped it on their own troops or Vietnamese civilians. Further, he says that there was only *one* casualty in their squadron, so Bob couldn't have seen his friends shot down.

Blackman encountered the same kind of credibility gap when he talked to Bob in person about Vietnam a few years later. "The way he described a particular mission was like night and day compared to how I would describe it," he says. "He described it as more intense, more horrifying, more dramatic."

•   •   •

In Midland, Bob had started out working as a laborer, but was soon promoted to field supervisor, a white-collar job with a company car and a good salary. He started calling Sandra, trying to convince her to move to Midland. Sandra was apprehensive about leaving her house, her job, and her family; but Bob eventually talked her into the move. In early 1975 she sold the house on Gunsmith and drove to Midland with Gary Wayne, towing a trailer with her Appaloosa horse.

Midland was a fresh start for Bob and Sandra: they bought a house, joined the local Baptist church, enrolled Gary Wayne in swimming classes at the YMCA and in kindergarten that fall. It was the first time in years that Sandra hadn't worked full-time, so she had time for horseback riding. She also became good friends with Sammy Baker's wife, Dreanne.

Sandra was very happy in Midland, but Bob was having problems at work. Growing up, he had been compulsive about his clothes and his appearance, but he had started dressing so sloppily that Sammy Baker felt compelled to talk to him about it on several occasions. And Bob was becoming more and more distracted. He told Baker that he was driving down the highway one day at a hundred miles an hour, when he suddenly slammed on the brakes and skidded to a stop, burning so much rubber that there were bald spots on all four tires. "I don't know why I did it," he said.

•   •   •

On Thanksgiving Day, 1975, Sandra cooked a big turkey dinner; then she and Bob and Gary Wayne watched the annual Texas-Texas A&M football game on television. They went to bed, but Sandra woke up at three o'clock in the morning and realized that Bob was gone. He had packed his clothes and left in the camper. Sandra phoned Marjorie Eimann, and cried hysterically: "Mother, I woke up and Bob's not here!"

He stayed away for several weeks, then suddenly reappeared. As she would so many times, Sandra took him back. In fact, the reconciliation was so complete that they were remarried on December 18, 1975. She hadn't told anyone in her family about the divorce, so she also kept the marriage a secret.

In his absence, Bob had lost his job, and by Christmas they were broke. They moved back to College Station in February, 1976, arriving unannounced at Marjorie's house in a pouring rainstorm, with all of their belongings soaking wet in the back of an old pickup.

Bob made no effort to find work, and Marjorie couldn't support all of them on her modest income (she was still keeping children in her home); so Sandra suggested that they open a day-care center in the house next door, which Marjorie owned.

Happy Face Nursery opened its doors a few weeks later. Sandra painted a big yellow "smiley-face" on a sheet of plywood and mounted it in the front yard. Happy Face was licensed for thirty-one children, and being so close to the A&M campus, it was always full.

After two months of being cramped in Marjorie's front bedroom, Bob and Sandra started looking for a house to buy. They found one in Steep Hollow that had been vacant for months and had been vandalized: screens were ripped out, windows broken, the interior trashed, and fifty-five-gallon drums full of garbage were scattered around the property. The owner was offering an assumable mortgage, with a $10,000 down payment.

After their financial problems in Midland, there was no way Bob or Sandra could get a bank loan, so they would have to borrow the money from family or friends. On April 9, 1976, Marjorie was sitting in the living room and overheard Bob and Sandra in their bedroom arguing about the house. Bob kept getting louder and louder, until he finally stomped into the living room and asked Marjorie to loan him the $10,000.

"Bob, I don't have that kind of money," Marjorie replied.

Sandra walked up behind Bob. "Mother doesn't have $10,000, Bob," she said.

Without warning, Bob whirled around and grabbed Sandra, picked her up off the floor, and threw her across the living room. She sailed right through the screen door, over the front porch, and landed full-force on the sidewalk—an indication of Bob's tremendous strength.

When Bob stormed out into the front yard, Larry Eimann ran to get his shotgun, but Marjorie talked him out of shooting Bob. Sandra struggled back inside, and Marjorie locked all the doors and called the police. But Bob was gone by the time they arrived, and they told Marjorie there was nothing they could do unless she filed charges, which she decided not to do.

They spent the next twenty-four hours terrified that Bob might come back and kill them all. Instead, he left town, drove to Oral Roberts University in Oklahoma, and reappeared a week later. Sandra, who was bruised all over from her fall, once again took him back.

Bob eventually convinced his parents to loan him the $10,000 down payment, and the couple moved to Steep Hollow in the spring of 1976. It took weeks to fix up the house, but when they were through they had a lovely home on six and one-tenth acres of land, with pastures for Sandra's horse, running room for her dogs, a sunny spot for Bob's garden, and a nice little tank and community-owned park right behind their house.

Steep Hollow was a wonderful place for Gary Wayne to grow up: neighborhood kids swam and fished in the tank behind his house and rode their go-carts and bikes on the trails surrounding it. He became best friends with Butch White, one year younger, who lived directly across the tank.

Steep Hollow was also an ideal place for Sandra, who finally had the space to re-create Henry Arnold's Homeplace: she acquired calves, chickens, rabbits, goats, and more horses and dogs. *Lots* of dogs. Besides Tramp, her old poodle, she raised dalmatians, cocker spaniels, and shelties, and eventually started breeding purebred German shepherds, which she imported directly from Germany. By 1981, she owned thirteen dogs, and her shepherd puppies were selling for $250 apiece.

The problem at Steep Hollow was Bob. Other than the brief stint in Midland, he hadn't worked regularly in three years. He had declared zero taxable income (after deductions) on his 1974 income tax, $4,845 in 1975 (the year in Midland), and zero again in 1976.

Bob's temper was as volatile as ever, and there was no telling what might set him off. He would get mad and start tearing up the house—breaking out windows, throwing tools or furniture or anything he could get his hands on. Whenever he threw a tantrum, Gary Wayne would run to his bedroom and hide behind his bed.

Sandra couldn't hide as easily, and according to her family and friends, Bob hit her on a few occasions.

Sometimes, after such eruptions, Bob would lie down on the floor and fall asleep, and be fine when he woke up. Other times he would take off and not come back for days: he once went to Idaho and sold World Book encyclopedias, and another time went to Virginia and stayed with an old marine buddy.

However, two frightening incidents in late 1976 convinced Sandra that she had to get help. One Sunday afternoon, Bob got mad and left again, and Marjorie drove out to Steep Hollow to console Sandra. Ten minutes after she arrived, Bob drove back up to the house. Knowing his temper, Marjorie ran out the front door just as he was coming in the back. She jumped in her car, and tore off down the long driveway. Bob ran to his bedroom and grabbed a gun; fought off Sandra, who tried to wrest it away from him; ran back outside, jumped in his car, and took off after Marjorie. Marjorie was going ninety miles an hour down FM 1179, and lost Bob by taking a shortcut to her brother's house, where she hid out all afternoon.

Then, a few days later, Bob was working in his garden and caught a salamander, which he placed in a bucket on the back porch. When Tramp, Sandra's old poodle, started sniffing at the tiny amphibian, Bob blew up. He went inside and got a gun, came back out, and shot Tramp right in front of Gary Wayne and Sandra, who were pleading with him to stop.

That was the last straw. Sandra convinced Bob to check himself into the Veterans Administration hospital in Houston. Sandra wasn't sure what was actually wrong with him: was it a nervous breakdown, or the result of Vietnam, or just Bob and his fits? When the VA doctors diagnosed him as paranoid schizophrenic, that added a new question: *Was he crazy?*

• • •

Schizophrenia is one of the most common, and least understood, of all mental illnesses, and affects an estimated two million Americans. It is often mistakenly equated with a split personality, as in *The Three Faces of Eve,* but that is actually a very rare condition among schizophrenics.

When Bob Black was diagnosed at the VA hospital in 1976,

schizophrenia was a catchall label for a host of mental problems. Freudian psychoanalysts had no objective criteria for distinguishing among mental illnesses, and diagnosed patients "by feel." A 1972 British study concluded that such methods were unreliable, subjective, and ripe for abuse. "If a person weighed a ton, moved like a blob, or behaved like a jerk, he could be diagnosed as schizophrenic," wrote Dr. Jerrold S. Maxmen, in his 1985 book *The New Psychiatry.*

In 1980 the publication of the *Diagnostic and Statistical Manual III* (DSM III) standardized the diagnosis of all mental disorders. Today, paranoid schizophrenia is diagnosed when a person experiences auditory or visual hallucinations or has delusions of being persecuted or controlled by external forces (for example, the CIA or extraterrestrials). In rarer cases, people may have delusions of grandeur: believing themselves to be Jesus Christ or the president of the United States or to have telepathic abilities.

While some schizophrenics never recover, many people experience a bout of schizophrenia and fully recover. In general, patients who were relatively successful in school, have no family history of schizophrenia, first exhibit symptoms in their twenties (as opposed to early adolescence), and whose symptoms were precipitated by recent major life events are considered to have a sixty to seventy percent chance of full recovery.

Today, Bob Black's symptoms—violent temper tantrums, moodiness and depression, repeatedly leaving home—would *not* be diagnosed as paranoid schizophrenia. And even accepting the validity of the VA hospital's diagnosis in 1976, he would be considered to have a sixty to seventy percent chance of recovery, given his past history.

•   •   •

Apparently, that is what happened. Bob came home from the hospital in early 1977, and for the first time since his discharge from the Marines, began to get his life together.

On March 16, 1977, he applied for a job at Harville Electric as an apprentice residential wireman. Harville, a locally owned company with about fifty employees, did residential and commercial wiring as well as service work. Bob was hired and joined the apprenticeship program of the International Brotherhood of Electrical Workers (IBEW), a three-year course leading to a journeyman's license.

He worked as a residential electrician—wiring new homes or making residential service calls. Bob was a perfectionist and became an excellent electrician. Harville received a number of complimentary letters from customers about his work.

With Bob working regularly for the first time in five years, and Sandra working at Happy Face, their taxable income climbed steadily from $16,000 in 1977 to $19,600 in 1978, $24,000 in 1979, $31,640 in 1980 (the year Bob became a journeyman), $33,746 in 1982, and $35,700 in 1983.

Bob and Sandra both liked to spend money, and they bought lots of pretty things: expensive jewelry (Sandra's aunt owned a jewelry store and gave them sizable discounts), nice furniture, a Mazda RX-7, a Ford El Camino, a $5,600 Kubota tractor, a big-screen TV set, and a VCR. In April, 1983, Bob bought a $7,800 Harley-Davidson FXRT, which he nicknamed "the Lone Eagle"; he also bought a used Honda 400 for Sandra so they could ride together in the Cavaliers (Sandra disliked motorcycles, but did it to please Bob).

Yet there were still problems in the marriage. Bob still pitched fits on a regular basis—often triggered by him damaging something on his Harley, which he tinkered with constantly, sometimes doing more harm than good. He also became more and more resentful of Sandra's dogs: He complained if she asked him to feed them or clean their kennel yet pressured her continually to breed the female shepherds—to make more money on the puppies. In fact, they named their home Bark-n-Holler—and over the driveway mounted a set of steer horns and a big sign with that name painted on it—because, as Gary Wayne explains, "The dogs would bark, and my dad would holler."

Sometimes he did more than just holler. Several times, he gave Sandra ultimatums to get rid of her horses, and a friend helped her hide them until Bob calmed down. When one horse suddenly got sick and died, Sandra's family suspected that Bob had poisoned him. And when her favorite German shepherd, Romal, who was extremely protective of Sandra, also died mysteriously in 1983, Bob was once again suspected. However, the family had no proof of his involvement in either incident.

He would also still take off when he got angry; he left Sandra at least six times between 1975 and 1984. Once, after a bad episode in August, 1978, Sandra even moved out herself. She and Gary Wayne moved in with Marjorie; and on August 8, Sandra called the College Station police department, reported that she was in the process of divorcing her husband, and asked to have an officer present when Bob brought her clothes to Winding Road. Bob delivered the clothes without incident, and they soon reconciled and Sandra moved back home.

• • •

Working at Harville had given Bob Black financial security and a respectable trade, but it hadn't replaced the heroic self-image that he had created for himself in the Marines. Apparently, it was not enough to be *Bob Black, residential electrician*—he needed to be something more. What he came up with were two entirely disparate images: *Ladies' man* and *scout leader*.

In Bryan–College Station, Bob developed a reputation as a crude, obnoxious, and totally indiscriminate womanizer. It didn't seem to matter if a woman was young or old, pretty or ugly, a family friend or a total stranger—at some point Bob would make a move on her. He came on to the wives and teenage daughters of his Steep Hollow neighbors, to Harville secretaries and A&M college girls, to a prominent doctor's wife and to biker girls. "Bob ran on anything wearing a skirt," says Chris Kirk, a Brazos county deputy sheriff.

And he did it anytime, anywhere, no matter how inappropriate the situation. At Harville's Christmas parties or dances, Bob would come on to women right in front of Sandra. "I don't remember Bob and Sandra ever coming to one of those where they didn't have a fight, and generally it was because Bob was mauling some woman on the dance floor," says Marilyn Soffar, Harville's vice-president at the time.

Bob prided himself on his vocabulary, but his pickup lines with women were as crude as any barfly's at closing time. Soffar recalls one time when Bob sent a vulgar greeting card to a Harville secretary, and the woman complained to Bob Harville, the owner. Another time, after Bob had done some electrical work at an A&M sorority, the housemother called Harville and asked that Bob not be sent back. As Soffar describes it: "I don't remember exactly what he was doing—spying on the girls through the bath vents, or something like that—but I thought it was a stupid thing for a grown man to do."

There was also an aggressive side to his antics. At least twice, he tried to force young women to have sex with him. One victim was seventeen-year-old Shannon Ware, the daughter of his across-the-street neighbor. Sandra had hired Ware to clean the house, and Bob came home, cornered her in the back bedroom, and made advances to her. "I told him he better get out of the house before his wife got there, and I never went back when Sandra wasn't there," Ware says. "He was evil."

He tried a similar approach with the twenty-one-year-old daughter of a coworker at Harville—pinning the woman, who was eight months pregnant at the time, in the bathroom of her trailer when no one was home. Fortunately, her sister and a friend drove up just then, and Bob left. "The man almost raped me," the woman told her sister.

Bob did have some success with women: he allegedly had one lengthy affair with a married woman, and had several one-night stands with biker girls. But his pickup attempts at Harville were so slobbering and ineffectual that he was considered a buffoon. And his reputation in the biker crowd was equally laughable. Candy Huber, the sister of Mark Huber, admits sleeping with Bob one time when he got her drunk, but says: "If you saw what some of the girls looked like who turned him *down*—one was a little skinny ugly thing, and *she* wouldn't go with him—you know he must have been hard up."

The more weight Sandra put on, the more Bob was obsessed with being a ladies' man. Sandra had gone from 112 pounds when they got married to a high of 173 pounds in 1979, and despite crash diets and Eskatrol pills, she usually hovered around 155 pounds.

Bob's attitude was a big part of her problem. "When she started losing weight and really looking good and buying new clothes, he would ruin it," says Shannon Ware. "He would rip her apart—call her a fat slob and tell her that she would never be attractive to anyone. She cried with me one day about it and said, 'I can't do this, I can't keep it up' because he had made her feel so bad about herself."

Marilyn Soffar attributes Bob's attitude to emotional immaturity: "Bob was an insanely jealous person, and he didn't *want* Sandra to be thin, because then he wouldn't have control. Sandra was his crutch. He knew she would always be there for him—and *only* for him—because she was fat."

Despite her weight, Sandra took great pains to look her best. "You never saw anyone who was nicer and more neat in her appearance," says Juanita Ware, her neighbor. "She had her hair done weekly, always had on makeup, and had started wearing contacts. She was an attractive woman."

The ultimate irony was that Bob was fat himself. He was only five feet seven inches tall (although he sometimes listed himself on job applications as five ten), weighed as much as 215 pounds, at times, and went to a doctor for weight-control measures on a number of occasions. "He had nothing to talk about as far as Sandra being fat," says Soffar. "He was pretty chunked-out himself."

•   •   •

At the same time that he was collecting tittie shots of biker girls and running on anything in a skirt, Bob Black was cultivating a very different image of himself in another sector of the Bryan community: *Adult scout leader.*

In October, 1981, he signed up Gary Wayne as a member of Boy Scout Troop 802, sponsored by the University Methodist Church. It was a Black family tradition: Bob had been an Eagle Scout, his brother had been an Eagle Scout, and now Gary Wayne was expected to carry on the heritage. Gary Wayne felt the pressure from the very beginning. "My dad was the one that signed me up and bought all my stuff," says Gary Wayne. "And he was always pushing me."

Troop 802 was extremely active and well organized. The troop had a twenty-year veteran scoutmaster, a highly involved executive board, and a half-dozen fathers who served as assistant scoutmasters. Very quickly, Bob joined their ranks, which gave him the opportunity to buy his own scout uniform—olive-green shirt, khaki shorts, red kerchief—and wear the hallowed Eagle pin on his shirt. Once again, he was back in uniform.

Under Bob's guidance and constantly hovering presence, Gary Wayne advanced quickly: He became a tenderfoot in February, 1982; second class in April, 1982; first class in August, 1982; star in May, 1983; and was on his way toward the coveted Eagle.

Bob was getting more and more involved too. In 1982 he converted an old bread truck, nicknamed "the Twinkie Truck," into a camper, and drove it nearly 4,000 miles that year on Boy Scout events—hauling scouts and camping equipment to and from various campouts and jamborees. In March, 1982, Bob also enrolled in the Wood Badge training program for adult scout leaders, and completed the course in March, 1983.

To the other adult leaders, Bob Black seemed like a wonderful guy with a burning zeal for scouting and a great rapport with the boys. "I watched him work with those kids for four years, and he was very patient," says one assistant scoutmaster. "If one of the kids was having a problem on a campout, Bob would take him aside, go for a walk, and talk to him. He had a way with the younger boys."

In Troop 802, each assistant scoutmaster took responsibility for merit badges in his particular field of expertise. Naturally, Bob was in charge of the electricity merit badge, but he also volunteered to teach the citizenship series—which was a requirement for the Eagle and included three of the most important merit badges in all of scouting: Citizenship in the Nation, Citizenship in the Community, and Citizenship in the World.

•   •   •

On March 30, 1982, Bob resigned from Harville Electric to take a job with the U.S. Postal Service. He told Marilyn Soffar that he was "burned out," and wanted a job where he'd be home every afternoon by three-thirty. In his resignation letter, he stated that he wanted "to devote more time to family priorities."

Apparently, those "family priorities" included killing his wife, because this was the period during which he asked Mark Huber and John-Boy Gorris to kill Sandra. And if the post-office job allowed him to be home at three-thirty, he devoted some of that extra time to chasing women, not to his family.

On May 1, 1982, Bob began working as a residential letter carrier with the Bryan post office. For a thirty-five-year-old self-proclaimed ladies' man with a beer belly and a deluded sense of his own attractiveness, it was too good to be true. He told one of his best friends that he loved the job because of all the "young ladies" he got to meet on his route.

But he couldn't handle it. Fourteen months later, on July 9, 1983, Bob resigned from the post office under a cloud of controversy. U.S. Postal Service personnel records are confidential, but a postal source confirmed that Bob resigned before he was fired—partly because of allegations stemming from his womanizing.

After five years of relative stability, he was sliding downhill once again, heading toward a final fall.

4

WHY DID SANDRA STAY with him? That is the question I asked over and over again. She knew that Bob was running around on her; she even warned Happy Face employees that he would come on to them. Her friends told her that he was no good. Her family would have supported her to get out.

So why did she stay?

The most obvious reason was Gary Wayne. She wanted her son to have his father, to grow up in a family environment, to have a "normal" home. Even with all of his faults, Bob was still Gary Wayne's daddy, and the boy loved him. In some ways, Gary Wayne was actually closer to Bob than to Sandra. She was there for him every day—feeding him, clothing him, driving him to school, meeting his basic needs—but Bob provided the more glamorous stimulation: deer hunting trips, Boy Scout expeditions, and fishing on the Brazos. And whenever Bob did something with him, it was always a big show, a major production, a glorious father-son adventure.

Sandra also stayed because she was afraid. Bob had hit her, and had tossed her through a screen door. Like many women locked into a cycle of abuse, Sandra was more afraid of the *unknown* violence—of what Bob *might* do if she left him—than she was of the *known* violence that she had already experienced.

Bob played on that fear. According to Sandra's friends, he had warned her that if she ever left he would find her and take Gary Wayne, and she would never see her son again. "I don't know if she thought Bob had supernatural powers," says Juanita Ware, "but one time she was thinking about leaving him and she came over here, very frightened, and said, 'The guy must have ESP.' Bob had called her that morning and said, 'You're not going anywhere, and you'll never go anywhere that I can't find you.' "

Her fear of Bob was one reason that Sandra started going to dog training classes at Action Dogs USA. Although *Schundzend* is a competition sport for attack dog training that Sandra got involved in as a hobby, she also wanted the dogs to protect her from Bob. "She was scared to death of him," says Dan Linder, owner of Action Dogs. "She really feared for her life, and would say, 'I want this dog to not like Bob.' "

While her fears were palpable, her own insecurities may have been more paralyzing. She was thirty-five years old, overweight, and afraid of starting over. "He was the only man she had ever been with" says her friend Martha Lee. Bob reinforced her insecurities. As Lee recalls: "Sandra said that Bob would tell her, 'No one else would want you.' "

Finally, she may have even stayed because of love. Whether she still loved him is the hardest question of all to answer. Certainly, after so many years together, there was a bond between them. She had been with him since she was eighteen and she had given birth to their son; and on his good days, Bob could still be Bob: Supportive, a good listener, and her friend. Even if she didn't love him as he was, she might have still loved him for the way he used to be. And love of *any* kind is hard to give up.

●   ●   ●

On May 18, 1983, Sandra Black signed up for Christian counseling at the Aldersgate United Methodist Church. On the application form, under present marital status, she put a question mark, and under the heading "major problem areas for which you would like assistance" she wrote: "marital problems!"

Sandra had her initial counseling session that day with Barbara Griswold, a professional youth and family counselor, whose office notes summarized the situation at Steep Hollow:

> Married to B who has been diagnosed schizophrenic and a
> history of violence & infidelity & refusing medication, she has

turned her affection to their son, dogs & horses. He has ordered her to get rid of animals & has left. Afraid to anger him
by filing for divorce again. Recom she file a statement conc his
threats, hire a lawyer & insist he get on medication before
moving back in. Recom Barney Davis, M.D.

On June 15 Bob had his first appointment with Dr. Barney
Davis, a local psychiatrist. Over the next nine months, Davis would
have ten sessions with Bob, with Sandra present for seven of them.
His office notes provide an "inside" look at Bob's mental state—
and the state of his marriage—in the months leading up to October, 1984. The record begins with the initial visit:

Mr. Black is a 36 year old married white male who vaguely
describes symptoms of feeling pressured, angry, and impulsive, these feelings dating back at least over the last number of
months. He has had job related difficulties with the Post Office
and is planning to quit that job soon, to return to his original
work as an electrician.* He had a prior episode of illness about
seven years ago at which time he was hospitalized at the VA
Hospital in Houston, receiving a diagnosis of Paranoid Schizophrenia.
In listening to his symptoms it is unclear whether he is having
recurrent schizophrenia or some other form of psychiatric
disturbance. I have asked him to come in the hospital for full
evaluation and he will arrange to do so within the next day.

The next day, Bob voluntarily checked himself into Bryan's
Greenleaf Psychiatric Hospital, where he underwent a battery of
physiological tests, the results of which were all within normal
limits. Davis concluded that Bob was suffering from atypical depression** with a secondary diagnosis of post-traumatic stress
syndrome, and started him on Triavil, an antidepressant drug.
Bob's condition improved, and he was discharged from the hospital on June 22, to be followed up on an outpatient basis.

* Bob went to work for his old supervisor at Harville, Gil Huber (Mark Huber's
father), who had started his own company, H&S Electric.
** DSM III defines atypical depression as either a sustained episode of depression in patients with residual schizophrenia, but without the psychotic symptoms;
or as depression that is too brief or intermittent to be classified as major depression or bipolar disorder (manic depression).

Three weeks later, Bob and Sandra had their first joint counseling session with Davis. The Triavil had been making Bob sleepy,
so Davis adjusted the dosage. He also noted:

Overall he feels significantly improved. His wife reports
there's been a gradual decrease in his explosive behavior. . . .
I'll see him again in several weeks at which time we'll start
marital therapy if the biological side is settled down.

Their next two sessions were relatively uneventful, but in
mid-September a major blowup occurred at Steep Hollow that
made Davis reevaluate his diagnosis of Bob's illness and radically
alter his treatment:

September 28, 1983: Several weeks ago I received a phone call
from Robert's wife stating that Robert had another flare-up.
He had been working on his motorcycle and the work was
going unsuccessfully and he erupted, breaking out several
windows in the house, threatening people around him, etc. He
refused to see me at that time, but things seemed to settle
down. Since that time, he has been restless, irritable and continues to show signs of *explosive personality disorder.* [emphasis
added] I met with him and his wife and we decided to go ahead
and try lithium carbonate in addition to the Triavil he currently
takes. We also began talking about his continual need to try to
escape bad situations that he sees as being overcontrolling or
evidence of his bad performance. They are to start the lithium
and check back with me next week and I will be seeing both of
them again in the next several weeks.

Apparently, Bob's latest fit convinced Davis that the problem
was more than just atypical depression and needed stronger treatment measures. According to DSM III, explosive personality disorder (also called intermittent explosive disorder) is diagnosed when
a person has had several violent episodes with behavior "grossly
out of proportion to any precipitating psychosocial stressor" that
result in "serious assault or destruction of property." The behavior must not be due to schizophrenia or other mental disorders,
and the person must show no signs of aggressiveness between
episodes. The condition is very rare, more common among men

than women, and the males are "likely to be seen in a correctional institution."

The new medication that Davis prescribed, lithium carbonate, is used most commonly to treat manic-depressives but is also successful at controlling violence in explosive personality types. First introduced in the U.S. in 1971, lithium attenuates the highs and lows of the manic-depressive cycle. However, there is a fine line between a therapeutic and a toxic dose, and patients must have their blood levels monitored on a regular basis.

By the next appointment on October 15, the situation had gotten even worse at Steep Hollow:

> Bob's wife came in stating that Bob had gotten angry with her and was planning to leave once again. He apparently is still taking the lithium, but has not yet gotten a blood count level. She also brought the son with Bob's understanding and knowledge, and I sat with both of them trying to explain a little bit about what was going on. I asked her to get Bob to get the lithium level and they will be calling me for results.

In fact, Bob did leave again in October, and one of the places he went was to Haskell for a high-school reunion. It was his first trip back to his hometown in nearly ten years, and he apparently decided to make a lasting impression on his old classmates: He arrived on his motorcycle in full biker regalia, wearing his Harley vest, a black leather jacket, black pants, and gold chains around his neck. With his full beard and shaggy hair, he was the closest thing that Haskell had ever seen to a real biker: *The Eagle Scout had become a Hell's Angel!*

It must have been a conscious decision. Bob could have just as easily returned home as one of his other personas: *Adult scout leader* or *residential electrician.* Or, if he had wanted an excuse to ride his motorcycle, he could have returned as the *Wednesday night Cavalier.* Instead, he put on the full leathers of Los Vagabonds, and went home as *Billy Badass.*

His old classmates were shocked, and some of their wives, who had never met him before, were frightened. "I really thought he was a bad guy," one recalls. "I thought to myself, 'This is a guy who has gone off the deep end—stay clear of him.' "

Bob couldn't pull off the Los Vagabonds act in Bryan because the real bikers knew he was a phony and laughed at him behind his back, but in Haskell no one knew any different. Or so he thought.

Even there, however, people were laughing at him. "One guy joked that Bobby had probably just rented the leather suit for the weekend," says Bill Blakely, his old math teacher.

Worse than being laughed at, he was ignored. "I just tried to ignore him, and I think that's what a majority of the people did," says Gary Druesdow, a former classmate. "I always thought Bobby was one brick short of carrying a full load."

At the homecoming football game on Friday night, Bob ran into Ed Hester, another old classmate and fellow Eagle Scout. Hester invited him over to his house after the game for a beer, and they sat up until two o'clock in the morning, talking and drinking. Bob talked mostly about his marital problems. "He was upset because he thought his wife was running around on him," Hester recalls. "He said she was Oriental—from Thailand or somewhere like that—and her uncle had taken her to Houston and had her working as a prostitute. Bobby said he was going to have to go get her back."

Of course, it was all a total fabrication. Just as he was pretending to be a biker, he was lying to his old scout buddy.

At a reunion dance on Saturday night, Bob got a chance to trot out another of his favorite images: *Ladies' man.* He ran into his old high school girlfriend and kept pestering her to dance, and to go for a ride on his motorcycle. Later that night, some of his classmates went to another dance in Old Glory, twenty miles away, and Bob showed up on his motorcycle with a younger woman. "He had this gal with him who everybody knew would run around with anybody," says Tim Burson. "It shocked me because he had told me he was married, and all about his family."

On October 24, 1983, after Bob returned from Haskell, he and Sandra went back to see Dr. Davis. A blood test had revealed that Bob's lithium level was below the minimum therapeutic level; so Davis increased his dose. He also noted:

> [Bob] asked to see me alone briefly during this session and in doing so, told me he really didn't know if he wanted to stay married anymore. I brought Sandra back in and we discussed

his frustrations and it seemed that the discussion of them allowed him a chance to feel a bit more comfortable. The plan is to continue medications as ordered, to get another lithium level, and to see me again as a couple in several weeks.

By the next session, the lithium had started to take effect.

November 16, 1983: Bob has done relatively well with no major upswings or downswings since last seen. . . . We focused some on Sandra today in pointing out to her that she fails to take adequate time for herself, tending to do all the chores around the house and then complaining because others don't help out. We then talked some about her weight and how her obesity may be a mechanism of being angry at her husband. We also talked about Weight Watchers as a possible alternative. Continue same medications. See again after the first of the year.

However, Bob stopped taking his medication (he had done the same thing when he was in the VA hospital), and the symptoms returned.

January 4, 1984: Bob asked to come in by himself without Sandra. He has had another rough couple of weeks apparently stimulated by the fact that he stopped taking his medications around Christmas time and was also assigned to a job that he did not like. The job business got straightened out today and he says he feels better although continuing evidence of depression is seen. I asked him to restart lithium along with the Triavil in lower dosages. We spent much of the time reflecting on his Vietnam experience and the sadness that that generated. See him again several weeks.

By the next session, the lithium had kicked in again, and Davis' notes for the next two sessions are almost euphoric: the medication was working, Bob and Sandra were talking about their problems, and he and Gary Wayne were planning a wonderful summer vacation.

February 1, 1984: Bob brought Sandra with me [sic]. The last month has gone very well and nobody can really figure out why. Current medication level includes one lithium tablet in the morning and two in the evening accompanied by Triavil 2/10 tablets prn for anxiety. They are working towards selling their home and getting a new piece of land. Generally no major conflicts so I shortened their session. See again in six weeks.

March 8, 1984: Bob came alone as Sandra got tied up with business. He reports that things are generally going well. He and his son are planning to take an extensive motorcycle vacation and Sandra may be joining them later. We were talking some about his dissatisfaction with his current life and how he was viewing that almost as a schizophrenic situation when, in fact, it sounds more like the typical fantasy life that most people have. He seemed relieved in the discussion of this. Also reporting some recent difficulty with gastric intolerance to lithium. I asked him to rearrange the scheduling and drop back to two tablets a day if need be. Check back in one month.

It was the final session. Bob never went back to Davis, and by mid-April, he was running wild.

5

John Wayne Hearn had been a regular reader of *Soldier of Fortune* magazine since its inception in 1975. Most months, he bought it on the newsstand and read it cover-to-cover: Robert K. Brown's "Command Guidance" editorial, the combat reports, the gun reviews, the personal narratives of Vietnam battles—*and* the classified ads in the back. Hearn liked SOF because it told him "who was shooting at whom" around the world in firsthand, on-the-scene reports, in a way that *Time* and *Newsweek* never did. He sometimes read other military adventure magazines—*Gung Ho, New Breed,* and *Le Mercenaire*—but *Soldier of Fortune* was the granddaddy of them all, and his favorite.

He had even attended SOF's 1983 annual convention at the Sahara Hotel in Las Vegas, which gave him a chance to dress up in cammies and lounge around the pool-bar with other Vietnam vets, telling old war stories and reliving glory days.

The SOF convention was awash with activities for military enthusiasts: there were briefings on Central America, Afghanistan, Grenada, and southern Africa; a huge military-arms expo, where you could buy everything from assault rifles to cammie bikinis and baby outfits; a $50,000 three-gun international shooting match; an impressive "firepower demonstration" in the desert, where SOF staffers shot up a mountainside with vintage machine guns and blew up old cars with dynamite and C-4; and an awards banquet on Saturday night with guest speakers Col. "Chargin' Charlie" Beckwith, the founder of Delta Force, and G. Gordon Liddy.

While he was in Las Vegas, Hearn talked to a few men who

seemed to be *real* soldiers of fortune—combat vets who were helping to train Nicaraguan *contras* in Honduran base camps—among
the hundreds of starry-eyed Walter Mittys and wanna-bes in their
brand-new, right-off-the-shelf cammies.

•   •   •

In March, 1984, shortly after Hearn and Paul Englett moved into
the Riverdale apartment, Englett ran a classified ad in the Atlanta
Constitution that read: "Ex-marine DI seeks warehouse supervisor
position." When the ad appeared, Englett received a mysterious
phone call from an unidentified man who asked questions about
Englett's time in the service and then started talking about patrio-
tism and "serving your country." Hearn, who had hurt his back
and was at home that day, was listening to the conversation on the
apartment's speaker phone. The man rambled on for over an hour,
asking Englett what he would do for his country. When he hung
up, Hearn told Englett that the man was trying to recruit him as a
mercenary.

Englett was skeptical, but when the guy called back a few days
later, his intentions became clearer: He said that he owned a
"country club" in Atlanta whose members paid a fee for two weeks
of combat training in the summer. After two summers of training,
the club would place them in a mercenary job overseas.

The phone call piqued Hearn's interest. From articles in *Soldier of Fortune,* he knew that a number of so-called merc schools
were operating in the Deep South (The Merc School in Birmingham, Alabama, and Cobray International War School in Powder
Springs, Georgia, were the best known), although most were more
like fantasy baseball camps for wanna-be Rambos than serious
combat training schools, and SOF publisher Bob Brown had
blasted them as rip-offs.

But Hearn also knew, from reading *Soldier of Fortune,* that there
were several *legitimate* paramilitary groups that had sprung up in
the wake of the 1982 Boland Amendment (which had cut off military funding for the Nicaraguan *contras*), and that were funneling
aid and supplies to the *contras.* President Reagan had given his
blessing to the private *contra*-aid network, declaring "I'm a *contra*
too," and a host of right-wing organizations had leaped to answer
the President's call: the U.S. Council for World Freedom, headed

by retired Army Maj. Gen. John Singlaub; retired Air Force Brig. Gen. Heine Aderholt's Air Commando Association; World Medical Relief; Friends of the Americas; Caribbean Basin Security Group; and Civilian Military Assistance, founded by Tommy Posey, a former army corporal from Decatur, Alabama.

Soldier of Fortune publisher Bob Brown was also heavily involved in the *contra* support network: He had sent teams of SOF "advisors" to Honduras to train *contra* troops, had established SOF's El Salvador/Nicaragua Defense Fund, and had helped set up another aid group—Refugee Relief International, Inc.

By the spring of 1984, the pro-*contra* movement in the U.S. was operating at a fever pitch: Singlaub was crisscrossing the country, raising millions from conservative benefactors; Oliver North was hustling money from Saudi Arabia and orchestrating top-secret meetings with *contra* leaders in Miami; and the streets of Tegucigalpa, the capital of Honduras, were crawling with CIA operatives, NSC couriers, and cammie-clad Vietnam vets like Tommy Posey—"heroes and zeros," as *Newsweek* called them—who were flocking to enlist in President Reagan's "private war."

John Wayne Hearn wanted a piece of the action. He supported President Reagan, supported the *contras,* and wasn't above making a few bucks for a good cause. He figured that he had at least as much combat experience as Posey and his CMA cronies (two of whom, Dana Parker and James Powell, would be shot down over Nicaragua and killed in September, 1984). If guys like Posey were cashing in, why shouldn't he? Rather than paying money to some bogus merc school, why not put his own Marine Corps training to use?

Hearn had also heard that experienced combat vets could make $200 a day, or more, as bodyguards for business executives, rock stars, movie celebrities, and the like. Unlike the SOF wannabes, he had no romantic illusions about combat and didn't want to put himself in a position to get killed, but if he could make $200 a day for protecting some bigshot oil executive—or even more for training the *contras*—why not?

After years of reading the personal-services ads in *Soldier of Fortune,* he didn't have to search out an employment agency to put his new career plans into action. He had seen ads for bodyguard work in SOF before—along with other ads that seemed to offer *anything* imaginable:

MERC FOR HIRE. Anything anywhere if the price is right. Send description.

EX-MARINE, Vietnam Vet, with devious, discreet mind, seeks dirty work. Anything, anywhere.

MR. EMPLOYER: Ex-Ranger, 3 years Vietnam, will do anything for money, from bodyguard to ?. Call Earl

GENTLEMAN THAT IS BORED in peace is looking for a bit of excitement. Within the boundaries of law if possible; has nothing against "crime" if sufficiently interesting . . . Gentleman Peter.

From the wording of those kinds of ads, Hearn couldn't help but think that they were offers to commit illegal activities. Even though *he* wasn't looking for illegal work, there was no doubt in his mind that if he wanted to pursue his ideas about bodyguard work and training *contras, Soldier of Fortune* was the place to start.

He discussed his notion with Paul Englett: Why not run an ad in *Soldier of Fortune* and see what happens? It was cheap—only forty dollars for three months—so what did they have to lose? Englett didn't object, so Hearn drafted the ad copy:

EX-MARINES—67-69 'Nam Vets, Ex-DI, weapons specialist-jungle warfare, pilot, M.E., high-risk assignments, U.S. or overseas.

Hearn also included the phone number of his Riverdale apartment. He was the ex-marine weapons specialist, jungle warfare expert, and multiengine (M.E.) pilot, while Englett was the ex-DI (drill instructor). The ad was intended to do two things: advertise their availability for high-risk assignments in the U.S. or overseas, and recruit *other* Vietnam vets to provide such services under Hearn's leadership.

The first week of May, 1984, Hearn mailed the ad and a forty-dollar check to *Soldier of Fortune.* The magazine's ad department received his copy on May 9, and scheduled the ad for publication four months later—the normal lag time—in the September, 1984, issue.

John Wayne Hearn had four months to wait, to see if his life would change.

6

On Friday, April 13, 1984, Bob and Gary Wayne Black rode to Houston on Bob's motorcycle, the Lone Eagle, to visit his parents. There, for the first time in twelve years, Bob saw his first cousin, Teresa Black Heatherington.

Teresa is the daughter of Vannoy's younger brother, an oil company executive in Katy, a Houston suburb. She was home on vacation with her two young children, Nichole, age eight, and Jason, six, having left her husband, Ted Heatherington, back home in Apple Valley, California. That was no coincidence: Teresa and Ted, who was twenty-two years older, were having marital problems, and she was trying to sort out her feelings about a divorce.

Although Teresa was a native Texan, she had adopted the health-conscious southern California lifestyle: she lifted weights and took aerobic classes at a local gym, met her friends for hearty lunches at the cozy Apple Valley Inn, and was taking self-improvement courses—algebra, sociology, and philosophy—at a local college. The last time Bob had seen her, she had been a skinny sixteen-year-old girl welcoming him home from Vietnam, but now she was a fully developed twenty-seven-year-old woman: attractive, fair-skinned, with long legs and curly reddish-brown hair. She was also thin. *Very* thin. She weighed 113 pounds—almost exactly what Sandra had weighed when Bob married her.

Bob wasted no time in making a move: he invited Teresa for a motorcycle ride. It was the same ploy that he used with "little skinny ugly" biker girls in Bryan, who usually turned him down, but it worked with Teresa. Bob had always been a hero to her—the

dashing Marine Corps officer of her youth—and now, reeling from
a bad marriage, perhaps she wanted to believe that he still was. She
climbed on the back of the Lone Eagle, wrapped her lithe arms
around Bob's bulging gut, and they roared off into the night.

Later that evening, he took her to Gilley's Saloon in Pasadena,
then back to her parents' house in Katy. Inflamed with the scent of
the hunt, he spent Saturday night and all day Sunday at Teresa's
parents' house.

A friend once admonished me about the danger of getting
involved with married women, saying: "It's too easy—you just
figure out what they're lacking in their marriage and fill the void."
It didn't take Bob long to figure out what Teresa was lacking: he
got up Sunday morning and brought her a bouquet of flowers.
Before he left for Bryan that afternoon, he kissed her a few times—
and not "kissing cousin" pecks on the cheek.

He called her from Bryan on Thursday morning, before she
left to drive home; by then, their love affair was already blooming.
Teresa mailed him a letter on "I ♥ Texas" stationery her first night
on the road, from a motel in Fort Stockton, Texas, telling him how
good it felt "to be in the clouds." She arrived back home in Apple
Valley two days later, still carrying Bob's wilted flowers. (She had
to argue with a California agricultural inspector to take them
across the state line.)

Four days later, Ted Heatherington was standing at the
mailbox when *three* letters arrived from Bob, including one with a
photo of Bob and Teresa on his motorcycle. When he saw the
photo, Ted commented wryly that Bob and Teresa looked like they
were "on their honeymoon." He was joking, of course, but he
wouldn't have been if he had known Bob. Enclosed in one of the
letters was money that Bob had sent to Teresa to rent a secret post-
office box, so he could write to her without Ted's knowledge.

Teresa played along with the gambit: she not only rented the
post office box, but told Bob that she would send a decoy letter to
Bark-n-Holler (Bob had his *own* post office box in Bryan) to put
Sandra off their trail.

Ted Heatherington's remark about the "honeymoon" was
more prophetic than he could have possibly imagined: after one
weekend in Houston, a couple of motorcycle rides, and a few
passionate kisses, Bob was already pledging his undying love to

Teresa and *seriously* proposing marriage. And Teresa was only slightly more restrained: her *one* concern was that their families—particularly her father—might not approve of a marriage of first cousins.

That taboo did not inhibit Bob in the least. If anything, the illicitness only added to the attraction. Bob assured Teresa that *his* father, Vannoy Black, would be "damn near as happy (probably more so) as I am" when he learned about their relationship, and would help to bring her father around.

Bob's *one* concern was to see Teresa again, and quickly. The summer before, he and Gary Wayne had taken a 3,600 mile motorcycle trip through Kansas, Nebraska, Iowa, South Dakota, and Montana. It had been a great adventure: they rode through a flash flood in Dallas, a tornado in Wichita, sixty mph crosswinds in Nebraska, and a snowstorm in South Dakota. They were planning a repeat trip for the summer of 1984. They were supposed to leave Bryan on June 1, ride crosscountry to Seattle, where they would store the Lone Eagle with a friend, and fly to Alaska! Bob wore a patch of the United States on his motorcycle jacket, and had colored in the states that he had already visited on his bike. Eventually, he hoped to make it to all fifty.

Bob had been talking up the Alaska trip to Gary Wayne for weeks: planning their route, making an itinerary, working on the bike. It was going to be another glorious father-son affair—a "vacation dream of rarity," as Bob described it to Teresa—which would prove once again what a fabulous dad he was.

But with Teresa in the picture, Bob made a sudden unilateral change in the itinerary: a 1,300-mile detour to Apple Valley, with a seven-day layover. To do that would reduce their time in Alaska to only a few days, but Bob was insistent. He wrote joyfully to Teresa, announcing their expected arrival on June 17.

Over the next two months, Bob and Teresa's love affair exploded with heat and passion. Bob's almost-daily letters grew longer and longer: an eight-pager on April 29, a fourteen-pager on April 30, a sixteen-pager on May 3. In addition, there were long phone calls on Sunday afternoons, while Ted Heatherington was at work: two and a half hours on April 29, three hours on May 6, and so on.

Bob pursued Teresa relentlessly, overwhelming her with

corny, melodramatic gestures of his love. He wrote a hundred "I love you's" at the end of one letter, filling a page and a half of paper. A few days later, while finishing a sixteen-page letter at 1:30 A.M., he protested that he was too exhausted to write a hundred "I love you's" again, but then did it anyway!—this time in four neat columns, like a repentant fifth grader writing "I will not talk in class."

Teresa's letters were less frequent, but equally passionate. She responded to his "I love you's" by filling a page with "I adore you. I love you very much"; told him that she had picked out "their song" ("Feels So Right" by Alabama); and sent him a series of "Silly Rabbit" greeting cards (the pet name they called each other).

On May 8, Teresa wrote her decoy letter to Bob at Steep Hollow, which began with the salutation "Dearest Cousin and Harley-Davidson Owner," instead of her usual "My Dearest Bob" or "Sweetheart." She thanked him for the motorcycle rides and the trip to Gilley's, extended a formal invitation for Bob and Gary Wayne to stay in Apple Valley, and even asked if Sandra couldn't come too. She included a few clandestine thrills for Bob, as well, saying that she would agree to his "serious, personal requests" as soon as he got to California.

Early on, Bob started leading Teresa to talk about sex, although, at first, he hid behind a veil of false modesty. He wrote that her willingness to talk about "s-e-x" would "help build my confidence," and claimed to have misgivings about their making love when he got to California, but would go along with it, given its "inevitability."

Soon, however, he dropped the veil and began pushing for graphic details: He asked her to describe her body, and challenged her to share the "kinkiest" thing she had ever done. When Teresa mentioned that she had some homemade nude photos of herself, Bob could hardly contain himself and began pleading anxiously with her to send "your nudies."

Teresa was slightly more inhibited talking about sex (she was usually responding to Bob's questions, rather than posing her own), but nonetheless, as an open-minded California woman, she *did* respond, which stimulated his lusty desires even more.

When he wasn't prompting Teresa about sex, Bob was often

scheming about money. He painted grandiose pictures of their future financial security, promised her a new car and a "plushly furnished" house, and suggested that with her support he might end up "very rich." His bombastic claims of financial prowess were particularly ironic coming from a man who didn't hold a regular job for nearly five years (from 1973-1977) and had depended on his wife to survive.

His letters oozed with paternalism and sexism: He often told Teresa that he was proud of her, using the tone of a father praising his "little girl," and appreciated her for doing things *he* wanted—for talking openly about sex, for being thin, and for saying she liked to cook (although he was quick to caution her that he disliked meatloaf).

He also laid subtle guilt trips on her: He chided her when he didn't receive any letters one week; begged her to show compassion for his "terrible terrible need" by making love to him as soon as he arrived in Apple Valley; and reminded her of his disappointment over not receiving her "nudies."

Their letters covered a wide range of topics: they exchanged lists of likes and dislikes for a mate (they both chose good sex partner as their top like, and Bob listed insincerity as one of his top dislikes). Bob also confessed his past marital infidelities, but swore that he would never stray again and then, in the next sentence, begged Teresa again to send her "nudies."

•   •   •

As the motorcycle trip drew closer, Bob considered dumping Gary Wayne and going to California by himself. He talked to Gary Wayne about the trip, hoping that his enthusiasm had waned. But Gary Wayne had his heart set on it, so Bob backed off. In fact, displaying his usual ceremonial flair, he ordered a copy of *Zen and the Art of Motorcycle Maintenance,* which he planned to give to Gary Wayne when they crossed the Continental Divide.

They never made it. Bob ended up leaving Gary Wayne at home after all. Because of Bob's insistence on going to Apple Valley, and the Saturday layover requirements on cheap flights from Seattle to Alaska, Bob and Gary Wayne would have ended up spending only a few *hours* in Alaska. On top of that, Bob wanted *Sandra* to pay for the tickets, and when she refused, he blew up.

The trip became such a sore point that Gary Wayne eventually decided not to go—with Sandra's blessing—and that made Bob even angrier.

Gary Wayne assumed that the trip was off altogether, until he saw Bob cleaning out his important papers from his rolltop desk. When the boy told Sandra about it, she said, "He's probably leaving again," but Gary Wayne insisted that it wasn't so.

Unfortunately, it was. Bob had already told his boss, Gil Huber, that he was leaving Sandra for good, and he had hauled several truckloads of his stuff—guns, motorcycle parts, tools, and boxes of *Playboy* magazines—to the home of *David* Huber (Gil Huber's son and Mark Huber's younger brother, who was Bob's "helper" at H&S Electric), and stored them in his spare bedroom.

On Friday, May 25, Sandra and Gary Wayne returned home from Happy Face and saw Bob's motorcycle packed and ready to go. Bob sat them down at the dining room table and told them he was leaving because he wanted his freedom. He gave Sandra a vase of roses and Gary Wayne the copy of *Zen and the Art of Motorcycle Maintenance*, inscribed:

> To my beloved son, Gary Wayne Black.
> You will always be with me, and I will
> love you forever.
>
> > Dad

Sandra and Gary Wayne cried and pleaded with him to stay, but Bob marched outside, gave them each a hug, climbed on the Lone Eagle, and rode away. He hadn't told them where he was going, or if he was ever coming back.

Four days later, he arrived surreptitiously in Apple Valley, without Ted Heatherington's knowledge. According to the official itinerary, Bob wasn't supposed to arrive until June 15, so he spent the next two weeks in hiding at the Ponderosa Ranch, a local motel. When Teresa left work (she was a part-time teacher's aide at an elementary school) she would drive to his motel, where they made love, acting out the "s-e-x" fantasies they had rehearsed on the phone. Teresa left in time to meet her children at their school-bus stop and be home when Ted got off work at 3:00 P.M.

On June 15, as expected, Bob drove up to the Heatherington

home with his motorcycle fully loaded, as if he had just driven crosscountry. Ted Heatherington welcomed him into his home, and Bob spent the next week there, sleeping in his guest room every night, and with his wife every afternoon.

At the end of the week, Bob said his heartfelt good-byes, climbed on the Lone Eagle, and pretended to leave for Texas. In fact, he moved into a cabin in the desert outside of Apple Valley, and he and Teresa took their love affair back underground. Bob even used her children to maintain the deception: He wrote post-cards to her son and daughter and sent the cards to a friend in Bryan, who then mailed them back to California, so they would have a Bryan postmark.

After a month of wild lovemaking, Bob was soaring: he was losing weight; was tanned and fitter than he had been in years; and was planning to go back to college, land a white-collar job, and move back to Hawaii.

He and Teresa were still seeing each other regularly, but Bob also resumed sending her love letters, which were filled with vivid descriptions of their lovemaking sessions, suggestions for the future ("Are you familiar with prostatic massage?"), and feverish, late-night fantasies. He was pushing Teresa to daring heights: He took several rolls of color photographs of the two of them in acrobatic sexual poses, and they went shopping for vibrators at a sex shop.

The only damper on his euphoria was that he was quickly running out of money. He had applied for a job with Roadway Express, a nationwide trucking firm, but as the days passed with no news, his money woes mounted: His health insurance expired, the front-wheel bearing on his Harley started going out, and he was running short of money for food. Increasingly depressed, he debated selling his jewelry and his prized gun collection, and even proposed a harebrained idea of trying to establish his pedigree as an American Indian, based on the unconfirmed stories of distant Indian blood in his family (he didn't even know what tribe), which could entitle him to free land and medical service.

He also fretted about what might happen if Sandra divorced him, complaining that Texas's divorce laws would "impossibly burden" him with debts, and about paying child support for Gary

Wayne: "I would prefer *our* family (Bob, Teresa, and her two children) to not carry that burden."

•   •   •

On July 10, 1984, Sandra Black filed a petition for divorce in the 85th District Court of Brazos County. Gary Wayne did his best to talk her out of it—he still wanted his daddy and hoped that there was a chance to work things out—but Sandra had finally had enough. She still had no idea where Bob was, or if he was gone for good. He had called one time that summer, to tell her that he was sleeping in a launderette and to beg for money.

In Bob's absence, Sandra's family had rallied around her, and her friends were encouraging her to finally go through with the divorce. Texas law requires a sixty-day waiting period; so unless Bob contested it, the divorce would become final on September 8, 1984.

Sandra had discovered that men found her interesting—perhaps even attractive. Martha Lee had introduced her to a thirty-four-year-old Aggie who loved horses as much as Sandra did. Several times, she and Martha Lee had trailered their horses to the man's property, outside of town, to go horseback riding. At this point, it was just a friendship—the man wasn't interested in Sandra romantically—but it was a tremendous boost to her self-esteem, after all the years of Bob's put-downs, to know that she could make male friends.

At last, Sandra was creating a life of her own—without Bob.

•   •   •

Sandra Black wasn't the only one filing for divorce. In late July, Teresa Heatherington started interviewing divorce lawyers—with Bob's able assistance. Once they settled on an attorney, Bob gave the man a gold pendant with a large diamond as collateral for her bill—*without* Teresa's knowledge. Bob was still taking care of his little girl.

Getting a divorce in California was more complicated than in Texas (there was a six-month waiting period, instead of sixty days), but divorcing Ted wasn't nearly as stressful for Teresa as dealing with her parents. In late June, they had learned about her relationship with Bob, and reacted just as she had feared: Her father called to express his furious disapproval, and her mother, a born-again Christian, wrote a scathing thirteen-page letter citing chapter and verse on the "unbiblical" nature of the relationship.

By mid-August, Bob and Teresa were two lovers under siege by a cruel world. They were like a modern-day Romeo and Juliet—albeit a thirty-eight-year-old Romeo with a beer belly and a twenty-eight-year-old Juliet from la-la land—their love weighed down by Teresa's parents and Bob's money woes.

It all came to a head on Tuesday, August 21, when Teresa had divorce papers served on Ted, and the two of them ended up in a huge argument at one-thirty in the morning. All the while, Bob was crouching in the bushes outside their sliding-glass bedroom door, preparing to "rescue" Teresa if need be.

The incident gave Bob a chance to show off his protective capabilities to Teresa's parents, and he wrote a chilling eight-page letter to her mother the next day: Ted was depicted as a grotesque animal, and Teresa as having been in mortal danger. Not surprisingly, Bob's account of his own role—although he actually did nothing—was full of heroic imagery, valiant self-sacrifice, and fearless bravado.

He ended the letter with two pages of testimony about his religious beliefs, in which he claimed to have had a personal encounter with the Holy Spirit that made him "unshakable" in his belief that he was saved and going to heaven.

But the letter did him no good. The next day, August 23, Teresa caved in to the mounting pressures from her parents and decided to try to salvage her marriage. She sent a frantic note to Bob (via her best friend), telling him that Ted was back home; she said that she needed "time and space to work out things by myself" and urged him to go home to Texas.

The next morning, Teresa came to his cabin to say good-bye. But Bob carried her across the threshold, made love to her one last time, and begged her to marry him in the future. Teresa started crying, and said she would.

Bob packed the Lone Eagle and left for Bryan that afternoon, but the relationship was far from over.

7

GARY WAYNE was so excited when he heard that his dad was coming home that he ran outside and cleaned up Bob's motorcycle shed, which had been accumulating junk all summer. Bob had called Sandra on Friday from Blythe, California—195 miles out of Apple Valley—to tell her that he was on his way. Sandra told him to "come on over," and told Gary Wayne that his father would be home that weekend.

Bob didn't make it until Monday, after fighting heavy rainstorms and strong head winds in New Mexico. He also had mechanical problems with the Lone Eagle: the bike ran hot the entire trip, and Bob limped into Bark-n-Holler with a burned valve. When he pulled up in the driveway, Gary Wayne ran out to meet him. "I was so happy to see him," he recalls. "I hoped everything would be fine and dandy again."

It wasn't. Bob and Sandra got into an argument, and Bob left an hour later to find a place to stay. He stopped to see David Huber, his young helper from H&S Electric. "He told me he had a lot of fun in California and I should have gone with him," says Huber.

Bob didn't let on to Huber how anguished he was over leaving Teresa, who he had written *three times* on the way home, including once from a rest area outside Las Cruces, New Mexico, where he asked beseechingly "Why did I leave???" and told her that until she married him there would be "utter loneliness and unhappiness" in his life.

In fact, Teresa was already having second thoughts about

staying with Ted. She wrote to Bob on Tuesday, August 28, berating herself for "how royally I have screwed up everything" and assured him that he was still her "knight in shining armor." The next day, she mailed him a greeting card that read: "The little girl in me wants to take tiny steps. . . . The big girl in me wants to run to you."

The big girl started running the very next day. On August 30, she wrote Bob saying that Ted had decided *not* to contest the divorce and had agreed to give her custody of the children, to sell their house and split the equity, and, most importantly to Teresa, to *not* tell her parents the "intimate details" about her affair with Bob. Teresa called Bob the next day and promised to move to Bryan as soon as her house sold. With Bob and Sandra's divorce scheduled to become final on September 8, they could be together by October!

Bob's excitement was dampened by his intensifying money woes: he was so broke that he wrote back to her on a Kentucky Fried Chicken napkin and shared his despondency over the Lone Eagle, which needed a major engine overhaul. Bob wrote that he hoped Sandra would feel sorry for him and help him out.

He knew her well. When Sandra learned of his calamity with the motorcycle, she gave him seventy dollars, loaned him her car to tow the bike to the Harley shop, and invited him to stay at Bark-n-Holler for a week, until he could afford a place of his own (Bob had already talked to Marilyn Soffar, and had been rehired at Harville Electric, beginning September 4).

Bob took Sandra up on her offer but assured Teresa that he would sleep in the spare bedroom, so "yours and my love isn't threatened at this time even if appearances don't bear that out with the neighbors." In fact, the neighbors *were* confused: Juanita Ware was so frustrated that Sandra had taken Bob back that she hardly spoke to her for the next four months.

And "appearances" were also confusing to Gary Wayne, who was still hoping that everything would be "fine and dandy." During the next few days, he and Bob went golfing and bicycling together, worked out at 24-Hour Gyms of Texas, and barbecued two piglets that they had butchered in the spring. Bob and Sandra were getting along amicably themselves: they were talking about maintaining a friendship after the divorce, and Sandra even offered to let Bob sleep at Happy Face until he could afford an apartment.

But the amicability ended on August 30, when Sandra found an unfinished love letter in a kitchen drawer. It began "My Dearest Darling T-Baby" (Bob's pet name for Teresa). Even though she was reconciled to the divorce, the letter was a crushing blow: it was obvious that Bob was in love with another woman.

She didn't know who T-Baby was and told Bob she didn't want to know, but he insisted on telling her that it was Teresa. Sandra went into a tirade, accusing Bob and Teresa of being so "sick" that they had gravitated to each other through mutual weakness. She was so incredulous that Bob would be having an affair with his first cousin that she made him phone Teresa, and when she wasn't home, Sandra called Teresa's father, who confirmed the relationship.

That night, Marjorie Eimann noticed lights on next door at Happy Face; she walked over and found Sandra crying. "What's wrong, Sandra?" she asked.

"I can't tell you, Mother," Sandra replied, sobbing. "I'm going to get a motel room and spend the night."

"You don't need to do that, Sandra—I've got three bedrooms," Marjorie offered.

"No, Mother, I want to be alone," she said. "When I get better I'll talk to you."

Monday morning, Sandra came and opened the nursery, but was too upset to work. She spent the day with her aunt Mary McCulloch and came back to Marjorie's house that evening and sat down in the kitchen.

"Mother, do the initials T.B. mean anything to you?" she asked.

"No, Sandra," Marjorie replied.

"Well, what's wrong with me is that Bob wrote a love letter to *Teresa Black* and put it in my kitchen drawer so I would find it."

Marjorie was flabbergasted. *Teresa Black?* The skinny little pigtailed girl who used to come over to Vannoy and Ivonne Black's house and drink lemonade? Yes, Sandra said, it was true.

When she got home that night, Bob had left her a note:

Sandy, I love you so very much and I am hurting like never
before. I would indeed change my mind and stay, but
knowing I would eventually leave again, I can't bring myself
to continuously hurt you. Please forgive me, my sweetheart.

• • •

On August 31, Bob moved into Happy Face. He slept on a table,
and left in the morning before the children arrived. On September
4, he started working at Harville, but was still so short of money
that Sandra loaned him another fifty or sixty dollars; Teresa sent
him twenty dollars, for food, and he talked to a local gun shop
owner about selling his gun collection on consignment.

Bob and Teresa had returned to writing almost daily letters,
and phoning on Sundays and Wednesdays. Bob placed the calls
from a pay phone at A&M's Memorial Student Center (MSC). As
always, Bob's letters were replete with steamy sexual passages; and
when his rolls of "sex photos" came back from the developer on
September 4, he and Teresa exchanged drooling critiques of their
favorite shots.

On the surface, Bob was acting extremely congenial toward
Sandra (he made some electrical repairs at Happy Face and fixed
Marjorie Eimann's air-conditioner) but his animosity toward her
was just below the surface. When she told him about her new male
friend—the horse-lover Martha Lee had introduced her to—Bob
graciously offered his advice on how to attract the man romantically but then turned around and told Teresa that he planned to
use the relationship against Sandra as a "tit for tat" justification of
their affair.

Bob was being equally two-faced with Gary Wayne. He told
Teresa that he planned to have a father-son talk with Gary Wayne
to "slip some sly psychology on him" and "covertly" adjust his
attitude toward their relationship.

While he was at it, he also tried to "slip some sly psychology"
on Teresa's father, who was still pressuring her to end the affair. At
Teresa's urging, Bob composed a long letter to his uncle, working
on it feverishly at the nursery late at night, editing and reediting it.
Addressing the most critical issue—his past infidelities—Bob
reached back to his youth, to the highest standard of honor he
could find:

In order to convince you beyond question that I will never
renig I am making an oath to you now in writing that has
been reserved by me for only the most solemn, sincere and
binding occasions . . . and I regard it as the ultimate when
I tell you 'As an eagle scout, I give my Scouts' Honor that
I will fulfill my oaths of marriage to your daughter.'

He was thirty-seven-years-old, using the Eagle Scout oath to
justify marrying his first cousin. It wasn't exactly what Lord Baden-
Powell, the founder of the Boy Scouts, had in mind.

                              •   •   •

It didn't take Gordon Matheson long to figure out that Bob Black
had a girlfriend. Matheson, the general superintendent at Harville
Electric, noticed Bob making long phone calls in the office after
work and writing letters in Marilyn Soffar's office after she'd gone
home. *It has to be a woman,* Matheson thought.

A burly man with blond hair, a bushy mustache, and a gregari-
ous personality, Matheson had only been at Harville for nine
months and hadn't known Bob during his earlier stint with the
company. But he liked him right off the bat. "You couldn't help but
like Bob Black," Matheson recalls. "He always had a smile on his
face, and any corny joke you told he'd think was just the funniest
thing that ever hit the wind."

Part of a superintendent's job is to keep up employee morale,
and Matheson tried to take an interest in his workers' problems.
He noticed that when Bob got off the phone he would seem depressed; so one afternoon Matheson asked him what was wrong.
Bob told him the whole story: He hated his wife, he was in love with
his cousin Teresa, and wanted to marry her.

Matheson was having an extramarital affair himself and
shared that secret with Bob. "It kinda threw us together," he says.
"I could sympathize with him, and he could sympathize with me."

Bob started ranting about all the things he hated about Sandra: She was a bitch, she was ugly, she was fat. "That was the main
thing—she was fat," says Matheson. "Bob thought he was a ladies'
man, and it shot down his whole image of himself."

When Bob finished, Matheson told him: "Look, if it's that
bad, divorce her."

"I am," Bob replied.

• • •

Over the next four weeks, Bob bent Matheson's ear two or three times a week—before work, after work, any time he saw him. The conversations were always the same: He hated Sandra, he loved Teresa, he had to have her. "I've never seen anybody as obsessed with a woman as he was," Matheson says. "I mean, he was *really* obsessed. All I heard was how much he loved Teresa and wanted to be with her, but she wouldn't leave her husband and her two kids. She was going to, and then she wasn't—it went back and forth."

Then, one afternoon, Bob suddenly started talking about Vietnam. He told Matheson that he had seen many people killed in the war, but it really hadn't bothered him.

"How do you think *you* would feel about killing someone?" he asked.

Matheson had never been in the military (he had scar tissue on his lungs and bad knees from playing football), but he said, "Well, if I was in a war, I don't feel like it would bother me to kill someone."

Bob agreed, and dropped the subject—for then.

• • •

On Tuesday, September 11, Teresa's house sold. It was the final hurdle standing between Bob and her, and with the closing scheduled for thirty days later, she could be in Bryan by October 12!

Teresa wrote to Bob that morning, but was so anxious to tell him the good news that for the next two afternoons she called his favorite pay phone at the MSC at fifteen-minute intervals, hoping to catch him there. Bob didn't get the news until Friday, however, when Teresa's letter arrived. He rushed out and bought thirty dollars' worth of quarters in anticipation of their Sunday night phone call.

For the next week, Bob's euphoria was boundless: he opened a joint checking account, began searching for a house to rent, checked with the A&M legal department on whether first cousins could marry in Texas (*"Yes,* dear, 1st cousins can marry," he reported blissfully), and mailed Teresa a cassette recording of Ravel's *Bolero,* with the comment: "Just wait 'til we make love to this!!!!!" On September 19, he asked her: "Are you as excited as I am that each day now brings us closer to our dreams?"

The answer was no. Teresa was once again buckling to the pressure from her parents—and from Ted, who was begging her for another chance. In a letter to Bob, Teresa shared her concerns over her children's reaction to the divorce; she complained of waking in the middle of the night, feeling smothered and confused; and she said she needed to "clear the cobwebs from my poorly functioning brain."

With Teresa having fallen strangely silent—a week passed with no letters or phone calls—Bob's doubts were starting to creep in. "Where are you anyhow?" he asked plaintively in a September 20 letter, and complained that his morale was "exceedingly low."

It all came crashing down on Saturday, September 22, when Bob received Teresa's letter. He stayed up until 2:00 A.M. writing a frantic four-page reply: he chided her for wavering and reminded her of how much *he* had been suffering. Then he switched gears, hoping to draw on the sexual fervor of their relationship to steel Teresa's resolve: he described new sexual "firsts" that he was looking forward to, thanked her for telling him about using their "toy" (the vibrator), and begged her to send him "another pair of your panties please." He signed the letter "To thine own self be true—B."

But his pleadings did no good. Teresa called him the last week of September and said that she wanted to end the relationship. Bob responded by threatening to kill himself, but Teresa had heard Ted say the same thing, and she didn't take Bob's threat seriously.

She underestimated her cousin's flair for the dramatic.

That night, Bob allegedly took a bunch of unidentified pills. The dose wasn't enough to kill him, but he was still groggy when he showed up at work the next morning. He told Gordon Matheson that he had tried to kill himself, but Matheson wasn't overly sympathetic. "I think maybe he was trying to get me to feel sorry for him," he says. "If he had really meant to do it, he wouldn't have told me about it."

Bob had better luck with Sandra, who was so upset about the suicide attempt that she called Teresa. Teresa apologized for her relationship with Bob, to which Sandra responded, "If it hadn't been you, it would have been somebody else." She asked Teresa to come to Bryan and end the relationship in person, rather than over the phone, and Teresa agreed.

If Bob *was* trying to get attention, he had succeeded. Teresa flew into Houston on Saturday (Bob's parents helped foot the bill), and Bob picked her up at the airport on the Lone Eagle—which was newly repaired. They spent Saturday night at his parents' house and on Sunday, rode the motorcycle to Bryan-College Station. Bob took her to church, and then they tromped around the A&M campus.

Sandra's plan backfired, however. By the time Teresa flew home on Monday, the love affair was back in full swing. Teresa promised Bob that she would leave Ted, move to Bryan, and allow her divorce to become final on February 23, 1985. On the plane home, she wrote Bob a letter stating that she felt "an inner peace" about their love, and ended it: "I'm an Aggies girl."

That same day, Bob signed a six-month lease on a three-bedroom house at 1108 Bittle Lane, near downtown Bryan. On the rental form, he listed his marital status as divorced, put Teresa down as his fiancée, and explained that he needed the house "for bride and family."

Bittle Lane is in an industrialized section of Bryan. The cheap tract houses were fairly new, but they would look run-down five years after they were built. Bob's "dream house" wasn't exactly a dump, but close. It was quite a comedown from Bark-n-Holler and the "plushly furnished" house that he had promised Teresa.

•   •   •

On October 3, Bob Black walked into Gordon Matheson's office and announced that he was quitting. Matheson was relieved. Bob's obsession with Teresa had started affecting his work, and it was also taking up too much of Matheson's time. "I had reached my saturation point," he says.

After Bob's "suicide attempt" the week before, Matheson had started looking for an excuse to let him go. "That was just about the straw that broke the camel's back," he says, "and I think *he* saw the handwriting on the wall."

That morning, Bob told him, "I don't feel like I'm doing a good job for you. I'm gonna try to find a job somewhere else."

"Well, if that's the way you feel, I'm sorry to see you go," Matheson replied.

The next time Gordon Matheson saw him, Bob Black wouldn't be asking him to just *listen* to his problems with Sandra and Teresa—he would be asking him to solve them.

• • •

Within a week Teresa was vacillating once again. Bob had a phone installed at Bittle Lane, and made *sixteen* phone calls to Apple Valley in that one week, trying to reassure her. But on October 9, Teresa wrote and told him that it was over.

She would go back and forth several more times in the next month and keep leading him on sexually—she sealed her envelopes with lipstick kisses and told him "Without you, the toy is, at best, just a convenience." By mid-October, Bob decided to take matters into his own hands. If he was going to have Teresa, Sandra would have to die.

Part Five

HIGH-RISK ASSIGNMENT

Anytime you try a decent crime you got 50 ways
you can fuck up. If you think of 25 of them, then
you're a genius—and you ain't no genius.

—*Mickey Rourke to*
William Hurt in Body Heat

1

"PLEASE CALL Debbie."

The message was on John Wayne Hearn's telephone-answering machine when he got home on Saturday, October 27, 1984. He had received hundreds of similar messages in the three months since his personal-services ad had first appeared in *Soldier of Fortune,* but this one intrigued him. To begin with, it was a woman. A fairly young woman, he guessed, from the sound of her voice. Of course, there was no way to tell what she looked like, but she certainly *sounded* good on the phone. *Real* good.

Hearn dialed the number, but got no answer. *Too bad,* he thought. The woman had a sexy purr in her voice, and sounded like the kind of woman he'd like to meet. But he didn't have time to dwell on it. There were other calls to make. *Lots* of them. His ad had generated more excitement, and had given him more of a sense of purpose than anything since Vietnam. It couldn't have come at a better time.

• • •

It was a wanna-be's wet dream.

Even with four months of anticipation, Hearn was totally unprepared for what happened in early August, when his telephone started ringing. The September issue of *Soldier of Fortune* hadn't even hit the newsstands when the calls began.

They trickled in at first, one or two a day, but within a few weeks his phone was ringing off the hook. Paul Englett had moved

153

back with his wife in July; so Hearn was on his own, and soon the calls were overwhelming him: ten, fifteen, twenty calls per day!

As soon as he walked in the door, the phone would start ringing: daytime, nighttime, weekends, it didn't seem to matter. He couldn't sleep, couldn't eat in peace, couldn't even watch TV without constant interruptions. He bought a telephone-answering machine, but not even that solved his problem: when he came home the answering machine would be backlogged with messages to return.

On the surface, the calls were a pain in the ass, but on a deeper psychological level, this incredible response was flattering to Hearn's sagging ego. Sitting in his barren Atlanta apartment, he was suddenly transported to a nether world of intrigue and political machinations that he had only experienced vicariously through the pages of *Soldier of Fortune*. Now he was part of that world, living out his fantasies every day.

Out of curiosity, and to assuage his own ego, Hearn started returning the phone calls. He made his first return call on August 13: a fifteen-minute call to Nebraska. Three days later, he placed a call to Kansas. Four days after that, he made five calls—two each to New York and Illinois and one to Maryland—and he was off and running.

As expected, some callers were Vietnam vets looking for work, but the vast majority were people who wanted to hire *him* for high-risk assignments. And they didn't mean bodyguard work or *contra* training. Not hardly. The most popular request, by far, was murder-for-hire. Nothing else was even close.

Hearn was dumbfounded. He might have been a loser in love, a mama's boy and a sad-sack kind of guy, but he was no criminal. He had no criminal record and had never been in trouble with the law (except for a minor scrap with the ex-husband of one of his wives), but people were suddenly treating him like a professional hit man. Total strangers were calling him up and asking him to kill people right over the phone. The requests were straightforward, unblinking, and completely businesslike: "I want you to kill somebody, how much would you charge?"

"Do what?" he gasped, the first time someone asked.

The requests for other criminal activities were equally staggering: kidnappings, bombings, jailbreaks, assaults, political assassinations, overthrowing foreign governments, transporting un-marked packages and large caches of money, buying and selling illegal weapons.

Some requests sounded almost too bizarre to be true: a wealthy lawyer, who was sterile, offered him $200 a day to make love to his young wife, who wanted a baby; a group of Oregon farmers wanted him to blow up the Bagwhan Shree Rajneesh camp in Oregon; a flaky woman who claimed to be the ex-girlfriend of Martha Raye's ex-husband wanted him to beat up the man's current lover.

Others had a disturbing note of reality: a man from Alexandria, Virginia, called repeatedly, offering to sell Hearn illegal silencers (he was so persistent that Hearn worried that he was an FBI agent); a Vietnam vet called asking for work, and told him, "I'll kill my own mother if the price is right"; a California man offered him the use of a 500-ton freighter, anytime he wanted it, to fight communism; and another man called with SAM missiles for sale.

The calls came from all over the world: Canada, England, Germany, Israel, France, Turkey, Greece, among other places. As they poured in, Hearn recovered from his initial shock and began to sort out in his mind which jobs he would consider, and which ones he wouldn't. The murder-for-hire requests he just listened to and made no response, but some of the other calls intrigued him.

In early August, he received a call from a man who identified himself as L.C. Mitchell from Toronto, Ontario. Mitchell wanted Hearn to organize a coup d'etat to overthrow the government of Guyana, a small South American nation that became infamous in November, 1978, when Jim Jones and 900 members of his People's Temple committed mass suicide.

Mitchell claimed to represent Guyanese ex-patriots living in Toronto who were dissatisfied with the government of President Forbes Burnham. A self-styled Marxist, Burnham had been elected in 1964 (allegedly with CIA assistance) and had nationalized the country's principal industries—bauxite and sugar—which set off an exodus of businessmen and intellectuals, who had emigrated at the rate of 16,000 per year.

Whether or not L.C. Mitchell was for real, Toronto *does* have a large contingent of Guyanese ex-patriots (the country was formerly a British colony), and some of them had already made one attempt to overthrow Burnham. In December, 1983, five Guyanese men from Toronto had been arrested by U.S. Customs officials in Middleburg Heights, Ohio, and had been charged with plotting a coup against Burnham. The five men had attempted to buy $34,900 worth of weapons and explosives from men they thought were Cleveland mobsters, who turned out to be undercover customs agents.

Apparently, L.C. Mitchell was initiating a second attempt. After their first phone call, he wrote a follow-up letter to Hearn on August 17, 1984, in which he referred to "delivering a 'pink slip' to a civil servant," and suggested shooting down Burnham's presidential helicopter, and burning the National Phone Exchange and the General Headquarters building (both of which were wooden), which would cut off communication and throw the country into chaos. He also described the fighting capabilities of the Army, the National Police Force, and four private armies of "religio/politico fanatics" that he claimed were controlled by Burnham (in fact, Burnham *was* supported by the House of Israel, an armed religious cult), along with a fifth private army that "managed to commit mass murder and suicide"—an obvious reference to Jim Jones.

Hearn was tempted. It wasn't the bodyguard work or *contra* training that he had advertised for, and he knew that such a mission would be clearly illegal. But Mitchell had claimed that a U.S. congressional investigation had described Guyana's private armies as "hit squads" and "thugs." How much trouble could he get into for overthrowing *that* kind of government, Hearn wondered? Why, he might end up being a hero, for helping an oppressed people throw off the shackles of tyranny. On a more mercenary plane, Mitchell had hinted that there was big money behind the coup—a figure of $100,000 had been mentioned.

Hearn's problem was that to carry out a mission of that size, he needed an organization—a trained cadre of combat veterans. It was time to get serious about his new career.

•   •   •

On Tuesday, October 23, Hearn signed a year-long contract with Message World, a computerized answering service in Atlanta. Beginning November 1, whenever he was out of town, all phone calls to his Riverdale apartment could be call-forwarded to Message

World. Then by punching in the proper codes, he could retrieve the messages from anywhere in the country, or leave a new outgoing message telling callers where to reach him.

That same day, he called *Soldier of Fortune* and renewed his personal-services ad for an additional three months—covering the January, February, and March '85 issues. He dropped "ex-DI" from the ad copy, since Paul Englett was no longer involved, and added the phone number of Message World and the name that he had invented for his new organization: World Security Group.

Reflecting his growing sense of self-importance, Hearn had also created an impressive new title for himself: *Colonel* John Hearn. The leader of World Security Group couldn't be a lowly E-5 sergeant. Nossir, he would be Col. Hearn from then on.

He was taking his leadership responsibilities very seriously. Also on Tuesday, he ordered $54.90 worth of books from Paladin Press, which advertised every month in SOF (the Paladin ad was placed prominently in the magazine, opposite Bob Brown's "Command Guidance" editorial). Hearn chose titles that reflected his new professional interests: *How To Kill, Vol. 1, Get Even: The Complete Book of Dirty Tricks, How To Make Disposable Silencers, Survival Evasions and Escape, Exotic Weapons, CIA Methods for Explosives Preparation, The AR-7 Exotic Weapons System.*

Hearn's new self-confidence carried over to his personal life as well: in late August, he had quit driving for Old Dominion and had taken a higher-paying job with another Atlanta-based trucking firm—Transus (formerly Georgia Highway Express); and he had started dating *two* different women, one of whom was a friend of Paul Englett's wife. The second was a woman from Atlanta named Judy with whom he had struck up a conversation on the CB radio while driving on Interstate 20; he had then met her for dinner at a nearby Waffle House.

By late October, Hearn had allegedly carried out a number of "missions" through World Security Group, and more were looming on the horizon. An anonymous caller from Atlanta had offered to pay him $500 a month to deliver an occasional package to cities that Hearn was driving to for Transus. The man sent him a key to a storage locker at Atlanta's Greyhound bus station, where he was to pick up the packages and after delivering them, his pay. According to Hearn, he made three such deliveries: two to Memphis and one to Chicago. Each time, he had picked up an unmarked package wrapped in brown paper, approximately twelve inches long and eight inches wide; driven to Memphis or Chicago; then left the package overnight on the seat of his unlocked truck cab, parked at his motel. The packages were gone the next morning. From their size and weight, Hearn had assumed that they contained drugs, but he had never looked.

He had numerous other missions to choose from, if he wanted them. Wild-eyed wanna-bes were a dime a dozen in the paramilitary subculture, but licensed pilots like Hearn were hard to find. The job offers had continued to pour in: a Kansas man wanted him to fly into eastern Iowa, pick up a large cache of money—dirty money, Hearn assumed—using an "air hook" (a grappling hook fastened to the end of a 100-foot-long rope), and deliver it to Kansas City; another anonymous caller, who was apparently involved in the *contra*-supply network, offered to pay him $5,000 to fly a plane loaded with M-16's to south Texas (from there they would be flown on to Honduras); an oil company wanted him to supply ten bodyguards for its operation in Lebanon; and the Guyana mission was still in the works.

Hearn was also receiving phone calls every day from Vietnam vets who were anxious to go to work for him—men who hadn't found anything as meaningful or fulfilling as their tours in Vietnam.

When they called, Hearn told them to send him a resumé and a copy of their DD-214 form, the military discharge paper that would prove they had served in Vietnam. He wanted only combat vets—no desk jockeys. So far, he had collected nearly one hundred resumés and DD-214's, which he kept on file in his apartment.

One of the first, which was postmarked August 10 and addressed to "Doc John" at Hearn's Riverdale address, was from an ex-Green Beret in Pennsylvania who claimed to have been a mercenary in Haiti, El Salvador, and Cuba, listed himself as an expert in "gorilla warfare," and printed "Money is the name of the game" across the bottom of the page in a childish scrawl.

In mid-October, Hearn had received a phone call from another Vietnam vet, asking about work. This man, a retired Marine Corps captain from Bryan, Texas, said that his name was Bob Black.

• • •

Late Saturday night, October 27, Hearn tried once again to call
"Debbie," the seductive-sounding woman who had left him a message. There was still no answer. If the woman hadn't sounded so
good on the phone, he would have just blown it off. But from the
area code, he knew that she lived nearby—somewhere in north
Florida.

2

On Tuesday, October 23, 1984, Cecil Batie, a thirty-two-year-old foreman for Asplundh Tree Service in Gainesville, Florida, checked his nine-year-old son Brad out of school early. When his ex-wife, Marlene Sims Watson, who had temporary custody of Brad, found out about it, all hell broke loose. She immediately called the Alachua County Sheriff's Department and filed a complaint.

It was the latest skirmish in a bitter fourteen-month custody battle between Cecil and Marlene. Less than three months later, Cecil Batie would be dead.

•　•　•

Gainesville is *not* the Florida pictured in travel guides or tourist brochures. This is north central Florida, a region of towering pine forests, magnificent live oaks dripping with Spanish moss, sandy marshes of palmetto and scrub oak, and gently flowing rivers—the Suwannee and the Santa Fe—their waters black with tannic acid from the cypress trees along their banks. Here, live oaks, long leaf pines, and cypress still outnumber the Yankee "snowbirds," high-rise condominiums, and gaudy tourist attractions that have overwhelmed the southern half of the state.

In 1883 Carl Webber, a writer inspired by the beauty of the area, described Gainesville as the "Eden of the South," sitting "like a queen upon the southern brow of the hill portion of the state." Today, however, to most tourists speeding down Interstate 75 on their way to Disney World or the beaches of the Gold Coast,

Webber's Eden is merely a quick gas stop or a convenient exit to Wendy's or McDonald's.

Geographically, Gainesville is one hundred miles north of Disney World but only sixty miles south of the Georgia state line; that is a meaningful distinction. Culturally, Gainesville has more in common with south Georgia than with south Florida, and it is more akin politically to Jacksonville, its overgrown but still-redneck-under-the-collar neighbor to the north, than to Orlando, Miami, or Tampa.

This is farm country. Reagan country, at least in the 1980 and 1984 presidential elections, despite an overwhelming Democratic electorate. It is also "Gator Country," as the billboards remind you when you approach the city. The reference is to the two-legged orange-and-blue variety, although an abundance of four-legged ones inhabits the nearby rivers and swamps. Gainesville is home to the University of Florida, and on autumn Saturday afternoons 80,000 orange-and-blue-clad devotees fill Florida Field to cheer on their beleaguered football gladiators (the Gators were on NCAA probation during much of the 1980s for recruiting violations).

The university is the town's only major economy. Gainesville is too far inland to attract the resort trade, too cold in the winter for citrus, and too hot in the summer for transplanted Yankees. Carl Webber must have stayed out in the sun too long when he declared Gainesville's muggy summers to be "a perfect feast to the soul."

When the Florida Legislature voted to locate the state university there in 1906, Gainesville had a thriving phosphate industry and a varied agricultural base in Sea Island cotton, watermelons, strawberries, and assorted truck crops. It was also a national center for the "Chautauqua movement," and William Jennings Bryan and other notables had lectured there. More important to the legislators, however, it was "a town without a saloon or a disorderly house."

Today, those teetotaling legislators must be turning over in their graves. Although UF has several nationally ranked programs, a renowned teaching hospital, and more national merit scholars than any other university in the state, it has only recently shed its national image as a party school. In 1969, *Playboy* magazine ranked the University of Wisconsin as the top party school in the country, but *Playboy*'s judges said that UF wasn't included in the rankings because it was in a league by itself. By then, Gainesville, an other-wise sleepy southern town whose churchgoing residents hadn't allowed the sale of liquor until 1963, and wouldn't approve its sale on Sunday until 1973, had become known as Sin City.

It was a colossal paradox. If the college students and profes-sors had been surgically removed, Gainesville would have much more resembled Hog Town, its original name in the 1850s, than Sin City. It was as if 20,000 students had been bused in from Orlando, Miami, and Tampa as extras for a Hollywood movie: *Party Time in Hog Town.*

And party they did. The Atlantic beaches were only seventy-five miles away, the Gulf of Mexico only fifty, and UF's fraternities were potent enough to last a hundred years after "Greeks" had died out everywhere else in the country.

Today, with university enrollment at 34,000, Alachua County is the youngest county in the state, with a median age of 26.5 years. In August, 1990, Gainesville was terrorized by a serial killer who murdered five UF students—four women and one man—in a three-day killing spree.

•   •   •

The "Sin City" label was particularly ironic on Gainesville's south-east side, where Cecil Batie lived. Southeast Gainesville is the working-class side of town, across the tracks from the old Jackson-ville-Cedar Key railroad line that spawned the town in the first place. Most of Gainesville's new growth—upscale town houses, subdivisions, and shopping malls—is occurring on the northwest side, near the university and the Interstate, while southeast Gainesville is left behind, to wither and decay.

Both blacks and whites live in the area, although generally in separate neighborhoods: the blacks on the south side, bordering Waldo Road, and the whites on the east, off Hawthorne Road. The white areas are blue-collar, country-music-loving, pickups-in-the-front-yard neighborhoods. The residents have sometimes been called "white trash," but most are just hard-working rough-cut country folk. "They're *real*—they're not fake," says Lloyd Vip-perman, a Gainesville defense attorney who grew up in the neigh-borhood. "If they don't like you, they tell you . . . or shoot you.

They don't put on a facade and pretend to be something they're not. They're not yuppies!"

Cecil Batie grew up in a neighborhood that was known as Starvation Hill during the 1930s. It was a cruel joke—a bitter reminder of the failed Florida boom of the early 1920s, when a group of local businessmen, burning up with the real estate fever sweeping south Florida, platted out a marvelous new subdivision called Royal Pines Estates. The businessmen paved six miles of "winding, enchanting boulevards and avenues" through the piney woods, took out ads in newspapers all over the country, and waited for the profits to roll in. But when the boom went bust in 1926, only two houses had been built, and when the Great Depression hit six years later, Royal Pines Estates became Starvation Hill.

It isn't much of a hill, even by Florida standards: just a sandy rise covered with scraggly pines and scrub oaks. Hardly any vegetation will grow in the sandy soil, and the daily summer rains wash right through it, leaving the crackerbox houses dry as tinder in the sweltering afternoon heat.

In 1958, when V.R. and Lillie Belle Batie and their eight rambunctious children moved into an old house on S.E. 15th Avenue, one block off Kincaid Road, Starvation Hill quickly became known as Batie Hill. V.R. Batie (his real name was Verdie Ree, which, as a former neighbor says, "You have to have a bad Southern drawl to even pronounce") had been a tree surgeon in his native Alabama and soon opened Batie Tree Service in Gainesville.

The tree business was a tough way to make a living, even with eight kids to haul limbs and branches. V.R. ran the business out of the family's kitchen; while Lillie Belle, a thin, frail-looking woman with wiry strength, worked full-time as a lab technician at UF's Shands Teaching Hospital.

Cecil Lee Batie was born October 24, 1951. He was the fifth child, the youngest of four boys, and the runt of the litter. He was always short for his age, but he was strong and feisty and held his own in the fights that were common in the neighborhood. Altercations were part of life on Batie Hill—both at home and on the street. V.R. Batie believed the biblical admonition "spare the rod, spoil the child," and put his faith into action. "You could never prove our father wrong," says Myra Batie Monismith, the youngest of the Batie children. "He was always right, just because he was the father." A former employee of Batie Tree Service puts it more bluntly: "Old man Batie was a grouchy bastard; there was no pleasing him. He'd say, 'Son, you've done me a damn good job this week, I'm gonna give you a raise,' and when you got your paycheck there'd be an extra nickel. You'd just as soon he'd knock two of your front teeth out as say you was getting a raise."

Cecil started working for his father in the tree business when he was eight years old, after school and on weekends. When he wasn't working or in school, he was usually building go-carts that he raced down Thrill Hill, one street over. In 1968 he dropped out of high school to work for his father full-time (although he eventually got a GED). By then, the go-carts had given way to hot rods. Cecil bought a 1966 Ford Mustang that he souped up and raced around town.

Cecil had a bit of his old man's rowdy streak. He wouldn't back down from a drag race *or* a fistfight, if challenged. He liked to drink beer and frequented the local roadhouses, although as he got older he did most of his drinking at home, where he would sit in his backyard, get drunk, and sing along, badly, to Freddy Fender or Country Charley Pride records.

He was the dependable one in an often-contentious family. When Lillie Belle or one of the four Batie sisters needed something done, Cecil was the one they called. Despite his rugged exterior, Cecil had a sensitive side, which was most evident in his relationship with a pack of roughneck boys who lived on Batie Hill. The Guys, as they were called, were eight or ten years younger than Cecil, and were naturally attracted to his hot rods and go-carts. Instead of running them off, Cecil became their mentor and a surrogate father to one of the boys when his own father died.

One year, Cecil and the Guys spent six months working in old man Batie's barn, converting a junked Chevrolet Chevelle into a race car. When it was finished, the Chevelle still looked like an entry in a demolition derby, but Cecil proudly painted the names of all the Guys on its side—plus "Thanks for letting us use the barn" to mollify his daddy, and "Don't laugh, it's paid for." They towed it to a half-mile dirt track at Ellisville and entered it in a race, but after all their work, the Chevelle's engine blew up on the very first lap. "We were just a bunch of kids that, combined, probably didn't have an IQ of 100," Jimmy Dobbins recalls, laughing.

In 1972 Cecil was a brash, fun-loving, good-looking young southeast Gainesville rowdy with a hot car—all of the right qualifications for a successful ladies' man.

Then he met Marlene Sims.

She became his first, and *only*, real love. "Cecil made one mistake in his life," says Wayne Batie, his older brother, "and that was falling in love with Marlene." To his dying day, Cecil believed that it was a match made in heaven, but for the most part, it was played out in hell.

Marlene was fifteen years old, pudgy, pimply-faced and homely—hardly the best catch Cecil could have made. But one thing she had going for her was a remarkable ability to work her charms on men. It was a skill she may have learned from her sister Debbie, sixteen months older, who displayed the same prowess.

Debbie and Marlene are the only children of Frank and Iris Sims. It is *not* the typical American family. A Sims family portrait would more likely be painted by Willem de Kooning or Salvador Dalí than Norman Rockwell.

Frank Sims, born in 1933, is a beefy 240-pounder who had several youthful run-ins with the law: according to FBI records, he was arrested at age nineteen for passing hot checks in Silver City, New Mexico and was released to his father's custody; he was picked up six months later for being AWOL from the Army. His wife, the former Iris Williams, is a paunchy, bespectacled, dour-faced woman from Santa Rosa Beach, a tiny community in the Florida panhandle. The Williams clan lives out on Mack Bayou Road, where calls to the local sheriff's department are not uncommon: in November, 1982, Iris's relative, Johnnie Williams, was convicted along with a cohort, Richard Park, of the grisly murder of Ted Schery, a fifty-year-old janitor from nearby Destin.*

Iris quit school after the ninth grade, and gave birth to Debbie on January 5, 1956, when she was only sixteen. Marlene was born the following year, on May 22, 1957. Frank eventually became an

---

* While Williams and Schery were engaged in a homosexual act, Park started choking Schery from behind, then Williams slit his throat with a kitchen knife. They loaded his nude body into Williams' station wagon and drove to Mack Bayou Road, intending to chop off his hands with an ax and knock out his teeth, to hinder identification. But Williams' brother ran them off with a shotgun, so they dumped Schery's body in a field. The trial judge described the crime as "so savage and brutal it almost defies description," and sentenced Williams to life in prison.

insurance underwriter for the Florida Farm Bureau, a member-owned insurance company for farm families. He worked for the Farm Bureau for twenty years; among his colleagues, he was considered dependable and knowledgeable and he was well-liked. In the early seventies, after working in several north Florida field offices, Frank was transferred to the company's headquarters in Gainesville.

While Frank is genial and soft-spoken, Iris is gravel-voiced and abrasive. In the Sims family, Frank brought home the bacon, but Iris apparently wore the pants—and the girls took after their mother.

With hindsight, it would be easy to portray the Sims girls as ogres, but the truth is that they could both be charming and delightful, particularly with someone they were trying to impress. Both girls were high-school dropouts, but their talents were never in the classroom anyway. No, their real talents were with men. Apparently, they were honor roll students in flattery and flirtation, national merit scholars in coyness and teasing, and post-doctoral candidates in bed.

By conventional standards, neither was a likely candidate for sex kitten—they were fairly overweight and shapeless—but their lives are testimony to the principle that while men yearn for beauty, and lust after it from afar, raw sex is a far greater motivating force. They were hardly feminists, by any stretch of imagination, but in their own way the Sims girls turned sexism on its head, using sexual power for *their* ends. In the process, they cut a swath across southeast Gainesville, leaving a trail of broken hearts, pining men, and—eventually—murder in their wakes.

• • •

When Cecil Batie met Marlene in 1972, she was ready to get away from home. In short order, she got pregnant, quit school, and got her wish. They were married in April, 1973, and moved into a trailer around the corner from Cecil's parents, on a rutted dirt road. Their first son, Adam, was born five months later, on September 5, 1973.

The marriage was stormy and tempestuous, and lasted only two years. Shortly after their second son, Brad, was born on May 14, 1975, Cecil reportedly came home from work one day and discovered that Marlene had moved in with one of his best friends, Ralph Smith, who lived right down the street.

Apparently, Cecil never got over it. Even after Marlene divorced him in December, 1975, married Smith, and had a daughter by him, Cecil couldn't accept that the marriage was over. He wasn't a churchgoer, but he believed that he and Marlene were still married in the eyes of God.

Marlene knew that Cecil still loved her, and according to his family and friends, whenever Cecil started getting involved with another woman, Marlene would start coming around—just long enough to rekindle Cecil's hopes and run off the other woman. "Cecil dated some of the prettiest, nicest women you'd ever want to meet," says Jimmy Dobbins, one of his best friends. "I mean, Marlene looked like a hog compared to some of them, but she'd show up and say, 'Cecil, let's do something this weekend,' and he'd go, no matter what the consequences."

The custody problems began in 1978. After Marlene split up with Ralph Smith, she left the boys with Cecil, and Judge R.A. "Buzzy" Green gave Cecil permanent custody of them. From 1978 to 1983, Cecil raised the boys on his own, and the custody issue slowly escalated into a full-scale war.

It was exacerbated when Frank and Iris Sims moved into a trailer directly across the street from the Baties. Although Frank had a white-collar job, the Simses' lifestyle fit right in on Batie Hill. Frank was a pack rat, and his yard was soon cluttered with a half-dozen junk vehicles: a 1951 Plymouth, a 1961 Chevy truck, a 1971 International school bus, an old gas-company service truck, even a golf cart.

When V.R. Batie died of heart disease in 1981, Lillie Belle Batie moved out of the neighborhood. However, Cecil moved into his father's house, and several of his siblings still lived nearby. With the two families facing off across the street, the custody dispute became a blood feud, on the order of the Hatfields and McCoys.

The war erupted in late 1983, when Marlene filed a complaint with the Florida Department of Health and Rehabilitative Services (HRS), charging Cecil with physically abusing Adam, who was ten years old at the time. HRS investigators confirmed that Cecil had indeed struck Adam, and on October 10, 1983, HRS filed a "petition for dependency" in circuit court, to place Adam in protective custody. In court, Cecil admitted hitting Adam, and on November 15, Marlene was given temporary custody.

Cecil was devastated. He expressed remorse to his family, his friends, and his coworkers about letting his temper get the best of him. "Cecil could not eat for weeks because he was upset with himself for letting this happen," says Myra Monismith, his sister.

On the heels of her victory, Marlene filed a separate complaint alleging that Cecil had also abused Brad, the younger boy, with a wooden paddle. Cecil admitted using a paddle, but denied that he had used it abusively. Nonetheless, on December 6, 1983, Marlene was given temporary custody of Brad.

With two quick lightning strikes, Marlene had won custody— albeit only *temporary* custody, an important point that would come back to haunt her—of both boys. But then, incredibly, she turned around and *gave* Adam back to Cecil two weeks later. Adam was an unruly child, both at home and at school. So Marlene gave him back. Evidently, she wanted *custody,* but she didn't really want Adam.

In January, 1984, Jean Shepherd, the HRS caseworker assigned to the Batie case, informed Marlene that Adam could not be returned to Cecil without Judge Green's approval, or Marlene and Cecil would be in contempt of court.

Marlene did not take the news graciously. She had a highly developed vocabulary of obscenities and didn't hesitate using it with social workers. Shepherd would soon be hearing reports that Marlene had nicknamed her "the bitch from HRS," and Shepherd would later describe Marlene as "one of the most difficult clients I've ever worked with."

Shepherd was in a quandary. According to her, Marlene indicated she didn't want Adam, yet the court order prevented him from being with Cecil. As an interim solution, Judge Green gave temporary custody to Lillie Belle Batie. Cecil was allowed visitation privileges, but only under his mother's supervision.

Meanwhile, Shepherd was still seeking a permanent solution. She talked to other HRS caseworkers and to Adam's school guidance counselor, who were optimistic that Cecil could overcome his abuse patterns through therapy. Shepherd approached Cecil directly: would he be willing to enroll in parenting classes and go to a family therapist?

Cecil jumped at the offer. He enrolled in parenting classes and in June, 1984, began weekly therapy sessions with Dr. Andres Nazario, Jr. He made other changes in his life: he began coaching Adam's baseball team at the Southeast Boys Club and cut way back on his beer drinking, which was already down from his rowdier days.

Shepherd and Nazario were both impressed by Cecil's efforts to face his problems. But not Marlene. When Joyce Sherman, Adam's guidance counselor, made a remark about how hard Cecil was trying to improve, Marlene launched into an angry tirade: she blamed Cecil for the contempt of court problem and said that he couldn't control Adam any more than she could.

At one point, Jean Shepherd suggested to Marlene that *she* go to counseling with Cecil, but she bluntly refused and told Shepherd that from then on HRS should communicate with her only through her attorney.

Marlene wasn't sitting idly by, however. In July, 1984, she married Larry Watson, a local carpenter. Apparently, Watson was head-over-heels in love with her, but Marlene later admitted to a friend that she had only married Watson to give the appearance of a stable family environment.

Marlene and Watson moved to Hawthorne, twenty miles east of Gainesville, but she still spent a lot of time at her parents' trailer. She and Cecil kept getting into terrible arguments, and Jean Shepherd was trying to keep them apart. According to Shepherd, Cecil had told her on numerous occasions that Marlene had threatened to kill him. He had good reason to be alarmed: The Simses' trailer was stocked like an armed fortress. Frank and Iris had guns placed throughout the trailer: two rifles were propped behind a living room chair, a Luger pistol was placed above the fireplace, the washroom closet contained five or six old shotguns or rifles, and Iris kept a pistol in the nightstand beside her bed.

Cecil had also complained bitterly about Marlene and Iris's drug use. He claimed that Marlene was hanging around with known drug dealers and that she was using illegal drugs, although he never provided any proof. He also told Shepherd that Iris's prescription-drug use was a bad influence on the boys. Iris, who was admitted to North Florida Regional Hospital ten times in six years, suffered from a host of maladies. According to a close friend of the family, she was a walking inventory of various prescription drugs: Percodan, Dilaudid, Fiorinal, Desyrel, and codeine. This same friend described her as a "junkie"; her own attorney commented on her prescription-drug abuse, and she was hospitalized in 1985, with "probable abuse of Dilaudid and Percodan" listed as one of the diagnoses.

In August, 1984, HRS reassessed Cecil's parenting skills, and Judge Green awarded him temporary custody of Adam. With that, the situation on Batie Hill became as volatile as the Ocala National Forest that surrounded Gainesville, which had been plagued all year with raging brushfires. All that was needed was a spark to start a major conflagration.

• • •

The spark occurred on October 23, when Cecil picked up Brad from school. Why he did it remains a mystery. Cecil's birthday was the next day, so perhaps he wanted to do something special with Brad. Or maybe he did it just to irritate Marlene. If that was the case, it certainly worked.

That afternoon, Marlene filed a complaint with the sheriff's department, then went straight to her attorney, Harold Silver, who drafted a motion for emergency hearing. He charged that Cecil had "spirited the child away from school," and that Brad was "terrified" of Cecil after having been beaten with the wooden paddle. At 4:45 P.M., Judge Stephen Mickle ordered Cecil to return Brad to Marlene, which he did that night.

Marlene and Silver were back in Mickle's courtroom at 9 o'clock the next morning, trying to get *permanent* custody of Brad (Marlene only had *temporary* custody). But Judge Mickle's review of the court records turned up a surprising discovery: *Cecil* still had legal custody of Brad; HRS had never officially placed Brad in protective custody of the state. Mickle told Silver that he would have to go before Judge Green, who had originally heard the case, to make any change in custody. Further, he ruled that if Silver couldn't get an emergency hearing before Green, then Brad would have to be returned to Cecil.

While Silver scrambled to petition Green for an emergency

hearing, Marlene spent the afternoon riding around with her sister, Debbie. Every half hour, Marlene called Silver's office to find out if there was any word. Finally, at 4:30 P.M., Silver delivered the bad news: There was no way to get an emergency hearing with Green, and it could take weeks to schedule a formal hearing. In the interim, she would have to return Brad to Cecil.

Marlene was incredulous. She told Debbie that she couldn't understand how the court could make her give back Brad or why Cecil would keep the boy against his will. Debbie was supportive and told her that Cecil didn't really love the boys but was just doing this to get back at her. As they drove back to Hawthorne, Marlene was still raging, and she told Debbie: "I hate Cecil Batie and wish he was dead."

At that moment, Debbie apparently decided to solve her little sister's problem.

3

On October 30, 1984, at 5:27
p.m., John Wayne Hearn tried calling Debbie again. This time,
finally, he got an answer.

"Sun Bank," a woman said, in a businesslike voice.

Hearn immediately realized why his previous calls had gone
unanswered: He had been calling a bank at night and on the weekend. "Is Debbie there?" he asked.

"This is Debbie," the woman replied.

"Uh . . . this is *John,*" he said. "You've left several messages
on my answering machine . . . ?"

"Oh, right," Debbie said perkily. "I wasn't going to leave any
more messages—I didn't think you were going to call me back."
She said it teasingly, with a little pout in her voice.

"Well, I'm calling." Hearn retorted. He liked this woman
already. "Exactly what was it you wanted?"

"Oh . . . I just wanted to know if you'll do anything that's
illegal or against the law?" she said coyly.

Even if he would, Hearn wasn't stupid enough to say so over
the phone. "No ma'am, I won't. I'm sorry."

"Well, okay then; I guess I can't use you," Debbie said
brusquely, as if she might hang up.

Hearn jumped in quickly, reacting to the implied slight to his
manhood: "Wait now—what is it you wanted?"

"Well . . ." she said, "my sister has a problem with her ex-
husband."

"What kind of problem?"

"See, she has custody of her kids, but he came and took them away, and I just wanted to know if you could come get them back?"

"Sure, I can do that," Hearn replied confidently. "As long as the kids *want* to go back, that's not illegal. Now I can't *hurt* the man, but I can get the kids." In fact, he had no intention of doing any such thing. He was just trying to keep Debbie on the line. She still might turn out to be fat and ugly, but Hearn didn't think so. She sounded like a woman who knew how to play the game—and enjoyed it. To John Wayne Hearn, deep in the throes of a post-Elaine binge of "middle-aged craziness"—dating two women and eager for more—Debbie sounded like his kind of woman.

"How old are they?" he asked.

"Nine and eleven."

"Well, they're old enough to know what they want. That's no problem."

"How much would it cost?" Debbie asked.

"Well, it's gonna be expensive," Hearn said. It was a throw-away line that showed his inexperience. He hadn't even asked where the children were located—they could have been in California for all he knew.

Debbie pressed the point: "How much is expensive?"

Hearn grabbed a figure out of his head. "About thirty thousand dollars."

"Hmm," Debbie said. "I'll have to call you back."

"Fine," Hearn said.

Debbie said good-bye and hung up.

The entire conversation had lasted one minute; it was the most important minute of Hearn's life.

Reflecting on the call, he doubted that the woman could come up with the $30,000, but he wasn't serious about the child-nabbing, even if she could. He was just trying to impress a woman who sounded *good* on the phone: feeding her a line of bull, embellishing his own experience and expertise, the way he did with other people all the time. He figured he'd never hear from her again.

•   •   •

Down in Gainesville, Debbie Banister was also reflecting on the phone call. Four days earlier, after leaving the first message on Hearn's answering machine, she had driven out to Marlene's trailer in Hawthorne, and, according to Marlene, told her that she had found a man who would kill Cecil Batie.

"Where did you find him?" Marlene asked.

"In *Soldier of Fortune* magazine." Debbie told Marlene that her husband subscribed to SOF. She said that she'd left a message on the man's recorder, and he was supposed to call her back.

Now that he had, Debbie could have gained several important insights into this ex-marine weapons specialist who had advertised his availability for high-risk assignments. Not about his expertise or experience, but about his personality.

In a one-minute phone call, Debbie might have been able to tell that this was a man who was susceptible to flattery and flirtation, and his macho attempts to impress her were all too apparent. Of course, he had fended off her initial probe about "doing anything illegal," but that part would come later.

John Wayne Hearn and Debbie Banister had both been playing a game of deception, but while Hearn was hoping to get laid, Debbie was playing a far deadlier game—one that he had never played before, that he could not win.

•   •   •

It was only natural that Debbie Banister was the one who had made the call. She was the take-charge person in the Sims family, the one with the business sense. Debbie was smarter than Marlene, and more capable than Iris. Marlene had a stronger motive to want Cecil dead, but she was too flighty and unstable to pull it off. And while Iris might have been vindictive enough, she was so absent-minded that she reportedly told a friend she couldn't remember what she had done two months before.

No, it had to be Debbie.

While Marlene and the Sims family were still mired in the "white trash" lifestyle of southeast Gainesville—living in ram-shackle trailers with junk cars in the backyard—Debbie had clawed her way to middle-class respectability. She had a responsible job in the Sun Bank loan-recovery department, a new $50,000 brick home in Starke, a late-model Oldsmobile Cutlass, a charge account at Maas Brothers, and money in the bank. She had achieved all of that with drive and determination to get what she wanted, no matter what stood in her way.

And she had done it all on her own. In 1973, she had dropped out of Gainesville High School during her junior year, moved out on her own, and gotten a job as a cashier at Pantry Pride. In December, 1974, at age eighteen, she married Billy Thigpen, a lanky, easygoing good old boy she had met in driver's ed class.

Thigpen's ambition in life was to be an auto mechanic, but Debbie wanted more than that; and six months after they were married, she went looking for it: She started having an affair with Joe Banister, a thirty-one-year-old man she met in the checkout line at Pantry Pride.

Joe Banister was a symbol of everything that Billy Thigpen was not: While Thigpen had southeast Gainesville written all over him, Banister came from a solid middle-class family, owned a nice home in respectable northeast Gainesville, had a good-paying union job with Western Electric, and drove a Corvette.

For him, Debbie Sims was a contradiction of all the respectable tendencies in his life. Banister had come of age in the slumbering fifties, in a family that could have been Ozzie and Harriet's next-door neighbors: it was a white bread, mashed potatoes, and "Hi, Mom, I'm home" childhood.

Debbie Sims's family, on the other hand, was more like what *The Beverly Hillbillies* might have been if Roman Polanski had directed it: Granny popping Percodans in the kitchen, Ellie Mae smoking pot in the hall, and Jethro diddling Miss Hathaway under the swimming-pool cabana.

Joe Banister was the oldest of two children; his sister, Lana, was three years younger. His father, Ceree Banister, worked at the University of Florida as the equipment manager for the athletics department. His mother, Ruth, worked part-time at Ruddy's Department Store, but was home in the afternoon with the kids.

Ceree Banister was painfully quiet—the children knew it must be important when he said something—but hard working and dependable. Ruth, who was as outgoing as her husband was reserved, was nurturing and overprotective. She never learned to drive, never learned to swim, and never quite trusted those who did. "If you go near the water you'll drown," was her attitude, and she sheltered her kids from the dangers of the world. "It's a wonder we ever grew up," Lana recalls today.

Joe took after his dad. He was quiet and reserved, and spent a lot of time alone in his room or shooting baskets by himself after school. He never had a lot of friends, but the ones he did have remained close to him throughout his life. Lana teased him that he was "born an old man," and in many ways, he was. Ceree Banister always got sideline passes to UF football games, and most boys would have been thrilled to rub shoulders with Gator football heroes. Joe went to the games, almost out of obligation to his father, but to him it was no big deal.

He was almost disgustingly responsible about money. Lana was always broke, but Joe saved his weekly allowance and used it to buy a Cushman motor scooter in junior high, which he used on his afternoon paper route, delivering the Gainesville *Sun.*

In high school, he fell in love for the first time—with *cars.* Using his savings, he bought an old Ford, a late-1940s model, which Lana calls "the ugliest thing I've ever seen." But Joe fixed it up, and cruised the A&W Root Beer stand on 13th Street with his buddies.

When he graduated from Gainesville High School in 1961, he was a stocky five feet eight inches tall, with a ubiquitous flattop, a fairly bad case of acne, and the same shy, taciturn personality. He was an average student, ran track, and belonged to the trade education club, whose motto began "I believe in the dignity of work." It fit him well.

His father insisted that he enroll at UF, but after two years he quit and joined the Air Force. He spent the next five years in Bitburg, Germany, working on electrical systems in jets.

He returned to Gainesville in 1968, got a job with Western Electric (installing electromagnetic switches in telephone systems), bought a house around the corner from his parents, and married the preacher's daughter, who lived next door. "Good old Joe," so steady and dependable, stayed at the same job for seventeen years, but the marriage turned out to be less stable, and they soon divorced. On the rebound, he married a beautiful young woman with long blond hair, but they split up in 1973, and she reportedly cleaned out the house and moved to Las Vegas.

Debbie Sims was all the things his mother would have disapproved of: Scandalously young, married, flirtatious, foul-mouthed, wildly inappropriate, and decidedly unladylike. That may have been part of the attraction. Joe Banister already owned a Corvette

—a symbol of rebellion against the numbing respectability of his life—but he needed Debbie to go for the full ride.

One afternoon, Billy Thigpen got a phone call from a friend, who asked: "Do you know a guy named Joe Banister?" Billy said no, and his friend responded, "Well, he sure knows your wife. He's got her picture on top of his TV set."

When Debbie got home that night, Thigpen confronted her with the accusation, and she responded by moving out of the house. But Thigpen had been raised to believe that when you're married you stick it out; so after a few weeks he told Debbie that he would give her a second chance, and she moved back in. Apparently, she didn't stop seeing Joe Banister—she just became more clever about not getting caught.

Debbie was making other changes in her life: She got her GED at an adult education center, enlisted in the Army Reserve, and got a job as a telephone installer at Western Electric (an interesting coincidence, since Joe Banister worked for the same company).

Despite her heightened vigilance, Billy Thigpen eventually caught her running around with Joe Banister again. One afternoon, he was returning home earlier than expected from a hunting trip and noticed Debbie's car parked at a neighborhood park. He pulled over and waited, and eventually, Joe came driving up with Debbie in his car. Caught red-handed, Debbie defiantly moved out of the house for a second time.

Once more, Thigpen decided to give her another chance. He got a job offer as a truck driver in Marianna, eighty miles west of Tallahassee, and asked Debbie to go with him. They moved to Cottondale, just outside of Marianna, where Debbie had a friend.

After six months, Thigpen assumed that everything was going fine: Debbie was working in the emergency room at Jackson County Hospital and had transferred from the Army Reserve into an Air National Guard unit in Dothan, Alabama, thirty miles across the state line. Then one morning he got up before Debbie and went into the kitchen to make breakfast. There weren't enough eggs and bacon in the refrigerator, so he reached into Debbie's purse for some money to go to the store. Inside, he found a stack of letters from Joe Banister, addressed to a secret post-office box that Debbie had rented.

Even for old-fashioned Billy Thigpen, that was the last straw.

He told Debbie that he was leaving, but, according to Thigpen, she kept him so broke for the next few weeks that he couldn't move. When he finally got home to Gainesville, he had two dollars in his pocket. He filed for divorce under Florida's no-fault divorce law, but Debbie wouldn't sign the papers until he hired a lawyer and threatened legal action. After three separations in three years of marriage, they were finally divorced on May 1, 1978. It is a chapter of Billy Thigpen's life that he is still trying to forget.

•   •   •

Debbie remained in Cottondale for a few months, received her honorable discharge from the Air National Guard (as a sergeant), then returned to Gainesville and moved in with Joe Banister. On November 4, 1978, they were married in a small ceremony at his house.

If Joe's family was shocked by his affair with a married woman, they were truly scandalized by Debbie's behavior once she became his wife. Every Sunday at noon, the family would gather at Ceree and Ruth's house for a big Sunday dinner. The first few months, Debbie was on her best behavior—trying to show her new in-laws what she thought they wanted to see—but soon her true personality emerged: She made crude, off-color remarks at the dinner table, told vulgar jokes, and wore cutoff shorts and halter tops without a bra, which shocked the staid Banister family.

Her behavior soon became an embarrassment outside the Banister home. Joe's sister, Lana, worked in a dentist's office, and one afternoon when her car was in the shop, she asked Debbie to give her a ride home. Debbie arrived at the dentist's office "barefoot as a yard dog," according to Lana, wearing cutoff shorts with her butt hanging out, her waist-length hair soaking wet from the shower, and carrying a can of beer. After that, Lana started introducing her simply as "Debbie Banister"—not "Debbie Banister, my sister-in-law."

In February, 1980, Debbie gave birth to a daughter, Amanda Jean. A son, John Ceree, was born the following year. Joe had always wanted children and became a doting father, but his mother and sister were appalled by Debbie's mothering techniques, or the lack thereof. According to Lana, Debbie bought the children tons of new clothes but dressed them in sweaters in the middle of summer and short sleeves in the dead of winter. Amanda and John always seemed to have colds, which Joe's family attributed to Debbie's lack of proper care.

Joe wanted her to stay home with the children, but Debbie was hardly the stay-at-home type, and returned to work soon after Amanda was born. She started working at Atlantic Loan Company for Wayne Kelly, who later hired her at Sun Bank.

In 1980 Joe and Debbie bought a lot in the Deerwood subdivision in Starke, thirty miles north of Gainesville, and built a house next door to Joe's good friend and coworker David Bennett.

Every Sunday, the family still gathered at Ruth and Ceree's house for Sunday dinner, but Debbie was always in a hurry, always on the go. She would eat and run, or leave the kids with Joe while she went to town. To Lana, her behavior was always perplexing, and sometimes bizarre. "Debbie would drop off the kids and say, 'I need to run to the grocery store,' and come back five hours later with no groceries," Lana recalls.

Although Joe Banister had given her financial security and two beautiful children, good old Joe had turned out to be as bland and dull as Billy Thigpen. Indeed, Joe and Billy were a lot alike: quiet, low-key, easy to control, but thoroughly unexciting. Once their illicit love affair became legal, once the Corvette became just another family car, the thrill was gone.

As a symbol of her rebellion against married life, Debbie went off one day with Marlene and returned home sporting a butterfly tattoo, fluttering brazenly above her left breast. Marlene had one, too (which shocked no one), but for Debbie Banister, a mother of two, married into a respectable family from Gainesville's northeast side, it was scandalous. She could have hidden it under high-neck blouses, but instead she flaunted it, wearing sleeveless sundresses and tank tops that announced to the world: "I will not be tamed!"

• • •

And she wasn't. Soon, she began running around on Joe Banister, the same way she had run around on Billy Thigpen. She had changed jobs again (she had twelve jobs in twelve years), and was working for U.S. Life Financial Company (now Norwest Financial), developing loan packages and doing credit investigations. Her boss, Kenneth Parrish, remembers her as a "fantastic employee."

She was outgoing, efficient, and well liked—by customers and co-workers alike. Perhaps a bit risqué, with her tattoo and sundresses, and quite flirtatious with male customers, but Parrish really didn't mind that. After all, a little harmless flirtation was good for business. But when Debbie started openly dating one customer—a Florida highway patrolman who stopped by regularly to make payments on his account—Parrish had a problem. Debbie and the trooper started going out to lunch so often, and so openly, that it became grist for the office gossip mill—and Parrish decided to intervene. He told Debbie that he wasn't concerned about what she did in her personal life, but as a U.S. Life employee, it didn't look good for her to be dating a customer. Without denying the relationship, Debbie politely suggested to Parrish that it was none of his business.

•　•　•

When John Wayne Hearn got off the phone with Debbie Banister on October 30, he immediately made six other phone calls, including two to Vietnam vets who had responded to his *Soldier of Fortune* ad. Then he called his wife Elaine, who was scheduled to enter the hospital in Columbia, South Carolina, the following day. Although they had been separated since February, he and Elaine still talked periodically on the phone and still discussed getting back together for one more try. Hearn was dating two other women, but keeping all of his options open.

The next afternoon he left for Columbia, 211 miles away. On Saturday morning, he went to the hospital to see Elaine. She wanted him to make a decision about their marriage—were they going to try to make another go of it, or was it over?—but Hearn was more interested in talking about his new business ventures. He told her that he was thinking about buying land in South Carolina to open a "war games" franchise (customers fight mock battles, shooting dye-filled pellets), and also mentioned that a woman from Florida had called him and wanted to hire him to get her kids back from her ex-husband. Hearn asked Elaine how she would feel, assuming they got back together, if he got a call from a woman in the middle of the night and had to go out and do a job like that.

Lying in her hospital bed, Elaine didn't take him seriously. In the five years they had been married, she had heard too many big stories from Hearn—too many schemes that had never panned out. Once, in Oklahoma, he had decided to become a flea-market dealer and had sunk nearly $1,000 on junk—knickknacks, air fresheners, Christmas trinkets, little bottles of perfume—that he never sold. He was always dreaming, always talking big.

But Hearn was insistent. "I'm going into the mercenary business," he told her. "You know, killing people for money."

"That's crazy, Johnny," she told him.

•   •   •

When he left to return to Atlanta, Elaine thought they had agreed to get back together and try one more time. Hearn confirmed that when he called her the next week, and again the following week. But then she didn't hear from him until Christmas.

No wonder. John Wayne Hearn had more exciting things on his mind than his faltering marriage. Like Debbie Banister.

She had left another message on his answering machine while he was gone, and he called her back Monday morning from Tampa, Florida, where he had hauled a load for Transus.

This time, they talked for two minutes. Debbie told him, "We're not going to be able to raise the thirty thousand."

"Okay, no problem," he said.

She called him back later that day and said, "I think we can get a little less than thirty thousand."

"How much less?" Hearn asked.

"Well, I don't know."

Hearn couldn't have cared less about the money—he didn't intend to do the child-nabbing anyway—and he just wanted to meet Debbie. "I'll tell you what, Debbie, I'll do it for you for fifteen thousand dollars."

"Okay, I think we can get that," she said.

"Fine," he replied, feigning self-assurance.

That week, November 5 through November 8, Hearn was hauling loads all over Florida, "making turns" between Orlando, Fort Myers, Tampa, and Jacksonville. At night, he would call Message World from his motel room, retrieve his messages, and make return calls. Mostly, though, he thought about Debbie. What was he going to do if she really came up with the $15,000? One option was to take the money and run. After all, any woman stupid enough to give him $15,000 without knowing anything about him deserved to get ripped off. And what could she do, report him to the police?

But Debbie sounded so *good* on the phone—that was the hook. Hearn wanted to meet her at least one time and find out what she looked like. Who knew, something might happen between them. After that, he could still take the money and run.

When he got home to Atlanta on Thursday, he called Debbie at Sun Bank. They talked for thirty-nine minutes—their longest conversation so far. Hearn made his pitch: "Listen, before all this comes down, I would like to meet you in person. Just to find out if we're *comfortable* with each other, before we make the deal."

"Fine," Debbie said. "Where do you want to meet?"

Now Hearn had his chance. After fantasizing about this woman for over a week, she had agreed to meet him—and wanted *him* to pick the spot. So where did Hearn suggest for this rendezvous? Perhaps a quiet, candlelit, romantic little out-of-the-way place? Let's see . . . how about Shoney's Big Boy?

That's right. Shoney's was the best he could do. After all, this was the same truck-driving Romeo who had met Judy, his Atlanta girlfriend, at the Waffle House on Interstate 20.

He suggested that they meet at the Shoney's on Interstate 75 in Cordele, Georgia. His choice was hardly romantic, but it was utterly practical: Cordele was approximately halfway between Gainesville and Atlanta, and Hearn had eaten there many times on his way to Florida.

They set the date for noon on the following Monday, November 12. Debbie added the one touch of romance, telling Hearn that she would be wearing a blue dress, in the tradition of John Dillinger's "woman in red."

Hearn called her again the next morning to finalize the plans. On Sunday, he called Transus and asked to have his name taken off the dispatch board for Monday (he was an "extra board driver"; so he didn't have a regular run).

On the morning of the momentous rendezvous, Hearn drove to the Atlanta airport and rented a Volkswagen Rabbit from Budget Rent-a-Car. It was hardly the best car to impress a woman, but Hearn didn't want Debbie Banister to get the license number of his pickup truck—just in case. His romantic hopes hadn't totally clouded his judgment—the leader of World Security Group had to be cautious.

He drove the 145 miles to Cordele and arrived at Shoney's about 11:30 A.M. He told the hostess that he was expecting a lady in the next thirty or forty minutes and asked for a table in the glassed-in patio of the restaurant, where he would have a full view of the parking lot. Then he waited.

About 12:20 P.M., a woman in a light-blue Oldsmobile Cutlass pulled into the Shoney's parking lot. Hearn recognized the Florida inspection sticker on the front windshield. *That's got to be her,* he thought. The door opened and a fairly young woman in a blue dress stepped out of the car and walked toward the restaurant.

Hmmm, not bad, Hearn thought to himself. *Maybe a few pounds overweight, but all in all, not bad.*

This mystery woman who had occupied his thoughts for the past two weeks appeared to be in her late twenties and had reddish-brown hair cropped short on the sides but shoulder length and wispy in back. She had long school-girl bangs that were combed straight down over her forehead, giving her face an unflattering ovalness—a bowl-like roundness—that accentuated her extra weight. She was small-breasted, with matronly hips and fleshy arms. But, at age thirty-eight, overweight and dumpy himself, Hearn couldn't be too picky.

In a chivalrous flourish, he met her at the front door, introduced himself, and ushered her to their table. They chitchatted for a few minutes, then ordered dinner: Hearn selected a chicken and rice dish, and Debbie—in a nice touch—deferred to his judgment and ordered the same.

While they waited for their food, they talked about themselves —haltingly, at first, then more openly. Hearn had proposed this as a social meeting, to get to know each other before the child-nabbing, so he wasn't about to bring up *that* topic. After a woman drove 150 miles to meet him, child-nabbing was the furthest thing from his mind. Ironically, the same was true for Debbie. She was apparently scoping out Hearn for a much bigger job than child-nabbing; so she didn't bring it up either.

They continued talking over dinner. Hearn had never been shy talking about himself, and Debbie was a good listener. He told her about his job, his Marine Corps career, his photography business, his custody battle over his son—and Debbie seemed genuinely interested. She talked about herself too: her job at Sun Bank and her two beautiful children.

Debbie told him that she didn't have to be home until evening (she had arranged for her husband to pick up the kids from daycare); so they had the whole afternoon to kill. Cordele is only forty miles from Plains, the home of former president Jimmy Carter; so Hearn suggested that they drive over and tour Carter's house.

"Sure, why not?" Debbie responded.

They piled into Hearn's rented VW Rabbit and headed for Plains. Driving down the deserted back roads of south Georgia, they shared more about their lives: Hearn talked about his problems with Elaine, her reluctance to raise his son (Elaine had four children of her own and thought that Wayne should be with his natural mother), her lack of understanding about Vietnam and his flashbacks. Again, Debbie was sympathetic and said that she couldn't understand Elaine's attitude. And she talked about her problems with Joe Banister: she said that he came home from work and sat in his chair all night, drinking beer. It was just what Hearn wanted to hear: she was married, but unhappily so.

In Plains, they toured the visitor's center and the president's house. Hearn, the fledgling photographer, always carried his camera, and he took pictures of the Carter house, and of Debbie posing in front of it.

It was only about three o'clock when they finished the tour, so they drove on to Albany, fifty miles south of Plains. The excuse Debbie had given Joe for why she couldn't pick up the kids was that she needed to go shopping for them; so she and Hearn went to the Albany mall, where Debbie bought several outfits for her kids.

At five o'clock, they started back to Cordele. They drove through the peaceful Georgia countryside, past quaint farmhouses with wraparound porches and peaked tin roofs; huge pecan groves, barren and somber in the stark winter twilight; parched fields of corn, stillborn and shriveled from the summer drought. The afternoon had gone splendidly, so far, but Hearn was thinking how nice it would be if things went even further. Sitting inches away from Debbie in the tiny Rabbit, he was enveloped by her presence—her breasts, so close and inviting, her hair, the scent of her perfume. Before he realized it, he had an erection bulging in his jeans. He tried to hide it by shifting in his seat and tugging at his pants.

"You having a problem?" Debbie asked with a grin.

"Yeah, I'm having a problem," Hearn admitted, laughing. *This is a sexy woman,* Hearn thought, *She knows exactly what's going on and likes it!*

They arrived back at Shoney's about 6:00 P.M. It was a two-hour drive to Gainesville; so Debbie would already be late getting home, but she still didn't leave. Instead, they went back inside, sat down, and ordered supper. Halfway through the meal, Hearn was looking down at his plate when Debbie called out his name, in a sweet, tender voice: "John."

He looked up, and Debbie leaned across the table—she came all the way out of her seat—and kissed him on the end of the nose.

"What was that for?" Hearn asked, taken aback.

"Just because I wanted to," Debbie said, beaming.

Hearn shook his head and smiled. *Damn,* he thought to himself. This woman was like no one he had ever met.

It was nearly seven o'clock when they finished eating, and by then, Debbie was very late. Hearn walked her out to her car, and sat down beside her in the passenger seat to say good-bye. He leaned over and kissed her—not on the end of the nose but passionately—and she responded. Hearn was ready to go across the street and get a motel room, but Debbie was already so late. . . .

All the way home to Atlanta, he was filled with desire and wonder and the afterglow of Debbie Banister. Ever since he was fourteen years old, when Mary Watson first told him about Joe Pickett, she had promised him: "Someday you'll meet someone just as special as your father was to me." Since then he had fallen in love many times—always quickly, always hoping to fulfill his mother's prophecy, the way he had tried to fulfill all her other expectations of him. But none of the other loves had ever worked out, and now Mary Watson was convinced that no woman was good enough for her son.

But after one day with Debbie Banister—after the way she listened to him, the way she smiled at him, the way she climbed across the table to kiss him on the end of the nose—John Wayne Hearn was falling once again . . . hoping this would finally be the one.

4

BOB BLACK was like a new man when he moved back to Bark-n-Holler in October, 1984. He told Sandra that his relationship with Teresa was all over, and he asked to move back home. Sandra, who was still feeling sorry for him after the suicide attempt, said yes.

He was flat broke, after quitting Harville and shelling out $475 in rent and deposits for the Bittle Lane house, but he told Sandra that he was tired of electrical work and wanted to do something different. He interviewed for several jobs and ended up taking one selling restaurant equipment for a company in Tyler, Texas. He borrowed Sandra's car and drove to Tyler for three weeks of training, then came home and started making sales calls on his friends (he tried to sell an ice machine to Marilyn Soffar).

With his sights set on a white-collar career, Bob took to wearing a sport shirt and tie and carrying a briefcase wherever he went. He made an appointment with the dean of admissions at A&M, to talk about reentering college and completing his degree, and told Gary Wayne that even at age thirty-eight, he was going to try out for the Aggie football team's Twelfth Man squad (nonscholarship walk-ons who play on the kick-off coverage team).

Bob was still writing and phoning Teresa on the sly, but he did such a good job of convincing Sandra that the affair was over that she told her attorney to cancel the divorce.

• • •

The first time Bob asked David Huber to kill Sandra it was just before Halloween. Huber, the twenty-one-year-old younger brother of Mark Huber, and Bob's former helper at H&S Electric, was Bob's closest friend at the time. He was working as a maintenance man in the A&M Corps dormitory, and Bob would often drop by campus at lunchtime to visit. They would go to the Memorial Student Center cafeteria and ogle the college girls. Leering at women was the main basis of their friendship. As Huber recalls, "Bob would say, 'Look at that bitch over there,' do his laugh, and say, 'I wonder how long it'd take me to get in her pants?' "

When Bob returned from California in August, the only clue Huber had that he was any different was that he seemed less interested in gawking at the coeds. "He wasn't slobbering all over himself if something sweet walked by," Huber says.

Still, Bob didn't step out of his ladies' man role completely: he told Huber that he had met a "great lady" in California named Teresa, but didn't mention that she was his cousin or that they were planning to get married or that he had rented the house on Bittle Lane. "I would have thought that the *last* thing he would want was to be married again," says Huber. "The word 'love' never came up [regarding Teresa]. He still had me convinced that *I* was naive, that love didn't exist. He really liked this line from the movie *St. Elmo's Fire:* 'Love is a myth which creates the delusion of marriage, leading to the reality of divorce.' He really liked that one."

One afternoon, Bob and Huber were hanging out at lunchtime in the A&M Quad, when Bob started complaining about Sandra. "I just don't know what I'm going to do," he said, according to Huber. "I can't leave her, I can't divorce her, what else can I do? I lost my ass the first time we got divorced, and everything we own is in her name. I don't want to lose my setup."

He went on and on, whining about his predicament: "I just don't know what I'm gonna do. I guess there's nothing else I can do, is there? What would you do if you couldn't divorce her?"

Bob sounded so pitiful that Huber tried to make a joke. "Well, you can always knock her off, Rocky," he said.

Bob's eyes suddenly lit up, and he glanced furtively around the Quad to make sure that no one could overhear them. "We ought to discuss this matter in further detail," he said under his breath.

Today, Huber thinks that Bob was setting him up. "Bob was afraid to come right out and say 'I want Sandra dead,' " he says. "He wanted it to be *my* idea. I think he thought he was putting one over on me."

At first, Huber thought he was joking. Bob Black was a funny guy, and they shared a number of running jokes, most of them somewhat raunchy. When Huber got home that afternoon, he told his wife Janie, "You won't believe what that crazy Bob said to me today. He wants me to kill his wife. Can you believe that?"

Janie Huber didn't think it was funny. She already thought that Bob was a bad influence on Huber because of his womanizing. "I hope you realize how crazy this is," she said. "You should get away from him and never speak to him again."

"Yeah, you're right," Huber said grudgingly, but Janie knew he wasn't serious.

Huber's relationship with Bob had always been puzzling to Janie Huber. Bob was almost twice Huber's age, but he had taken him under his wing at H&S Electric. "It always bothered me because it seemed like Bob wanted David as a friend more than David wanted Bob," says Janie, who has since divorced Huber and remarried.

Huber admits that he looked up to Bob as a father figure, but not even Huber trusted Bob completely: he warned Janie, who was blond and pretty, to never be alone with him. "Bob never actually tried to come on to me," she says, "but he would always smile bigger and talk a little friendlier when David was in the other room."

The only thing that Bob and Huber really had in common was that they had both been in the Marines, but even that was peculiar. Huber had joined the Marine Corps in 1981; but with one year remaining on his enlistment, he started having payroll problems at Camp Lejeune (he didn't get a paycheck for several months) and went AWOL. He moved back to Bryan and went to work for his father at H&S Electric. The Marine Corps had never caught him.

"David acted like it was a big deal that he and Bob were marines," says Janie. "But it never seemed right to me because Bob had been an officer and David was AWOL. Whenever I complained about Bob, it was always, 'Well he's a marine, he understands me.' " (Bob was one of the few people in Bryan who knew that Huber was AWOL.)

In addition to their lunchtime meetings on campus, Bob would drop by Huber's apartment two or three afternoons a week, and they would buy a bottle of wine and sit out in the front yard, drinking and talking. It was two ex-marines—one an AWOL enlisted man and the other a flight officer who the Corps had let go—getting drunk on cheap wine and reminiscing about "the Band of Brothers."

One of their favorite topics was *Soldier of Fortune* magazine, which Bob subscribed to. He ridiculed most of the stories about mercs, except for those about Col. "Mad Mike" Hoare, the most famous merc of all (Hoare had led an army of Belgian Congo mercenaries against secessionist Katanga in the mid-1960s). "Bob talked about 'Mad Mike' like he was his old friend," says Huber, "but otherwise it was, 'Look at this asshole.' "

Bob was equally sarcastic about SOF's personal-services ads. "Who would go through a magazine to hire a hit man?" he asked Huber. "That's the way to really hang yourself."

•   •   •

In mid-October, when Bob Black called John Wayne Hearn the first time, he said that he was selling restaurant equipment but wasn't making much money and wanted to quit. He asked Hearn about going to work for World Security Group.

As he did with all vets who called, Hearn asked Bob if he had served in Vietnam. Bob said yes and told him what outfit he'd served in. Hearn said that he didn't have any work at the time but told Bob to send him his DD-214 form.

Bob called a few weeks later, asking again about work. Hearn told him the same thing: He didn't have anything for him. Still, Bob kept calling. Almost every time Hearn came home, there was another call from him. Hearn kept telling him, "No, I don't have anything," but Bob kept calling anyway—chatting him up, buddying up to him, acting like they were old friends. It was as if there was something else he wanted . . . something he wasn't saying.

•   •   •

A few days after their first conversation about killing Sandra, Bob stopped by the A&M campus to see David Huber again. This time, he had a new plan, which he didn't wait for Huber to suggest: He wanted to kill Ted Heatherington. "Bob started thinking that if Teresa's husband was killed maybe he could afford a divorce," Huber explains.

According to Huber, Bob already had the details worked out: He and Huber would drive to California over the Thanksgiving holidays, go late at night to the Greyhound bus station where Ted worked, hit him over the head with a baseball bat, rob the cash register (to make it look like a burglary), then dump him down an abandoned well outside of town and pour concrete over him.

At this point, Huber realized that Bob wasn't joking. It was the first time Bob had mentioned that Teresa was his cousin, and Huber tried to ease the tension with a joke. "What's this about marrying your cousin?" he teased. "You're gonna have babies born with three ears."

Bob laughed but kept talking about the plan. "Even when he was dead serious, he'd still laugh," Huber says.

To prove just how serious he was, Bob called Huber a few days later and told him, "If you want to see Teresa, go to the MSC mailroom and ask for a package for David Huber." When Huber went to the mailroom, there was a thick envelope waiting for him: inside were Bob's prized photos of Teresa and him in acrobatic sexual poses.

Huber was stunned. "I was expecting maybe some tittie shots, but these would have made Larry Flynt blush," he recalls. "Bob was showing off Teresa to me. . . . I remember thinking how weird it was. It was like he had seen too many movies."

As Thanksgiving drew closer, Bob kept talking about killing Ted Heatherington: going over the itinerary, drilling Huber like it was a military operation. He was so consumed with the idea that he even mentioned it to Huber's next-door neighbors—Randy and Gemma Sowders—when he ran into the young couple at a gas station. "I've either got to kill my girlfriend's husband or Sandra," he told them.

Gemma Sowders was a friend of Sandra's, had once worked for her at Happy Face, and had been to Bark-n-Holler many times to ride horses. But Bob's reputation protected him: Gemma

Sowders thought he was kidding. "He was not a serious person," she would say later.

•   •   •

Meanwhile, out in California, Teresa was as indecisive as ever. During the first two weeks of November she sent Bob a flurry of letters that were filled with sexual innuendos but then, on November 14, wrote: "Sadly, sadly I know it's true . . . we can't go on this way forever." She delivered the coup de grâce three days before Thanksgiving, when she wrote Bob that "the Lord is not giving me the power to split this family."

Bob's religious fervor had come back to haunt him: he had taken Teresa to church with him in Bryan and convinced her to start attending church when she got back home, but now she was using religion as a justification for staying with Ted.

She ended her letter with appreciations for Vannoy and Ivonne Black, for their "unconditional acceptance"; for Sandra ("She is a good woman!"); and finally, for Bob, whom she promised to love forever. It was over . . . sort of.

5

John Wayne Hearn's love affair with Debbie Banister burst wide open after their November 12 meeting in Cordele. Hearn called her the very next day, and from then on, they would talk on the phone two or three times a day (in the next week, they talked eleven times!). Hearn was out of town that week—driving to Memphis, Chicago, and Cincinnati—so sometimes he would call Debbie at work, and she would call him back on Sun Bank's WATS line. Other times, she called Message World, found out where to reach him, and called him at his motel.

All Hearn wanted to talk about was seeing her again, but Debbie suddenly raised the issue of the child-nabbing again. Cordele had been a social meeting, but it was time to get back to business. She mailed Hearn a photograph of Cecil Batie and the two boys, taken at the beach, so that Hearn would know what they looked like. But there was still the problem of money. In one of their phone calls, Debbie told him that $15,000 was still too much, and asked whether he would do it for less. Hearn didn't care about the money—he just wanted to see her. "Okay, Debbie, I'll do it for ten thousand," he said.

"Great," she said.

• • •

From the very beginning, Debbie had been keeping her family apprised of her negotiations with Hearn. After her first phone call with Hearn, she had gone to her parents' trailer for lunch. Marlene was there too, and, as usual, they all started complaining about

192

Cecil Batie. The custody battle was building to a head, as Judge Green had scheduled a hearing about permanent custody of Brad for January 8, 1985.

According to Marlene's recounting of this conversation, Debbie asked, "What it would mean to y'all to be rid of Cecil Batie?"

"I don't know; what are you talking about?" Frank Sims replied. "I'd like for him to be out of our lives."

"I can get Cecil killed for thirty-thousand dollars," Debbie said. "I met a nice man who's a professional mercenary. He works out of the country."

"Where'd you meet him?" Iris popped up.

"I'm not telling you any of the details," Debbie replied. "But I like him a lot, and he likes me, and I think I can get him to kill Cecil for a lot less than thirty thousand."

"How do you know he won't just take a potshot at Cecil when he's got the kids in the van?" Marlene asked. "I don't want that."

"No, it won't be done that way," Debbie assured her. "He's an expert in martial arts—he could kill Cecil with his bare hands, for that matter. He's a professional."

. . .

After Hearn agreed to do the *child-nabbing* for $10,000, Debbie went back to her parents' trailer to report the good news. Again, according to Marlene's version of events, Debbie announced: "The price for killing Cecil has gone down to ten thousand."

"Whatsa matter, Debbie, you lost your touch?" Iris teased her. "Why won't he do it for free, seeing how he does this kind of thing for a living?"

"No, I don't want him to do it for free," she said. "The price is ten thousand."

The next problem was where to get the money.

Debbie turned to Marlene. "Are you still the beneficiary of Cecil's life insurance policy?"

"I think so," Marlene replied.

"How much is it for?" Debbie asked.

"I'm not sure—it's either fifteen or thirty thousand dollars," Marlene replied.

"Find out," Debbie ordered her.

"Will he take some land instead?" Frank suggested (the Simses owned several lots in Alachua and Walton counties). "That way, if the insurance isn't in Marlene's name, he's still got the land."

"I don't know, I'll ask him," said Debbie.

Despite Iris's sarcastic remark, Debbie Banister hadn't lost her touch. Not at all. As far as John Wayne Hearn knew, he was still negotiating about a child-nabbing, not a murder. But Debbie had other plans.

• • •

Hearn was back home in Atlanta on November 19 and 20, and talked to Debbie seven times in those two days (including one call for fifty-eight minutes, and another for forty-six). Debbie asked if he'd take some land instead of money, but Hearn said, no, he wanted cash.

Debbie had to come up with a way to raise the money. "Listen, John," she said, "if somebody wanted to burn a house down so nobody could find out how they did it, do you know how to do it?"

"Sure," Hearn replied cockily. He was happy to show off his knowledge, and he suggested two different methods: loosen an indoor gas fitting and place a lit candle in a back bedroom or pour lacquer thinner over the floor and set a lit candle in the middle of it; when the candle burned down the lacquer thinner would ignite.

Debbie thanked him and said good-bye.

On November 21, the day before Thanksgiving, Iris and Marlene decided to drive to Santa Rosa Beach to pick up Iris's mother, Ivory Williams, and bring her back to Gainesville for the winter. Iris's father had died in August, and Mrs. Williams was having a difficult time adjusting. She had called Iris that morning and didn't sound very good on the phone. Iris and Frank decided that she could stay with them until spring.

Marlene called Debbie at Sun Bank. According to Marlene, they had the following conversation: "Me and Momma are gonna go get Grandma today and bring her back here," she said. "You want to go with us?"

Debbie said yes, then added: "Wouldn't it be a shame if Grandma's house burned down?"

"Yeah, it would," Marlene agreed.

It was the perfect solution. Mrs. Williams lived in an old wooden house that her husband had built twenty-five years before, and that was overinsured for $30,000. And the policyholder was not Mrs. Williams but *Iris Sims*. If the house burned down, Iris would collect a quick $30,000. And there would be no problem with the insurance company paying off: the policy was carried by Florida Farm Bureau and had been written by Frank Sims.

• • •

Two days before Thanksgiving, David Huber told Bob Black that he wasn't going with him to California to kill Teresa's husband. Bob got mad, called him chickenshit, and stomped off.

As Huber recalls: "Any other time he'd say, 'Let's go get a bottle of wine,' and after the wine was gone he'd say, 'Well, I gotta go home.' But this time it was 'You chickenshit!'—and he left, no good-bye or nothing."

Bob didn't stay mad long. He was back at Huber's house the following evening, and the plan had suddenly reverted to killing Sandra. Bob said that he still loved her too much to do it himself; so Huber would have to do the dirty work. And Bob insisted that Gary Wayne be with *him* when it happened. "He wanted to shield it from Gary Wayne, so he wouldn't think Bob had anything to do with it," says Huber. "I can't stress it enough, that was the one thing that was always present: 'Gary mustn't know.' "

From then on, every time Bob came to see Huber—which was every day or every other day—he talked about killing Sandra. *Every* time. It was just a normal part of the conversation, like talking about the weather. "He'd say 'How was your day; did you hear about what happened to so-and-so; Sandra needs to be killed and here's how,' " says Huber. "Then we'd drink some more wine, and he'd say 'Did you hear about what this guy did? Well, I gotta go.' It wasn't really a dominating part of the conversation, but it was there in every conversation."

Bob came up with all kinds of schemes to kill her, some more outlandish than others: in one, Huber was supposed to hide in the Blacks' house until Sandra came home, then put a choke hold on her until she passed out, drag her to the paint shed, where Bob would have left an open can of kerosene and a drop light with a broken bulb. Huber was supposed to hit the circuit breaker, which would supposedly short out the lightbulb and start a fire. While all of this was going on, Bob would be jumping on the trampoline with Gary Wayne!

There were others: Huber could steal a truck and run Sandra

off the road while she and Bob were out for a Sunday ride on their motorcycles; or hit her in the head with a baseball bat, drive her to a nearby bridge, where Bob would meet him on *her* Honda, and dump Sandra *and* the motorcycle off the bridge; or blow up her barn while she was inside feeding her horses.

When Huber went home and told Janie what Bob was suggesting, *she* blew up. "This is crazy!" she yelled. "You can't have a friend who says things like this." She gave Huber an ultimatum: "If you want to stay married to me, stay away from Bob and don't ever talk about it again."

Instead of breaking off the friendship, Huber just started seeing Bob on the sly. "I had no other friends in that town that I could trust," Huber says. "I wasn't about to lose a good friendship over that."

Bob tried to win over Janie by inviting the Hubers to dinner at Steep Hollow, but she was too uncomfortable to go. "I could not see myself sitting at the table with them, knowing he was talking about having Sandra killed," she explains. She even suggested that Huber go to the police, but he insisted that Bob was just blowing off steam.

The truth was, not only did Huber know that *Bob* was serious about killing Sandra, but so was *he.* Bob had promised him $5,000 cash, and Huber—with a baby on the way and no maternity health-insurance coverage—was desperate for money. "Bob was talking me into it, and he knew it," he says.

Besides the $5,000, Bob offered another inducement: He told Huber that there would be "a big red present" under his Christmas tree if he killed Sandra. Huber knew that the big red present could mean only one thing: Bob's red Harley-Davidson, which Huber had been coveting for months.

Bob had turned Huber on to Harleys: he had let him ride his, had taken him to the Harley shop in Lufkin to look at new bikes, and had offered to cosign a loan so that Huber could buy one. He had also introduced his young friend to the biker scene: he had taken him to the local biker bars and to Harley swap meets, where, as usual, Bob took along his camera to take tittie shots. "Some people collect stamps, Bob liked to collect pictures of girls' titties," says Huber.

Bob knew that Huber wanted a Harley more than anything in the world—and the offer had the desired effect: "Honestly, I could have used the motorcycle at the time," Huber now admits. "From the stuff I've seen in the Marine Corps—death, murder—it does nothing to me. I don't really agree with it, but it wouldn't bother me. I mean, you're trained to kill people in the service, so what's the difference? You can either get paid your fifty cents an hour in the service or get a motorcycle for the same thing."

Yeah, right.

One afternoon, Bob stopped by campus and Huber introduced him to one of his coworkers. After Bob left, the man said, "There's something weird about your friend,"

"Yeah," Huber agreed, "he wants to have his old lady killed."

"Are you serious?" the man exclaimed. "That's soap-opera stuff."

"Don't say anything about it," Huber said. "There's nothing to worry about. Bob's just a shell-shocked Vietnam vet living a fantasy life."

"You've got a shithead for a friend," the man said.

• • •

As the days went by, Bob kept stopping by campus to see Huber, and kept talking about killing Sandra. Several times, Huber told him that he was thinking too much about it; Bob agreed and dropped the subject for a few days. But soon the running jokes started up again, and Bob was back at it. He said that he had paid Huber's older brother Mark $500 to kill Sandra several years earlier and suggested that Huber could make good on his brother's debt. Huber told him he could forget that.

Bob kept coming up with more and more elaborate schemes for how to do the job. In one, Bob would call Sandra out to his motorcycle shed, where Huber would push the motorcycle on top of her, pin her underneath it, and start a fire. "I didn't agree with that one because the motorcycle that I'd be getting for doing it would be burned up," Huber says frankly.

Bob's most brutal scheme was for Huber to ransack the house to make it look like a burglary, then shoot Sandra with one of Bob's pistols. According to Huber, Bob also told him, "If you want to rape her, go ahead," but cautioned him to wear surgical gloves so he wouldn't leave fingerprints and to "wipe everything up," so the police couldn't determine his blood type from his semen.

"I told him I wasn't into that," Huber says.

• • •

Out at Steep Hollow, things were so "fine and dandy" that Sandra and Gary Wayne couldn't quite believe it. Bob was like a new person: considerate, loving, even-tempered. "He was the perfect person," says Gary Wayne. "He didn't get upset with things as easily as he used to. Seemed like he was trying to straighten out his life."

After all that had happened in the past, Sandra was skeptical at first, but Bob gradually won her over with a series of romantic gestures. First, he bought her a new van. Sandra and Marjorie were sitting at Happy Face one afternoon when Bob drove up in a brand new 1985 Chevrolet custom van. "Sandra and I both like to went through the floor," Marjorie recalls.

Bob took them outside and gave them the grand tour. The van was loaded with floor-to-ceiling carpeting, captain's chairs, a bar, an AM-FM cassette player, even a television set. Bob was out of work again, but he had a financing plan all figured out: Sandra could *lease* the van from Tom Light Chevrolet for $275 a month— for Happy Face Nursery. That way, she could claim it as a business expense. They came back inside, Sandra signed the papers, and the van was hers.

Next, Bob started on the bathrooms at Bark-n-Holler: remodeling them, regrouting the tile, installing new trim. He was a perfectionist, and wasn't satisfied until everything was exactly right. Then he moved on to his next project: a new barn for her horses. He bought lumber and siding and roofing shingles, and started building a beautiful new barn. He just couldn't seem to do enough for Sandra.

• • •

Debbie, Marlene, and Iris left for Santa Rosa Beach around 6:00 P.M. on Wednesday, November 21, 1984. It was a five-hour drive to Walton County, in the Florida panhandle. Debbie drove her Oldsmobile, and Marlene rode with Iris in the Simses' 1984 Toyota pickup.

Marlene has given the following description of what transpired on their trip: When they reached Perry, eighty-five miles from Gainesville, Marlene got into Debbie's car so that they could finalize their plans about burning Grandma's house. Debbie

shared John Wayne Hearn's suggestion about loosening a gas fitting, but Marlene was afraid of gas; so they settled on Hearn's
second proposal: lacquer thinner.

• • •

When they reached Freeport, Marlene got back in the truck and
told Iris what they were planning to do. How did Iris Sims react to
this shocking news that her daughters were going to burn down
her mother's house, which her father had built twenty-five years
before? According to Marlene, Iris said: "Be careful," and offered
to give them a key to the house. (Iris and Debbie have never
admitted any involvement in, and have never been charged with,
burning the house.)

They arrived in Santa Rosa Beach late Wednesday night and
went to bed. According to Marlene, the next morning, she and
Debbie drove to a K mart in nearby Fort Walton Beach, bought one
gallon each of lacquer thinner and varnish remover, and stored
them in Iris' truck. Then they packed up Grandma's clothes, her
favorite photographs, and her cat, and left for Gainesville about
2:00 P.M. They debated stopping at Iris's brother's house so that
Grandma could enjoy Thanksgiving dinner, but they were in a
hurry—so they drove on home to Gainesville.

When they got back to the Sims trailer about 8:00 P.M., they
unloaded Grandma's belongings and packed her off to bed. Then,
according to Marlene, Iris told Frank what the girls were planning
to do, and he obligingly gave Marlene a flashlight and some extra
cash, and told her to be careful to not get a speeding ticket anywhere near Walton County, which could place them in the area that
night. (Frank has never admitted any involvement in the arson, and
has never been charged with it.)

Debbie and Marlene left in the Simses' pickup about 8:45 P.M.
to drive back to Santa Rosa Beach. They stopped once to buy a
package of hot dogs for their grandmother's dog, in case he started
barking, and arrived in Santa Rosa Beach about 1:30 A.M.

Mack Bayou Road is on a narrow peninsula that borders
Choctawhatchee Bay. It's a low, swampy area with scrub pines and
palmettos—a perfect breeding ground for rattlesnakes, mosquitos,
and sand gnats. A maze of narrow dirt roads winds through the
woods, with ramshackle trailers and old houses stacked along a
beautiful bay.

According to Marlene, she and Debbie backed the truck in on a side road—ready for a quick getaway—and hiked through the woods to Grandma's house, carrying their gallon cans of lacquer thinner and varnish remover. They fed the package of hot dogs to the dog, then went through the house in opposite directions, pouring solvent all over the floor. They backtracked over each other's paths to mix the two solutions, and poured an extra amount around the gas heater, to make sure it would explode.

Then they crept back outside, locked the door, and sneaked around to the bathroom window. Marlene cut a hole in the screen with her pocketknife, and they started pushing lit matches through the hole. But the solvent wouldn't catch. By then, the dog had started barking, and Marlene got scared and panicked. She gave Debbie her cigarette lighter and ran back to the truck.

As usual, it was up to Debbie. According to Marlene, Debbie lit a paper towel, stuffed it through the window, and the solvent exploded. Debbie ran back through the woods, Marlene picked her up on the side of the road, and they took off.

Two neighbors were awakened by the blaze. They ran outside, saw the house engulfed in flames, and thinking that Mrs. Williams was asleep inside, ran next door to awaken Iris's brother, Norman Williams. He assured them that his mother wasn't inside, and called the volunteer fire department.

Marlene and Debbie sped down U.S. 98, heading toward the Choctawhatchee Bay bridge, eight miles away. They pulled off onto a dirt road long enough for Marlene to jump out and toss the empty solvent cans into the woods. Before they reached the bridge, they heard sirens and saw fire trucks racing to the scene. As they drove over the bridge, they looked back across the bay and saw flames lighting up the night sky; then they drove the back roads home to Gainesville.

•   •   •

At 4:30 A.M., J.R. McCardle, an investigator for the state fire marshal, arrived at Mack Bayou Road. Ivory Williams' house had been totally destroyed. McCardle interviewed Norman Williams and the neighbors, took photographs of the still-smoldering house, and noted in his report: "Further investigation is necessary. Case remains open."

•   •   •

Mrs. Williams was already awake when Debbie and Marlene arrived back at the Simses' trailer around eight o'clock Friday morning. She assumed that her granddaughters had come to visit her,
and didn't suspect that they had been gone all night. According to
Marlene, she returned the key to Iris, told her and Frank that the
house was burned, and she and Debbie went home to sleep.

•   •   •

At 9:30 A.M., Norman Williams called to report the tragic news. He
had waited that long so as not to upset Mrs. Williams first thing in
the morning, but there was no way to *avoid* upsetting her: there was
nothing left of her house but the concrete block foundation, and
nothing left of her mementoes of a lifetime but the charred remains of her dinette chairs and table, a living room sofa, and her
old pedal-style Singer sewing machine.

•   •   •

John Wayne Hearn had Debbie Banister on the brain. During a ten-
day period, from November 26 to December 5, he and Debbie
called each other *twenty-one* times. He had become so bold that he
had even started calling her at home in Starke—in the morning,
after Joe Banister had left for work. Debbie had become such an
obsession that he was neglecting World Security Group: during the
same period, he made only four calls regarding his SOF ad.

On Wednesday, December 5, Hearn made his long-awaited
visit to Gainesville. He had been "making turns" in Florida all
week, and after completing a run from Tampa to Jacksonville, he
rented a car and drove the seventy miles to Gainesville.

Debbie had given him directions to Sun Bank; he went
straight there, and she introduced him to the women she worked
with. When she got off work that afternoon, they went to eat at
Skeeter's—"the Home of the Big Bisquit and Friendly People."
Debbie asked him where he was staying, and suggested the Hilltop
Motel, just down the street from the restaurant. Hearn followed
her there. He told the desk clerk that he needed a room for two and
checked into room 107, which cost twenty-five dollars for the
night.

Hearn's heart was pounding with anticipation as Debbie followed him into the room. After a month of building sexual tension, this new romance was finally going to be consummated. A married woman doesn't go to a cheap motel with a man if she doesn't intend to go all the way. He knew he was home free.

They sat down on the bed and talked for a few minutes, then Debbie asked, "Do you mind if I get comfortable?" It was a line right out of the movies. The oldest cliché in the world. It was perfect.

"No, I don't mind," Hearn replied.

Debbie got up and walked into the bathroom, and came out five minutes later carrying her dress. *Whoa!* Hearn thought. Every time he thought that he had this woman figured out, she completely blew his mind. She had joked about his erection in the car, kissed him on the end of the nose in Shoney's—and now this.

And it was just the beginning. Debbie Banister took him to bed and fucked his brains out. She made love to him like no woman had ever done before—not his four wives, not his many girlfriends, not even the whores in Vietnam. Debbie did everything herself. She wouldn't *let* him do anything, except lie back and enjoy it. She worked her way down his body with her tongue and her lips and her breasts, never using her hands. She took him to the edge of ecstasy—and beyond. In a twenty-five-dollar room in the Hilltop Motel, John Wayne Hearn made it over the top. He was over the hill, and gone.

•   •   •

On December 6, 1984, Ray Jenkins, a claims adjustor for the Florida Farm Bureau, went to the Simses' trailer to question Ivory Williams about the fire. Jenkins had already received a written report from the Farm Bureau's adjustor in Walton County, David Butler, who had reported that there had been some recent disagreements between Mrs. Williams and youngsters in the neighborhood. (According to Norman Williams, she had complained to the Walton County Sheriff's Department the day before the fire.) Butler was suspicious that the fire might have been set by the children in retaliation, and he was also concerned that "certain members of the Williams family have been involved in crime and drugs." He urged Jenkins to "carefully question" Mrs. Williams.

However, when Jenkins arrived at the Simses' trailer, Iris was very insistent that he *not* talk to Mrs. Williams. She told him not to even mention the fire to Mrs. Williams, since that might upset her. Jenkins was in a bind: On one hand, he had a suspicious fire to investigate; on the other hand, Frank Sims was fairly high up in the Farm Bureau hierarchy—certainly higher than *he* was. Faced with those limitations, Jenkins chose to question Iris instead. He tape recorded the interview, which is excerpted below:

• • •

Jenkins: "Ah, what was the date and time of this fire? Do you know?"

Iris: "We left there, I guess about noon Thanksgiving Day, and we arrived down here about eight o'clock that night. And I didn't know anything about it until I was called the next day."

Jenkins: "Okay. Did you, or did you help close up, or did you close up her house? Who, you know, as you left, ah . . .

Iris: "Ah, yes. We—we all did. We, you know, picked up a few things, ah, in order to set her up down here partially, you know, just mainly her, you know, pictures and stuff that she always . . . she always carries those, no matter where she goes."

Jenkins: "Okay. Do you know who first discovered the fire?"

Iris: "I think it was the neighbor across the—right down below Mama."

Jenkins: "And who notified you?"

Iris: "My brother."

Jenkins: "Ah, what did he say, what did he describe and so on?"

Iris: "I don't know if he talked to me first, or if he talked to Frank. Ah, but I think his, just, you know, in general, Mama's house burnt down last night. He was pretty well real upset."

The interview only lasted nine minutes. Jenkins never asked any questions about problems with the neighborhood children.

• • •

Mary Watson had seen many women come and go in John Wayne Hearn's life. She tried to keep an open mind whenever he met a new one—that is, until the woman did him wrong, which, in Mary's mind, they always did.

This time, Hearn swore it would be different. "Mom, I have met the most *different* woman," he told her in early December. He said that his new love, Debbie, was good-looking, had a great job in the loan department of a bank, and had two lovely children. When Mary asked how he had met her, Hearn lied and said that she had contacted him about doing a photography portfolio on her daughter Amanda. He just couldn't stop raving about her. "She's the sweetest lady, Mom," he said. "You'll love her to death."

•   •   •

On December 7, 1984—Pearl Harbor Day, fittingly enough—Mary Watson got a chance to find out for herself, when Debbie Banister called her at home on Sun Bank's WATS line. It is doubtful that Debbie had any idea of how dominant Mary Watson was in Hearn's life, but nonetheless she wanted to make a good impression. She showed the proper blend of politeness and deference toward the older woman, and handled Mary's gentle probes with subtlety and grace: she told her that she and her two children lived alone in a nice house in Starke, that her take-home pay from Sun Bank was about $340 every two weeks, and that she paid seventy dollars a week for day-care. When Mary asked about her husband, Debbie said that he was "deceased," then tactfully changed the subject.

The phone call lasted seven minutes. Hearn called Mary an hour later, and asked her what she thought of Debbie.

"She seems nice," Mary said.

Debbie had won the first skirmish between the two women. But Mary Watson, like the U.S. after Pearl Harbor, had not yet begun to mobilize her forces, and soon they would be at war.

•   •   •

On December 13, 1984, Ray Jenkins recommended that Florida Farm Bureau pay the $30,000 claim on Ivory Williams' house.

David Butler, the Walton County adjustor, was still not convinced that the fire was an accident. He had requested a state fire marshal's report, but he knew that could take months to complete. Butler was young and fairly new with the company, however, and he didn't want to ruffle any feathers with the higher-ups, all of whom knew Frank Sims.

In a memo to his boss, he concluded: "I do not believe Frank Sims, his wife, or his mother-in-law had anything to do with the fire! I do, however, feel there are some bad apples in Frank's wife's

family in this area!'' With that, he closed out his investigation of
the case.

• • •

When it came to romance, John Wayne Hearn had always been a
fast mover, but he had met his match in Debbie Banister. In the
past, *he* had always been the initiator, the one rushing to get involved, but Debbie seemed as hot for him as he was for her. In the
two days after he left Gainesville, she called him *nine* times!

Hearn was ready to push it to the limit. On Sunday, December
9, he went to the Eastern Airlines counter at the Atlanta airport
and bought a $168 round-trip ticket from Gainesville to Atlanta,
made out to Debbie Banister. The reservation called for Debbie to
fly up on Friday morning and return home on Sunday afternoon.

Debbie told Joe Banister that she was going to Disney World
with Marlene and her kids for the weekend. She told the same story
to her boss, Wayne Kelly, in order to get Friday off. Kelly's wife
asked her to buy a monkey puppet for her while she was at Disney
World, and Debbie promised that she would. Friday morning, Marlene dropped her off at the Gainesville airport, then hid Debbie's
car at her trailer so Joe wouldn't see it.

Hearn picked her up at the Atlanta airport about 11:30 A.M.
He was so eager to impress her that he had bought himself a new
bed; but his apartment was still almost barren—there was just a
small table, two old dinette chairs, a television set, and his floodlights and studio backdrops. The new bed was all he really needed,
however.

It was a big weekend in Atlanta: MARTA (the Metro Area
Rapid Transit Authority), the city's high-speed rail system, had just
opened five new stations, and the public was invited to ride free all
weekend. Hearn and Debbie spent the day riding MARTA from
one end of Atlanta to the other. It was as if the city was there just
for them—two young lovers in love. That night, they ate at a nice
restaurant in a shopping mall, where Debbie also found a monkey
puppet like the ones sold at Disney World and bought it for her
boss' wife.

Hearn, the incurable romantic, topped off the evening with a
surprise: a $400 necklace that he had bought for Debbie at Zales
Jewelers, where he had an account.

On Saturday, Hearn introduced Debbie to the manager of his

apartment complex, Eunice Weeks, a young woman with whom he had become friendly in the ten months he had lived in Riverdale. Weeks was engaged to be married in April, 1985, and Hearn had agreed to take the wedding photos. He had already told Weeks that he and Debbie were going to get married themselves, and so on Saturday he took Debbie to the office to show her off.

Later that day, Weeks and her fiancé came up to Hearn's apartment so that he could take a photo of them for their Christmas cards. While Hearn was setting up his camera equipment, Weeks and Debbie had had a chance to talk woman-to-woman. Debbie showed her the necklace that Hearn had given her and told her all about their trip to Plains, Georgia, to see Jimmy Carter's house. She also talked about her two children and said that they lived in a big house that her "deceased husband" had left her. "But I'm going to sell it," she told Weeks, "so John and I can build a home in South Carolina."

To Weeks, Debbie and Hearn seemed very much in love.

After Hearn finished taking photographs of Weeks and her fiancé, Weeks suggested, "Why don't you let me take a picture of you and Debbie?"

So Hearn and Debbie posed for the camera: they were holding hands, with his left arm encircling Debbie's thick waist. She was wearing a blue dress with white polka dots, and Hearn was in jeans and an olive-drab Marine Corps T-shirt. Eunice Weeks took several shots. In one, Debbie looks somewhat impatient, with a tight-lipped smile, but Hearn is grinning like the carefree warrior he had once been. He looks like his old self again, happier than he had ever been.

•   •   •

Saturday night, Hearn made a few phone calls about his SOF ad. He was probably showing off for Debbie, who, according to Hearn, was fascinated and titillated by his clandestine World Security job offers.

One of the return calls he made was to Bob Black, who was still bugging him about work. Hearn told him the same thing that he'd told him before: "I don't have anything for you."

•   •   •

Before Debbie left to go home, Hearn asked her to marry him. She was complaining about Joe Banister, and told Hearn that she was going to divorce him.

"Well, when you get divorced, let's get married," Hearn said. He told her that he was going to move to Gainesville in January to be near her, asked her to find him an apartment, and gave her a hundred-dollar check for the deposit. Debbie said that she would start looking for a place.

•   •   •

When Marlene picked her up at the Gainesville airport on Sunday afternoon, Debbie showed off the necklace that Hearn had given her and told her that they were in love.

Events would begin moving very rapidly.

•   •   •

It only took Debbie one day to find an apartment. On Monday, December 17, she put down a hundred-dollar deposit for Hearn at the Prairie View Apartments, located south of Gainesville, overlooking the Payne's Prairie Wildlife Preserve. Payne's Prairie is a huge swamp that was once a lake, and the Prairie View Apartments appear to have undergone a similar transformation: it looks like it was once a cheap motel, now rented out as apartments.

Debbie told the manager, Tom Hurd, that Hearn would be moving to Gainesville on January 1, 1985, and Hurd assigned him apartment 30, a one-bedroom efficiency that rented for $230 per month.

•   •   •

Hearn was on the road for Transus the entire next week—in Memphis, Tupelo, Pensacola, and Birmingham. He talked to Debbie four times while he was gone, and when he got home on Saturday, there was a letter waiting for him. It was written on flowery stationery, in the halting grammar of a high-school dropout:

December 19, 1984

Dear John,

   Just a few short lines to say hello and I have read your recent letter over & over again, it sounds so good.

I would much rather be with you right now instead of sitting here trying to do some work! If I were with you, I am sure we could find a lot of things to be doing—if you know what I mean. It all begins with a kiss, then a big hug, then. . . .

I am looking forward to seeing you as soon as can [sic] and being with you—not to leave again.

I know we both have things we must take care of first, so I'll be patient—however I am counting the days and the minutes—

Well, I'll close for now—Be sweet as you are & don't forget the X-mas cards for your family & give Wayne a hug for me—

Love
Deb

•   •   •

David Huber turned chickenshit again, two weeks before Christmas, and told Bob Black that he wasn't going to kill Sandra for him. Huber said that he didn't need the law after him, with him being AWOL and Janie seven months pregnant. "I'm finally starting to get my shit together," he explained.

"You're a chickenshit," Bob said angrily, and stomped off.

Once again, though, Bob didn't stay mad for long. The big red present got dropped, but the next time he saw Huber they came up with a new plan together, to kill Sandra. "I don't know if this would be incriminating or not," Huber says anxiously, "but one of our plans was that he would get a life insurance policy and we'd wait at least a year."

With Janie almost due, Huber had less time for Bob and only saw him once a week or less. However, Bob always reminded him that the new plan was still in effect. "Only fifty-two more weeks," he would say cheerfully. "Only fifty-one more weeks. Only fifty more weeks . . ."

•   •   •

It was a wonderful Christmas at Steep Hollow.

Bob surprised Sandra by giving her a beautiful diamond for her wedding ring. When they got married in 1967, he had only been able to afford a small diamond, but this was a huge stone—

almost one carat. On Christmas Eve, Bob included Gary Wayne in the surprise by having him sneak out to the El Camino and bring the present inside.

On Christmas morning, Sandra was speechless when she opened it. The diamond was so gorgeous—and such a symbol of Bob's new commitment. How he intended to pay for it was a bit puzzling, since he still didn't have a job. When Sandra rode out to Action Dogs that week with Martha Lee, she showed her the ring, and remarked, "I just don't know where Bob got the money."

● ● ●

Bob didn't seem to be worried about money. He also bought a special Christmas present for Teresa: a Bible. Teresa wrote and told him that nothing else "would have touched me so deeply." Even though their love affair was supposedly over, they were still calling and writing on the sly. Teresa even maintained the subterfuge on Christmas: she sent *two* Christmas cards—an official one to Steep Hollow, which she signed for her whole family, and a second one to Bob's post-office box, addressed to "My Dearest Darling Bob," which described "sneaking kisses" and whispering "I love you's" in his ear.

In fact, their relationship still wasn't settled. A week before Christmas, Bob had quizzed her about their future together. And Teresa sent a Christmas letter to Vannoy and Ivonne Black, thanking Vannoy for his support—"You would have made me a terrific daddy!" she wrote—and explaining that even though she was back with Ted, their divorce was still pending. Nothing would be final, she wrote, until February 23, 1985.

● ● ●

Don't get Marlene Sims mad at you. That's the lesson Larry Watson should have learned on December 21, 1984, when she ran over him with a van. Watson ended up in an intensive care unit with permanent damage to his optic nerve, which left him, as the old joke goes, "blind in one eye and can't see out of the other."

Unfortunately, it was no joke.

The day of the accident, Watson had stopped at a bar after work and apparently had a few too many drinks. He called Marlene, who was at the Simses' trailer (she had spent the day Christmas shopping), and asked her to stop on her way home and pick him up—which she did.

Here the story gets murky. Watson has steadfastly refused to tell his side of the story (even to his family), and says that he only remembers what Marlene told him. According to her version, she took him home and put him to bed, then got back in her van, intending to go to an auction with her parents. As she circled in front of the house, Larry ran out in front of her and she accidentally hit him. She claims that his head smashed into the windshield, then he bounced off, hit the side-mounted mirror, and fell to the ground, where she ran over him.

The honeymoon was over for Larry Watson.

Some of his relatives hadn't even met his new bride until they arrived at the ICU waiting room. Marlene was there, along with her sister, Debbie Banister, who put Larry's family on notice right away. "If you people have come down here to cause any trouble for Marlene, I want you to know I have an excellent attorney," she said.

It was a strange introduction. Until then, his relatives had no reason to be suspicious of Marlene, but they suddenly began to wonder: is there something she's trying to hide?

While Debbie was pushy and aggressive, Marlene seemed almost too friendly. She invited Larry's sister-in-law to go into the ICU to see Larry. It was a ghastly sight: His head was swollen to twice its normal size, and one eyeball was bulging out of its socket. Oddly, though, for a man who had just been run over by a van, he had no cuts on his face and no marks anywhere else on his body. It looked more like he had been beaten in the head.

The family's suspicions were heightened when they saw the van: the windshield on the driver's side was shattered way up at the top, as if a baseball had been thrown through it. Larry Watson is a very short man, and his family wondered how his head could have hit that high on the windshield. Had he *leaped* into the van?

But Larry wasn't talking. And today, for whatever reasons, he still isn't. "I ended up blind, and I feel lucky at that," is all he will say.

• • •

On December 22, John Wayne Hearn took a thirty-day leave of absence from Transus. He lied to his supervisor and told him that he had some "family problems" he needed to take care of regarding custody of his son. He told Eunice Weeks part of the truth—that he was moving to Gainesville to be with Debbie Banister—but lied and said that he was going to be doing all of the photography work for Sun Bank's national advertising campaigns.

He couldn't lie as easily to himself. He had only $304 in his checking account and $90.24 in savings, plus his last paycheck from Transus, $411.89. It was barely enough to last him a month. Which is why he was hedging his bets: he didn't give up his Riverdale apartment and took only a leave of absence from Transus. He had thirty days to find out if he could make a living in Gainesville as a photographer (he actually had no leads for work) and, more importantly, to see if things were going to work out with Debbie.

That night, he called his mother to tell her about the move. "It's just for a month or so," he said, "until Debbie sells her house, and then we'll be getting married and moving to Columbia."

He also told her that he wouldn't be home on Christmas morning, because Debbie wanted him to stay in Gainesville, but he would drive to Columbia that night. "Mom, it won't hurt your feelings, will it?" he asked plaintively.

"Honey, we understand," Mary Watson replied, even though she really didn't.

Hearn spent Christmas Day in Gainesville. When he got home to Columbia that night, he was raving about Debbie Banister. "This woman really cares about me, Mom," he said. Debbie was perfect in every way: she was financially responsible, a model mother, a consummate housekeeper. "Mom, she even gets down on her hands and knees to scrub the floor, like you do," he said.

Mary Watson wanted to believe that Debbie was as good as she seemed. "I prayed," she says. "Oh, Lord, how I prayed, that he had finally found someone."

6

On December 27, Frank Sims suffered a serious heart attack and was admitted to North Florida Regional Hospital. He had been in poor health for years: He had been hospitalized in 1980 for rheumatoid arthritis (which eventually forced him to retire from the Farm Bureau) and again, in May, 1984, because of the side effects from his arthritis medication. The doctors at North Florida Regional determined that he had a blockage of his right dominant coronary artery, and recommended a cardiac catheterization.

• • •

With Frank in the hospital, the Sims women got down to business. Brad's custody hearing was less than two weeks away, and it was time to do something about Cecil Batie before it was too late.

The closer it got to the hearing, the more the situation had deteriorated. In early December, Cecil had invited Marlene to go to family counseling with him and the boys. Dr. Andres Nazario had suggested it, hoping to work with Cecil and Marlene on coparenting Adam and Brad.

Marlene did go to several sessions, but they were disastrous. She expressed such anger and hostility toward Cecil that Nazario had to ask Adam and Brad to leave the room. "The thing that stands out was her hostility toward Cecil," Nazario said later. "This was *serious* anger." According to Nazario, Marlene didn't directly threaten to kill Cecil, but she did say something like "I wish you were dead."

Christmas, as everyone knows, is a time when wishes come true.

Debbie Banister called John Wayne Hearn to tell him about her father's heart attack, and on December 29, Hearn drove down to Gainesville. He went first to the Simses' trailer. Debbie, Marlene, and Iris were all there, and the conversation quickly turned to Cecil Batie. The women started telling him about what a bastard Cecil was, about all of the terrible things he had done to them over the years, about how he got drunk and beat the boys with a two-by-four. Ever since the meeting in Cordele, Hearn had been hearing about what a rotten son of a bitch Cecil was—as a justification for the proposed child-snatching—but on this day, the venom reached a new level.

They kept complaining until, finally, Hearn had to say something. He couldn't just sit there like a helpless wimp. After all, he was *Colonel* John Hearn, the leader of World Security Group, a fearless mercenary, a professional gun-for-hire. That's who he had told Debbie he was. And that's who he had told himself he was, in recent months.

"Look," *Colonel* Hearn said confidently, "if y'all are having a problem with Cecil, why don't I just beat the hell out of him? Break an arm or leg or something, and he ain't gonna bother you no more."

"It won't do any good," Marlene replied. "He's too damn mean."

"That's right," Debbie agreed. "The only way he's ever gonna stop bothering us is if he's dead."

There, she had finally said it.

Hearn suddenly realized what kind of deep hole he was in. This was no amateurish child-nabbing operation with a piece of ass thrown in on the side. This was serious shit.

From that point on, everything changed. According to Hearn, Debbie no longer talked about "getting the kids back." No, from then on it was "get Cecil out of the way," or "get him out of our hair for good," or "we'll be glad when he's gone." She didn't say "kill him," but the implication was clear.

And she never asked Hearn to do it. Not directly. She never said "If you don't do this, I won't love you anymore." But Hearn could tell that she wanted *somebody* to do it. And since he was the man in her life, it was obvious that he was the one.

Most of the talking they did about Cecil Batie took place in bed. That's where they did *all* of their serious talking. Every day on her lunch hour, Debbie would leave Sun Bank and go straight to Hearn's motel room. They only had an hour, so they had the drill down pat: as soon as she walked in the door, off went their clothes, and they went straight to bed. They would make love, then lie in each other's arms and talk about their future—about getting married and moving to South Carolina and building their dream house—until it was time for Debbie to jump up, take a quick shower, and hurry back to work. There wasn't time to eat, but who cared?

But now, according to Hearn, instead of talking about their future, Debbie wanted to talk about Cecil. It was always the same refrain: "Cecil will never leave us alone until he's gone for good, somebody has to get him out of our hair, somebody has to do it." And although she never told Hearn that she expected him to be the one, he could sense her pulling back—sexually and emotionally—when he didn't respond. She would create a distance between them, a gap of unspoken expectations, of stillborn dreams.

Finally, one day, Hearn said it. They were in bed, as usual, after making love. After the best sex that Hearn had ever had in his life. The kind of sex he had dreamed about, with a woman who swore that she loved him and would be with him forever. The way Debbie was talking about Cecil, Hearn was afraid she might try it herself, or find someone who would bungle the job. He wanted to keep her out of trouble, to keep her for himself.

"Okay, I'll do it," he said at last.

•   •   •

Debbie had already sent Hearn the photo of Cecil at the beach with his kids, but sometimes photos don't do justice. So one afternoon, as they were driving to the Sims' trailer, she pointed out Cecil in his front yard, working on a car. "That's Cecil under the hood," she said. Hearn nodded. Now he knew his man.

Then Debbie started pushing him. She started talking about it every time they were together—in bed, out of bed, wherever: "How are you going to do it? When are you going to do it?" And according to Hearn, Iris started pushing him too. "Momma wants to know when you're gonna do it," Debbie asked. "Momma is getting nervous about the hearing; she wants to know when you're gonna do it."

"You go back and tell your momma it's none of her damn business," he replied angrily. "I'll do it when I get goddamn good and ready."

Hearn didn't like Iris Sims—or Marlene. He didn't like Iris's prescription drug use or Marlene's druggie friends. He didn't want either one to know anything about his plans, so they wouldn't do something stupid and give him away.

•   •   •

Hearn stayed in Gainesville for New Year's Eve, then drove back to Atlanta on January 1. It was a relief to get away—to escape from the relentless pressure to kill Cecil Batie. Hearn was wrestling with himself over whether he could actually do it. He had never killed anyone except in Vietnam, and then only at long range. Perhaps he could still get out of it, he thought. The Simses hadn't paid him any money yet, and maybe they would change their minds. And if they did, he could still take the money and run, the way he had originally planned.

He tried not to think about Cecil. Instead, he started making some return phone calls for his ad, which he had been neglecting terribly. One call was to Bob Black, who had left yet another message on his answering machine. Hearn had already decided not to hire Bob, even if he had any work, because of the way he had been pestering him.

Trying to get off the hook, Hearn said, "Look, Bob, let me ask you a question. I'm getting up another shipment of arms going to Nicaragua. If you know anybody that has any weapons for sale, and if I can work out a deal with them, I'll pay you a commission."

Bob said, "I've got a gun collection that I'd be willing to sell." He named what he had: a Ruger Mini-14, a Winchester 30/30 carbine, a Springfield M1A1 7.62mm rifle, a Weatherby .25-06 caliber rifle with a high-powered scope, a Charles Daly 12-gauge over/under shotgun, a Savage 20-gauge over/under shotgun, a Smith & Wesson .357 magnum pistol, and various others.

"How much would you give me for them?" Bob asked.

"I need to check around and find out what they're worth," Hearn said. "I'll get back to you."

• • •

On January 2, 1985, the Florida Farm Bureau issued a check for $29,900.00 (it was a $30,000 policy, less a $100 deductible), to Iris Sims. At 6:35 P.M., Debbie Banister called Hearn at his Riverdale apartment and told him that Iris had the check in her hands and that she would cash it the next day.

Hearn called the Tabor Motel in Gainesville to reserve a room, then packed his bags. Before he left, he called Bob Black again (at 7:09 P.M.) and offered him $5,000 for his gun collection. "That's all they're worth to me, Bob," he said.

"Okay, I'll take it," Bob said.

Hearn said that he would come to Bryan the following week to pick up the guns, then hung up. He left for Gainesville about 9:00 P.M. He was going back to kill Cecil Batie.

• • •

The next morning, Iris and Debbie went to Sun Bank to cash the insurance check. Because of the large amount, and the fact that Iris didn't have an account there, the bank wouldn't cash it without first having Iris's signature authenticated by a bank officer who knew her. Iris and Debbie drove to the Barnett Bank at Hawthorne Road and SE 27th Street—right around the corner from Batie Hill— where Iris and Frank banked. Cecil Batie banked there too, and he was popular with the tellers because he liked to cut the fool with them.

Iris endorsed the check in front of Gretta M. Smith, the branch manager, who signed below her name:

> The above signature of Iris Sims is a true and correct endorsement. She personally appeared before me well known to be the Same Iris Sims which placed her signature above.

Iris handed the check to Debbie.

"Great!" she said, according to Smith, and put it in her purse.

They drove back to Sun Bank and cashed the check: Iris bought an $8,136.41 cashier's check, which she used to pay off a loan on the Simses' 1984 Toyota pickup, then cashed the remainder—$21,700.00—in hundred-dollar bills. She gave $10,000 to Debbie in hundred-dollar bills, then, according to Marlene, carried the rest of the money home and stored it in her freezer. That same morning, Debbie obtained a safe deposit box at Sun Bank, in which she allegedly deposited the $10,000.

Ivory Williams, whose house had burned, got nothing.

• • •

At 11:00 A.M. on Thursday, January 3, Debbie went to Hearn's room at the Tabor Motel and handed him a sealed white envelope. He opened it and looked inside

"Are you going to count it?" Debbie asked.

"No," Hearn replied soberly. He already knew what was inside.

• • •

With Brad's custody hearing only four days away, Cecil needed to be killed that weekend. Marlene had already called him on Wednesday and asked if she could have Brad and Adam for the weekend. It was a strange request, since Marlene hadn't kept both boys at the same time for months. But Cecil had never denied her access to the boys, and he didn't this time either. Marlene said she'd pick them up at noon Friday.

Hearn was supposed to do it while the boys were out of the house.

On Friday, Marlene picked up the boys at noon, as scheduled. Cecil's sixty-five-year-old roommate, Carroll "Rusty" Gordon, was there when she arrived. Rusty was a twenty-year air force veteran who had a drinking problem. He had lived on and off with the Batie family for seventeen years and had moved in with Cecil before Christmas to look after the boys while Cecil was at work.

Friday morning, Cecil had asked Rusty to have some clean clothes ready for the boys when Marlene came, and he had two stacks folded neatly in the boys' bedroom. Rusty offered to get them for Marlene, but she insisted on doing it herself. She disappeared into the bedroom carrying two empty grocery bags. A few minutes later, Rusty was on his way to the bathroom and noticed that Marlene had gone into Cecil's bedroom. She came out a few minutes later with both sacks full of clothes—much more than she needed for one weekend, according to Rusty. (Marlene denies that she took more than a weekend's supply of clothes.)

"Rusty, what you need to do this weekend is go out and get a good drunk," Marlene said, according to Rusty.

"Naw, I've been too sick to get drunk," replied Rusty, who had been ill for several weeks. (He turned out to have throat cancer, which eventually killed him.)

Unbeknownst to Rusty, hidden at the bottom of one of the grocery sacks—and covered up with clothes—was a small metal file box that Cecil kept on his bedroom dresser, in which he stored his important papers. The week before, Debbie had asked Marlene to get it, on the assumption that Cecil's life insurance policy was inside.*

•   •   •

On Friday afternoon, Eleanor Tarounga, the HRS caseworker now handling the Batie case, made a final recommendation to Judge Green about custody of Brad. Normally, HRS was reluctant to split up siblings, but in this case Tarounga had decided to recommend "split custody": Cecil would get Adam, and Marlene would get Brad.

She called both Cecil and Marlene that afternoon, and told them her decision. Cecil took it well; he knew that Brad wasn't happy living with him. The week before, Cecil had told Rusty Gordon that he was going to give Brad back to Marlene, no matter what happened at the upcoming hearing.

For all intents and purposes, the custody battle was over. Marlene was going to get Brad, which is what she had wanted in the first place. So the motive for killing Cecil should have been gone. By then, however, a stronger motivation had entered the picture: money.

Marlene assumed that she was the beneficiary of Cecil's $30,000 life insurance policy. With double-indemnity, Marlene was expecting to receive $60,000 when Cecil was killed. The murder was still on.

---

* According to Hearn, Marlene was supposed to pay back the $10,000 to her parents when Cecil's life insurance came through.

• • •

John Wayne Hearn waited as long as he could before buying a gun —still hoping that Debbie and the Simses might change their minds. But the weekend was upon him, and he needed a murder weapon.

Friday night, he looked in the Gainesville *Sun* classified ads, under Sporting Goods. There, scattered among ads for used scuba gear, ten-speed bikes, a bumper pool table, and a Sears weight bench, were five ads for guns. Hearn skimmed over the first four— a Colt .45 pistol, a Beretta .22 automatic, a 12-gauge shotgun for $50, a Thompson Contender .44 magnum—and settled on the final ad:

> 12-GAUGE SHOTGUN. Winchester 1200, stainless 18-inch barrel, pistol grip. Excellent defensive weapon. $300.

The Winchester 1200 is a lightweight, pump-action, police-model shotgun with a pistol grip (it has no stock). It is designed for close range killing.

Hearn dialed the seller's phone number, and asked him about the gun. The man, a Gainesville librarian, had bought it to carry on his sailboat, and had never even fired it. Hearn got directions to his house, and drove over. He paid the man $300 in crisp one-hundred dollar bills, and left with the shotgun.

He had the $10,000, he had the gun, and he had an appointment for murder.

7

SATURDAY DAWNED CLEAR and
cold in Gainesville, with temperatures in the low 30's, and even
colder weather on the way. An Arctic front had roared into the
South the night before, dumping a foot of snow in parts of Arkansas, Tennessee, and Kentucky.

It was a nice morning to stay in bed and sleep late, but Cecil
Batie had to work. His Asplundh tree crew had been working
"four-tens" (four ten-hour days per week), but rain earlier in the
week had cost them a day, so they needed to work Saturday to get
in their forty hours.

While he was at work, things were hopping across the street at
the Simses' trailer. Frank Sims had come home from the hospital
that morning, after a successful cardiac catheterization two days
before. He was still weak, and heavily medicated, but was strong
enough to walk and talk.

In anticipation of Frank's return, Iris had reportedly sent her
mother, Ivory Williams, back home to Santa Rosa Beach—with no
house to live in. Mrs. Williams had been staying in Marlene's old
trailer, behind the Simses, but Iris phoned her brother and told
him to come get her. Mrs. Williams may have become suspicious of
the Simses. Before she left, she allegedly invited Cecil (whom she
had always liked) and Lillie Belle Batie down to the trailer. According to Mrs. Batie, she told them: "Something happened. I know
they burned my house."

John Wayne Hearn showed up at the Simses' trailer about
mid-morning, after trying to cover his tracks in the Gainesville

220

area: first he checked out of the Tabor Motel and moved to the Great Western Motel; then he drove to the Gainesville airport, rented an Oldsmobile Cutlass from National Car Rental, and left his pickup truck in the long-term parking lot. The Winchester 1200 was in the trunk of the car, encased in a waterproof gun case that he bought from Ranchers, a local sporting goods store.

When he got to the Simses, Frank started talking to him about guns and showed off his mini-arsenal of weapons: a Swedish Mauser, a German Luger, and various other old guns. Not to be outdone, Hearn said, "Let me show you one I just bought last night." He walked Frank outside and showed him the gleaming Winchester 1200 in the trunk of his Oldsmobile. According to Hearn, Frank didn't inquire why Hearn suddenly needed a stainless steel police-model shotgun, but simply admired it and went back inside.

Around 11:00 A.M., Hearn went roller skating with Debbie, Marlene, and their five children at the Sun Skate Center. Marlene brought along her neighbor in Hawthorne, Debbie Fox, along with *her* daughter and nephew.

The adults skated for a while, and then retired to the snack bar area and watched the kids. Debbie Fox noticed some curious behavior between the Sims girls and Hearn. According to her, Debbie and Marlene walked off by themselves to talk, and when they returned, Marlene acted very strange and remote. Then they moved with Hearn to a separate booth, and began talking earnestly. According to Hearn, they were going over a sketch of Cecil Batie's house drawn on a napkin, which Frank Sims had executed earlier. It was a detailed floor plan showing the layout of the rooms, the location of doors and windows, even the placement of living room furniture and kitchen appliances.

Debbie and Marlene allegedly went over the sketch with Hearn, pointing out where everything was located in the house (Marlene denies being present for this). Debbie warned him about Cecil's dogs, and wrote a note across the bottom of the napkin:

> puppy on porch
> & black & white dog may be near kitchen door
> (friendly when fed)

According to Hearn, Marlene pointed out that the back door opened directly into Cecil's bedroom, and told him that Cecil never locked it. All Hearn would have to do was open the door, step inside Cecil's room, and shoot him in bed.

•   •   •

Around 3:00 P.M., Marlene left to go pick up Larry Watson, who had just been released from the hospital, in care of his mother. The fact that he had been released at all, much less to his mother, who was gravely ill, was disturbing to his family. Watson was still in serious condition; only a week before, he had been transferred to Shands Teaching Hospital, the most sophisticated hospital in north Florida, for more extensive testing on his damaged optic nerve. But Larry had convinced his mother, who had come to visit him, to sign his release.

Some members of his family were already upset with Marlene for allegedly doing a disappearing act after Larry's transfer to Shands—where she visited him very rarely, according to family sources. They felt that if *anyone* should have released him from the hospital, it should have been his wife.

Larry had a fistful of prescriptions that needed to be filled, but Marlene picked him up from his mother's house and drove home to Hawthorne, twenty miles away, without filling them. Then she called his sister-in-law and said pitifully, "I don't know what I'm going to do. Larry has all these prescriptions, and I don't have any money. I'm here with the kids, and I don't have any food in the house."

"Well, Marlene, why did you drive all the way out to Hawthorne?" the sister-in-law asked irritably.

Larry's brother ended up driving to Hawthorne and giving Marlene a hundred dollars for the prescriptions, but by that time no drug stores were open. Larry went to bed with nothing but Tylenol, and didn't get his medications until the next day.

Marlene didn't seem overly concerned.

About 6:00 P.M., she took her kids next door to Debbie Fox's house for a wiener roast. At one point, Fox mentioned that *her* ex-husband was coming over the next day to pick up the children for a custody visit. According to her, Marlene said, as if thinking out loud: "I won't have him [Cecil] to worry about tomorrow."

In the meantime, Hearn and Debbie had returned to the Simses' trailer, where Hearn installed a telephone recording device on the phone. On his way to the bathroom he noticed a pistol case lying open on a dresser in Frank and Iris' bedroom. Inside were about a dozen 12-gauge shotgun shells loaded with No. 2 birdshot. Hearn stuffed four of them in his pocket. *Why buy shells if I don't need to,* he thought. For killing Cecil Batie, four shells would be plenty.

It was Debbie's birthday, so Hearn went to Zales Jewelers and bought her a ring. When she stopped by his motel that afternoon, he gave it to her—along with $5,000 of the $10,000 to put in her safe deposit box (on Friday, he had also wire-transferred $500 to his bank in Atlanta). Debbie kissed him one last time, said good-bye, then drove home to Starke.

Now Hearn was alone with his thoughts. Alone, with time to kill, before it was time *to* kill. He thought again about the take-the-money-and-run option—about just getting in the car and leaving. But he knew that if he did he would never see Debbie again. He would be giving up the greatest love of his life: the most understanding, the most affection, and the most incredible sex he had ever experienced. Sitting in his motel room, John Wayne Hearn ran through every excuse he could think of for leaving—and rejected them all. It all came down to Debbie Banister. He had told her that he was *bad*—a professional mercenary, an experienced gun-for-hire. She had given him the money, she had given him her body, and now he had to prove it.

So he stayed, and waited, and counted down the hours.

•   •   •

Cecil Batie got home late in the afternoon and soaked in the tub, relaxing after a hard day's work. Three friends from Asplundh— Jerry Duckworth, Michael Wilkerson, and David Campbell— dropped by the house to visit. Cecil's nineteen-year-old niece, Lauri Hudson, and her husband, Steve, who were living in Cecil's old trailer, were also there. The trailer had no heat, so Lauri and Steve had spent the afternoon huddling around Cecil's heater, with Rusty Gordon, staying warm.

Cecil's friends went home around 6:00 P.M. Cecil, Rusty, Lauri, and Steve watched TV until about 8:45, when Cecil decided to go out for a beer. He hardly ever went out drinking anymore, but he had something to celebrate that night: The custody battle was over. Even though it wasn't going to turn out the way he had hoped, Cecil knew in his heart that Brad would be happier with Marlene. At last, the long tortured fight over his sons was coming to an end—and that was worth a drink.

He called Gloria Parker, a woman he had been dating for a few months. His sister Myra had introduced him to Parker, and even though she teased him that Parker was "higher class" than the other women he had dated, Myra saw his interest in Parker as a sign that he was finally getting over Marlene.

Cecil asked Parker if she wanted to go to Whiskey River, a southeast Gainesville nightclub, for a drink. Parker lived on the opposite side of Gainesville, and she decided that she didn't want to go out. She and Cecil talked for another fifteen to twenty minutes, however. He was in a good mood, laughing and cutting up.

When he got off the phone with Parker, he invited Rusty, Lauri, and Steve Hudson to go with him instead. But they were watching the movie *Walking Tall* on television, and didn't want to leave. So Cecil decided to go alone. He put on a new pair of blue jeans, a red plaid shirt, his favorite brown vest, his cowboy boots, and a Levi's jacket, and left about 9:00 P.M.—for his last night on the town.

• • •

The time had come.

John Wayne Hearn left the Great Western Motel, drove to a convenience store and bought a pair of cotton gloves—which would leave no fingerprints. Then he drove out of Gainesville, into the countryside, until he found a deserted road. He pulled over, got the shotgun out of the trunk, and marched out into an empty field.

He had never fired a pistol-grip shotgun before, and he wanted to test-fire it before using it on Cecil. He loaded the four shells that he'd stolen from the Simses that afternoon. No. 2 birdshot is designed to kill small birds—doves and quail—without ripping them to pieces, but at close range, it's powerful enough to blow a man's face off. Hearn raised the gun into firing position: his left hand on the pump lever, his right hand braced against the pistol grip, anticipating the recoil. When he fired, the gun recoiled violently, harder than he had expected, and hurt his hand. He wasn't holding it tight enough. Next time he would know.

He got back in the car and headed for Batie Hill.

When he reached Kincaid Road, he drove slowly past SE 15th Avenue. Cecil's house was the second one from the corner, and he could see it from the road. Lights were on in the living room, but Cecil's black and orange Chevy van wasn't there.

Hearn drove on. He cruised up and down the streets of the neighborhood, retracing the skeletal remains of Royal Pines Estates, that bankrupt dream of decrepit businessmen now rotting in the ground. He turned down one of the unlit streets and pulled onto the shoulder, facing Kincaid Road, and cut the engine. It was pitch dark—a cold, moonless, winter night. Hearn checked his watch, then sat and waited—timing how often sheriff's deputies patrolled the area.

Sitting in darkness, his doubts surfaced again: *Why am I doing this?* he thought. *This is crazy.* He started up the car and drove back down Kincaid Road, past SE 15th Avenue, past the Winn Dixie shopping center, past the Barnett Bank, and turned left onto Hawthorne Road. He was driving slowly, mechanically, trying to concentrate. For fourteen years, he had made his living behind the wheel. It was the one place where he could forget himself. Go on automatic and drive all night. But he couldn't forget himself this night. He tried to rehearse the plan in his mind, but his mind wouldn't cooperate. At Waldo Road, he turned right and drove to the Gainesville airport, tracing his escape route. When he got to the airport he turned around, drove back to Batie Hill—then did it again and again. He was fighting the urge to run. Fighting the urge to stay. He drove on into the night.

•   •   •

Some of Cecil Batie's old friends were at Whiskey River that night —friends from the neighborhood, running buddies from his rowdier days. Randy Dobbins, the oldest of the three Dobbins brothers, who had grown up right next door to Cecil, was one of them. They had shared a lot of good times together: the junk Chevelle that they had worked on so hard for six months, which blew up on the first lap; the parties in Cecil's backyard, when he'd

let the underage boys sneak a few beers; the wild rides around
Dead Man's Curve in Cecil's hot rods; and the wild spills in his go-
cart on Thrill Hill. They had shared sad times too: when Dobbins'
father died in 1978, Cecil had left Santa Rosa Beach (where he was
visiting Marlene) at midnight and had driven straight through to
Gainesville, to be there for Randy and Jimmy and Donnie Dobbins.

Randy and Cecil had a few beers together and talked about
old times. Mostly, though, Cecil talked about his boys. He told
Dobbins about the custody hearing coming up on Tuesday, and
said that it looked like Marlene was going to get Brad, and he
would get Adam.

"Whatever makes the kids happy is fine with me," he said.
"Whoever gets them, I just hope the boys will be treated the way
they should be." Nursing a beer with his old friend and talking
about his boys, tears started welling up in Cecil's eyes.

Randy Dobbins felt sorry for his friend. "Cecil, there ain't
nothing I can do for you, buddy," he said, "but I wish you all the
luck in the world."

Cecil left Whiskey River about midnight. He and Dobbins
were supposed to be partners in a pool game, as soon as a table was
free, but Cecil suddenly changed his mind. "Randy, I think I'm
going to go home and go to bed," he said.

When he got home, Lauri and Steve Hudson had already
gone and Rusty Gordon was in bed. Cecil turned on the TV. He
loved old movies—particularly old westerns and war movies—and
had subscribed to cable TV just to pick up the Turner Broadcasting
System, which carried a lot of them.

He took off his plaid shirt and his vest and draped them over a
chair. He pulled off his cowboy boots and his socks and stretched
out on the couch. The house was chilly, so he unfolded an old
green electric blanket and pulled it up around his neck. At five feet
six inches he was short enough to stretch out completely on the old
flowered couch. He propped his right arm behind his head, laid
back to watch his movie, and slowly drifted off to sleep.

· · ·

At 1:30 A.M., John Wayne Hearn drove past the house with his
headlights off and pulled in behind Cecil's Asplundh truck on the
far side. He had already driven past the house two or three times

but hadn't stopped. Through the bay window in the living room he could see that the TV set was still on, but there was no picture—just white noise. The television station had gone off the air. Marlene had told him that Cecil sometimes got drunk and passed out on the couch, and Hearn assumed that was the case.

He sat in his car, running through the same arguments that he had been having with himself all night long. Once again, they all came down to the same thing: If he wanted Debbie, he had to do it. Still, he sat—for five minutes, ten minutes . . .

Finally, he opened the door and stepped outside, gripping the Winchester tightly in his right hand. He walked toward the rear of the house, heading for the back door, as planned. But suddenly, a dog started barking—the one Debbie had written the note about on the napkin: "black and white dog may be near the kitchen door, friendly when fed."

Hearn ran back to the car, jumped inside, and left. *Now what?* he thought anxiously. The dog had ruined his original plan. There was no way to go in the bedroom door. He would have to use the front door.

He drove around Gainesville for another hour, trying to work up his nerve all over again. Finally, he returned to the house around 3:00 A.M. This time, he stopped in front and pulled off on the side of the road. He got out and tiptoed to the front porch, the Winchester dangling in his right hand. The porch was cluttered with junk: an old air-conditioner, an ice chest half filled with sticks of lighter pine, an empty Pepsi bottle. Hearn stepped up to the bay window and looked inside. The white gauzelike curtains, sagging on their hooks, were partway open. In the soft backlighting from the TV set he could make out a body stretched out on the couch. It was Cecil. He was covered with a blanket, except for his face. Hearn had seen his photo, had seen him working on his car, but never up close. He stared down at him. Cecil looked so small under the blanket, almost like a child.

One minute passed.

As his eyes adjusted to the dim light, Hearn could make out other things in the room: a pack of Winstons on the coffee table, an ashtray filled with butts, an old pair of running shorts. *Two minutes.* Hearn kept staring. Across the room, on a cedar chest, were two framed photographs of Cecil and his boys. Beside it was the family

Christmas tree, still decorated. *Three minutes.* The lightweight Winchester felt as heavy as a sea anchor, weighing him down. *Four minutes.* He couldn't stop looking. *Take the money and run,* a voice screamed inside his head. *If I don't do it, I can't have Debbie,* a second voice replied. *Five minutes.*

He couldn't do it.

Hearn turned and lurched back to the car, sweating and shaking. He started the car and drove away. Fleeing Batie Hill. Fleeing the face he had seen in the window. Once again, he drove down Kincaid Road, down Hawthorne Road, down Waldo Road, heading to the airport. Driving aimlessly. His thoughts spinning in circles, turning back on themselves. But this time he kept going—past the airport, past Waldo, seventeen miles away, driving on toward Starke. He was going to Debbie's.

Of course.

On the outskirts of Starke, he turned into the Deerwood subdivision, followed the road to the end of the cul-de-sac, and pulled up in her driveway. The lights were all out. Debbie and Joe Banister and their two children were asleep. Hearn sat in the driveway, searching for strength. For clarity. He remembered her touch. Her skin. The smell of her hair. He thought about the plans they had made: the land in South Carolina, the beautiful log home, a blissful future together. He remembered her letter: "To be with you—not to leave again." Debbie's promises were the only dreams he had left: she had promised to divorce Joe, marry him, and live happily ever after.

Yes, it's true. It has to be.

He started the car and drove back to Gainesville. Driving fast and resolutely this time. Back to Batie Hill.

It was 5 A.M. when he arrived. If he was going to do it, he had to do it now. The sun would be coming up soon. People would be stirring. It was now or never.

He pulled up again in front of the house and cut the engine. He popped the plastic cover off the dome light, unscrewed the bulb, and opened the car door. Leaving the door ajar, he picked up the Winchester off the floorboard and crept silently back to the porch. His seven years of Marine Corps training had finally paid off. After three tours in Vietnam, he knew how to move silently in the night—an invisible killer.

Cecil was still asleep on the couch, but he had pulled the blanket completely over his face. That made it easier. Hearn didn't have to look at him. He stood over him, staring down. And now the choice was clear, his options certain: *If I don't do it, I can't have Debbie. If I don't do it, I can't have Debbie.* It was a chant, a catechism drumming in his head. *If I don't do it, I can't have Debbie. If I don't do it, I can't have Debbie. If I don't do it, I can't have Debbie.*

He raised the Winchester up over his head and pressed the barrel against the window, pointing down at a sharp angle toward Cecil's head. He braced himself, pushing hard against the window, preparing for the recoil. *If I don't do it, I can't have Debbie. If I don't do it, I can't have Debbie. If I don't do it, I can't—* Suddenly, there was a movement in front of him! Cecil Batie was stirring in his sleep— perhaps just moving, or perhaps waking up. Something clicked in Hearn's mind, and he was back in Vietnam: something was moving in the bush, rising out of the muck, rearing up toward him. He squeezed the trigger. The explosion thundered across Batie Hill, echoing off the crackerbox houses and the metal sides of the Simses' trailer right across the street. The first shot blew a perfect hole in the plate glass, sending hundreds of tiny shards of glass rocketing into the blanket, just ahead of the pellets of No. 2 birdshot that slammed into Cecil Batie's face.

Hearn was pushing so hard against the glass that when it broke he lurched forward, poked the gun through the hole, and in the same motion, pumped the gun and fired again. The acrid smell of gunpowder filled the night, enveloping him with its familiar bitter sweetness. His head swimming, he wheeled around, smashed his leg into the old air-conditioner, and ran blindly back to the car. He was running back to Debbie. Running away from himself.

8

IN THE EARLY MORNING hours of January 6, 1985, Hermit Ray Gann was sitting on the side of his bed, getting dressed to go hunting, when he heard two gunshots ring out across Batie Hill. An experienced hunter, Gann recognized the discharges of a shotgun: one loud blast followed, almost immediately, by a second—as if the shooter had fired once, reloaded as quickly as possible, and fired again. To Gann, who lived directly across the street from Cecil Batie and next door to Frank and Iris Sims, the shots sounded close by.

Instinctively, he glanced at the alarm clock beside his bed and noted the time—5:08 A.M.—and continued dressing. It was not unusual to hear gunshots on Batie Hill, and Gann figured that one of his neighbors had fired at a stray dog or cat. In either case, there was nothing to be concerned about. He finished dressing and left for the woods in order to be there before daylight to meet his hunting partner: Billy Batie, Cecil's oldest brother.

• • •

The gunshots awakened Kathy Kopman with a start. Her first thoughts were of her children, asleep in the bedroom on the west end of the house, next door to Cecil Batie's. It sounded like the shots had come from that direction; so Kopman hurried down the hall to check on them.

The children were sleeping soundly. Kopman stood over them for a few moments, to be sure, then returned to her bedroom. Still feeling uneasy about the gunshots, she called Time and

Temperature, the twenty-four-hour time-of-day service. "The time is 5:18," said the computer-generated voice.

Kopman could hear her rottweiler raising hell in the back-yard, barking and carrying on. On this night, the big dog was tied up in back of the house. If he had been loose, whoever had disturbed him would have had hell to pay.

•   •   •

Rusty Gordon was dead asleep when the first shot sounded. Asleep in the deep fog of a man who had slept off more than a few drunks in his life, although on this weekend he had rejected Marlene's suggestion that he pitch one.

The second shot broke through the fog. Rusty sat up and hollered to Cecil: "Bubba, who's shooting the place up out there?"

He rolled out of bed and padded down the hallway in his slippers. "What kind of damn fool is up here shooting this time of morning?" he grumbled to anyone who was listening.

When he reached the living room, he saw that the TV set was still on, with no picture, and that Cecil had once again fallen asleep on the couch. *Bubba's home,* Rusty thought to himself. The blanket was pulled all the way over his head, but there was nothing unusual about that; Cecil always slept covered up, even in the middle of summer.

It was still dark outside, but the TV set gave off enough light to see. Rusty picked his way across the living room, opened the front door, and stepped out onto the porch. He looked up and down the street, trying to see who had caused the commotion.

Seeing nothing, he closed the door, then quietly, so as not to wake Cecil, he tiptoed back across the living room, turned off the TV, and went back to bed.

•   •   •

Since his air force days, Rusty Gordon had been an early riser and usually woke up every morning at six o'clock. But because he was sick, he slept late that morning. It was after nine when the phone woke him. He stumbled into the kitchen to answer it.

It was Lillie Belle Batie, Cecil's mother. "Where's Ceebo?" she asked, using her affectionate nickname for her youngest son.

"In there on the couch," Rusty replied groggily. "It looks like we overslept. What time is it?"

"Nine-fifteen," Lillie Belle replied. "What time was Cecil planning to come over?" (Cecil and Rusty were supposed to trim up a hickory tree in her front yard that morning.)

"Hold on, I'll go wake him up," Rusty said. He laid the receiver on top of the refrigerator and walked to the couch. He leaned down and touched Cecil on the shoulder. "Wake up, Bubba," he said. There was no response.

Suddenly, Rusty noticed the hole in the plate-glass window just above the couch and the shards of glass sprinkled across the blanket. There were no other signs of anything wrong—no gaping holes in the blanket, no blood.

But when Rusty pulled back the edge of the blanket, he saw it: there was blood all over Cecil's face, blood puddled on his cheeks, blood caked in his beard. Rivulets of dried blood from two dozen wounds where the birdshot—dispersed by the plate glass—had exploded into his face.

Rusty ran back into the kitchen, told Mrs. Batie to sit down, and said that Cecil had been shot. Then he ran out of the house, screaming for his neighbor to call 911.

•   •   •

By the time Farnell Cole arrived, S.E. 15th Avenue was already filling up with vehicles: patrol cars, ambulances, the blue van of the crime-scene investigation unit. Cole pulled his unmarked car onto the shoulder, got out, tugged at the holster on his right hip, and zipped up his blue nylon jacket. It was a chilly morning, but the sun was shining brightly in a cloudless azure-blue sky.

It was a beautiful Sunday morning. A perfect day to putter around the house until the NFL play-off games that afternoon, when the Dolphins and Steelers would meet for the AFC championship, and the 49ers and Bears for the NFC's. A perfect day, that is, unless you happened to be the on-call investigator for the Alachua County Sheriff's Department's criminal investigation division (CID). Theoretically, at least, being on call meant that Cole could have stayed home and waited for the phone to ring, but it wasn't worth the aggravation. Something always came up. So he had gone on down to the CID office, a low-slung complex behind the ACSO's main building, which is where he was when the call came in: "Uniformed patrol has been dispatched to a homicide at 2839 S.E. 15th Avenue. The victim is a white male: Cecil Lee Batie."

Cole crossed the narrow street. Two uniformed deputies were stationed in front of the house. It had been four years since Cole had gotten his transfer from uniform patrol to CID, but he was still counting his blessings. Farnell Cole wasn't the kind of cop who had loved wearing a uniform—and the uniform had never loved him back. He was stocky and barrel-chested, with an uncooperative waistline that, even in his early thirties, was showing signs of getting out of control. In uniform he looked sort of pinched around the gills, like a jumbo shrimp with a peanut-sized head, just waiting for somebody to pinch it off. Cole looked much more at home in the faded blue jeans and sport shirt that he was wearing under his jacket on this day.

He stepped over the rope with a DO NOT ENTER sign dangling from it that had been stretched across the front yard to cordon off the house. An orange Mercury Torino fastback was parked in the driveway. A hot rod, Cole noted. In southeast Gainesville, a hot car and a cold corpse usually meant one thing: a woman. Two rowdies started fighting over a woman and one got killed. Or the woman did it herself, sometimes: got in a fight with her old man and blew him away. Either way, a woman was usually the cause.

Cops play hunches. They operate on gut instincts, on tendencies. You see certain things over and over, you start to recognize the patterns. You start anticipating the answer before you ask the question. When you guess right, you usually get your man. When you guess wrong, sometimes the wrong person goes to jail. It happens.

Cole knew the Batie family. Knew their reputation. They kept to themselves, and took care of their own problems. When the sheriff's department got called, it was usually because the Baties were raising hell or fighting among themselves. One of them got too drunk and started a fight, but when it was over everybody was happy again, and that was the end of it. A murder did not fit the pattern.

Several other deputies were standing on the porch, along with

Nancy Neely, the crime scene investigator. They were waiting on
Cole. From here on out, until a suspect was arrested and sent to
trial, this would be his baby. The house, the body, the evidence—it
was all under his direction. Cole believed in the hands-on approach to his work. He would even be on one end of the stretcher
when they loaded Cecil Batie's body in the ambulance for the trip
to the morgue.

He asked if the house had been sealed, and was assured that it
had. The paramedics had arrived at 9:30 A.M. and pronounced the
victim dead, and three deputies—Kittel, Avera, and Brinsco—had
arrived one minute later and sealed off the house. Cole had to be
meticulous, even fanatical, about such details. If one person
carelessly tampered with the evidence, the whole case could be
blown.

Cole opened the screen door and stepped inside. The living
room was musty with the smell of death. The victim was lying on a
couch, covered by a green blanket. Only the top of his head was
visible. Neely told him that the paramedics had pulled down the
blanket to check for a pulse, but otherwise the body was undis-
turbed. Cole told her to go ahead and start taking photographs,
without moving the blanket. "And somebody call Charlie Sanders," he added.

Cole walked back outside and looked at the four-inch hole in
the window. A spent shotgun casing had already been found in the
corner of the porch. Cole looked from the hole to the body, and
back again. He had seen other southeast Gainesville murders in his
six years on the force. He had practically grown up with them: his
father had been a Gainesville cop for thirty years, and Cole had
followed in the old man's footsteps. But something was wrong
here. Terribly wrong. This one did not fit any of the tendencies or
patterns. This was no barroom brawl that had spilled out into the
street. No gunfight between competing rowdies. No crime of passion between jealous lovers. This was a cold-blooded assassination.

Out in the street, standing behind the security rope, Cole
recognized Billy Batie, the victim's brother. He knew Billy from the
family's tree business, and walked over to talk to him. Billy Batie
did not yet know that Cecil was dead. The family only knew that he
had been shot; they had heard no other details. Billy Batie is not

the kind of man to whom you would want to have to deliver that news. He is the roughest of the Batie boys, and the most like his daddy. "Billy's a mountain man," says his brother Wayne. He fits the part: He is rough-hewn and shaggy, and looks like he just came out of the woods.

On this morning he actually had. When Cole told him that Cecil was dead, Billy was understandably angry and upset. When he calmed down, Cole asked him, "Who would have a reason to kill Cecil?"

Billy Batie didn't hesitate. He said that there was only one person who had a reason to kill Cecil, only one person who had anything to gain from it: his ex-wife, Marlene Sims Watson.

Five minutes after arriving on the scene, Farnell Cole had his first suspect.

•   •   •

Sgt. Charlie Sanders knew when they called him at home on a Sunday morning that he wouldn't be seeing his wife and kids again for a while. In a homicide investigation, the first forty-eight hours are critical. If you don't get on the trail quickly, suspects disappear, memories fade, and the trail slips away. Sanders knew that if Farnell Cole was having him paged at home it had to be a bad one and for the next few days they would be working around-the-clock.

Sanders arrived at Batie Hill at 11:20 A.M., and Cole quickly briefed him on the situation. The two men had started with the sheriff's department the same year, 1978, and had worked together ever since Cole transferred to CID in 1980. Officially, Sanders was Cole's supervisor, but they worked as a team. There was a Mutt and Jeff quality about them: Cole is burly and bulldog tough, while Sanders is razor-thin and wiry, with a thick drawl and a streak of country philosopher: he prides himself on his ability to read people.

Now that Sanders had arrived, the investigation began in earnest. Lori Naslund, an assistant medical examiner, removed the blanket from Cecil Batie's body. Cole and Sanders moved closer to study the wounds. One thing was immediately apparent: There must have been more than one shot. One had obviously hit Cecil full in the face: there were over two-dozen entry wounds in his face, several of his front teeth were shattered, and the cotton wadding from the shotgun shell was actually resting in his mouth. But there was also a gaping hole in his left shoulder, and an even larger one —five inches in diameter—on the left side of his neck. From the amount of blood that had drenched the couch, that shot had apparently severed the jugular vein.

Looking at the spread-out pattern of wounds on Cecil's face, Cole and Sanders surmised that those had been caused by the first shot, which had passed through the plate glass window. The gaping wounds in the neck and shoulder were characteristic of a shotgun blast at point-blank range.

They went outside and looked at the hole in the window. With only one hole and two shots, the killer had to have fired once, then poked the barrel through the hole for the second shot. And with only one spent shell-casing on the porch, they could eliminate the use of an automatic shotgun, which ejects its shells automatically. They figured they were looking either for a pump or a manual loader.

Sanders agreed with Cole that the crime didn't fit the neighborhood. In southeast Gainesville, people usually settled their differences face-to-face. If two men got into a gunfight and one shot the other, he would usually be waiting for the cops when they arrived, hand them the smoking gun, and say, "I just killed the son of a bitch." Shooting Cecil Batie twice through a window while he was asleep on the couch did not fit the style of southeast Gainesville. Right away, Cole and Sanders speculated that it had to be an outside job.

•   •   •

As usual, the Banister family gathered at Ruth and Ceree's house for Sunday dinner. Ruth always had the meal on the table at twelve o'clock sharp. Joe brought Amanda and John, but Debbie arrived an hour late, just as they were finishing.

"You wouldn't believe who got killed last night," Debbie said, wearing a big grin.

"Who, Debbie?" Lana asked.

"Old Cecil Batie," she announced smugly. "Somebody blew the son of a bitch away with a 12-gauge shotgun."

Once again, the Banisters were shocked, as much by Debbie's mouth as by the announcement itself.

"How horrible," Lana exclaimed.

"Oh, he had it coming," Debbie responded. "I knew sooner or later it would happen to him."

Later, when Debbie and Lana were doing dishes in the kitchen, Lana commented, "Those poor kids."

Debbie shrugged it off. "They're better off without him," she said.

This woman has a mean streak a mile wide, Lana thought.

• • •

John Wayne Hearn's escape plan, which he had rehearsed so often before the murder, failed miserably. When he got to the Gainesville airport after shooting Cecil Batie, he stashed the Winchester 1200 under a big bush and went to turn in his rental car, only to discover, to his surprise, that National Car Rental was closed until 8:00 A.M. Hearn had assumed, without checking, that it would be open all night, but the Gainesville airport was so small that everything shut down at 11:00 P.M.

Hearn went inside the terminal and sat down in the waiting area. The only other people there were a couple of Eastern Airlines baggage handlers and an old black shoeshine man. To pass the time, Hearn had his boots shined.

Finally, at 8:00 A.M., he turned in the Oldsmobile, retrieved his pickup truck, and picked up the Winchester on his way out of town. He arrived in Atlanta about 1:00 P.M. Sunday, and immediately called the Simses. "How's Frank?" he asked. Hearn was concerned that the killing might affect Frank's heart.

"Frank's fine," Iris told him, "but all hell has broken out up the street. The Baties are yelling that Cecil is dead."

Hearn then called Judy, the woman he had met at the Waffle House on Interstate 20 months before. He hadn't seen her since before Christmas, but he needed to get Cecil Batie off his mind—and, more important, to establish an alibi. He went over to Judy's apartment and spent the afternoon and evening with her. He told her that he wouldn't be seeing her anymore because he was moving to Florida to be with his new love (he even showed her a picture of Debbie Banister and her two children) but was enough of a smooth-talker to convince Judy to let him spend the night.

Monday morning, he left Judy's apartment and went to the

Tara State Bank and deposited $1,500.00 cash—part of the $10,000 that Debbie Banister had paid him to kill Cecil Batie. That evening, he boarded a flight for Houston.

He was on his way to meet Bob Black.

9

BOB BLACK was following his plan to the letter. In early December, while he was still selling restaurant equipment, he had paid a sales call on Donald J. Ballard, who owned a local convenience store called Howdy Corners *and* a life insurance company, Williams, Ballard and Associates. Bob had met Ballard in 1983, and had done the wiring on Howdy Corners when it was being constructed.

Ostensibly, Bob was trying to sell Ballard an ice machine, but Ballard, who has a reputation as an aggressive salesman, turned the tables and tried to make a sale himself. He told Bob that he could save money on his life insurance policy, and at the same time increase his coverage, by converting from a whole life policy to term life. He also suggested that Bob consider working as an associate with his company, because he could make good money selling insurance, even on a part-time basis. Ballard promised to call him after the Christmas holidays to explore both ideas.

In early January, Ballard followed up on his promise: He called Bob at home and scheduled an appointment with him. Bob went to Ballard's office with the three existing life insurance policies that he and Sandra had, which were carried by Fidelity Union Life Insurance Company in Dallas: one for $1,500, one for $25,000, and a second $25,000 policy with an accidental death rider that would double the coverage to $50,000. The total of all three was $76,500.

Ballard reviewed the policies, then repeated his pitch about the benefits of converting to term life. Bob said that he liked the idea but that Ballard would have to convince Sandra since she would be the one writing the check. They agreed that Ballard would come to Steep Hollow and make his presentation to Sandra.

Ballard also brought up the idea of Bob going to work for him as an associate, selling insurance on the side. The timing was perfect: Bob was having little success selling restaurant equipment, and was looking for a new career. First, though, he had to get licensed. To sell insurance in Texas, a person must pass an exam and be licensed by the state. Coincidentally, Ballard conducted a forty-hour study course through his office, to prepare new associates for the state exam. Bob decided to enroll.

The first phase of Bob and David Huber's plan—to get a big insurance policy on Sandra and wait a year—was under way. However, it was coming together so quickly, and so effortlessly, that Bob decided not to wait. Teresa's divorce was still pending until February 23. He needed to do it before then, while Teresa was still available. His only problem was finding somebody to do the job. Huber had already turned chickenshit on him twice, and might do it again. Bob needed a more reliable hit man. He needed a professional.

• • •

Hearn arrived in Houston about 11:00 P.M. on Monday, January 7, 1985. Before leaving Atlanta, he had called his sister, Ann, who lived outside of Houston, and told her that he would be going to Bryan to talk to a Mr. Black about buying his gun collection for $5,000. He asked Ann if he could store the guns at her house, since he couldn't take them home with him on the plane, and then come back later and pick them up.

"I guess so," Ann replied. It seemed like a strange request, since she had never known Hearn to have *any* interest in guns, much less be dealing in them. It was the first time Ann had even heard from her brother in nearly two years. Hearn had gotten mad at her on his last visit and hadn't spoken to her since. But that was typical: Ann felt that he communicated with her when he needed something from her but otherwise ignored her.

When he arrived at the Houston airport, he rented a white Camaro Z-28 from National Car Rental, and made the two-hour drive to Bryan-College Station. He checked into the Ponderosa Motel, just outside of town, where Bob Black had told him to stay.

First thing in the morning, at 6:35 A.M. Texas time (CST), he called Debbie Banister at home in Starke. He was so dependent on Debbie, that he couldn't do *anything* without talking to her first.

Bob Black arrived at the Ponderosa Motel around 10:30 A.M. They introduced themselves and talked briefly. Bob said that he had some errands he needed to run, and suggested that Hearn meet him at his home around noon to look at the guns. He drew a map of how to get to Bark-n-Holler.

Hearn called Debbie again at 12:19 P.M., then left for Steep Hollow. When he arrived, Bob was outside washing his El Camino. They went inside, sat down at the dining room table, and had a glass of iced tea. Bob showed Hearn his DD-214 form (he had never mailed it), which proved that he had been a Marine Corps officer in Vietnam.

Then Bob started bringing out his guns from the master bedroom and the attic. He showed Hearn his stainless-steel Mini-14, his M1A1, his Winchester 30/30 carbine, and the many others. Before Hearn left Atlanta, he had asked Bob to write out a sales receipt for the guns, made out to D.A. Banister. Bob already had the receipt typed up, and had also listed on it his diamond ring, which he wanted to sell:

> January 7, 1985. Buyer: D.A. Banister
> Seller: R.V. Black, Jr.
> Diamond Ring appraised 12 Oct 82
> M1A1
> Mini-14
> Winchester
> Weatherby
> S&W 19

After examining the guns, Hearn repeated his offer of $5,000. Bob said that he felt the guns were worth more—at least $6,000.

"They aren't worth that much to me," Hearn argued.

Bob insisted that he needed $6,000, and offered to throw in Gary Wayne's guns to sweeten the deal.

"I'll have to think it over," Hearn told him. They agreed to meet the next morning at the Jack-in-the-Box, where Hearn would give him a final answer.

With the negotiations at a friendly standoff, Bob changed the subject. "You know," he said, "if my old lady wasn't around, I wouldn't have to be selling my guns."

"What are you talking about?" Hearn asked.

Bob explained that he had a girlfriend named Teresa in California. "We're childhood sweethearts," he said, "and if my wife weren't around, Teresa and I could get married." He added that he had some insurance on his wife, and with her out of the way, he would have all the money he needed. "I've been trying to think of a way to get rid of my wife," he said.

Two days after killing Cecil Batie, this was not a conversation that John Wayne Hearn wanted to hear. Bob went on to say that he and a friend had been planning to kill her, but the friend had backed out at the last minute. The plan was for Bob to hit her in the head, put her in her van, drive it to the Highway 6 bypass, set the cruise control, aim it for a bridge abutment, then jump from the van into his El Camino.

"I need somebody to drive my car," Bob said.

"I don't want to hear about it," Hearn said nervously, and left.

That afternoon, he called Debbie Banister again—for the third time that day. He called her again the next morning, before he left for the Jack-in-the-Box to meet Bob Black. Hearn bought breakfast for himself *and* for Bob, who complained that he had no money. They sat down in a booth to eat. Hearn said that he wouldn't pay $6,000 for the gun collection, but would only give Bob the $5,000 they had agreed on.

Bob was adamant. "I've got to have $6,000," he insisted.

Hearn blew up. "You fucked me, Bob," he said angrily. "You cost me money to come all the way out here, then backed out of the deal."

Bob started backpedaling and said that he'd accept the $5,000 after all, but Hearn was still angry. "I don't want your damn guns, Bob," he said. "I won't even come out here and talk to you again for less than a thousand dollars, just for my expenses."

He left Bryan and drove back to Houston.

That evening, Hearn went to see his sister. "Did you buy the gun collection?" Ann asked.

SOF publisher Robert
K. Brown modeling a
Soviet Red Army sable
hat at the 1989 *Soldier
of Fortune* convention
in Las Vegas.

Bob, Sandra, and
Gary Wayne Black
dressed in Civil War
period costumes.
Photo was taken
about 1980.

Bob Black and Teresa Heatherington on his motorcycle, the "Lone Eagle," in April, 1984, shortly after their love affair began.

Debbie Banister posing in front of John Wayne Hearn's apartment in Gainesville, Florida. Hearn took the photo himself.

Debbie Banister
standing over her
husband's grave,
holding a red rose.
The photo was taken
by the man who killed
him—John Wayne
Hearn.

John Wayne Hearn with
his son, Wayne, and his
mother, Mary Watson,
two days after his arrest.
Photo was taken in the
Brazos County jail,
March 17, 1985.

John Wayne Hearn in
Vietnam, about 1967.

Hearn in Vietnam,
about 1967.

Hearn in Vietnam, posing
behind an M-60 machine
gun, about 1967.

Hearn in his Marine Corps uniform, shortly after he enlisted in 1964.

Hearn in his ROTC uniform from San Jacinto High School, Houston, Texas. Photo was taken in 1961.

Mary Watson holding her infant son, John Wayne Hearn, in October, 1945.

John Hearn, approximately four years old, playing in his front yard in Houston.

Debbie Banister posing in front of John Wayne Hearn's apartment in Gainesville, Florida. Hearn took the photos himself.

Debbie Banister at her desk in the Sun Bank loan recovery department. At right are flowers sent to her by John Wayne Hearn, who also took this photo.

Sandra Black, approximately four years old, with her father and mother, Glen and Marjorie Eimann.

Bob and Sandra Black were married on Christmas Eve, 1967. *Left to right:* Bob's paternal grandmother, Bob, Sandra, and her maternal grandmother, Liddie B. Arnold.

Bob Black as a lieutenant in the Marine Corps, about 1969.

Sandra Black on the beach at Kaneohe, Hawaii, in 1970. She and Bob spent seventeen months there—it was the happiest time of their marriage.

Bob and Sandra Black at the Marine Corps Air Station in Kaneohe, Hawaii. Their house had been selected as House of the Month.

Sandra, Gary Wayne, and Bob in College Station, 1971, after returning from Hawaii and before Bob went to Vietnam.

Sandra Black working
Chauncy at Action
Dogs USA. Trainer
Dan Linder is at left.
This photo was taken
a few weeks before
her death.

Bob and Gary Wayne
Black showing off two
deer they killed on a
successful deer hunt.
About 1982.

Sandra Black on the dining room floor of her home in Steep Hollow, February 21, 1985. This is what Gary Wayne Black saw when his father sent him into the house.

Gary Wayne and Bob Black, only minutes after Bob was sentenced to Death Row, February 26, 1986.

Bob Black *(center)* with his family, only minutes after he was sentenced to Death Row. *Left to right:* Bob's younger brother Gary, his son Gary Wayne, Bob, Ivonne Black, and Vannoy Black.

Joe Banister, shortly before his death.

Marlene Sims, seventeen and pregnant in 1974.

Debbie Banister being arrested on April 15, 1985. *Left to right:* Farnell Cole, Debbie, her daughter Amanda, Don Denton, Iris Sims, Wiley Clark, and Marlene Sims Watson, who is holding Debbie's son John. *(Photo courtesy of WCJB-TV)*

Cecil Batie playing his guitar, with photos of his sons on the wall behind him.

Bob Black *(in foreground)* being escorted to Death Row on February 26, 1986. *Back row, left to right:* Brazos County Sheriff Ronnie Miller, unidentified officer, and Investigator Chris Kirk. *(Photo:* Houston Chronicle)

Gary Wayne Black and Marjorie Eimann answering reporters' questions after their lawsuit against *Soldier of Fortune* magazine. Behind them, *left to right:* Larry Eimann, Ron Franklin (with his arm on Gary Wayne), and Graham Hill. *(Photo:* Houston Chronicle)

Soldier of Fortune publisher Robert K. Brown reacting to the verdict in the Eimann case, March 3, 1988. *(Photo:* Houston Chronicle)

SOF defense attorney Larry Thompson, who had hoped the Eimann case would never go to trial. *(Photo:* Houston Chronicle)

"Naw, he wanted more money," Hearn replied.

Ann was relieved; she hadn't wanted to keep guns in her house anyway. That evening, Hearn took her out to eat at a local truck stop and paid for the meal with money he had earned by killing Cecil Batie. All he talked about was Debbie Banister. He told Ann that he loved her and she loved him, that Debbie was going to sell her house, and that they were going to get married and build a $100,000 five-bedroom log home in South Carolina.

"Is Debbie divorced?" Ann asked.

"No, her husband's dead," he replied.

"What happened to him?"

"I don't know, I've never asked about it," he said.

"Well, I'm glad you've found somebody to make you happy," Ann said. "You've had as hard a time as I have." (Ann has been married five times herself.)

Hearn left at eleven o'clock to catch his plane back to Atlanta.

• • •

Farnell Cole and Charlie Sanders worked around-the-clock for nearly seventy-two hours, questioning Cecil Batie's family, friends, neighbors, coworkers, and everyone else they could before the tracks got cold. They asked everyone the same question—"Who could have had a reason to kill him?" Everyone gave them the same answer—Marlene.

On January 6, the day of the murder, Cole interviewed Randy Dobbins, Eleanor Tarounga, Gloria Parker, and Rusty Gordon. Rusty, who was terribly shaken by Cecil's death, told him about Marlene taking all of the boys' clothes on Friday, and telling him to "pitch a drunk."

Later that afternoon, Cole questioned Frank and Iris Sims. They said that they were both home Saturday night, but hadn't heard any shots. The only motive they could suggest for the killing was that, according to them, Adam Batie had roughed up a black boy several years before, and perhaps the boy's parents had killed Cecil in retaliation.

Before leaving, Cole told Frank and Iris that he wanted to talk to Marlene. At 9:00 P.M., she arrived at the CID office with her mother. It was Cole and Sanders' first opportunity to assess their only viable lead in the case. Marlene denied any involvement in

Cecil's death, but she wasn't exactly remorseful about it. "Don't get me wrong," she said, according to Cole, "I didn't have anything to do with it, but I'm glad he's dead."

Marlene was a wealth of information when it came to naming *other* potential suspects: she suggested a half-dozen, including Gloria Parker's ex-husband, Billy Batie (who had gotten in an argument with Cecil several years before), and hot rodders on S.E. 15th Avenue, with whom Cecil had gotten angry.

Marlene herself had an airtight alibi: She had been home in Hawthorne all night, as her neighbors, Larry Watson, and Larry's brother (who had brought her the $100) could attest to.*

On Monday afternoon, the medical examiner's office completed the autopsy on Cecil Batie, which strengthened Cole and Sanders' theory that there had been more than one shot. Dr. Carolyn Hopkins found numerous entry wounds scattered over Cecil's neck, thorax, arms, scalp, and face (some of which contained embedded glass) and removed a total of 154 birdshot pellets from his body. She noted that the left jugular vein was severed, numerous pellets were lodged in the skull and the base of the brain, and the right basal ganglia had the "consistency of freshly ground meat."

Cole phoned the Gator Skeet Club, and found out that a Remington 3″ magnum shell loaded with No. 2 birdshot (the type of casing found on the porch) held anywhere from 124 to 158 pellets. With 154 pellets found in Cecil's body alone, and dozens of others in or under the couch (some had blown right through it), there had to have been two shots.

Over the next three days, additional information came to light that pointed toward Marlene as the prime suspect. One of her neighbors in Hawthorne, Joanne Justice, told Cole that the day after Cecil took Brad out of school, in October, Marlene had come to her trailer to use the phone. According to Justice, Marlene had been drinking and was "raving mad," and declared, "Before I will let Cecil take my kids from me, I'll kill him and leave." Then she

---

* According to Larry's sister-in-law, Marlene had dumped Larry at his mother's house the morning of the murder, with his unfilled prescriptions and with only twenty of the hundred dollars that his brother had given her. Larry hardly saw her at all for the next few weeks; she removed her things from Hawthorne and moved back into her trailer behind her parents.

looked at Justice and said, "You didn't hear me say that—understand?" (Marlene denies saying this.)

The Batie family also reported that Cecil's metal file box, which contained all of his important papers, was missing. For years, Marlene had been the beneficiary of his life insurance policy. In July, 1984, however, Cecil had made his sister Myra the beneficiary. Apparently, this was news to Marlene: within days of the murder, she reportedly called Cecil's insurance agent demanding payment (Marlene claims that Debbie made the calls), then had her attorney contact him as well.

Cole also received reports of Marlene's prior drug usage: Beth Bottle, a former roommate and the daughter of Marlene's close friend Pat Bouchette, told him that Marlene had used drugs supplied to her by a boyfriend who would "do anything" for Marlene, including kill people. She claimed that Marlene had used speed, Quaaludes, pot, and LSD, in addition to prescription drugs that she got from Iris Sims. (Two years later, Marlene stated that she was not using any drugs.) Furthermore, Bottle stated that Marlene herself was "perfectly capable of killing someone" or having them killed.

By January 10, Cole and Sanders had identified seven potential suspects who might have had a reason to kill Cecil Batie, including Marlene. The list included all of the "leads" that Marlene had so helpfully supplied. Cole and Sanders asked the other six suspects to take a polygraph test. Each of them agreed, and each of them passed.

It was time to pay another visit to Marlene.

On Thursday evening, January 10, Cole and Sanders arrived unannounced at Marlene's trailer. She invited them in, and was pleasant and friendly—at first. Cole told her the status of the investigation: Seven suspects had been identified, the other six had each passed a polygraph, and that left her as the prime suspect. "Would you be willing to take a polygraph?" he asked.

"I'd be more than happy to," she replied, according to Cole.

Cole said that he had a polygraph examiner standing by, and if she wanted to get it out of the way, they could do it immediately.

"No problem," Marlene said. She asked Cole to watch her children while she went next door and asked her mother to baby-sit.

When she returned ten minutes later—accompanied by Iris—
all of the pleasantries were gone. The women cussed out Cole and
Sanders for "accusing" Marlene of the murder. In addition, Marlene said that she had called her attorney and she would *not* take a
polygraph.

Cole and Sanders started to leave, but before they did, Cole
made a promise to Marlene. "I will see to it that you are arrested
and convicted of the murder of Cecil Batie," he said.

Immediately after the investigators left, there was a flurry of
phone calls between the Simses' trailer and Debbie Banister's
house in Starke. From then on, *Debbie* would be taking charge.

The next afternoon, Charlie Sanders made one last attempt to
talk to Marlene. He called the Simses' trailer and asked Marlene to
come down to the ACSO. Surprisingly, she agreed. Marlene
showed up at 5:45 P.M.—not with her mother or her attorney but
with her sister, Debbie Banister. Since she was now clearly the
prime suspect in the case, Sanders "mirandized" her, as required
by Federal law, and began the interview.

A funny thing happened. Almost every time he asked a question, *Debbie* would answer for Marlene. It was as if Debbie was
afraid that Marlene might say something stupid. Sanders made a
mental note to find out more about this sister.

Marlene still insisted that she had had nothing to do with
Cecil's murder. She repeated her litany of other people who could
have done it, and again refused to take a polygraph.

"Marlene, I don't understand that," Sanders said. "You told
me at first that you'd take the polygraph, and now you say you
won't. You sit here and tell me you had nothing to do with it
whatsoever, and you don't know who did it. If you didn't do it, and
you don't have any knowledge of it, why won't you take the polygraph?"

Marlene got huffy and told him to call her lawyer if he had any
more questions, that the interview was over.

As the women got up to leave, Sanders said, "Marlene, regardless of what happens today, there will come a day—and it
won't be too long—when we'll talk again. And next time, the talk
will be a *lot* different. I believe you had something to do with it, and
I'll find out. You can count on it."

Marlene paused for a moment and looked back at him. San-

ders had the feeling that she wanted to talk to him and that if
Debbie had not been there, she might have. But Debbie *was* there,
and quickly led her away.

That afternoon, as usual, Cole and Sanders got together to
update each other on the case. They were both tired and frustrated. They had a prime suspect and a compelling motive, but no
hard evidence. Everything pointed to Marlene, but she had an
alibi. But if she hadn't done it, who had? After six days, all they
really had was a hole in a window, an empty shell casing, and a
dead body.

10

THERE WAS A LETTER waiting for
John Wayne Hearn when he got home from Texas:

Jan. 8, 1985

Dear John,

Just a few pages to say hi and to let you know that I love
you very very much.

When I saw this card it reminded me of our up-coming
trip together and the starting of our lives together. I am
sure that the property will be just as beautiful as the
picture on this card. Even if we moved to the flat desert, it
would be the prettiest place I've ever been as long as you
are at my side.

You will never know how much I love you as there is no
way I can prove it to you, and nothing I can buy or say to
convince you of how much you mean to me. I will have you
—no ifs, ands, or butts about it.

I worry about you. I dream about you & I see your face
when I close my eyes.

What I want most of all is my life with you—
uncomplicated, simple and forever—just making you happy
& making love.

I'll close for now and get back to work.

Love,
Debra

• • •

Bob Black was getting desperate. David Huber had turned chickenshit on him. John Wayne Hearn had not responded to his indirect solicitation of help. He had to find someone—someone dependable—to help him with his plan.

In January, shortly after Hearn's trip to Texas, Bob called Gordon Matheson, his old superintendent at Harville Electric. It was about 8 A.M., and Matheson was still in the office checking blueprints for upcoming jobs and calling suppliers. It was the first time that he had heard from Bob Black since he had quit in October.

"Gordon, can I come over and talk to you for a few minutes?" Bob asked.

"Sure, Bob, come on over," Matheson replied. He assumed that Bob wanted to talk about the same old thing: how much he loved Teresa and hated his wife.

When Bob arrived at Harville thirty minutes later, Matheson led him into the dayroom and poured himself a cup of coffee. He offered one to Bob.

Bob shook his head. "Let's go outside," he said nervously.

Matheson pointed toward his empty office. "We can use my office."

"No, I'd rather go outside," Bob said.

They walked out into the parking lot and stood between two Harville service trucks. Bob looked at the ground and shuffled his feet. "Gordon, I really need you to help me," he said plaintively. "You're the only one I know that I can come to."

"Well, sure, Bob, I'll be glad to help you out if I can," Matheson said. "What is it you want?"

Bob looked at the ground again. Matheson had never seen him so nervous and struggling for words. "All I need you to do is drive a truck for me."

"Drive a truck?"

"Yeah, you drive your truck alongside my van, and I'm going to put my van on cruise control and jump out of it into your truck."

"Say what?" Matheson chuckled. "Whatsa matter, Bob, don't you like your van?" He thought Bob was trying to collect on his insurance.

"No," Bob said, looking even more uncomfortable. "My wife's gonna be in the van."

Matheson didn't say anything. He was used to hearing all kinds of crazy shit on construction sites. Roughneck men say outrageous things when they're hot and tired. He stared at Bob for a few seconds, sizing him up, trying to decide if he was serious. Finally, he said, "Bob, let me just explain to you how stupid that sounds, okay? Now, for example, if she's in the van and you jump into the back of my truck—what happens if she don't *die* in the wreck?"

Bob's shuffling stopped. He raised his head and looked Matheson straight in the eye. "Then I'll get out of the truck and beat her in the head with a club," he said unflinchingly.

At that point, looking eyeball-to-eyeball, Matheson knew that Bob was serious. *This guy has gone completely off the deep end,* he thought. "Bob, do you realize what you're saying?" Matheson asked.

"Yeah." Bob told him that he was taking out a $100,000 insurance policy on Sandra and would give him half of it.

Matheson still couldn't believe what he was hearing. "Bob, do you realize what you're asking me to do?"

"Yeah, I do," Bob said.

Matheson exploded. "I want to tell you one fucking thing, Bob—there's a lot of things in this world I *would* do, and I could sure use fifty thousand dollars, but I ain't *stupid* enough to try to kill somebody!"

Bob immediately backed off. "Okay, don't worry about it, Gordon. Just forget it."

But Matheson was incensed that Bob would think that he was the kind of person who would kill somebody. "I can't believe you'd think I'd do such a thing," he said angrily.

"I'm sorry," Bob said, backpedaling. "You're a friend, Gordon, and I'm sorry I even asked you. Don't worry about it; I've got some marine buddies that will take care of it for me."

Bob climbed on his Harley, fired it up, and rode away.

Matheson went back inside and tried to work, but Bob's request was gnawing at him. Finally, he walked over to Marilyn Soffar's office. "Marilyn, do I look like the kind of person who could kill somebody?" he asked.

She laughed. "Naw, Gordon, not really."

"No, I'm serious—do you take me for a killer?" He told her what had just happened.

Soffar already thought that Bob Black was out of touch with reality, and this just confirmed it.

"Do you think I ought to go to the police?" Matheson asked.

"What are they gonna do?" she replied cynically. "Bob would just deny it, and it would be your word against his."

"Well, should I at least call Sandra?"

"I don't think Sandra would believe you," she said. "This is so off-the-wall, Bob will never go through with it. And there's no sense causing a big stink now that they're back together."

"So what should I do?" Matheson asked.

"I'd stay away from him," Soffar suggested.

Matheson returned to his office, determined to do just that.

●   ●   ●

On January 17, John Wayne Hearn loaded his meager belongings in a U-Haul trailer and drove to Gainesville. He moved into the Prairie View Apartments, the complex that Debbie had picked out for him on the south side of town.

He had told his mother that he was going to be working for Sun Bank—repossessing airplanes and doing photography work—but that was a lie. The chances of an inexperienced newcomer establishing a freelance photography business in a town the size of Gainesville were almost nil. He still had $5,000 in Debbie's safe deposit box, but the way he ran through money—especially when he was in love—it wouldn't last long.

In truth, there was only one way that he could hope to make any money: through his ad in *Soldier of Fortune.* Even that was iffy. He had been neglecting his World Security calls for two months, ever since his love affair began with Debbie Banister. Since Christmas, he had made only *seven* SOF-related long distance calls, and two of those had been to Bob Black.

Now he had to get serious again. He had a phone installed in his Prairie View apartment, left the new number with Message World, and started hitting the phones: he made seven return calls in the first three days he was in Gainesville.

Colonel Hearn was back in business.

In fact, Col. Hearn had a new controlling partner in World

Security Group: Debbie Banister. She had become his business manager. She would call Message World and retrieve his phone calls herself, and she even recorded a new outgoing message in her sexiest voice: *"This is World Security Group. Colonel Hearn is unavailable at this time, but you can leave a message and he will get back to you as soon as possible."*

Debbie would make return calls on Sun Bank's WATS line, and screen out the flakes from the legitimate callers before Hearn ever talked to them. According to Hearn, she even started running computerized credit checks on the callers to find out about their assets.

By this time, Debbie had taken over *every* aspect of Hearn's life. She had the remainder of his $5,000 in her safe deposit box, and she doled it out to him like a mother giving a child a weekly allowance.

The truth was, Debbie *was* like his mother. It was a role that Hearn had been practicing all his life. Like a dog that flops on the ground when a bigger, stronger dog shows up, he was trained to roll over and play "Mama's boy." He knew both facets of the role: how to *please* Mama by being a good boy—doing what he was told, buying her presents, telling her that he loved her—and how to *get* things from Mama with his little boy whine, his pouting lip, his temper tantrums. The only difference, in this case, was that if he was a good boy for Debbie Banister, she would take him to bed and blow his mind with her wild lovemaking. And boy-howdy, did he ever want to be a good boy!

For Debbie, this was the opportunity that she had been waiting for all her life. Her marriage to Billy Thigpen had been utterly boring; her marriage to Joe Banister was numbingly respectable, which was almost worse; but *this!*—this was exhilarating. At last, the butterfly above her left breast was spreading its wings and flying free. There was only one obstacle in the way of total freedom: Joe Banister. And Debbie had a plan for him too.

•   •   •

Joe Banister was worth a lot more money dead than alive. He had a $49,000 life insurance policy through Minnesota Mutual, plus $60,000 in death benefits and annuities from Western Electric—a total of $109,000. And, as opposed to Cecil Batie, there was no doubt about his beneficiary: It was his loving wife, Debbie Banister.

• • •

Once John Wayne Hearn settled permanently in Gainesville, his love affair with Debbie took on a regular routine: In the morning, Hearn would call her—either in Starke, after Joe left for work, or at Sun Bank—and at lunchtime they would either meet at Hearn's apartment to make love or at the Simses' trailer to eat lunch. Hearn would park his truck behind the trailer to avoid attracting attention.

But then something alarming happened: Debbie started showing up for their afternoon trysts with bruises. They were in bed when Hearn noticed the first one: a small bruise over her breast.

"How'd you get that?" he asked.

Debbie said that she didn't want to talk about it, but Hearn persisted. "Tell me what happened."

"Joe hit me," she whimpered.

Hearn, who had always been insanely jealous, erupted: "He hit you??!!"

Yes, Debbie said. Joe had been drinking and hit her. She thought he suspected that she was having an affair.

Over the next few days, Debbie showed up with more bruises —on her arms, her legs, her shoulder—and Hearn's jealous rage built to a frenzy. This was the woman he intended to marry, and he wasn't going to let anybody—particularly her *husband*—beat on her.

A few days later, they were at the Simses' trailer for lunch, and Debbie was complaining about Joe. Iris Sims spoke up: "If Joe finds out you're seeing John, he's gonna kill you."

Hearn couldn't contain himself any longer. "If he doesn't stop beating on her, *I'm* gonna kill the son of a bitch!" he cried.

It was what Debbie Banister had been waiting for. She knew now that Hearn was capable of murder—he had done it once already. In the car, after leaving the trailer, she said, according to Hearn, "I can see right now that it's gonna come down to him or me. I'm not going to drag my kids through a custody battle like Marlene did. I don't care if it's you that does it, or if I have to find

somebody else, but that's the only way we're going to be together."

Hearn nodded. It had to be done. And *he* knew that he was
capable too. Debbie didn't need to find someone else.

•   •   •

On Wednesday, January 23, 1985, Hearn opened an account with
Gainesville Florist. That afternoon, he had a half-dozen assorted
roses delivered to Debbie Banister at the Sun Bank loan recovery
department. The enclosed card read "Beautiful flowers for a beautiful girl" and was signed "J.W.H."

•   •   •

Over the next few days Debbie and Hearn started discussing different ways to kill Joe Banister. One idea was to get him out of town,
to avoid suspicion, and run him off the road. That week, Debbie
called Joe's boss at Western Electric, Jimmy Singletary, and asked
him to temporarily transfer Joe to Tampa.

"Joe needs to be by himself for a while," she explained.

Singletary was dumbfounded. Usually, when he got a call
from an employee's wife, it was to ask him to keep her husband *at
home*, not to send him away.

Debbie assured him that there was nothing wrong at home.
"Joe just needs some time by himself," she said.

That also struck Singletary as odd, since he hadn't asked
about their home situation. For the past few months, Joe had been
working out of town anyway—either in Palatka (forty-five miles
south of Starke) or in Yankeetown (on the Gulf Coast, eighty-five
miles from Starke). A few weeks before, Singletary had suggested
to Joe that he get a motel room in Yankeetown and stay there
overnight, rather than make the long drive back to Starke. But Joe
had said no, he wanted to be home at night with his kids.

Knowing how Joe felt about his family, Singletary couldn't
understand why his wife suddenly wanted him gone—and he ignored Debbie's strange request.

•   •   •

It had been two weeks since Hearn had seen his son, so he drove
home to Columbia on Saturday, January 26, for the weekend. His

truck wasn't running too well, and he rented a car to make the 350-mile trip. On Sunday morning, as usual, he called Debbie Banister. But this would not be their usual phone call: on this morning, they would be plotting Joe Banister's death. With Singletary refusing to send him out of town, they had devised another plan: to kill Joe on his way home from work.

Mary Watson had an extension phone in her radio room, which was hooked up to a cassette tape recorder and a $24.95 telephone recording control device from Radio Shack. Hearn had installed the system in 1982, at the height of the ugly custody battle with his ex-wife, in order to record *her* calls (in South Carolina, it's legal to record phone calls without the other party's knowledge). Any time the phone was picked up, the recorder automatically came on. Mary still used it to record conversations with her in-laws or relatives, and would then play back the tapes for her children. She had a box full of old tapes in the radio-room closet.

Hearn had told Frank and Iris Sims about the system, and they were so impressed that he had installed an identical device on *their* phone. So when he called Debbie at 11:37 A.M. at the Sims trailer, it could have been "recorder wars," with simultaneous recordings being made on both ends of the line. Over time, however, a tape recorder becomes a part of the landscape, and sometimes a person forgets about it. John Wayne Hearn and Debbie Banister will be paying for their forgetfulness for the rest of their lives.

The recorded conversation begins with Hearn pressing Debbie to tell him that she loves him. "Why can't you tell me?" he demands.

"I can't," Debbie says.

"Why?"

"Someone is listening on the phone." Debbie's children, John and Amanda, were in the room with her.

Hearn keeps insisting. "Yeah, tell me you love me."

"Okay . . . what else?" she says, trying to change the subject.

"I'm waiting," he says, pouting.

Debbie snickers. "You are aggravating, you know that? Amanda is sitting right here too. Right behind me."

There's a long pause. "All right," Hearn says, giving in.

"Oh, no," Debbie says, teasing him. "I see that lip swelling out. Those eyes getting narrowed . . . Are you there?"

"Yeah, I'm here," he responds, still pouting.

"I do love you," she says quickly, with a playful laugh. "That is what pisses you off, isn't it?"

"Yeah, it's about time you said it."

Debbie starts talking about Amanda's health, but Hearn soon brings her back to their love affair. "Were you going to our place to call today?" he asks, referring to his Prairie View apartment.

"Yeah."

"Are you going to take Amanda and John with you?"

"Yeah."

"Okay. I don't think they'll say anything about the pictures in there, huh?" Hearn had photos of Debbie all over the apartment.

"Yeah—John said something about 'Big John' yesterday."

"To who?"

"Joe."

"Uh-oh," Hearn cries, with mock alarm. "What was said?"

"He looked at me because John was sitting in the backseat and said something about, you know, 'Meet Big John?' And his daddy looked at him and he said 'We know that you're Big John,' and he said, 'No, no!' That's what Joe thought he said, but that's not what he said. He said '*Big John.*' "

Hearn starts chuckling.

Debbie continues: "[Joe] thought he said, '*Me* Big John.' He said, 'No, no, Big John's at home.' "

Hearn lets out a delighted guffaw.

"I said, 'John, just sit down there and shut up.' I'm sitting here going, 'Okay, *I'm* driving, so if he hits me I'll put him in the ditch.' "

Hearn laughs again. "So what was said when you got home?"

"Nothing."

"Nothing at all?" he asks, disappointed.

"No, he was drinking when I got home."

"Oh."

Debbie chatters on for several seconds, but Hearn breaks in: "I love you." He says it in a whimper, like a three-year-old child. "I miss you," he adds in the same tone of voice.

Debbie doesn't respond, and changes the subject again. "Where is your mother?" she asks.

"In the other room. Yeah, I'm gonna work on the plans today." Hearn is referring to the floor plan for their log home, which they had purchased from Jim Barna Log Homes in Tennessee.

They talk about the house plans, and about when Hearn plans to return to Gainesville. Then Debbie asks her son if he wants to talk to "Big John."

"Who's he?" the boy replies, loud enough to be heard.

"He said 'Who's he?' " Debbie says, laughing.

"He better *not* be saying 'Who is he,' " Hearn responds, his feelings hurt.

Iris Sims is also in the room, and she makes a comment, which Debbie repeats. "Mama said Big John is Big John Stud. She is gonna call you BJS."

"Huh?"

"Mama said 'Big John Stud,' " she repeats.

"Oh."

"Is your face turning red?" she teases.

"No," Hearn says.

"You caused that yourself, you know."

"Good," he brags. "Well, you *like* it don't you? I mean, anybody can do it six times between the night and the morning, I mean, they ought to be called something." He breaks into a full-throated laugh, proud of himself.

"Shut up, this is on a recorder, you know?" Debbie says, reminding him about the Simses' tape recorder.

Hearn laughs even harder. "Oh! Oh, my God!" he cackles.

"Yeah, that's right," Debbie encourages him. "Mama said, 'Talk some more, talk some more—she's gonna go in there and listen.' "

"Oh, well," he says, with an "Aw, shucks" tone of voice.

" 'Oh, well' yourself."

"They are going to question you about what I just said, and you better tell them the truth," he says.

"Nooo," Debbie replies.

Hearn talks to Amanda for a few seconds. Then Debbie comes back on, and the conversation shifts to Joe Banister.

"Yeah, he got a transfer Monday and Tuesday to Yankeetown," Debbie says.

"Dang," Hearn mutters under his breath. "Where to?"

"Um . . . Yankeetown."

Hearn's voice drops several notches, becoming solemn and deadly serious. "Well, he'll be back home both them nights, won't he?"

"Uh-huh . . ."

"Well, that's okay." His voice is hard and cold—no longer that of a whimpering little boy but a tough Marine Corps weapons specialist preparing for a mission.

Debbie breaks the somber mood: "Mama said to tell you that Marlene says she wants a present."

"Huh?"

"She wants a birthday present early. Her birthday's in May, but she would like something earlier. . . . Marlene—"

"Yeah."

"Yeah, she says not real expensive—about six-one or six-two, about a hundred and eighty or ninety pounds." Debbie is referring to the Vietnam vets who have been answering Hearn's ad.

"Yeah, well, tell her the one—I'm sorry about. I, I just couldn't do nothing about that."

"I might have known."

"Well, I've got plenty of pictures coming in the mail, so we'll just pick one," he says, chuckling.

"Well, let me go," Debbie says. "I'll talk to you later, okay?"

"What time later?"

"This afternoon."

"I know this afternoon, but—"

"Don't pin me down to a time," Debbie interjects. " 'Cause all I'll do is not make it, and then you'll be mad."

"Well," Hearns says reluctantly, "you going to our house to call then?"

"Yeah, if I talk to you," she teases. "You could come back and see me. . . ."

"I can leave in the next ten minutes," he says quickly, accepting the challenge.

"No-oo," Debbie groans. "I'll see you later. I'll talk to you later, okay?"

"I love you," Hearn says, whining again.

"Bye."

"You be careful, okay?"

"I will. . . ."

"I love you," he repeats.

"Okay," Debbie says matter-of-factly.

There is a long pause while Hearn waits, hopefully, for her to respond. "You could at least say 'Me too,' Butthole," he says angrily. "They wouldn't know what you're talking about."

Debbie laughs again, toying with him.

"Makes me mad when you don't," he fumes.

There's a four-second pause, but Debbie still doesn't respond. Finally, she yells at her daughter. "Amanda, Amanda! She's chomping her teeth in my ears."

That reminds Hearn of something. "Oh!" he says, "Do you know that you grind your teeth together when you're asleep?"

"I do?" Debbie asks.

"Yes, you do—"

"I know."

"Yes, you do."

"I do," she admits.

"I know you do," he says, snickering.

"I know I do," she agrees, laughing at herself. "I grind my teeth. . . ."

"They just 'squeek, squeek, squeek.' And I *listen*." He laughs again.

"I do if I'm nervous."

"Well, what was you nervous about?"

"Probably 'cause you chase me all over the bed. . . ." She giggles.

"No," he protests. " 'Cause you should have been pretty damn relaxed."

"Yeah," she says, teasing. "I'll talk to you later."

"I love you," he says again.

"Bye."

"Talk to you later."

"Bye."

"Bye."

The conversation ended at 11:52 A.M.

But they weren't through for the day. At 6:16 P.M., Debbie called Hearn from his Prairie View apartment. This time, they were plotting Joe Banister's death. Their plan was for Hearn to follow Joe home from work and run him off the road.

" 'Cause he will not have a rider with him," Debbie says.

"When?" Hearn asks. "This week?"

"Uh-huh."

"Okay." Hearn's voice is heavy and resigned, half an octave lower than normal.

"Because the guy that was riding with him is going on vacation."

"Okay," he says. It is the voice of a frightened man trying to work up his nerve. Cops have an expression for it: "You can hear his asshole pucker." And you can almost hear Hearn's cinching up tight: "squeek, squeek, squeek."

Suddenly, Mary Watson walks into the room. "Is that Sweetpea?" she asks. It is her nickname for Debbie.

"Uh-huh," Hearn replies quickly. His voice returns to its normal pitch. Mama has caught him being bad, and he's playing innocent.

"While I was out did the phone ring?" Mary asks.

"Yeah," he says.

"Tell her hi," Mary says.

"Hi," Hearn says sweetly to Debbie. "She says hi."

"Hi," Mary calls out, from across the room.

"I was standing by when it rang and I picked it up," Hearn explains to her. After Mary leaves the radio room, Hearn waits a full five seconds, until she's out of earshot.

Debbie starts talking first, but most of what she says is garbled. ". . . if they investigate it . . ."

"Uh-huh," Hearn says. Now that his mother is gone, his voice has dropped back down.

"I don't care about him," Debbie says. "You do whatever you need to do, if you think it's necessary."

"Well, according to you, the sooner the better, right?"

"According to me?"

"Uh-huh."

"I been telling you that for a long time," she says.

"Well, you were the one that was scared about the time not

being right," Hearn says. (Marlene had allegedly been begging Debbie not to kill Joe so soon after Cecil Batie's death.) "Have you got over that fear?"

"No . . . Oh, yeah, I did."

"You sure?"

"Yeah, but not the other."

"Okay," Hearn says. He sounds very sober. He has made up his mind. "Okay . . . Well, I'll just tell you this, the way I got it figured it will be an accident."

"Good."

"I just got to follow him, check the road out, you know, maybe two mornings in a row."

"Okay."

Hearn coughs loudly, clearing his throat. "So he won't, he'll be leaving, uh . . . he'll be leaving early Monday and Tuesday, right?"

"Yeah."

"And he'll leave early—"

"He'll leave early, not as early, but he will leave [unintelligible]."

"Okay."

"See, like Monday he'll leave around five or five-thirty," she says.

"Yeah."

"But, um, the other days he ain't gonna leave work until . . . at least six. It's about an hour drive."

"Okay . . . well." Hearn takes a deep breath. "Uh, may have to bend my pickup up a little bit."

Debbie mumbles something unintelligible.

"Yeah," Hearn responds.

"There are several bridges," she volunteers.

"I know," he says. "That's the reason I'm gonna, you know, go to check this out. But I'd rather discuss it with you, you know? I know you said you didn't want to know, but hell, you know what's gonna happen—you might as well know anyway. Because I need to know approximately which way he goes and all this."

"Yeah . . ."

"Well, since I won't have the car [his rental car] all week, I'll, you know—I'm gonna do it and if I find some place where I may be able to do it, then . . ." Hearn clears his throat. " 'Cause I can't stand this anymore. I gotta have you." He sounds desperate, his voice breaking with emotion. "I gotta, I gotta be with you. I'm tired of being alone. I've got to have you and my kids."

With icy precision, Debbie closes the deal: "Friday night, put the icing on the cake—is that what you're telling me?" There is no hint of wavering in *her* voice. This is a business transaction.

"Yeah," Hearn replies dully.

• • •

They talked one more time that afternoon, after Debbie had called Message World to check Hearn's messages. It was a brief conversation, and at the end, Debbie tells him: "Let me go and I'll talk to you later."

"All right, I love you," he says.

She still won't tell him. "Sleep tight, John."

"Oh, I *can't*," he whimpers, "I *won't*."

"Why?"

"I'm too far from you," he moans. He sounds like a parent talking baby talk to an infant. "You know it? I'm just too damn . . . I just, I gotta be with you." Suddenly, he drops the baby talk. "And I don't mean you in Starke and me in Gainesville. I have *got* to be with you. So I hope you're gonna be able to go with that after everything goes down."

"That's what's best," Debbie says.

"What do you mean, it's best?"

She mumbles something about timing.

"I don't know about the week or two," Hearn replies. "Maybe a week."

Debbie's response is garbled, but apparently has to do with how they will explain Hearn's presence after the murder.

"I can be your long-lost cousin or something," he suggests, his voice breaking. He is about to cry. "Baby-sitter for Amanda and John while you're gone, taking care of everything."

"I got to go," Debbie says.

"I love you," he moans again. "You can't tell me?"

"Unh-uh."

"Oh—Amanda's sitting there in your lap? Well, I don't care,

let her know it too." He wants Debbie to shout it to the world. "You gonna call me when you get to work, or . . . ?"

"I'll call you when I get to work."

"I love you," he whimpers. "I'll talk to you later, baby. Hey, you be real careful going home. I don't want anything to happen to my two favorite ladies."

"You just think about the other night," Debbie says. She knows exactly how to drive him wild.

"Oh, God!" he groans. "Hey, *you* think about it too. You think about it *real real* hard."

Debbie tells him again that she has to go.

"Okay," he says.

"Bye," she says.

"Love you?" He puts a question mark at the end, still hoping she'll respond.

"Bye," she says flatly.

"Bye-bye," he says, and hangs up.

•   •   •

At almost the exact same time, in Bryan, Texas, Don Ballard was making a sales call at Bark-n-Holler. Since Bob Black had warned him that Sandra would be the one writing the check for any new policy, Ballard had come prepared. He had drawn up two charts: one showed the advantages, both in premium costs and death benefits, of converting the Blacks' existing whole life policies to a comparable term life policy; and the second chart showed three different insurance packages that they could choose from. Plan One had $75,000 coverage on Bob and $50,000 on Sandra; Plan Two had $100,000 on Bob and $75,000 on Sandra; and Plan Three had $125,000 on Bob and $75,000 on Sandra.

When Ballard got to Steep Hollow, Bob and Sandra invited him into the living room, where he made his presentation. As he had hoped, Sandra saw the benefits of converting to term life, so Ballard pulled out his second chart, with the three different plans.

Here, something very unexpected happened: Bob and Sandra decided to buy $100,000 coverage on Sandra, even though that was $25,000 more than the *maximum* Ballard had recommended for her. Don Ballard was no fool, however, and he didn't refuse Sandra's check when she wrote it.

He had them complete and sign an application for a $100,000 term life policy with Massachusetts Indemnity and Life Insurance Company (MILCO). Before leaving, he also had them sign cancellation letters on their three existing policies with Fidelity Union. Ballard said that the new MILCO policy would take effect immediately, although it could take three to four weeks for the company to process the paperwork. He promised to hold on to the cancellation letters until the MILCO policy arrived, to insure that their coverage never lapsed. What that meant, he explained, was that for the next three to four weeks, *all* of the policies would be in effect.

Don Ballard shook hands with Bob and Sandra, and left Steep Hollow with Sandra's check in his pocket. As Debbie Banister might have said, that "put the icing on the cake."

11

On Tuesday morning, January 29, John Wayne Hearn drove back to Gainesville in his rental car. Over the next four days, he and Debbie raced ahead with their plans for Joe Banister's death.

On Wednesday, Hearn picked up Debbie's car at Sun Bank, took it to a car wash, then drove it to his apartment. There, he opened the trunk and removed Joe Banister's AR-7 rifle, which, according to Hearn, Debbie had left there for him. For a man who had never had any interest in guns, he was building up a collection in a hurry.

The Charter Arms AR-7 Explorer Rifle is an extremely versatile weapon. This .22 caliber "survival rifle" weighs a mere two-and-a-half pounds, and its barrel, receiver, and magazine can be quickly disassembled and stored inside its waterproof stock. It's a semiautomatic that holds eight shells, although Paladin Press sells a book that shows how to convert it to fully automatic (which Hearn had already ordered).

With its compact size, the AR-7 was the perfect weapon for what Hearn was planning to do: if for some reason he couldn't run Joe Banister off the road, he was going to shoot him with his own gun.

Hearn hid the gun under the front seat of his truck and drove Debbie's car back to the bank. To show his appreciation, he stopped by Gainesville Florist and ordered a twenty-dollar bouquet of flowers—six yellow sweethearts—which were delivered to

Debbie at the bank that afternoon. She called him that evening—
from a pay phone at the Pantry Pride in Starke—to say thanks.

Hearn had planned Cecil Batie's murder on his own, but *this*
one was Debbie's, and she planned it out, down to the smallest
detail. Instead of running Joe off the road on his way home from
work, Hearn claims that Debbie substituted a bold new plan: Get
Joe over to a friend's house on Saturday night, get him drunk, and
Hearn could run him off the road on the way home.

Early Friday morning, she put the plan into action. At 6:52
A.M., after Joe had left for work, Debbie called Patsy Adkins, the
wife of Bobby Adkins, one of Joe's best friends. Joe and Bobby had
worked together since 1968, and often got together to go deer
hunting, to work on each other's trucks, or to just talk and drink
beer. The Adkinses lived in Palatka, forty-five miles south of Starke
on State Road 100. It was a two-lane country highway—the perfect
spot.

Debbie told Patsy Adkins that Joe had been depressed lately,
and she suggested that Bobby invite Joe to come over Saturday
morning and help him with whatever project he had going (Bobby
was often working on his truck or his boat). "Joe needs to get out of
the house," Debbie explained. She said that she wanted to go
shopping on Saturday morning for Joe's birthday present (although his birthday wasn't until May) but she would drive over
Saturday afternoon and they could all go out to eat that night.

"Sounds fine to me," Patsy replied. "We don't have any
plans."

"Why don't *you* call Joe and talk to him about it," Debbie said.
"He's more likely to do it if you ask him. And I'll call Bobby at work
and get him to talk to Joe too."

"Fine," Patsy said.

Two minutes after Debbie hung up with Patsy Adkins, Hearn
called her at home, and they talked for sixteen minutes. The plan
was working. When she got to work, Debbie called Bobby Adkins
and repeated the same story. "Maybe we could even go out dancing," she suggested. She told Bobby that she wanted to buy something special for Joe's birthday to cheer him up. "Could you find
out if he'd like an Uzi?" she asked.

Bobby agreed to call Joe and invite him over on Saturday.

Later Friday morning, Debbie had a visitor at the bank: John

Wayne Hearn. Debbie had made no attempt to hide their affair: she kept Hearn's flowers perched on top of her desk, and he dropped by nearly every day to see her. She had introduced him to her coworkers, and Hearn had even taken photographs of Debbie with two of them.

On Friday, Hearn hung out in her office for several hours, and was there when Joe Banister called around noon. Joe didn't mention anything to Debbie about Patsy or Bobby calling him, but he called her again that afternoon, after talking to both of them. Joe told Debbie that he was going over to Bobby's about ten o'clock Saturday morning, to help him install some electrical outriggers on his fishing boat. Debbie said that she would find a babysitter for the kids, and would come over to Palatka later, after cleaning house and doing some shopping in town.

Everything was falling into place.

That afternoon, after work, Debbie went to Hearn's apartment and they made love. He saw another bruise on her and pleaded with her to pack her things and leave Joe.

"I'm not losing everything I've worked so hard for," she replied. If she divorced Joe, she risked losing the house, the car, and $109,000 in insurance benefits.

Friday evening, Hearn drove State Road 100 between Palatka and Starke, looking for a suitable spot to run Joe off the road. Outside of Florahome, he found a deep ravine on the right hand side of the road. It was a hundred-foot wide, thirty-foot deep, rock-lined crevasse with no guard rail. He would do it there.

•   •   •

On Saturday morning, February 2, Joe Banister got up, showered, and left for Palatka about nine-fifteen, driving his 1984 Ford Escort, a blue two-door hatchback. He was dressed in old blue jeans and a work shirt (Debbie was going to take him some dressier clothes for dinner). Around his neck was a gold chain with a telephone medallion, and he had a gold bracelet on his left wrist. As usual, he was wearing his wedding ring, along with an ornate gold ring with four inset diamonds that Debbie had had custom-made for him at Marquise Jewelers.

At 9:25 A.M., immediately after he left, Debbie called Hearn collect (it was a long distance call from Starke to Gainesville), and he called her back direct. Instead of going shopping for Joe's birthday, Debbie was going to spend the afternoon with her lover.

At 10:28, she called the Adkinses to make sure that Joe had arrived safely, and said that she wouldn't be there until at least five o'clock. Around eleven, she left for Gainesville. She dropped off her kids at Marlene's trailer, and arrived at Hearn's apartment around noon. They ran some errands, ordered take-out food from the In-n-Out drive-in, and carried it back to Hearn's apartment to eat.

They spent the afternoon making love—it was the last time they would have to be secretive about it—and finalizing their plans. According to Hearn, he was supposed to follow Debbie to Palatka, wait near the Adkinses' house until they all returned from dinner, then follow Joe and run him off the road into the Florahome ravine.

Around 4:30, Debbie took a shower, and Hearn went outside and got the AR-7 out of his pickup truck. When she came out, the rifle was lying on the kitchen table. "What's that for?" she asked.

"If something goes wrong, I'll have to shoot him," he replied.

"I want it to be as painless as possible," she said, according to Hearn.

At 4:43 P.M., she called the Adkinses and asked Patsy if they were waiting for her. No, Patsy replied, Bobby and Joe were out on the river. Debbie said that she was just leaving, and should be in Palatka around six o'clock. They left shortly afterward: with Debbie in the lead, Hearn following in his pickup, and the AR-7 under the front seat.

•   •   •

Joe Banister and Bobby Adkins spent the morning replacing a water hose on Patsy's car, and then installed the outriggers on Bobby's twenty-one-foot Chris-Craft, which he used for offshore grouper fishing. Joe seemed moody and listless, as if he had something on his mind. Bobby Adkins, a boisterous, back-slapping type, tried to cheer him up, but couldn't. Bobby had the feeling that something was really eating at Joe.

Whenever they got together, Bobby and Joe always had a few beers. It was part of their routine. Bobby's friends even teased him that his hand was shaped like a beer can, because he always seemed to be holding one. But Joe was in such a foul mood on Saturday morning that he didn't want to drink. He didn't have his first Budweiser until 2:00 P.M., and only drank three or four cans the entire day—which was few enough for Bobby to rib him about it.

"I've given up beer and gone to straight whiskey," Joe explained dourly.

Around 3:00 P.M., Bobby suggested that they take his boat out on the St. Johns River, five miles away. So Joe, Bobby, Bobby's son, and son-in-law all went for a boat ride. Joe wasn't any more talkative on the river. In fact, he laid down under the bow, to get out of the wind, and stayed there the whole trip.

Something really seemed to be bothering him. Something that he *wanted* to talk about, but didn't quite know how. He talked a little bit about how much he loved his kids, and hinted that his marriage wasn't going smoothly—but Bobby felt that there was something else he wanted to say.

• • •

Bobby Adkins wasn't the first person to notice it. The previous Sunday, the Banister family had gathered at Ruth and Ceree's house for their usual Sunday dinner. Debbie was off somewhere running around with the kids, so Joe was there by himself. He was always quiet, but he was even quieter than usual that day. He sat on the living room couch and hardly said a word.

Lana, his sister, got out her camera and started taking pictures. She tried to get Joe to smile, but he wouldn't. So she took the picture anyway: Joe is slouched on the couch, staring morosely into the camera, looking very sad.

Afterward, he said, "You know, Lana, you're really a good sister."

It was unusual for Joe to pass out compliments, even when he was in a *good* mood. Lana thought that he was teasing her, and made a smart-aleck reply.

"No, I'm serious," he said, "I know if anything ever happened to me, you'd take good care of my kids."

Lana still thought he was kidding. "No, I wouldn't," she retorted, "I'd put them out on the street."

"No, I mean it," he said.

"Of course I'd take care of your kids," she said.

Joe seemed so out of character that Lana had an eerie feeling something was weighing on him. Was there something going on at home, she wondered.

•   •   •

Gainesville is not that big a town. It's hard to hide a love affair, even if a person tries to be discreet. People get around. They see things. They tell their friends. The word travels fast. The phone company office is right downtown. So is Sun Bank. Employees of both went to lunch at the same time.

Had Joe found out about Debbie's affair? Or had he found out about her involvement in Cecil Batie's murder? If he *had,* he was the kind of man who might have turned her in himself.

•   •   •

Hearn pulled in beside Debbie's car in the parking lot of the Jiffy Store at state roads 19 and 20, a major intersection three miles west of Palatka. He got out, walked over to her car, and leaned down to talk.

"I'm not sure exactly where their house is," she said, "but it's somewhere off 19. I gotta go look." She told him to wait for her at the Jiffy Store, and she would meet him there after they returned from dinner. Joe would have to go past the store on his way home.

But after she left, Hearn decided to follow her so that he would know where the Adkinses' house was located. He tailed her down State Road 19 for three or four miles, but Debbie couldn't find the house. Finally, she stopped at a Handy Way convenience store, and phoned the Adkinses.

Hearn pulled into the parking lot and asked her what was wrong.

"Get the hell out of here," Debbie cried. "Joe is on the way up here to meet me."

Hearn drove back to the Jiffy Store. Across the street was a Texaco gas station, which was closed for the night. It was set back off the highway, with a clear view of the Jiffy Store and State Road 19. Hearn backed his truck into the driveway—where it would be inconspicuous—and waited.

He knew he had two or three hours to kill. Patsy Adkins had told Debbie that she had made reservations at Corky Bell's seafood restaurant in Green Cove Springs, thirty-five miles away. To drive there, have a few drinks, eat a leisurely dinner, and drive back would take about three hours. Hearn stretched out in the front seat of his truck. He was feeling none of the anxiety that he had felt about killing Cecil Batie. This one was easy to rationalize: He wanted Debbie, Debbie said that Joe was beating her, and she wouldn't divorce him. What other choice was there?

In Vietnam, Hearn had learned to catch little catnaps in the bush—to just flop down in the jungle and forget about the horror that awaited him. He leaned his head against the window, closed his eyes, and quickly fell asleep.

• • •

Debbie Banister was especially loving to Joe that night. The Banisters and Adkinses rode together in Debbie's car to Green Cove Springs—with Debbie driving, Patsy up front with her, and Joe and Bobby sitting in the backseat, sharing a beer.

They arrived at Corky Bell's about 7:45 P.M. and ordered dinner. Debbie seemed very concerned about Joe having a good time and smothered him with affection. She even fed him lobster off her plate. *Debbie's really watching out for him,* Patsy thought to herself. *Things must be good between them.*

Joe drank two more beers with his dinner. In fact, everyone was drinking beer—except Debbie, who ordered iced tea.

They left the restaurant about 9:15. Joe seemed more relaxed than he had been all day, after a wonderful meal with his wife and his good friends. When they reached Palatka, Debbie turned on State Road 20, drove three miles to State Road 19, and turned left at the Jiffy Store. They arrived back at the Adkinses' house at 10:00 P.M.

• • •

Hearn recognized Debbie's car when it passed. He saw a paper bunny rabbit, which Amanda had made at school, hanging from the rear-view mirror. Instead of waiting at the Jiffy Store as he was supposed to, he pulled out behind her car, following at a safe distance. He tailed them to the Adkinses' house—a contemporary log home like the one that he and Debbie were planning to build—

located at the end of a dirt road. Hearn cut his headlights, parked on the side of the road, just beyond the house, and waited.

Debbie and Joe and the Adkinses went inside. Joe got a drink of water, and Debbie went to the bathroom. Then they all sat on the front porch for a few minutes. Joe was yawning, and looked very tired.

"Are you all right?" Debbie asked worriedly.

"I'm just tired," Joe replied.

Debbie seemed *very* concerned about his condition to drive. It was as if she wanted to make sure that he didn't have an accident on the way home. "If you want to spend the night here, I'll go get the kids and go on home," she said.

Joe brushed off the suggestion. "I'm fine," he said.

This was a man who commuted every day to Yankeetown—eighty-five miles each way—to sleep in his own bed at night. Joe had drunk seven or eight beers since two o'clock, but he was used to drinking much more than that and not showing the effects. But Debbie wasn't convinced. She asked Bobby Adkins what he had given Joe to dilate his eyes.

"I don't know, maybe alcohol will do that do you," he replied, thinking she was joking. Bobby didn't think that Joe showed any signs of being too impaired to drive.

Finally, around 10:30 P.M., Joe and Debbie left, in separate cars. Debbie went first, with Joe right behind her—and John Wayne Hearn following behind him. When they turned left onto State Road 19, Hearn pulled out around Joe, passed him, and raced to catch up with Debbie. When he reached the Jiffy Store, she was already inside, buying a thirty-nine-cent Icee.

"Are you sure you want to go through with this?" he asked.

"You better hurry up or you'll miss him," she replied coldly, according to Hearn. "He's right behind me."

Hearn ran back to his truck and took off in pursuit of Joe, who had already passed the store. Hearn got caught at a traffic light, and didn't catch up to Joe until they reached State Road 100, the road to Starke.

Then it was just the two of them, with forty miles of two-lane road. Joe Banister was in an underpowered four-cylinder Ford Escort, while Hearn was in a full-sized GMC pickup with a 350-cubic-inch V-8. He could have overtaken Joe at any time, but he was waiting for the ravine at Florahome, sixteen miles away. It would be easy: Just pull in front of him and force him off the road; Joe would nose-dive straight into the ravine. "I may have to bend my pickup up a little," Hearn had told Debbie on the phone.

As usual, Joe Banister was driving fifty-five miles per hour. Everybody else in the world might speed, but good old Joe drove the speed limit. Hearn followed several car lengths behind him, resolute and determined, a hunter stalking his prey.

Finally, they reached Florahome, a hole in the road with no traffic light. Hearn edged closer, waiting to make his move. Joe had slowed to forty-five miles per hour. *He's drunk,* Hearn thought.

Ahead, the ravine came into view, at the bottom of a small hill. As they started down it, Hearn stomped the accelerator, and the big four-barrel carburetor kicked in. The truck roared up behind the Escort, right on its tail, and Hearn jerked the truck into the passing lane.

Suddenly, coming over the hill from the other direction—a set of headlights! *Jesus Christ, it was a car!* The vehicle was bearing down on him. Frantically, Hearn glanced at the ravine at the bottom of the hill. Was there still time? No way—it would be suicide. He let off the accelerator, pumped the brakes, and eased back into the right lane.

A blast of wind from the other car buffeted him as it passed. Joe Banister was already beyond the ravine, heading up the hill. "Damn!" Hearn yelled angrily. The ravine was the only spot between Palatka and Starke that would work. From there on, the road was flat and open. He would have to use his fallback plan. It was the only way.

Hearn reached under the front seat and pulled out the AR-7. With one hand, he pried the butt cap off the end of the stock and pulled out the barrel, the receiver, and the magazine. He slipped the receiver into its slot in the stock and tightened the wing nut, then fit the barrel into the receiver, and tightened the barrel nut finger-tight. That was all there was to it. For a man who had been a professional truck driver for fourteen years, logging 100,000 miles a year, steering an 8,000-pound semi with one hand, this was a snap.

He pulled back the charging handle to cock the gun, and it was ready. The magazine was loaded with eight .22-caliber Long

Rifle cartridges, which had been in the gun when he took it. He was going to shoot Joe with his own gun, and his own bullets.

First, though, he had to wait for the right opportunity. On a Saturday night there was a steady trickle of cars on State Road 100. Equally frustrating, there was a series of small towns, one right after the other: Grandin, Putnam Hill, Lake Geneva, and Keystone Heights. The towns were only two or three miles apart, and every time the traffic cleared, another town loomed up ahead.

Hearn was starting to get antsy. This had turned into a marathon hunt. A long-distance stalking. Almost forty-five minutes had passed since they had left the Adkinses' house, and Joe Banister was still poking along at fifty-five mph. They passed through Theressa, another little pissant community, and Hearn dropped farther behind—a quarter of a mile behind the Escort—and pulled out his road atlas. He peered at it in the murky glare of the truck's dome light, trying to make it out. From Theressa, it looked to be only seven or eight more miles to Starke. The closer he got, the worse the traffic would become. He had to do it soon.

Suddenly, when he looked back up, Joe Banister was gone! The red taillights of the Escort had disappeared! Panicked, Hearn looked in the rear-view mirror. About two hundred feet behind him, he saw a road cutting off to the east, barely visible in the streetlight of a small country store. Hearn had passed it without even noticing. Joe must have turned there!

Hearn whipped the truck around and sped back toward the intersection. There was a sign for County Road 18—so obscure that it wasn't even labeled on his atlas. Hearn turned right and saw the Escort's taillights flickering ahead of him, a half-mile away. He floored the accelerator and raced after them. The road was barely eighteen feet wide, an old farm-to-market road in the middle of nowhere. There were a few scattered farmhouses, but no streetlights, no barricades, and no traffic.

He was gaining quickly on the Escort, as the big V-8 gobbled up the asphalt. For the first time, the reality of what he was doing broke through the numbness. *You don't have to do this,* he thought. But he was too far down the road to turn back now. *No, it's gotta be done this way,* he told himself. *It's gotta be done.*

He was almost on top of Joe Banister. He reached across and rolled down the passenger-side window, which formed a perfect firing stock. He picked up the AR-7 off the seat and laid the barrel in the cradle of the window.

There were no cars coming. The road was straight for the next quarter of a mile. Up ahead was a small bridge over a ditch. Hearn pulled out into the left-hand lane. He was driving with his left hand, holding the gun with his right. Joe Banister was still poking along at forty-five miles an hour. Hearn could see him hunched over the steering wheel, plodding on toward home. He pulled even with the Escort. The end of the AR-7's barrel was only three feet from Joe Banister's head, on a direct line. Hearn pulled the trigger once, then fired again. Joe Banister never looked up.

Hearn kept driving. In the rear-view mirror he saw the Escort swerve off the road and into a ditch, then lurch back across the road and into a ditch on the other side. He slowed and looked back. The car wasn't moving. Hearn knew that he had hit Joe at least once—but was he dead? The only way to be sure was to go back and check; maybe put another bullet in his head to finish him off. Should he go back, or keep driving? He wasn't sure.

12

DEBRA MOWRY, a thirty-two-year-old Melrose woman, had been visiting her parents in Hampton, a tiny community on County Road 18. She left their house about 11:30 P.M. to drive home. It was a chilly night, and Mowry was wearing a sweater to ward off the cold. A misty rain was falling and there was patchy fog along 18.

About a mile before the intersection of State Road 100, she saw a car with its headlights on straddling a ditch on the right-hand side of the road. Mowry drove on by, but then turned around, worried that someone might need help. She parked on the shoulder of the road and walked up to the passenger side of the car. The motor was still running. She saw a blue bundle lying in the passenger seat. It looked like a sleeping bag or a bag of laundry.

Mowry walked up and down the road, calling out in case anyone needed help, until she got spooked and left. She stopped at a pay phone at Edward's grocery, on the corner of State Road 100, and told the operator that she needed to report an accident. The operator mistakenly dialed the Clay County Sheriff's Department (Mowry was actually in adjoining Bradford County), and the call was answered at 11:42 P.M. by Sally McCoy, the graveyard shift dispatcher, who recorded the conversation.

"Clay County sheriff's office, McCoy."

"Hi, I'm just off of Highway 100, where State Road 18 intersects," Mowry says.

"Yes, ma'am?"

"And I just passed a car that's gone off the road and it's embedded in the ditch. It's still running, the lights are on. . . ."

"And it's on 100?"

"No, it's on 18. I just turned off of 18 onto 100."

McCoy realizes that Mowry is in Bradford County, and says that she'll relay the call. "Any description?" she asks.

"It looks like a little Pinto or Chevette or something like that," Mowry says. "It's so dark I couldn't tell, but it's going toward Hampton, it's off on the west. . . . I went back to see if I could help, and there's nobody in the car. . . ."

"Okay, but the lights are on and the motor's running?"

"The lights are on and the motor's running."

"Okay, hold on just a moment. . . ." McCoy radioed the Bradford County Sheriff's Department and relayed the information, and the Bradford County dispatcher said they would check it out.

•   •   •

Deputy David Aderholt arrived on the scene at 11:52 P.M. Aderholt was in his mid-twenties, with a baby face that made him look even younger. He had only been working for the sheriff's department for a year and a half. That night, he had a friend riding with him: Don York, a trained emergency medical technician.

Aderholt and York walked up to the blue Ford Escort. The ditch that it was straddling was half filled with water. The window on the driver's side was partially broken out, and jagged pieces of glass still hung in the window frame. Aderholt looked inside and saw the driver slumped across the gearshift console, with his head hanging down on the floor of the passenger side. He hurried back to his squad car, radioed for an ambulance and the Florida Highway Patrol (FHP), then returned to the Escort.

Aderholt opened the passenger door—which was closest to the driver's head—and checked the victim for a pulse. He couldn't detect one, but York thought that he felt a faint one. Two other deputies had arrived by then, and the four men pulled the victim out of the car. They laid him on the ground, on top of a raincoat, and began cardiopulmonary resuscitation. There was blood coming from his nose and left ear, and blood matted on the back of his head.

At 12:06 A.M., the Bradford County rescue unit arrived and took over CPR, but it was futile. At 12:17, paramedic Bill O'Neal pronounced the victim dead.

•   •   •

John Wayne Hearn was almost back to Gainesville when he passed Debbie Banister's car going the other way, toward Starke. He turned around and hurried to catch up with her. Debbie was driving fast, as always. In fact, a Florida highway patrolman had already stopped her for speeding that night on her way home from Palatka.

Hearn finally caught up with her and flagged her over. He walked up to her car, and saw Amanda and John asleep in the backseat. "It's done," he said soberly. "It's over with."

"I don't want to know a goddamn thing about it," Debbie said, according to Hearn. She told him about being stopped by the trooper and said that she had to get home.

When Hearn got back to his apartment at 12:15, the first thing he did was call Debbie. He usually only called her at home in the morning, when he knew Joe Banister would be gone, but he no longer needed to worry about that. "Are you all right?" he asked.

"Yeah, I just walked in," Debbie replied. "I've got to get the kids out of the car and put them to bed."

The conversation lasted one minute.

•   •   •

Being stopped by the trooper had given Debbie a partial alibi, but not an airtight one. At 12:21 A.M., she called the Adkinses' house, waking them up. She told Bobby that Joe hadn't arrived home yet and asked if he had turned around and gone back to their house. Bobby said no, but told her that if Joe didn't arrive in the next thirty minutes to call him back and he would go look for him.

Debbie then called the Florida Highway Patrol and told the dispatcher that she was worried because her husband wasn't home. "I'm not an irate wife complaining about my husband being out partying," she explained. The dispatcher said that she would call around and see if there had been any accidents.

What else could a concerned wife do? She had called the Adkinses, she had called the highway patrol . . . well, she could talk to her lover. At 12:31 A.M., Hearn called her again, and they talked this time for six minutes.

•   •   •

It was always a luxury for Don Denton to have a free Saturday night at home. As chief investigator for the Bradford County Sheriff's Department, Denton was on call twenty-four hours a day, seven days a week, and was automatically notified of every major felony in the county.

Even if he didn't get called by the sheriff's department, Denton still had to work on Saturday nights—for his *second* job as a Methodist minister. It might seem like an odd combination—cop and preacher—but not in Bradford County; Denton was one of *three* preachers employed by the sheriff's department.

Denton had felt the call to preach long before he became a cop. The Ohio native had moved to Gainesville in 1968, after a seven-year stint in the Navy, and had worked his way through UF as a "student pastor." Many of the hundred-plus Methodist congregations in the Gainesville district are small rural congregations— legacies of the old Methodist circuit riders—that depend on local preachers who, like Denton, are licensed but not ordained.

Denton got a job at the Bradford County jail through a member of his church, a local deputy sheriff, and gradually worked his way up: from deputy to chief investigator (he was actually the *only* investigator on the nine-person force), and eventually, to director of operations.

Along the way, he had never stopped preaching. In fact, he looks a lot more like a preacher than a cop: portly, balding, soft-spoken, with a gentle laugh and a fatherly manner.

Denton had spent this Saturday evening, like every other one that he was at home, fine-tuning his Sunday sermon. But after he received the dispatch call, he was at County Road 18 within minutes.

He walked over to look at the victim, still stretched out on the ground, who had been identified as John Joseph Banister, age forty-one, from Starke. None of the officers knew him, so Denton figured that he had to be a newcomer to town. Starke was small enough so that someone would have known him otherwise. Denton noticed two jagged cuts on the back of his head, near the base of his skull, about three inches apart. They did not appear to be bullet wounds; they looked more like cuts from the broken glass.

Denton walked over to talk to Trooper Donald Roberts of the Florida Highway Patrol, a veteran traffic-homicide investigator, who was already taking photographs, measuring tire marks, and diagramming the path the Escort had taken. From the broken glass on the highway and the tire tracks, it was apparent that the car had left the road approximately twenty feet after the window had shattered, then crossed a shallow ditch, and headed up the embankment toward the tree line. It had turned before it got to the trees, traveled 385 feet along the ditch, parallel to the road. At one point, there was a large clump of myrtle bushes directly in its path, but the car had veered around it—as if still being controlled by the driver—then struck the embankment, recrossed the highway, and ended up in the ditch on the other side. There were no indications of excessive speed, drunk driving, or loss of control; and the *only* damage to the car, other than the broken window, was a slight buckle of the left-front fender, where the car had struck the ditch embankment.

To Denton, the physical evidence was puzzling. The driver's window had obviously been shattered *before* the car had left the road, but by what? The most likely answer was Banister's head, which would explain the two jagged cuts on the back of it. But what had caused *that*? Had he suffered a heart attack and somehow thrown himself against the window? And if it wasn't a heart attack, what *had* killed him? The collision with the ditch embankment seemed too minor to have been fatal.

It was almost two o'clock Sunday morning. Denton knew that he couldn't get an autopsy until Monday. After consulting with Roberts, he decided to have the Escort towed to the Bradford County jail, where it would remain sealed until the autopsy. Until they knew for certain what had killed Joe Banister, the highway patrol would work the case like a traffic accident.

Don Denton watched as the EMT's loaded Banister's body into the ambulance and left for the morgue, then stood by while a tow truck hauled the Escort out of the muddy ditch. In the luggage compartment of the hatchback were an AM/FM radio, a Western

Electric toolbox, a fluorescent droplight, a racquet-ball racquet, and a November, 1984, issue of *Soldier of Fortune* magazine.

•   •   •

Sergeant Winston Barber arrived at the Banister home at 1:20 A.M. As a FHP supervisor, he had drawn the distasteful job of informing the victim's wife that her husband was dead. It was a ceremony that Barber had performed nearly ninety times in his twenty-three years on the patrol, and he knew how to do it quickly and professionally.

First, Barber woke up Banister's next-door neighbors—the Bennetts and the Coles—and asked them to accompany him when he informed the widow. Debbie Banister answered the door in her nightgown. Barber introduced himself and asked if he could come in. He told Debbie to sit down, then informed her that her husband had been involved in a traffic accident and had not survived.

Debbie rubbed her eyes and began crying softly—although she didn't start sobbing—and asked Barber what had happened. He explained that it had been a single-car collision on County Road 18, and that her husband's car had left the road and hit a ditch embankment. Because of unanswered questions at the scene, it was unclear whether the accident itself had been the cause of death. Barber said that the body had been removed to the medical examiner's office in Gainesville for an autopsy.

Suddenly, Debbie's demeanor changed. She reacted more strongly to Barber's announcement about the autopsy than she had to the death itself. "No, he'll be cut up!" she cried hysterically.

Barber tried to reassure her, but Debbie was inconsolable. He made sure that her neighbors were going to stay with her, and made a quick exit. After twenty-three years and nearly ninety such visits, it was the *first* time that Winston Barber had ever encountered that kind of reaction to an autopsy from a grieving widow.

•   •   •

As with any death, there were a lot of phone calls to make. At 1:26 A.M. David Bennett called the Adkinses from Debbie's house and told them that Joe was dead. Then Debbie called Lana Halbrook, Joe's sister, and informed her. The Bennetts drove Debbie into Gainesville to break the news to Ruth and Ceree Banister. She spent an hour and a half with her shocked in-laws, then the Bennetts drove her back home and said good night.

With the official calls out of the way, Debbie had calls of her own to make. At 4:30 A.M. she called John Wayne Hearn and told him that the police had been there and that Joe had been killed in a traffic accident. Debbie cried on and off throughout the thirteen-minute conversation, playing the role of the grieving widow to the hilt. Hearn couldn't understand why she was pulling that act with *him*. For the first time, he let himself think the unthinkable: *Am I being set up?* But no, he was too much in love to believe it.

They still weren't through with their phone calls: at 7:46 A.M. Hearn called Debbie again, and they talked for four minutes; then she called him at 8:25 for another eleven minutes; and he called her one last time at 10:39 for another three minutes. It was their *sixth* phone conversation in the ten and a half hours immediately following Joe Banister's death. If Starke and Gainesville had been a few miles closer, those would have been local calls. They would have never shown up on their phone bills, and no one would have ever known.

•   •   •

With Joe Banister finally out of the way, John Wayne Hearn was anxious to get on with his new life. On Monday, February 4, one day after the murder, he filed divorce papers on Elaine Hearn. Debbie Banister had sent him to *her* attorney, Val Bates, to have the papers drawn up, and Hearn lied and claimed to have been a Florida resident for more than six months. Soon, there would be nothing standing in their way.

That same morning, he accompanied Debbie, Marlene, and her best friend Pat Bouchette to make Joe's funeral arrangements. Debbie asked Bouchette to come along because she had recently made some funeral arrangements herself, and Frank Sims was still too weak to go.

Debbie's eyes were so red and blistered from crying that Hearn had to drive. They went to Copelands Funeral Home, where Debbie and Bouchette scheduled Joe's funeral for Thursday at 10 A.M.

On the way home, Debbie insisted on stopping at Marquise Jewelers, to tell the owner, Mel Tussinger, that Joe had been killed.

Debbie had been a customer of Tussinger's since she was in high school, when she had opened a "teen account." Tussinger had sold her bridal sets when she married Billy Thigpen *and* Joe Banister, and had sold her lots of other jewelry, including the custom ring that Joe Banister always wore. In fact, Tussinger knew the whole Sims family: Marlene, Frank, and Iris all shopped there. So did Joe Banister, who had bought a set of earrings and a charm for Debbie at Christmas.

Tussinger offered his condolences to Debbie and promised to come to the funeral. Still, he was surprised that Debbie had made a special stop to tell him about Joe. She was a long-time customer but not a friend. "She must really want everyone to know," he thought after she left.

Afterward, they stopped for lunch at Leonardo's Pizza, near the UF campus. For weeks, Pat Bouchette had been hearing from Marlene about Debbie's new boyfriend and had met Hearn once, briefly, at Marlene's trailer. Marlene had relayed lots of juicy gossip about Hearn: he worked undercover for the government, did jobs "across the pond," and had different sets of identification. But this was Bouchette's first chance to really talk to him; so she questioned him about his background.

"I've got a degree in aeronautical engineering," he bragged. "That's airplanes, you know."

Hearn was doing his normal embellishing act, to impress someone he didn't know. Bouchette was nonplussed; she thought he was a suspicious character and decided to check him out.

• • •

On Monday afternoon the medical examiner's office in Gainesville called Don Denton and told him that Joe Banister had died from a gunshot wound to the head. Dr. William Hamilton had removed a mushroom-shaped, small-caliber bullet from the right cerebral hemisphere of his brain.

There were actually *two* gunshot wounds: the jagged cuts on the back of his head were the entry and exit holes of one bullet, which had apparently passed through the driver's window (which explained the ragged entry hole) and grazed the back of the head, just below the surface, causing only superficial damage; the other wound was caused by a penetrating shot above the left ear that went straight through both cerebral hemispheres—the major halves of the brain—and killed him. The second wound was only visible after Hamilton had shaved the hair in that area.

Hamilton concluded that the grazing shot would have felt like being hit over the head with a Coke bottle or slipping on a banana peel and hitting your head. There would have been pain, shock, surprise, and a temporary stunning. The penetrating wound would have produced immediate unconsciousness and within a few minutes, death. It was possible that Joe Banister could have still controlled his car after the first shot—to steer around the myrtle bushes, for instance—but not after the second.

The autopsy also revealed that Joe's blood-alcohol level was .14 percent at the time of his death, above Florida's legal limit of .10 percent. Ironically, Hamilton also found that he was suffering from severe arteriosclerosis: there was a ninety-five-percent blockage of the left coronary artery, and sixty- to seventy-percent blockages in several other major arteries. Without surgery, Joe Banister would have probably died from a heart attack within six months.

Suddenly, Don Denton had a murder on his hands.

That afternoon, he met with Trooper Roberts, David Aderholt, and Wiley Clark, an investigator for the state attorney's office in Starke. In Florida counties, the local sheriff's department is responsible for *investigating* criminal cases, but the state attorney *prosecutes* them. Particularly in small counties like Bradford, there is a close working relationship between the two.

Denton and Clark had always worked together on major cases since Clark had first arrived in Starke in December, 1976. Clark brought a wealth of big-time investigative experience to a small-town office: He had been a Gainesville cop, a crime-scene investigator, a member of a regional narcotics task force, and an investigator for a statewide organized-crime unit. Clark was used to hopping on a plane in the morning and flying to Miami to track a lead, flying to Atlanta that afternoon to meet with the FBI, and returning home the same day. He knew how to coordinate investigations with other counties, other states, and the FBI.

Wiley Clark is a smart, savvy, hard-nosed cop. After sixteen years of dealing with the criminal mind—from lowlifes on the street to mafioso kingpins—he has a cynicism about human nature. Medium height, slightly built, in his mid-forties, he walks with the

catlike gait of a football scatback. He is an immaculate dresser—
always outfitted stylishly in sport coat, button-down shirt, and club
tie—as befits his role as the president of the Starke Rotary Club.
Strapped just above his ankle, discreetly hidden by his pant leg, is a
.38 revolver—a quick reminder that this Rotary president is, above
all, a cop.

Denton and Clark were starting from scratch: they knew nothing about Joe Banister except that he had a wife and two kids and a
small-caliber bullet in his head. Their first move was to call the
Florida Department of Law Enforcement (FDLE) in Jacksonville
and request that its portable crime lab be sent to Starke to check
out the Escort and the crime scene.

Then, sitting in Denton's office in the Bradford County
Courthouse, they speculated about what might have happened out
on County Road 18 late Saturday night. With what little evidence
they had so far, all they could come up with were wild possibilities:
the surrounding woods were a popular hunting area, and there was
a one-in-a-million chance that Banister had been killed by a stray
bullet; there had been several random shootings on Interstate 75
in the past year, and Banister could have been the latest victim;
finally, a University of Florida fraternity had been having a party at
a nearby house, and perhaps the frat boys had gotten out of control.

They were grasping at straws, and they knew it. That afternoon, Denton and Joe Uebelher, a FDLE agent, drove to the medical examiner's office in Gainesville to retrieve the bullet that had
been removed from Joe Banister's brain. It appeared to be a .22-
caliber, although they wouldn't know for sure until it was tested at
the FDLE Laboratory.*

Don Denton decided to pay a call on Joe Banister's widow.
Even for a Methodist minister, it was a delicate situation: to tell a
distraught young widow, still in shock over losing her husband,
that he had, in fact, been murdered. Denton planned to stay no
more than five or ten minutes—just long enough to explain the
autopsy results, find out what Joe Banister had done on Saturday,

---

* The FDLE lab confirmed that it was a .22 bullet. Also, the FDLE portable crime
lab discovered a second .22 bullet near the rear window of Joe Banister's car. It
was badly deformed—consistent with a bullet that had shattered the driver's
window and passed through the back of Joe's head.

and if anyone had a grudge against him. Later, at a less intrusive time, he would schedule a longer interview.

Denton made a few phone calls, located Debbie at Ruth and Ceree Banister's house, and asked if he could come see her. He and Uebelher arrived at the Banisters' home at 4:20 P.M. The house was crowded with friends and kinfolks who had gathered there, in the Southern tradition, to be with Ruth and Ceree. Denton asked Debbie if they could talk to her in private. She led them into Ruth's bedroom and closed the door. Debbie sat down on one side of the bed and Denton and Uebelher sat on the other.

Denton told her about the autopsy results, and Debbie began to cry softly—again, she didn't sob and didn't lose her composure. When she calmed down, Denton asked her if Joe had owned any guns, and Debbie quickly rattled them off: a Mini-14 rifle, a .45 revolver, and a .22 pistol, which she often carried herself. Believing that the fatal bullet was a .22, Denton made a note to return to that point later.

First, though, he asked Debbie what Joe had done on Saturday. "Well, let me start on Friday morning," she said, and proceeded to recount, in great detail, how she had called Patsy and Bobby Adkins and arranged the Saturday get-together in Palatka. She ran through the whole weekend—providing an almost hour-by-hour breakdown—and had all the times down pat. She was particularly detailed about *her* schedule: her various phone calls to the Adkinses, getting stopped by the trooper on her way home, picking up her kids from Marlene's at 11:30, and calling the highway patrol.

The longer Debbie rattled on, the more puzzled Don Denton became. He had dealt with many grieving widows, and most had trouble remembering *any* details in the wake of such a tragedy. As Debbie kept talking, Denton's five- or ten-minute interview stretched into thirty minutes, an hour, an hour and a half. Periodically, as if on cue, she would tear up for a few moments, and then, with stoic resolve, regain her composure.

Since she didn't mind talking, Denton kept asking questions. Debbie jabbered on about Joe's two ex-wives, his friends, his drinking habits. She said that they had a wonderful relationship, that they got along well and hadn't had any arguments, and that although Joe had a temper, he "kept it within himself." Denton asked if he had ever hit her, and Debbie said no, that she had told him she would shoot him if he ever did. He had no enemies, and she could think of no one who would want him dead. In passing, she also mentioned that about a month earlier (which would have been right after Cecil Batie's death) she had asked Joe to check on his life insurance policies to make sure that neither of his ex-wives were still listed as his beneficiary.

Finally, Denton brought her back to Joe's guns. Again, Debbie mentioned the .22 pistol, the .45, and the Mini-14, then remembered that Joe also owned another "old gun" of some kind. She apologized for not knowing much about weapons, but described it as having a "little wheel" that turned and the shells were "in the little wheel." She never mentioned Joe's AR-7.

Denton pressed her about the .22—where was it kept, was she sure it was still there, and when was the last time she had seen it? Debbie said that she kept it in a closet and was sure it was still there, she had just seen it that morning. Denton asked her to check again and call him back.

He was long past ready to leave, but Debbie had some questions of her own: she wanted to know more details about the autopsy. It was a miraculous recovery for a woman who had become hysterical at the mere mention of an autopsy by Winston Barber, but now Debbie wanted to know exactly where Joe had been shot, what caliber weapon was used, and how many bullets they had found. Denton wanted to spare her the gory details, and started hemming and hawing, but Debbie *really* wanted to know.

When Denton and Uebelher finally left the house, Denton thought that Debbie Banister was the strangest grieving widow he had ever encountered—either as a cop *or* a preacher. And although her behavior wasn't enough to make her an official suspect, it was enough to remind Denton of the cardinal rule of homicide investigation: "When a husband or wife gets killed, the spouse usually did it."

13

CHARLIE SANDERS heard about Joe Banister's murder Monday night on the eleven o'clock news. WCJB-TV, the Gainesville station, reported that Banister had died from gunshot wounds to the head rather than in a traffic accident as originally thought.

Sanders pondered this startling new piece of information. It had been four weeks since Cecil Batie's murder, and Sanders and Farnell Cole were still stymied in their investigation. They were sure that Marlene had been involved, but she had a lock-tight alibi and couldn't have done it herself. And they hadn't identified anyone else who could have done it for her.

But this news about Debbie's husband was almost unbelievable: two sisters, two dead husbands. Could it be a coincidence?

Sanders fell asleep and woke up in the middle of the night in a cold sweat. He sat straight up in bed and reached over and shook his wife awake.

"What is it?" she asked, frightened.

"I know who did it," he sputtered.

"Did what?" his wife asked.

"Killed Cecil," he replied. "The whole family is involved in this thing, I just know it. They've gotta be."

• • •

As soon as he got to work on Tuesday morning, Sanders called Don Denton. The two men knew each other well: they had worked a brutal homicide together several years before.*

"Don, we've got a serious problem we need to talk about," Sanders said. He explained about Cecil Batie's murder in January and the connections between Debbie Banister and the Sims family. At first, Denton wasn't really interested. He had never heard of Cecil Batie, and he had his hands full with the Banister case. But Sanders insisted on coming to Starke that day to meet with him.

When he got off the phone, Sanders called Farnell Cole at home. Cole had been working late on the Batie case and was still asleep.

"Have you read the paper yet?" Sanders asked.

"No, why?" Cole replied groggily.

"Cecil's brother-in-law was shot and killed Saturday night in Starke."

"You're kidding!" said Cole, suddenly awake.

"Nope. It was Debbie Banister's husband. Somebody shot him while he was driving down the road in his car. I just called Don Denton; we're going up there this morning to talk to him."

"I imagine we are," Cole said wryly.

• • •

The meeting was held in Denton's office, with Sanders, Cole, Denton, and Wiley Clark. The Gainesville investigators had brought their files, and they laid out the Cecil Batie case. By the time they had finished, Denton and Clark were convinced that there was either a connection between the two murders or the strangest set of coincidences in the world. From that point on, the two investigations were joined, and the four men became one team. For the next six weeks, they would work together on the most complicated and bizarre case that any of them had ever seen.

Their first break came that very afternoon: a sheriff's deputy from Jonesboro, Georgia (an Atlanta suburb) called the Bradford County Sheriff's Department and reported that a Pat Bouchette

---

* A Starke horse trainer was murdered, his head and hands were chopped off, and his body was thrown near Cross Creek, the home of Marjorie Kinnan Rawlings, the author of *The Yearling*. A detective magazine ran a story about it entitled "The Headless Horseman from Cross Creek."

had phoned him that afternoon, had given him a Georgia tag number, and had asked who it was registered to. The deputy had assumed that Bouchette was a Florida police officer, but when he realized she wasn't, he explained that auto registrations were not public information in Georgia. Bouchette then suggested that *he* call the Bradford County sheriff. There had been two murders in recent weeks, she said, and there was a suspicious guy running around Gainesville in a pickup truck. His name was John Hearn.

• • •

On Tuesday afternoon, Debbie showed up at Ruth and Ceree Banister's house with a stranger, whom she introduced to her in-laws as "John Hearn, my cousin from South Carolina." It was exactly what Hearn had suggested in their January 27 phone call.

Joe's sister Lana was suspicious immediately. She had never heard Debbie talk about any long-lost cousin from South Carolina, and Debbie and Hearn seemed a little too friendly for cousins: the way he looked longingly at her, the knowing glances that passed between them, their expressions when their eyes met. And Debbie's children kept jumping in his lap, as if they already knew him. Amanda and John were not the kind of children to go to a stranger, yet they were hanging all over Hearn. Three weeks earlier, Amanda had made a comment about going roller skating with Aunt Marlene and Big John; Lana hadn't paid any attention to it at the time, but now she began to wonder.

Cousin or not, Hearn tried his best to fit in with Joe's family. He had his camera with him and offered to take pictures of Joe's out-of-town relatives. He was snapping pictures right and left: individual shots, a group shot of the entire family in the front yard, photos of Lana and her husband. He was so courteous, so helpful, so eager to please: "Okay, everybody look this way and say cheese!"

At the end of the day he even gave Lana's husband one of his business cards:

John Hearn

Insurance Photography, Weddings,
Sporting Events and Aerial Photography

Was he thinking about adding funerals and wakes to his repertoire?

• • •

The investigation moved quickly in the next few days. On Wednesday, February 6, Jimmy Singletary, Joe Banister's supervisor at
Western Electric, reported that Debbie was the one who had arranged for Joe to go to the Adkinses' house in a separate car and
also mentioned her strange request to have Joe transferred out of
town the week before.

That afternoon, Wiley Clark subpoenaed Marlene Sims Watson, to question her about what time Debbie had picked up
Amanda and John on Saturday night. An investigator from Gainesville served her with the subpoena at her parents' trailer. Marlene
remarked: "I expected to be served by my buddy Cole on the other
case, not this one. I'm not worried about this subpoena. I need to
get with Debbie on the times, but I know exactly what time she
picked the kids up that night."

"What time was that?" the investigator asked.

"Ten minutes after twelve," Marlene replied.

Iris Sims chimed in. "Yes, I remember, too, because the kids
were acting up and we wanted Debbie to come get them because
they were being a terror."

On Monday, Debbie had told Don Denton that she had picked
up the kids around eleven-thirty, and had arrived home at twelve-
fifteen. The story was already breaking down.

• • •

On Thursday morning, Joe Banister was buried at Hillcrest Cemetery in Gainesville. He had always disliked suits, so Debbie had him
buried in a sport shirt and slacks. She sat beside Lana Halbrook in
the front row and wept openly throughout the service. Bobby
Adkins gave a moving eulogy that had many people in tears in the
packed funeral home. Standing at the back of the crowd was Sgt.
Charlie Sanders, who was there (as he and Cole had been at Cecil
Batie's funeral) to check the guest book and look for suspicious
characters.

One person that he didn't pay much attention to was a big
hulking man with a camera who seemed to be part of the family: he

had driven Debbie to the funeral, signed the guest book right under Frank, Iris, and Marlene, and even taken photos at the graveside service. This was John Wayne Hearn.

•   •   •

After the funeral, Hearn accompanied Debbie back to Ruth and Ceree Banister's house, where he ate dinner and took more photos. He tried to get Bobby and Patsy Adkins to let him take their picture, too, but Bobby refused. Later that afternoon, Hearn returned to the cemetery with Debbie and Ruth Banister. By then, Joe's grave had been filled in and smoothed over, and the red clay was completely covered with the funeral wreaths and flower arrangements sent by his friends and relatives.

Once again, Hearn got out his camera and took pictures of Debbie and Ruth standing behind the grave with the flowers arrayed in front of them. In one shot, Debbie is standing alone, her red-rimmed eyes hidden behind sunglasses, holding a single red rose over her heart. It is a touching portrait of a grieving widow at her dead husband's grave—taken by the man who killed him.

•   •   •

Thursday afternoon, Denton, Clark, Cole, and Sanders conducted a surreptitious interview at the ACSO with an informant on the Batie case: Ralph Smith, Marlene's second husband. Smith was not informing out of a sense of civic duty, but out of fear. To put it bluntly, he was afraid for his life: Cecil Batie was dead, Joe Banister was dead, Larry Watson was permanently blinded, and Smith figured that he was the next one in line. He was especially worried because Marlene had suddenly started cozying up to him after Cecil's death. Smith was so frightened that he had reportedly boarded up his windows with plywood.

He knew from personal experience that Marlene was capable of violence: he later claimed that she had tried to "whip" him on several occasions, had attacked him with a claw hammer, and had once run to her car to get a pistol—but, he recalled, "I took my young butt out the way."

After Cecil's death, there had been rumors on Batie Hill that Smith might have done it himself, because of their past differences (Marlene had left Cecil to move in with Smith), but he had taken a polygraph test and passed it. Since he was welcome in the Simses' trailer, Smith had been keeping the cops informed of activities there, but had not yet provided any useful information. This time, he delivered: he reported that there was "a new guy" hanging around with Debbie Banister, who Marlene had identified as Debbie's boyfriend. He drove a pickup truck and parked it behind the Simses' trailer, where it couldn't be seen.

Smith knew him only as "the new guy," but his cousin Billy "Roach" Rhodes* had actually gone up to him and asked his name. The new guy had replied: "My name's John Hearn."

．　　●　　■

Thursday evening, Lana Halbrook called Don Denton at the Bradford County Sheriff's Department. She had met him once before, on Monday, when the autopsy results came in, and had appreciated Denton's gentle manner and obvious concern for the family. Lana felt that she could trust him, and Denton had told her to call if she heard anything that might help the case. This evening, Lana had one question for him: "Who is John Hearn?"

●　　●　　●

That was the same question Denton asked Debbie Banister the next morning, when she accompanied Marlene to the Bradford County Courthouse for Marlene's subpoenaed appearance. While Marlene was being questioned on the second floor by Assistant State Attorney Tom Elwell, Debbie popped into Denton's office, one floor below.

Denton mentioned that he had typed up his interview notes from their conversation on Monday, and Debbie asked if she could take a look at them. She went over them meticulously and pointed out a half-dozen typographical errors; Denton penciled in the corrections. Once again, he was bewildered; he had never had a grieving widow correct his interview notes.

When he asked about Hearn, Debbie admitted that he was not her cousin. She said that he was a friend of her family's, but mostly

---

* "Roach" Rhodes was another colorful character on Batie Hill. According to Smith, the night Cecil was murdered, Roach got drunk and fell asleep in a box beside Smith's wood heater, where his dog usually slept. "He beat the dog to the box," Smith explained.

of hers. She explained that she had told the Banisters the cousin story in order to not upset them by bringing a strange man into their house. She claimed that she had met Hearn seven years earlier, when she was separated from Billy Thigpen and living in Cottondale, at an air national guard meeting in Dothan, Alabama. According to her, Hearn was a photographer in Atlanta, had come to Gainesville in December because of Frank Sims's heart attack, and had moved into the Prairie View Apartments in January.

In fact, the Cottondale story was a complete hoax, which Debbie, Hearn, Marlene, Frank, and Iris had concocted prior to Marlene's questioning by the state's attorney. They had picked Cottondale because Debbie had lived there by herself for a few months (so no one could dispute the story) and had attended Air National Guard meetings in Dothan—and Hearn had once worked for Wiley Sanders Truck Lines in Troy, Alabama, and often made runs to Dothan. However, the story would fall completely apart if anyone bothered to check the dates: Debbie had lived in Cottondale in 1978, while Hearn had worked for Wiley Sanders in 1980.

Just as she had on Monday, Debbie had some questions for Denton: she wanted to know more details of how Joe had been killed. Denton told her that it appeared as if someone had pulled alongside him and fired one shot through the driver's window, then walked up to the Escort after it crashed and fired the fatal shot. At that, Debbie went berserk. She started screaming that it couldn't have happened that way. "The ground was too muddy!" she yelled. When Denton reminded her that she had told him earlier that she hadn't been to the scene, Debbie got very snappy, said that other people had *told* her that there was mud all over the place, and immediately ended the interview.

• • •

Upstairs, Marlene was having a hard time with Tom Elwell, the chief state attorney in the Starke office. Short, bald, and politically ambitious, Elwell had tried fifty-two first-degree murder cases in his eleven years as a prosecutor. He was grilling Marlene about what time Debbie had picked up her kids, and about John Hearn. The pressure was getting to Marlene: she gave times that were inconsistent with Debbie's, and also admitted that Hearn was not a cousin.

Hearn and Debbie were outside waiting for Marlene in the parking lot, but she was so flustered after the interview that she took off; they looked all over for her, but she was gone. Without Debbie's constant presence, Marlene was starting to crack.

• • •

On Saturday, February 9, Farnell Cole and Charlie Sanders turned up the heat another notch. The previous day, Lillie Belle Batie had reported that Adam Batie, Cecil's oldest son, had seen Cecil's missing metal file box sitting on Frank Sims' bedroom dresser the day of Cecil's murder.

Cole immediately drew up an affidavit for a search warrant. He listed the contents of the box, as described by Mrs. Batie: the titles to Cecil's vehicles, the abstract of title to his lot, his divorce decree from Marlene, and various custody documents.

Saturday morning, Cole and Sanders showed up at the Simses' trailer with the search warrant. Iris told them, "Go ahead and search, you won't find anything that interests you."

The officers didn't find the file box, but Cole did find the abstract of title to Cecil's lot buried in a stack of papers on the dining room buffet. Until then, Iris had been extremely cordial, but she suddenly became very nervous. "Oh, look," she said to Frank, "he found Cecil's old abstract."

Iris claimed that Cecil had given them the abstract years before for safekeeping, but attached to it was a receipt for taxes that had been paid recently by Lillie Belle Batie. Cole photographed the abstract and seized it as evidence.

• • •

John Wayne Hearn was scrambling to come up with an alibi. *Debbie* had an alibi for Joe Banister's murder, *Marlene* had an alibi for Cecil Batie, but he didn't have an alibi for either one. He knew it was only a matter of time before the Bradford County investigators called him in for questioning. He needed someone to vouch for his whereabouts. Someone to bail him out.

So, he turned to the one person who had bailed him out of trouble his whole life: his mother. Mary Watson had barged past

the MP's at Parris Island, had gotten him pulled out of a rice paddy
in Vietnam, had found him a truck-driving job when he got discharged from the Marines, and had taken him under her wing
when his marriages folded. Now Hearn would ask her to lie to
protect him from a murder rap.

He started preparing her for that on Saturday morning, when
he called her from a Gainesville pay phone (he was afraid that his
apartment phone was tapped). Before he could ask Mary to lie to
protect him, he had to lie to her. At this point, Mary Watson didn't
know that Joe Banister had been killed. In fact, she didn't know
that Joe Banister even *existed.* Since December, Hearn and Debbie
had been telling her that Debbie's husband was deceased—so how
could Hearn explain his sudden murder one week earlier?

He couldn't. To cover up *that* lie, Hearn had to tell another
one—that it was *Cecil Batie* who was killed the previous week and
that Cecil is the person the investigators are asking about. As usual
Mary Watson's tape recorder was rolling, and this excerpt of the
conversation begins with Mary asking Hearn about the investigator's questioning of Debbie:

"They've talked to her and they've talked to the Sims family
and now they want to talk to you?" she asks.

"Yeah, well, and a hundred other people in between," Hearn
replies.

"Hmm . . . well, was he in drugs or something?" Mary asks,
referring to Cecil Batie.

"Yeah—heavy. Plus he had *thousands* of enemies here in this
town. . . . There wasn't anybody that he hadn't tried to run over
or run down in this town."

"Oh . . ."

"I didn't know him, but this is what I've been told."

"Uh-huh, well . . ."

"So just remember those dates," Hearn says.

"Twenty-sixth to the first of February?" Mary asks. Hearn
wants her to say that he was in Columbia from January 26 to
February 1, when he actually left for Florida on January 29.

"Yeah, I came up there and spent the week with Wayne."

"Yeah, okay."

There is a double irony here: Hearn is telling Mary that he

needs an alibi for *Cecil's* murder instead of Joe's, but he has his dates all wrong: Joe wasn't killed until Saturday, February *2*—so Mary saying that he left for Gainesville on February *1* would do him no good at all.

"Well, is Debbie pretty upset by it?" Mary asks.

"Yeah, she's scared to death that they are gonna try to link me to it, and that's the reason that she doesn't want anybody to know that she knows me—you know, as far as me and her, you know, being together."

"Uh-huh."

"They all think that I'm just a good friend of hers."

"Yeah . . ." Mary sounds skeptical. "Well, if they know all about you, honey, they would know whether or not you were dating her."

"No, they don't!" Hearn says peevishly.

"Okay."

"They don't! They've asked her, they've asked everybody, and nobody knows." Of course, Hearn was deluding himself: three people had already identified him as Debbie's boyfriend.

He tells her about the long custody battle between Cecil and Marlene. "So because all this has happened," he says, "they are trying to lay it on Marlena [sic] or somebody Marlena knows."

"Yeah."

"I have only met Marlena . . ." he pauses, preparing a lie, *"twice."*

"Uh-huh . . . and this happened before you met her?" Mary asks.

"Yeah," he says hesitantly, lying again. "I didn't meet her sister till I moved down here."

He tells her about Marlene being questioned by the police. "Then they brought up my name: 'Well, who is John Hearn? How long have you known him? Where did he come from? How long has he been in Gainesville? Blah, blah, blah, blah, blah.' You know, over and over and over and over."

"Yeah."

"And she told them, 'I don't know him. I know who he is, he's a friend of my dad's and my sister's, but I don't know him.' "

"Oh, me," Mary sighs. She is worried. "Well I don't see how they could link you to him if you didn't know him. . . ."

"I'm *here*," he says soberly.

"And not working," Mary adds.

"I'm *here*."

"Yeah, well . . ."

"If anything's asked, as far as you know I'm living on the money I've saved. I'll probably be coming, moving to Columbia at the end of this month."

"Uh-huh. Well, you might be better to go ahead and move now."

"No-oo, I'm not running from it!" Hearn says with determination, his voice rising. "If I run from it, they're gonna say, 'He did it, let's go get him.'"

"Yeah."

"No, I'm not running till they clear me of it."

He explains that the cops are trying to link Debbie and Marlene to the murder. "But . . . they have no clues. Nobody knows, the man was asleep on his couch and somebody walked up to the front window and did him in." He says it with no emotion, with no clue that *he* was that somebody.

"Unh-unh-unh," Mary says disapprovingly.

"What time did I get there Saturday night?" he asks. "It was about eight or nine o'clock, wasn't it?"

"Yeah," Mary agrees.

"Okay," Hearn says, "so I got there about eight or nine o'clock Saturday night, you know. . . ."

"Yeah."

"But instead of me telling them I left to come back Tuesday, you know. . . ."

"Yeah."

"I didn't leave till Friday."

"Uh-huh, until the first?" Mary asks, double-checking.

"Until the first."

"Okay."

"This is the only way that I know that I'm gonna be in the clear. And I'm sure they're going to be calling you."

"Uh-huh, okay . . . all right."

Hearn talks to his son for a few seconds, and tells him that he and Debbie Banister and her two kids will be coming to Columbia on February 18. Then Mary comes back on the phone. She's had some time to think about what Hearn has said, and now she is really worried. She asks Hearn if he is going to try to avoid being questioned by the police.

"No, I'm going down there," he says. "I'm gonna *volunteer* to go in today. They told Debbie and Marlena, both, they were gonna pick me up for questioning. Well, I'm gonna call *them* I'm gonna volunteer to go on my own . . . In other words, I don't want them looking for me. I'll go to them . . . 'cause I don't have anything to hide."

"Yeah."

"It's just, I have nothing to show where I'm at." He tells her that the Gainesville cops were going to charge Ralph Smith with the murder, until he came up with an alibi. "Well, see, I don't have an alibi," he says. "I don't have nothing at all to say where the hell I was at. . . ."

"Uh-huh."

There is a weighty five-second pause. "Except *this*," he says plaintively. The message is clear: It is up to Mary to pull him through.

"Yeah." Mary sighs loudly. "Unh-unh-unh."

Then Hearn starts rambling about his Atlanta phone bill, which would prove that he was in Atlanta "on the sixth. And it either happened the sixth or the fifth, I'm not sure which," he says. "Or it could have been the fourth. I don't know, you know, somewhere in there. But, you know, I wasn't even *here*."

He is so rattled that he doesn't realize what he's doing: He's talking about his *January* phone bill, not his February bill, which hasn't arrived yet. And the call he made from Atlanta "on the sixth" was when he called the Simses to find out if Cecil Batie was dead. Without realizing it, he's suddenly talking about the actual date that Cecil was murdered. Even with his mother, his story is breaking down.

Later in the conversation, she asks him about his *Soldier of Fortune* ad: "Well, does your ad in the paper . . . are you implicated with that some way?"

"No," Hearn says.

"No?" she asks.

"No," he says sullenly. "Not at all."

"Okay."

"Not at all."

"Okay . . . You don't run an ad anymore?" she asks.

"Yeah, I run an ad, but I get all the calls here."

"Uh-huh. Okay."

He tells her that the cops know about his ad, but if they ask her what he does for a living, she should tell them that he's a freelance photographer and a truck driver.

"Well, what about the moneys you got for getting that plane?" Mary asks. She is referring to another of his lies: He told her that he was going to Texas in January to repossess a plane for Sun Bank, when in fact he was making his first trip to meet Bob Black.

His voice drops. "Don't worry about it. Just don't say nothing about it."

"Okay . . ."

" 'Cause that was an under-the-board type thing."

"Uh-huh. Okay."

"More or less what that was, that was a theft from a thiever."

"Uh-huh."

"It was all done under the board."

"They don't know about that?"

"No," he says firmly, wanting her to drop the subject.

He takes her through the alibi script one more time, then adds: "See, now, if they ask you about a girlfriend, you tell them that you don't know if I have any girlfriends."

"Uh-huh."

"You tell them that the only girlfriend I have is the one that lives in Atlanta, or somewhere around Atlanta—which is Judy."

"Uh-huh, okay," Mary says.

•   •   •

Immediately after hanging up with his mother, Hearn called Judy, the girlfriend in Atlanta. It was the first time that she had heard from him since January 6, when Hearn had informed her that he wouldn't be seeing her anymore because he was moving to Florida to be with his new love. Out of the blue, Hearn called and apologized for walking out on her and chatted for eighteen minutes. Hearn had used Judy for an alibi on January 6, and now he was firming up his alibi before talking to the police.

Then he was ready. On Saturday afternoon Debbie Banister

called Don Denton and told him that Hearn had moved into her house, and would be there if he was needed for questioning.

•   •   •

On Monday, February 11, Don Denton called the FDLE office in Jacksonville and asked for help in obtaining background information on a John Wayne Hearn. FDLE called the Georgia Bureau of Investigation, which provided Hearn's driver's license number and vital statistics, and also reported that he was the owner-operator of World Security Group.

That afternoon, Denton talked to a GBI special agent who said that Hearn had been running an ad in *Soldier of Fortune,* and that the FBI was attempting to run a sting operation on him, enticing him to buy illegal silencers. Denton got the name of the FBI agent who was handling the case.

When Denton told Wiley Clark what he had learned, Clark immediately called Charlie Sanders and Farnell Cole in Gainesville. "Y'all be careful now, we don't know who this guy is," Clark warned them. "He could be really bad."

14

JOHN WAYNE HEARN had his first interview with Denton and Clark on Wednesday, February 13. Denton had called Debbie that morning, and told her that they would like to talk to Hearn that afternoon. She said that she would contact him and have him come in.

The last thing Hearn did before going to the courthouse was stop at a pay phone and call Mary Watson, to make sure they had their stories straight.

He arrived at the sheriff's department at 3:30 P.M. At first glance, he fit the profile of the "bad" mercenary that Denton and Clark had heard about from the GBI: at six-one and 240 pounds, he dwarfed Clark; yet he spoke in a soft, high-pitched voice and answered "Yes, sir" and "No, sir" like his mother and the Marine Corps had taught him to do.

Wiley Clark, a tough-as-nails interrogator, asked the questions, while Denton, a meticulous detail man, took copious notes. After some general background questions, Clark homed in on Hearn's relationship with Debbie Banister.

Hearn had rehearsed the Cottondale story, and delivered it perfectly, adding some embellishments of his own: He and Debbie had met at a Dothan truck stop while she was attending an air national guard meeting; he had stayed overnight at her house in Cottondale several times, but he had always slept on the couch; he had called her a few times since then and had had dinner with her once, in 1980. He insisted that the only reason he had come to Gainesville in December, and moved down in January, was because

302

of Frank Sims' heart attack. "I would do anything for that man," he said.

Hearn was adamant that his relationship with Debbie was "purely platonic." He insisted that she had never visited him in Atlanta, he had never phoned her at home, and had never called her at work until after he moved to Gainesville. As far as he knew, Debbie and Joe Banister had had a "perfect marriage," and he hadn't talked to her about Joe's death because anytime that was mentioned she began to cry. The reason he had been so visible since Joe's death was to help with the funeral—because Frank Sims was too weak to help and Debbie's eyes were too messed up for her to drive.

Then Clark asked him to explain his whereabouts on the weekend of Joe Banister's death. Hearn had been practicing for this too: he told Clark that the most important thing in his life was his "little boy," who he visited at least every other weekend, without fail. He said that he had left Gainesville around 3:00 P.M. on Saturday, February 2, and arrived in Columbia about 9:00 P.M. He spent the weekend at his mom's house, drove back to Gainesville in his pickup truck on Monday afternoon, and didn't know about Joe's death until he returned (Hearn had finally got his dates straightened out on Joe's murder.)

He went on to say that he was planning to move back to Columbia at the end of the month—since he couldn't get any photography jobs in Gainesville—and had already given fifteen days' notice at the Prairie View Apartments.

At that point, Wiley Clark backed up and had Hearn talk about his life in more detail: his childhood, his family, his Marine Corps career, his three tours in Vietnam, his marriages, his truck-driving jobs. Near the end, he told them about having a pilot's license, and how he had always wanted to be a commercial pilot. "But I'm too old now," he said. "All my dreams are down the tube."

•   •   •

Before leaving, Hearn agreed to come back the next day. The second interview began at 10:00 A.M. Thursday. This time, Wiley Clark pressed Hearn for details about the weekend of Joe Banister's death: What time had he left for Columbia, what route had he taken, what had he done while he was at home?

In the past, Hearn had lied to make himself look good, but now he was lying to avoid the electric chair. He said that he had gotten up Saturday morning and packed, worked on his truck, talked to his landlord, and left for Columbia about 3:00 P.M. On Sunday, he had taken his son roller skating and installed a temperature gauge on his adopted brother Jimmy's car.

Clark was still trying to get a reading on Hearn—to figure out how he thought, what made him tick. He asked Hearn about his friends, but he didn't really have any friends. Hearn said that he lived by himself, he didn't drink, he didn't go to bars, and he didn't socialize with people who did. When Clark asked him about girlfriends, Hearn named the two women who he had dated in Atlanta, including Judy. Clark asked if he belonged to any veterans organizations, trying to lead him into talking about World Security Group, but Hearn said no. He said that he still had trouble dealing with Vietnam, still had flashbacks and nightmares, and had gone to a counselor in Oklahoma for delayed-stress syndrome. Suddenly, talking about Vietnam, he broke down and started crying.

Denton and Clark looked at each other. Here was this big hulking ex-marine, who they *knew* was a professional gun-for-hire, and *suspected* was a two-time murderer, blubbering like a baby. Was it real or was it an act? It would not be the last time that Denton and Clark would ask themselves that question.

•   •   •

Immediately after the interview, Hearn left the courthouse, drove two miles to a KOA Campground, and called his mother from the pay phone. He went over his alibi story one more time: he had come home on Saturday, had taken Wayne roller skating on Sunday, and had fixed Jimmy's car. He warned her that the investigators would probably be calling her.

When he hung up, he called Bob Black at home in Steep Hollow, and told him that he would help him kill his wife. Since his first trip to Bryan in January, Hearn had called Bob once, on January 23, and Debbie had talked to him several other times. In fact, according to Hearn, Debbie had taken over the negotiations with Bob, as she had taken over the rest of his life. And Debbie was ready to expand the business. In February, according to Hearn, she sent in a new ad to *Soldier of Fortune:*

> PROFESSIONAL FOR HIRE: Weapons specialist, Jungle Warfare, Pilot, Highly skilled Individuals or Teams—Discreet and Confidential. Will go anywhere, do anything US and Overseas, WSG

Soldier of Fortune's ad department wrote back and said that it was deleting the words "will go anywhere, do anything"—in keeping with its new ad policy—and substituting "any assignments." The ad would appear for the first time in the June, 1985, issue.

Hearn and Debbie were going into the business of murder for hire.

Since January, Debbie had been working on Hearn about Bob Black's request. "All he wants you to do is drive a car," she kept saying, according to Hearn. "For ten thousand dollars, that's all you have to do. We need the money for the down payment on the house. All he wants you to do is drive a car."

Finally, Hearn had agreed. With Denton and Clark nipping at his heels, it was a good time to get out of town. So he called Bob on Thursday and told him that he would come to Bryan, but only if Bob sent him a $1,000 cashier's check ahead of time, as expense money for his first trip to Texas, and had a second $1,000 cash waiting for him when he arrived, as expense money for this second trip.

Bob agreed, and said that he would mail the $1,000 check that day. Hearn told him to send it to his mom's address in Columbia because he would be going home on Saturday.

Hearn talked to Bob Black for ten minutes, then immediately called Debbie at Sun Bank and told her that the deal had gone down. He was going back to Texas.

• • •

Later that morning, Bob Black went to the Western National Bank and bought a $1,000 cashier's check, made out to John Hearn, along with a personal money order for $1,000. He paid cash for both transactions (he reportedly got a cash advance on his credit card).

Bob then wrote the following letter to Hearn:

12:08 pm 14 Feb 85 Thurs. C.S.T.

Skipper—

Here's a cashier's check and I have with me a personal money order for the same amount now.

My office number is 409-xxx-xxxx and I should be there from 0830–1200 Friday; at home shortly before and after; and leaving for Galveston/Houston around 3:00 p.m. If there is *any* way you could schedule your plans to coincide with my being alabied [sic] out-of-town this weekend, it would help considerably; first, I could easily take Gary Wayne with me for the weekend, whereas my being gone later in the week would put him riding with her at practically all times. Second, it will take some fast talk to arrange being gone from work as well as home on. . . . probably Thursday.

No hard feelings if you can't; I understand. Also, don't want to push it down to the wire—23 Feb.

B.

The office phone number he listed was for Don Ballard's insurance company, where Bob was "working" part-time, studying for the state insurance exam. He was supposed to go with Ballard to an insurance convention in Galveston on the weekend of February 15 to 17, and had asked Gary Wayne to go. The last sentence: "don't want to push it down to the wire—23 Feb." apparently refers to the date that Teresa's divorce was scheduled to become final.

Bob mailed the letter, with the enclosed $1,000 cashier's check, to Mary Watson's address that afternoon by Federal Express.

Part Six

MAMA'S BOY

I believe you could look the whole world over
and not find any woman good enough for my
son.

—*Mary Watson*

1

MARY WATSON was frightened
and confused. The stories that Hearn and Debbie Banister had
been telling her made no sense. Even more upsetting, Mary was
feeling shut out of Hearn's life. In the past, *she* had been the one he
confided in about his wives; but now he was confiding in Debbie,
and Mary couldn't get through.

The worst was still to come. On Friday, February 15, two
investigators from Florida arrived at her house: Don Denton and
Wiley Clark. They had left Starke early that morning and driven
the 350 miles to Columbia to test John Wayne Hearn's alibi.

Mary was not afraid of police officers. To the contrary: she was
an ardent police buff. She had founded a local citizen's alert team
(an offshoot of her interest in CB radios) that had worked side-by-
side with local law enforcement—keeping tabs on suspects, assist-
ing with stake-outs, relaying vital information. She was well known
in the Richland County Sheriff's Department, and was friends with
one investigator, with whom she talked on the phone all the time.

But these officers from Florida were questioning her about
her son's involvement in a murder. And not *Cecil Batie*'s murder,
but *Joe Banister*'s. That threw her off-stride from the beginning.
Mary thought that Debbie's husband was "deceased" long ago.
What kind of terrible trouble has Johnny gotten himself into? she wondered.

Don Denton, a polite, soft-spoken man, did most of the questioning, while Wiley Clark sat across the room, staring at her with
an impenetrable look.

"Mrs. Watson, when was the last time your son was home?" Denton asked.

"I'm not sure exactly," Mary replied, "but he comes home every other weekend, without fail, to visit his son."

"Was he here on February second?"

"Well, date-wise, I can't tell you, but I can go back to the calendar," she said. She got out her calendar and studied it. "Yes, he probably was home that weekend, because it's every other weekend, if not every weekend."

"Are you sure?" Denton asked.

She looked at the calendar again. "Yes, possibly so. Because he is due to come home *this* weekend. He told Wayne he's coming and will take him skating."

Suddenly, Wiley Clark spoke up from across the room. "No, Mrs. Watson, he was *not* here on February second," he said brusquely. "He was on a telephone calling you to make up an alibi for him."

Mary bridled. "No, sir, he wasn't," she said stubbornly. If there was one thing that would set off Mary Watson, it was calling her—*or* her son—a liar.

Denton spoke again, calmly and deliberately. "Do you remember what you ate that weekend?"

"Well, normally we have something quick that you can hold over, like spaghetti or chili. I made some chili that upset Johnny's stomach not too long ago. That was probably the weekend I fed him that bad chili."

"All right," Denton said, making a note. "Mrs. Watson, do you know a Debbie Banister?"

"No, sir, I don't know the woman," Mary replied. It wasn't an outright lie, in her mind: she had *talked* to Debbie on the phone, but hadn't actually *met* her in person.

"You do too, Mrs. Watson," Clark cut in. "Debbie Banister has been here in your home."

"No, sir, she has not!"

"She has too, Mrs. Watson," he fired back.

The more Clark pushed her, the more bullish she became, and the more protective of her son. "I guess I was scared," she admits today. "I wouldn't volunteer any information. If they asked me a question, I avoided it."

According to Denton's interview notes, Mary insisted—at least three different times—that Hearn was home on February 2. She claimed that he had arrived around 7:00 or 8:00 P.M. on Saturday, had taken Wayne roller skating on Sunday, had worked on Jimmy's car, and had left on Monday after taking Wayne to school. It was the same story that Hearn had told them in Starke.

•   •   •

Shortly after the investigators left, a Federal Express van pulled up in Mary Watson's driveway to deliver a letter addressed to John Hearn. The letter was from a Bob Black in Bryan, Texas. Mary signed for it and carried it inside.

Then the phone rang: it was Hearn, calling from Debbie's house in Starke. Mary told him about Denton and Clark's visit. Hearn wanted to know what they had asked and what she had told them. Mary demanded some answers herself, and Hearn promised to explain everything when he and Debbie got to Columbia on Saturday. Then Mary told him about the Federal Express letter.

"Well, what is it, Mom?" he asked.

"I don't know, honey, I'll just open it up and see," she said.

She opened the envelope and started to read the letter aloud, but she heard Debbie ask Hearn if what *she* was expecting had arrived.

"Shut up, Debbie," Hearn snapped. He came back on the line. "Mom, don't worry about it. I'll look at it when we get there."

After he hung up, Mary read the letter anyway. She looked at the $1,000 cashier's check. *Who is Skipper?* she wondered. She had received a phone call the night before from a man who called himself Skipper and asked for Hearn. *Something is not right,* she thought.

Friday evening, Mary received another phone call from "Skipper," wanting to talk to Hearn. When Tom Watson got home from work, Mary showed him the letter and told him about the phone calls. "Tom, something is not right," she said. They talked it over, and decided to make a photocopy of the letter and check.

Early Saturday morning they went to the laundry plant where Tom works as a maintenance man and photocopied the letter and the cashier's check. Mary took the copies home and placed them in a desk drawer, just in case she ever needed them.

• • •

Hearn, Debbie, Amanda, and John arrived at Mary's house around 11:00 A.M. on Saturday, February 16. After everyone was introduced, Hearn got the Federal Express envelope out of Mary's mail holder, opened it, and pulled out the cashier's check. According to Mary Watson, Debbie snatched it out of his hand and ran out into the backyard, saying gleefully, "All I want is to find a jewelry store."

Prior to their visit, Mary had discussed sleeping arrangements with Hearn, and had suggested that Debbie and her kids sleep in the radio room, while Hearn share a bunk bed with Wayne. But Saturday evening, Hearn told her sheepishly that Debbie had said he was "out of his mind" if he thought she was going to sleep without him and had insisted on sleeping together. Mary was offended—her son had never slept with a woman he wasn't married to in *her* house—but she gave in. Hearn and Debbie took the radio room, and Amanda and John slept with Wayne.

The visit lasted four days. Hearn and Debbie went shopping, took the kids roller skating, went flying on two different occasions, and looked for property for their house and for the "war games" franchise that Hearn still wanted to open. They were like a family: Debbie's kids were already calling Hearn "Daddy," two weeks after Joe Banister's death.

The more time Mary Watson spent with Debbie, however, the more troubled she became. Hearn seemed totally mesmerized by her, as if he were hypnotized or drugged. Debbie ordered him around like a robot. She pushed a button, and Hearn obeyed: "John, bathe the children," "John, put the kids to bed," "John, do this," "John, do that." Mary had dominated Hearn's life for years, but it upset her to see him controlled by another woman.

One night, Debbie cooked spaghetti and filled two bowls for Amanda and John but ignored Wayne, who was sitting at the kitchen table. Hearn was backed up against the microwave, staring transfixed at Debbie, and didn't even notice that his son was sitting empty handed at the table. Finally, Tom Watson got up and fixed Wayne a bowl of spaghetti.

Hearn had promised to explain everything about Joe Banister's death, but when Mary asked him about it the first night, he said, "We'll talk after the children are asleep." That night passed, and the next, with no explanation. More strange things were happening: Marlene called collect on Monday afternoon, and there were other suspicious calls, which Debbie took in the radio room. Mary heard Debbie and Hearn whispering about Bryan, Texas.

Finally, Mary had had enough. On Monday night, she confronted Hearn and Debbie, demanding answers about Joe Banister's death. Debbie started telling the same story that she had told Don Denton: Joe was a good father, a good husband, and they had no real problems.

"Then why are you with my son?" Mary asked. "Why has all this happened?"

Debbie stuck with her story: she had told Joe's family that Hearn was her cousin because no one would believe that they were just friends.

"But you're *not* just friends!" Mary said. "Y'all have been dating since before Christmas! And you told me your husband was deceased."

Still, Debbie was unflappable. She launched into her well-worn version of the night Joe died: he had been drinking, she had tried to get him to stay over at the Adkinses', but he had insisted on driving home; and she had been stopped by a trooper on the way home.

Mary was fed up. "So you had nothing to do with your husband's death?"

"No, of course not," Debbie replied.

"Well, why do they think Johnny's involved?"

"Because *he* doesn't have an alibi," Debbie said. "I have an alibi, but Johnny doesn't."

Exactly.

Mary changed the subject. "What's all this talk about Bryan, Texas?"

Debbie explained that Hearn had to go back to Bryan to repossess a plane—it was the same deal that had fallen through in January. She said that she was thinking about going with him, but probably shouldn't.

"Well, maybe you could stay here with Mom," Hearn suggested.

"No," Mary said angrily. "I think she better take her butt back to Florida."

•   •   •

Tuesday morning, Hearn took Debbie flying again; then they packed the car and drove to Atlanta. They went to the Tara State Bank, where Hearn cashed Bob Black's $1,000 cashier's check, and also made Debbie a signatory on his checking and savings accounts (as Debra A. Hearn). From there, they drove to the Day's Inn at the airport, and rented a room for the night. At 4:06 P.M., Hearn called Bob Black one last time to tell him that he was on his way. Bob told him not to stay in Bryan-College Station but to get a motel in Navasota, twenty miles away, and call him Wednesday morning.

Later that evening, Hearn started getting cold feet. He told Debbie, "I don't feel right about going out there. This woman has done nothing wrong. Joe was beating the hell out of you, so maybe I can justify that. Cecil was beating the hell out of his kids, so maybe I can justify that. But this woman has done nothing to nobody."

"You already killed two people," Debbie responded, according to Hearn. "You shouldn't have a conscience."

At 10:00 P.M., she dropped him off at the airport and he caught a 10:45 Delta flight to Houston.

•   •   •

Hearn checked into the Vanguard Motel in Navasota around 3:00 A.M. on Wednesday, February 20, 1985. He signed the register under his real name, and listed himself as a representative of World Security. It was not a smart move for a man who was planning to commit a murder the next day; but then Hearn had already left a paper trail across Florida, Georgia, South Carolina, and Texas that a three-year-old could follow.

He called Bob Black that morning, and Bob arrived at the motel about eleven o'clock. The first thing he did was give Hearn a $1,000 personal money order, but Hearn handed it right back to him: The money order wasn't made out to anyone and Hearn didn't want to cash it in his own name. All of a sudden, he was worried about the paper trail. Bob said that he would cash it himself and have the money for him that afternoon.

Then they sat down to discuss the murder. Right off the bat, according to Hearn, Bob announced that he had decided that he couldn't actually kill Sandra himself, so Hearn would have to do it alone. At the last minute, Bob had turned chickenshit, just like David Huber had twice before. Hearn was angry about it, but not angry enough to leave. After all, he had already come this far, he had the $2,000 in expense money, and how would he explain it to Debbie?

With Bob out of the picture, they had to come up with a new way to do it. Bob suggested one of the schemes that he had proposed to the Huber brothers: Hearn could run her off the road on her way home. The best time to do it, he said, would be Thursday night, on her way home from Action Dogs. But Hearn nixed that idea; he said there was too much traffic on Highway 6.

Bob proposed another idea: Sandra and her mother walked every afternoon at Texas A&M, and Hearn could shoot her while they were walking.

"You know, it sure would be nice if you got rid of her mother while you're at it," Bob said. "That way I could have the nursery. I'll give you another five thousand to kill her too."

He drew Hearn a map showing the location of Happy Face and the A&M exercise trail and asked him to check it out. Bob said that he had to be at work by noon and suggested that they meet for lunch at 2 P.M. at the Chicken Oil to finalize the plan.

•   •   •

The Chicken Oil is about as far from a fern bar as you can get: the exterior is rough-hewn lumber, the roof is rusting tin, the interior is jammed with polyurethaned wooden tables and ladder-back chairs. The walls, the fireplace mantel, and every inch of available floor space are cluttered with a menagerie of Texas icons: old gas pumps; a drugstore Indian hawking cigars; deer antlers; stuffed prairie dogs; and the mounted heads of two buffalo, three moose, and a moth-eaten alligator. Depression-era signs advertise Pearl Beer ("Brewed with Pure Artesian Water"), Cherry Julep, Triple XXX Root Beer, Getty Oil, and the Lion Oil Company.

It is a favorite hangout for A&M students, who come to shoot pool, drink long-neck beers or sodas in wide-mouth fruit jars, and eat chicken-fried steak sandwiches, while George Strait croons "All My Ex's Live in Texas" on the juke box.

On the wall of the men's room, just above the sink, a Jesus lover with mixed-up priorities has scrawled:

> *I am the way, the truth, and the life:*
> *No man cometh unto the Father, but by me.*
>
> *John 14:6*

But an ardent Aggie fan scratched through "John 14:6" and replaced it with "Jackie Sherrill." At the Chicken Oil, A&M's ex-football coach still gets top billing over Jesus Christ any day of the week. *"Gig 'em, Ags!"*

In that setting, John Wayne Hearn and Bob Black—two pot-bellied, over-the-hill ex-marines—sat at a table, plotting a murder.

First, Bob gave Hearn an envelope containing ten one-hundred-dollar bills; he had cashed the money order. They still had the bothersome matter of how to kill Sandra. Hearn said that shooting Sandra at the exercise track was out of the question, because it was right out in public. And he wasn't going to kill Marjorie Eimann. After all, she was a grandmother.

No problem, Bob said. He had no shortage of murder schemes for Sandra. After all, he had been plotting it, on and off, for nearly three years. He pulled out another one from his repertoire: to make it look like a burglary. Bob told Hearn that there had been a rash of burglaries in Bryan recently—thefts of VCR's, TV's, and stereos—so they could ransack the house and make it look as if Sandra had walked in on a burglary-in-progress.

Hearn agreed.

It was too late to do it that night, so Bob said he would set it up for Thursday. They agreed to meet the next morning at the Vanguard Motel.

Wednesday night, Hearn decided to leave. He drove to Houston, made his fateful stop at the Goodyear blimp, then called Debbie, who, according to Hearn, gave him a pep talk. "You're not having second thoughts, are you?" she said. "Don't lose your gut, keep up your nerve, you can do it."

•   •   •

Thursday morning was cloudy and overcast in the Brazos Valley, with dense fog that hung over the barren farmlands. The fog and overcast skies gave the morning a wintry feel—a reminder of the "Siberian Express" that had roared into Texas the first week of February, bringing snow, sleet, and fierce ice storms that had forced the closing of Bryan's schools. Still, the harbingers of spring were everywhere: temperatures had been in the seventies all week; gardeners were rototilling their beds, getting ready for Washington's Birthday, the traditional spring planting date; fishermen were tuning up their outboards and making up new catfish lines in anticipation of sneaking down to the Brazos after work and putting in a few lines; and many families were planning to drive to Houston that weekend for the kickoff of the Houston Livestock Show and Rodeo, an eighteen-day extravaganza in the Astrodome, featuring the world's largest rodeo, a chili cook-off, and concerts by such country stars as Willie Nelson, Lee Greenwood, the Judds, and Charley Pride.

Over on the A&M campus, spring was also in the air: the Aggie baseball team's season opener was on Saturday; students were gearing up for Spring Break and their annual descent on the beaches of Padre Island: and 1,357 Aggie lovebirds had just set a new world kissing record the previous week, by smooching non-stop for three minutes, thereby enshrining themselves in the Guinness Book of World Records.

But all was not joy in Aggieland: Aggie fans were moaning about the A&M basketball team's humiliating loss on Wednesday to—*"Wouldn't you know it!"*—the hated Texas Longhorns, who had staged a tremendous fourth quarter rally that knocked the Aggies out of first place in the Southwest Conference.

In Bryan's breakfast joints, between bites of eggs and grits businessmen were grumbling about the most recent delay in construction of the new Brazos County Courthouse, which was already a year behind schedule and a million dollars over budget, and were arguing about the latest controversy raging in Austin over whether the legislature should repeal the state's antiquated "blue laws," which outlawed weekend sales of beer, liquor, and a bizarre hodgepodge of forty other items, including cloth diapers and nails (although disposable diapers and hammers were legal).

John Wayne Hearn woke up early at the Vanguard Motel and

waited for Bob Black, who showed up about ten o'clock with a three-wheel motorcycle loaded in the back of his El Camino. Bob had the murder schedule all worked out: he had convinced Sandra to come home that afternoon before going to dog class, and Hearn would be waiting for her when she arrived. In the meantime, Bob would pick up Gary Wayne and run errands, stalling for time. He suggested that they meet at 4:00 P.M. at the Brazos Center on FM 1179 (the road to Steep Hollow); Hearn could leave his rental car there and ride to Steep Hollow with Bob. After shooting Sandra, Hearn could drive her van back to town, pick up his car, and make his escape.

Hearn agreed with the plan, and Bob left at 10:30 to go to work. Hearn had five and a half hours to kill. He went next door to a doughnut shop, bought a dozen doughnuts, and ate them. He checked out of the motel just before noon and drove to Conroe, forty miles away, where he found some log homes like the one he wanted to build and took pictures of them. He was still thinking about his future with Debbie Banister.

While he was out joyriding in the Texas countryside, Debbie called the Vanguard Motel *three* times that afternoon, looking for him, but he had already checked out.

The third member of this triumvirate, Bob Black, was solidifying his future as well: When he got to Don Ballard's office, he found that his new $100,000 MILCO life insurance policy had arrived in the morning mail. Bob signed a policy-delivery receipt, acknowledging receipt and acceptance of the policy. Now that the new policy had arrived, Ballard would be sending in the cancellation letters on Sandra's old policies in the next few days. But if she were killed *before* that, all four policies would still be in effect. Bob couldn't have timed it more perfectly.

•   •   •

John Wayne Hearn ate lunch in Conroe, then drove back to Bryan. He still had time to waste, so he drove over to the Brazos Center to check it out. He didn't like what he saw: There were very few cars in the parking lot, and his rented Pontiac Bonneville would be too conspicuous. He called Bob Black and explained the problem, and Bob suggested they meet at the Safeway on Briarcrest instead.

Hearn browsed in a pawn shop, looking for cameras, then drove to the Safeway and met Bob. He left his rental car in the middle of the parking lot, where it wouldn't be obvious, jumped in Bob's El Camino, and they headed for Steep Hollow.

Bob took a roundabout way home so that no one would see Hearn in the car. According to Hearn, on the way, Bob told him one little detail that he had neglected to mention: he was planning to send Gary Wayne into the house first, to find Sandra's body, which would give Bob a stronger alibi.

This man is sick, Hearn thought to himself. He had killed two people and was preparing to kill a third, but he would never do *that* to his own son. Once again, he thought about leaving, but it was too late. He was committed.

When they reached Bark-n-Holler, they sat down at the dining room table and had a glass of iced tea. It was almost like a social call. Bob called Sandra at Happy Face to find out when she would be home, then went into the bedroom and brought out the Ruger .22—Sandra's own gun—which he had bought for her in August, 1981, from Tri-State Sporting Goods in Bryan.

Bob gave Hearn a handful of Sandra's jewelry, as collateral, until the insurance policy paid off: a gold ring with a one-carat diamond surrounded by six one-quarter-carat diamonds; an $1,800 gold pendant with ten small diamonds and three sapphires, mounted on an eighteen-inch gold chain; a gold bracelet with an oval diamond surrounded by smaller diamonds.

Then they started ransacking the house. In the master bedroom, they rifled through Sandra's dresser and cedar chest, scattering her clothes and several small jewelry boxes across the floor. Even in the midst of such chaos, Bob showed his flair for the dramatic: in the middle of their bed he placed Sandra's empty jewelry box, the leather case to her Ruger .22, and a framed photo of himself. Beside it, lying on top of a dresser drawer, was the note that he had left for her on August 31:

> Sandy, I love you so very much and I am hurting like never
> before. I would indeed change my mind and stay, but
> knowing I would eventually leave again, I can't bring myself
> to continuously hurt you. Please forgive me, my sweetheart.

At 5:15, Bob left to pick up Gary Wayne, and Hearn finished ransacking the house by himself. He checked the pistol to make sure it was loaded, then his awful wait began: the panic, the thoughts of leaving, the voices arguing inside his head.

Finally, at 6:45, he saw Sandra's van pull into the driveway. Hearn hid behind the living room partition, with the gun cocked and ready. Over the barking of the dogs, he heard the van's doors open and close twice—once when Sandra put Chauncy's dog carrier in the van and a second time when she removed the electric skillet from the back—then the kitchen door swung open.

•   •   •

Sandra walked into the kitchen carrying the skillet, her brown leather purse slung over her shoulder. Hearn was watching her from behind the partition. She stopped at the end of the kitchen counter, only six feet away, with her back toward him. She set the skillet on the counter and plugged it in, then suddenly wheeled around—had she sensed him behind her, heard him breathing? She dropped her purse, stepped backward, and caught her left foot in the strap.

Hearn stepped out and fired. The bullet hit her behind her left ear, and she collapsed on the floor, almost hitting the dining room table. Hearn started running out of the house but suddenly realized that Sandra wasn't dead. He had assumed that if you shot someone in the head, they would die—but Sandra didn't die. She lay on the floor, her eyes closed, her hands over her mouth, gasping for breath.

Hearn had never killed anyone whom he had to look in the face. In Vietnam, he had killed at a distance, with an M-16 rifle, an M-60 machine gun, or an Ontos. Cecil Batie had been covered with a blanket. Joe Banister had been driving a car, looking the other way. But Sandra Black was lying on the floor in front of him, in obvious pain, gasping for life. Hearn stood over her, the gun dangling limply at his side—waiting, hoping she would die.

But she didn't. Hearn was going crazy. What should he do? Pick up the phone, call an ambulance, and say, "A woman's been shot, come help her!" Should he turn and run? Or should he shoot her again?

Instead, he waited—five, six, seven minutes, maybe more.*
The worst moments of his life. Standing over her, waiting. Trying
not to look. Trying not to hear her raspy breathing. Finally, when
he could no longer stand to see her suffer, he raised the gun and
shot her again. A kill shot, right between the eyes. At last, the
gasping stopped.

Hearn turned and bolted out of the house. Bob had told him
that Sandra always left her keys in the ignition, and he was thankful
that they were there. If he had had to go back inside and dig for
them in her purse . . . the thought was too horrible.

He started the van and drove down the long driveway. For
some reason, the dome light wouldn't go off. Hearn yanked the
cover off the light and unscrewed the bulb. When he turned left
onto Steep Hollow Circle, the rear door swung open. Sandra had
left it ajar, in order to unload the grocery bag filled with Blue Bell
ice cream. Hearn hit the brakes—and the door slammed shut.

He drove down Steep Hollow Circle, trying to stay calm. A
neighbor was outside working in his garden, even though it was
almost dark. Hearn turned left onto FM 1179 and drove back into
Bryan. He parked Sandra's van at the rear of the Safeway parking
lot, near a Dempsey trash bin. He got in his rental car, jumped on
the Highway 6 bypass, and headed back to Houston. Just outside of
Conroe, he slowed going over a bridge, opened the passenger
window, and tossed the Ruger pistol into Lake Conroe.

He turned in his rental car at the Houston airport at 8:52 P.M.,
caught a 9:30 P.M. Delta flight to Dallas, and called Debbie Banister
from the Dallas airport. Then he flew on to Atlanta, rented a car,
and drove home to Gainesville.

Although he didn't have the $10,000 that Bob Black had
promised him, he did have a special present for Debbie: Sandra's
jewelry. Debbie hurried down to Marquise Jewelers to have it
cleaned and appraised.

---

* The Brazos County coroner estimated that Sandra lived for seven or eight
minutes after the first shot. He based his estimate on the amount of fluid in her
lungs.

2

GARY WAYNE wanted to go home. He was running a fever, coughing, and feeling as miserable as a fifteen-year-old with a bad case of bronchitis could feel. It was damp and chilly outside, misting rain, and he wanted to hurry home and get into bed.

But he was also excited that his dad was finally making an effort to fix his three-wheeler, which had been broken down in the backyard for months. So he didn't complain when Bob wanted to stop at the Yamaha shop near Happy Face, and try to find a clutch cable for the motorcycle. Gary Wayne waited in the El Camino while Bob went inside and talked to the manager, who came outside and looked at the three-wheeler but said that he didn't have anything that would fit.

Bob then suggested that they try the U-Rent-M store in downtown Bryan, which sold parts for two-cycle engines. It was a three-mile drive down Texas Avenue, the main drag, in rush-hour traffic, and by the time they arrived it was after 6:00 P.M. and the store was closed.

By then, any energy that Gary Wayne had summoned up about the three-wheeler was gone. "I guess we'll go on to the house," Bob said, and the boy nodded thankfully.

But not quite. Bob decided to stop at the Bryan Post Office— three blocks from the U-Rent-M—to check his mail (he hadn't received anything from Teresa since Valentine's Day). He went inside and checked his box, which was empty.

322

"Now we'll go home," he assured Gary Wayne, who was slumped in the passenger seat, too sick to reply.

They drove back down Texas Avenue, retracing their route, heading toward FM 1179. It was still only 6:15, however, and John Wayne Hearn might not be through at Steep Hollow. When they reached Briarcrest Drive, Bob got a sudden urge to make *another* stop. "Would you mind if I stop and talk to my boss for a minute?" he asked. "I need to tell him I'm going to be late for the meeting tonight." Bob was supposed to attend one of Don Ballard's study classes at 7:30.

"I guess so," Gary Wayne said grudgingly. He didn't ask why Bob couldn't just phone Ballard when they got home, instead of having to tell him in person. So Bob turned around and drove all the way back across Bryan, then west on Highway 21 to Howdy Corners, Ballard's convenience store.

Once again, Gary Wayne waited in the truck while Bob went inside. It seemed like he was in there forever. Ballard wasn't even there, but Bob bought a soda and stood around talking to the clerk while he drank it. Bob Black was such a sociable guy. *Come on, let's go,* Gary Wayne thought to himself.

Finally, Bob came out, started up the El Camino, and headed back into town on 21. But instead of taking the Highway 6 bypass—the fastest route to FM 1179—he kept driving east on 21, heading way out into the country. He drove all the way to Kurten, nine miles away, then turned south on FM 2038, a winding back road that eventually intersected with FM 1179 three miles *north* of Steep Hollow, which meant that he would have to backtrack to get home.

As he drove, Bob started talking to Gary Wayne about his upcoming sixteenth birthday, which was still eight months away, in October. "Your mother and I have been planning to give you a Jeep Scrambler for your birthday," he said. "Would you like that?"

"Sure," Gary Wayne said, although he couldn't understand why his dad was blowing the surprise eight months early.

When they finally reached FM 1179, Bob asked Gary Wayne if he wanted to drive the rest of the way home. Gary Wayne was so sick that driving was the last thing he wanted to do, and he said no.

"Why not?" Bob asked.

"I don't feel good," the boy replied. "I want to go home."

Finally, they pulled into the driveway at Bark-n-Holler and drove up to the back door. Sandra's van was not there.

"Mother must have already gone to class," Gary Wayne said. Then he noticed that Chauncy was still in the kennel. "I guess she hasn't got home yet," he corrected himself.

"I guess so," Bob said.

They lifted the three-wheeler out of the back of the truck and Bob started walking off toward his motorcycle shed.

"Is it okay if I crank the three-wheeler up right quick?" Gary Wayne called after him. Even sick, he was so happy that his dad was finally fixing the motorcycle that he couldn't resist hearing it run, even for a minute.

"Go ahead," Bob replied.

Gary Wayne kick-started the motorcycle, revved it up, and let it run for a minute or two, until it warmed up. When Bob returned from the shed, Gary Wayne cut the motor and left the three-wheeler sitting in the yard.

They walked up on the back porch together. Bob put the key in the lock, but the door was already open. "That's funny," he said, "the house isn't even locked." He pushed the door open and told Gary Wayne, "Go on in."

The boy walked past his father into the darkened kitchen. There was barely enough light to see. He got halfway into the kitchen and stopped. In front of him was the most dreadful sight he would ever see: his mother's feet, poking out from behind the kitchen counter. Thankfully, that was all he saw—just her feet, stretched out on the floor toward him.

Gary Wayne looked back fearfully at his father, and Bob, as if on cue, came running into the house. He rushed up to Sandra's body, bent over her for a moment, then yelled: "Get out of the house, your mother's been killed! She has blood all over her face!"

They ran back outside, jumped in the El Camino, and raced down the long driveway and across Steep Hollow Circle to their neighbor's house, to call the police. The whole way, Gary Wayne was praying silently, repeating the same words over and over: *Please, Lord, don't let her be dead. Please, Lord, don't let her be dead. Please, Lord, don't let her be dead.*

•   •   •

Babe Ware had lived in Steep Hollow since the neighborhood was built in the early 1970s. A retired military man, and a veteran of World War II and Korea, Ware lived directly across from the Blacks. In a rural subdivision like Steep Hollow, with the houses laid out around the circle, the neighbors all knew each other, and waved as they passed on the road.

It was too small a neighborhood to hide your problems. Babe Ware knew about Bob and Sandra's marital problems: about Bob leaving her so many times; about his violent temper. Ware had been over to their house several times after Bob had thrown a fit and broken out windows.

Ware's wife was bedridden with cancer, so either he or his daughter-in-law Juanita, who lived next door, was always home. Because of that, Bob and Sandra had asked Ware to keep an eye on Bark-n-Holler when they were at work, although that was hardly necessary; Sandra's dogs raised holy hell if anyone other than the family went near the house.

Which is why he was so surprised when Bob showed up at his front door, with a shell-shocked Gary Wayne in tow, yelling that there was someone in their house and that Sandra was "lying in a pool of blood." Ware had been home all afternoon and had never heard the dogs bark.

Bob used Ware's phone to call the Brazos County Sheriff's Department (at 6:53 P.M.), and told the dispatcher, Chris Faulkner, the same thing: "There's someone in my house and my wife is lying in a pool of blood." Faulkner dispatched Deputy Larry Watson, Marjorie Eimann's neighbor, to the scene and also called M.L. Maddox, an off-duty deputy who lived on Steep Hollow Circle. Faulkner told Bob that a deputy was en route, and asked him if he had actually seen anyone in the house, or any other vehicles? Bob told him no.

"Okay, I'm going to put you on hold," Faulkner said, "but stay on the line until the deputy arrives."

Bob couldn't sit still, however. He turned to Babe Ware and asked if he could borrow a rifle. Ware brought out a hunting rifle, and Bob marched Gary Wayne out onto Ware's front porch and handed him the rifle. "Keep an eye on the driveway and shoot anybody who comes out," he ordered.

It wasn't enough to send his fifteen-year-old son in to find his mother's body, now Bob made Gary Wayne stand sentry, as if it were *his* responsibility to shoot his mother's killer. The boy sat all alone on Ware's porch, shivering in the chilly night air, peering into the quickly descending darkness, trying not to cry—because boys weren't supposed to cry, even if their mother was dead—and still repeating his silent prayer: *Please, Lord, don't let her be dead.* He didn't want to believe his father's words. Perhaps whoever was in the house had just hit her in the nose, and that's why she was bleeding so badly. Maybe that's all it was—a really bad nosebleed —that had caused the pool of blood his dad kept describing so dramatically to old man Ware and the dispatcher. *Please, Lord, don't let her be dead. Please, Lord, don't let her be dead. . . .*

•   •   •

Larry Watson thought that he was going to Steep Hollow to investigate a burglary-in-progress. That's how the dispatcher had described it: "a burglary-in-progress with a possible injury of an unknown type." He didn't realize until he got there that the "possible injury" was to Sandra Black, who kept his three children at Happy Face Nursery.

Watson pulled up to the Wares' house at the same time as Deputy M.L. Maddox, who lived around the corner. Bob Black came running out and once again repeated his favorite line: "Sandra is lying in a pool of blood." Bob jumped in Watson's car, and they drove down to the house with Maddox following them. On the way, Bob kept insisting that someone was still in the house.

Maddox and Watson parked by the back door and walked onto the porch with their guns drawn. Bob pointed to the still-open back door and said, "She's in there."

Larry Watson led the way, with Maddox right behind him— their guns at the ready. In the glare of Watson's flashlight, they saw Sandra sprawled on the dining room floor. Watson knelt down and checked for a pulse, but from the amount of blood and the massive head wounds, he knew that it was hopeless.

Suddenly, M.L. Maddox heard a noise behind them. He wheeled around and saw Bob standing in the doorway with a shotgun that he had taken down from a gun rack above the door. Maddox was frightened. He didn't really know Bob Black, except to wave at him on the road. He didn't know about his past violence or his marital problems, but he knew what all cops know: When the wife is killed, the husband usually did it. "Something inside me said, *He shouldn't be behind me with a shotgun,*" Maddox recalls.

While Bob "guarded" the entrance, Maddox and Watson searched the house, checking for the burglar that Bob kept insisting was there. They saw the ransacked bedrooms, the clothes on the floor, the overturned drawers—but no burglar and, strangely, no signs of forced entry. There were no broken windows or screens, no jimmied locks, no bunged-up doors. If a burglar had been there, how had he gotten in?

They returned to the kitchen and Watson checked the body again for a pulse. Bob insisted that he check a third time; so he did. "Bob, I'm sorry, but there's nothing we can do," Watson said.

"Won't CPR help?" Bob asked.

Watson shook his head. "I'm sorry, but nothing will help."

Bob started walking toward Sandra's body, but Watson stopped him. "I don't think you want to go in there," he said.

Bob staggered out on the back porch and sat down. "Oh, no," he moaned pitifully, and began to cry.

•   •   •

Across the street, Juanita Ware was doing laundry when a friend called her shortly after 7:00 P.M. and said, "There's been a shooting on Steep Hollow Circle."

Uh-oh, Sandra, Juanita thought to herself. She hurried next door to her father-in-law's. Bob was still across the street with the deputies, but Gary Wayne was sitting quietly in Babe Ware's living room—fighting back tears, still trying to be brave.

Babe Ware had a police scanner in his bedroom, and they could hear it crackling with static. Suddenly, across the airwaves, there was a call for Judge Carolyn Hensarling, the justice of the peace, to report to Steep Hollow Circle. Babe and Juanita Ware looked at each other. In Brazos County, a call for Judge Hensarling could mean only one thing: a dead body. Texas law requires a justice of the peace to officially pronounce someone dead and request an autopsy.

Without saying a word, Babe Ware stood up, walked into the bedroom, and switched off the scanner.

• • •

Bob returned to the Wares' house a few minutes later on foot. With tears in his eyes, he told Gary Wayne what he had most feared: his mother was dead. Finally, the boy broke down and cried.

Juanita Ware started to offer Bob her condolences, but before she could speak, Bob said: "Juanita, would you open the nursery for me in the morning?" Juanita Ware was flabbergasted. She had once worked at Happy Face, but had no intention of opening it up the morning after Sandra's death. She couldn't understand why Bob would be worrying about the day-care at a time like this.

Babe Ware got her off the hook by telling Bob that she had to stay with his wife. Then he tried to offer *his* condolences. "I've never been through this, Bob," the old man said, "so I don't know the right words to say."

"Well, us war vets, we know how to get through these things," Bob replied jauntily.

"No, I really don't," Ware said.

• • •

Larry Eimann had spent the afternoon rigging up catfish lines at a friend's house, in preparation for Spring Break, which he always spent fishing on the Brazos. Larry and his wife Mary had built a house in Steep Hollow in 1983, only two houses down from Sandra, in order to be close to her. They saw each other every day: Sandra picked up their three-year-old son, Randy, every morning on her way to work and kept him at Happy Face. She usually drove him home in the evenings, too, but on this particular evening, Mary had picked up Randy—and his beloved "Auntie" had come home alone.

When Larry and Mary walked in the front door about 7:30 P.M., their phone was ringing. It was Gary Wayne. "Come down to the Wares'," he said, "something has happened to my mother."

Larry jumped in his car and raced down to Bark-n-Holler. A deputy was guarding the front gate. "You can't go down there," he said, when Larry tried to get through.

"That's my sister down there!" Larry said angrily. "I'm going down there and see what happened!"

But the deputy wouldn't let him through. Then Bob and Gary

Wayne came out of the Wares' house. They were both crying, and no one had to tell Larry that Sandra was dead; he knew.

Bob was supposed to stay at Steep Hollow to talk to the investigators, so Larry loaded Gary Wayne in his car and took him back to his house. From there, he called his aunt Mary McCulloch. "Sandra has been murdered," he told her. "I've got to go tell Mother. Call the rest of the family and have them meet us there, but don't let her see their cars."

•   •   •

Marjorie Eimann always cleaned house on Thursday night. She was vacuuming her floors when she heard her dog barking wildly in the backyard. She went to the front window and looked out but saw nothing.

What she couldn't see (but the dog could) were the cars and pickup trucks that were quickly filling up Winding Road. Eight of her brothers and sisters had parked down the street, and the family members were huddling together in the darkness, waiting for Larry.

When he got there with Gary Wayne, they all walked up on Marjorie's front porch, with Larry in front and the others marshaled behind him for support. It was the hardest thing that Larry Eimann had ever done.

Marjorie knew that something was wrong as soon as she opened the door and saw her whole family. "What is it?" she asked.

"Mother, Sandra has been murdered," Larry said.

"What?" she gasped in disbelief.

"Somebody has murdered Sandra," he said.

"Where's Gary Wayne?" Marjorie asked. Those were the first words out of her mouth—the protective instincts of a grandmother: "Where's Gary Wayne?" The boy stepped forward out of the crowd, and she hugged him to her breast.

•   •   •

Glen Eimann had just left the Bryan Hospital after visiting a sick friend, and was on his way to Martin's Place for a beer when an announcement came on the radio: "A woman from Steep Hollow has been murdered."

God dern, that sounds like Sandra, he thought.

He went into Martin's, ordered a beer, and was drinking it
when the bartender told him that there was a phone call for him. It
was one of Sandra's uncles, telling him to come to Marjorie's
house.

"Is it Larry or Sandra?" Glen asked.

"Sandra."

"I'll be right over," he said.

•   •   •

Something smelled at Steep Hollow. Charlie Owen sensed it immediately. When he got to the scene at 7:30 P.M., he did what all
good criminal investigators do: He talked to the first deputies on
the scene, M.L. Maddox and Larry Watson. Watson was still pretty
shaken up that the victim was Sandra Black. They walked Owen
through the house, and explained what had happened.

The most likely scenario was that Sandra had been killed after
walking in on a burglary-in-progress, but that just didn't fit for
Bryan, Texas. Things like that happened all the time in Houston,
Dallas, or Fort Worth—but not in Bryan. Charlie Owen had been in
law enforcement for ten years in Brazos County, and had *never* seen
it. They just didn't have burglaries during which a homeowner gets
shot twice in the head, including a kill shot between the eyes—an
assassin's shot.

Sheriff Ronnie Miller arrived soon after Owen did, and the
deputies brought him up to date on what had occurred. Miller, a
huge man (six feet tall, and well over 300 pounds), had just taken
office in January, after a razor-thin election victory in November
that was still being challenged in court. The election challenge had
left a cloud hanging over Miller's head, and this was his first major
case—a gruesome homicide, right off the bat. Miller was a rookie
sheriff, but an experienced investigator: he had spent ten years as
an investigator in Bryan and College Station.

After a quick tour of the house, Miller agreed with Charlie
Owen: something smelled. First of all, why were there no signs of
forced entry? There were cobwebs on the outside of the windows,
there was dust on the windowsills, and the front door showed no
signs of being jimmied. Bob Black insisted that he had locked the
back door, which was solid glass, when he left that afternoon; so
how had the burglar gotten in?

And why were only certain things taken? Sandra's jewelry box was lying open on the bed and a few pieces of jewelry were missing, but why hadn't the burglar grabbed all of it? And there were other valuables—a VCR, a color TV, Bob's guns—that any self-respecting house burglar would have snatched immediately. Why would a burglar pass up a VCR and a color TV to go rummaging around in Sandra's underwear drawer?

The ransacked house was also suspicious. "It looks like a TV burglary," Miller said. Real burglars might dig through a drawer looking for money, but they didn't empty out drawers on a bed and throw clothes all over the room. It looked too intentional, too staged—like a put-up burglary.

There were other disturbing questions: How did the burglar get out to Steep Hollow in the first place? And when? Bob said that he had left the house at 5:15 to pick up Gary Wayne; and his next door neighbor Jack Kindt had seen Sandra arrive home about 6:30, and then he saw the van leave again, five to ten minutes later. That left only an hour and fifteen minutes for the burglar to have gotten into the house. But none of the neighbors had seen any strange vehicles in the neighborhood, or heard Sandra's dogs bark. Had the burglar *walked* to Steep Hollow from town? Walked seven miles down an open highway and into a rural neighborhood with only one entrance road—without being seen? It seemed preposterous.

But if he hadn't walked, then why had he stolen Sandra's van? At 7:40 P.M., the van was discovered in the Safeway parking lot by a reserve Bryan police officer. Inside were four melted cartons of Blue Bell ice cream, which Sandra had bought especially for Bob.

Finally, there was Bob Black himself. None of the cops really knew him, but he didn't show the kind of emotion that they expected from a husband whose wife had just been murdered. He started whimpering periodically, but it seemed forced and contrived.

All his life, Bob had been obsessed with showmanship, with projecting a certain image of himself—the ladies' man, the Eagle Scout, the martyred war hero—but at the most critical time in his life, when he most needed to impress people with his sincerity, he came across, once again, as a phony.

As Miller recalls: "Bob was out there with no emotion, no tears, saying, 'Oh, my gosh, what a tragedy. Who would do something like this? Boy, I'm standing behind y'all guys—we're gonna catch this person.' I looked at him and I could feel my hair stand up, and I thought, *Bullshit, man.*"

Bob didn't help himself any when the cops asked him how he had spent the afternoon. He rattled off all the stops he had made with Gary Wayne, and had the times down to the *minute:* they left Happy Face at 5:40, arrived at the Yamaha shop at 5:50, the U-Rent-M at 6:15, Howdy Corners at 6:30. It was too exact, too thought out—too phony.

"This guy's wife is laying in there dead, and ten minutes later he's telling me '5:50, 6:15, 6:30,' " Miller recalls. "I'm saying to myself, *'Shiiit, man, don't be so damn ignorant.' "*

As the questions piled up, Miller told his men, "We need to look real careful at this thing. This just doesn't feel like a burglary to me. It's just not fitting together—not even close."

An hour or so into the investigation, a deputy told Miller, "Somebody wants to talk to you at the front gate." Miller lumbered down to the driveway entrance and saw Aubrey Arnold, whom he had known for years. Arnold told him that he was Sandra Black's uncle, and said: "There's been some past violence in the family. Bob's left her many times, and they're just getting back together. You ought to take a look at that sorry sapsucker."

•   •   •

Word of Sandra Black's murder spread quickly around Brazos County. The local television station broadcast a report on the ten-o'clock news. Some people were less surprised than others.

Mark Andrew Huber, the biker to whom Bob had given $500 to kill her in 1982, was in the kitchen of his sister Candy's trailer when the newscast came on.

"Oh, my God, Andrew!" Candy yelled, "Bob Black just killed his old lady!"

Huber rushed into the living room to watch the report. "I can't believe the crazy motherfucker did it," he said. "I can't believe the crazy motherfucker did it."

•   •   •

Mark's younger brother, David Huber, to whom Bob had offered "a big red present" to kill her in 1984, heard the news from his wife, Janie, who called him at work. *He got somebody else to do it,* was Huber's reaction.

"Actually, I was kind of pissed off," he now admits. "My first thought was, 'So much for that Harley.' That's not a good thing to think, but that was actually my first thought: I'm not getting that bike."

•   •   •

Gordon Matheson knew that Bob had done it the moment he heard the newscast. The reporter said that Sandra Black had apparently been the victim of an interrupted burglary, but Matheson knew better. All he had to do was remember the look in Bob's eyes in January, as he stood in the Harville parking lot.

He really wished that he had done something back then.

•   •   •

Bob didn't arrive at Marjorie Eimann's house until 10:30 P.M. He was driven there by none other than Don Ballard, who had sold him the new $100,000 insurance policy on Sandra just three weeks before. Bob had called Ballard at 7:30 and asked him to come to Steep Hollow. "I need somebody with a friendly face," he said.

When they arrived at Winding Road, Ballard stayed outside on the front porch while Bob went in. By then, the house was filled with Marjorie's relatives. Dr. O.C. Cooper had come by and had given Gary Wayne and Marjorie sedatives, and Marjorie was sitting on the living room couch with a blanket over her legs, in shock. Her sister Jane Pate and brother Bill Arnold were sitting on either side of her.

Bob walked over to Marjorie and knelt down in front of her. "Mom, what are we going to do?" he whimpered. "We've lost our Sandy." Then he buried his head in her lap and cried.

Bill Arnold, a cantankerous, tough-talking cowboy, who was already convinced that Bob had killed her, replied gruffly: "Well, I don't know what *you* are going to do, but *we* are going to find out who did it. And if there's been any hanky-panky going on, we will find out about it!"

Bob kept his head bowed and didn't say a word, but Bill Arnold kept repeating the phrase, sprinkling in some choice language to drive home the point: "If there's been any hanky-panky shit going on, we will find out about it."

Jane Pate had not suspected Bob until that moment, but she suddenly became so frightened that she got up and went outside. "I was about ready to run," she recalls. "If someone had dropped a frying pan on the floor, I imagine I would have had a heart attack. He could have wiped us all out."

3

GARY WAYNE was in a fog for the
first few days after his mother's death. He and Bob and Bob's
parents, Vannoy and Ivonne Black, stayed at the E-Z Travel Motor
Inn on Texas Avenue, not far from Winding Road. The one thing
that burned through the fog most clearly was Bob's urgency to get
back to Bark-n-Holler. "He wanted to start living in the house
again *real real* bad, and I couldn't understand why," Gary Wayne
says.

Bob was *so* anxious, in fact, that he told Gary Wayne: "I'll get
my dad to go out there and talk to the cops, and *he'll* get them out
of the house."

It didn't work. The sheriff's department would have round-
the-clock security on Bark-n-Holler for the next seven days, as
Sheriff Miller's men combed through the house, searching for
evidence. Miller assigned Charlie Owen to handle the "people"
aspects of the case (tracking down leads, interviewing suspects,
talking to the neighbors) and put Investigator Chris Kirk in charge
of the crime scene.

It was an interesting combination. Owen, in his early forties,
is short, tanned, and wiry. He's a country boy from Lake Whitney,
Texas, who dresses the way Texas cops are supposed to: a huge
white cowboy hat, western shirt, black boots, and a gleaming stainless-steel 9mm pistol in a speed holster on his hip. He's flashy, fast-
talking and cocky—a little man with a white hat, a silver badge, and
a monster gun.

Owen was something of a media star in Brazos County. He

was in charge of the "crimestoppers" program, and appeared on the local TV news with the "crime of the week," offering a reward for tips or leads that led to an arrest. Crimestoppers received 100 to 150 calls per month, and Owen had developed hundreds of informants and contacts among Brazos County's criminal elements: the bikers, druggies, and hard-living street people.

Chris Kirk, on the other hand, is Joe College in a department full of Matt Dillon clones. He comes to work in stylish sport coats, starched dress shirts, perfectly-pressed slacks, with perhaps a red tie—the one touch of flash. In a bow to peer pressure, he does wear cowboy boots, which are impeccably shined. Tall, thin, blond haired, and reserved, Kirk looks like he would be more comfortable behind an A&M lectern than in a biker bar—and, in fact, he has a masters degree in forestry.

He found the ideal niche for his skills and temperament as an evidence technician—or "bag man," in the jargon of the trade. He's an admitted compulsive organizer—"Everything has its place," he says with a laugh—and you get the feeling that his home is a monument to neatness and order: shirts arranged in the closet by color; shoes lined up exactly, toes in a row; stereo records and CDs alphabetized within subcategories (pop, country, jazz); and a refrigerator where mold never grows in the vegetable bins. For him, bag man is the perfect job.

While Charlie Owen worked the streets, Chris Kirk methodically pored over every inch of Bark-n-Holler—photographing; inventorying; dusting for fingerprints; collecting evidence in large plastic baggies, each one labeled, dated, and initialed in the top left-hand corner in his tiny, neat hand: "CCKirk, BCSO."

•   •   •

Twenty-four hours into the investigation, Bob Black had emerged as the prime, and only *real*, suspect.

On Friday morning, Bill Arnold and Margaret Ann Mauro, Sandra's uncle and aunt, went to see Sheriff Miller. They told him about Bob's history of violence, which Miller was already aware of, but they also added two new details: Bob had recently taken out a big life insurance policy on Sandra, and in late September he had stopped by Mauro's jewelry store with a woman named Teresa Heatherington, whom he had introduced as his first cousin.

Friday afternoon, Charlie Owen interviewed Don Ballard, who confirmed that Bob had just bought a $100,000 insurance policy on Sandra. Suddenly, there were two possible motives for the murder: the insurance money and a potential love affair.

That evening, at 8:00 P.M., Bob voluntarily went to the sheriff's department, where he was questioned by Miller and Owen. "Bob, we hate to talk to you this way," Miller began, "but we have to eliminate you as a suspect. And needless to say, you *are* a suspect —because of the insurance policy, the past violence, and y'all just getting back together."

"Well now, Ronnie, I can understand where y'all might think that," Bob said pleasantly.

Miller had never met Bob before Thursday night, yet Bob was already acting like they were best friends. The sheriff was also surprised by Bob's mild reaction to being called a suspect. In most cases, a man whose wife had just been shot in the head would go nuts if he were accused of doing it, but Bob showed no emotion.

Miller asked Bob to go over again what he'd done on Thursday. "Sure," Bob said. "Can I borrow a sheet of paper?"

"A sheet of paper?" Miller asked.

"Yeah, I get confused if I don't write things down," Bob explained.

Miller handed him a legal pad and a pen, and Bob started writing out a detailed summary of the day, giving a running commentary as he went along: after Sandra left for work he read the newspaper; then went to his office about 10:30 A.M.; left there at 12:05 P.M.; arrived back home at 12:25; fixed dinner and cleaned the house; left again at 4:00 P.M. to dump the trash; drove to Nash's grocery on Briarcrest to buy gas, a Coke, and a small box of Tide; returned home and did a load of laundry; called Sandra at Happy Face at 4:50 and she called him back at 5:10.

Miller and Owen exchanged knowing looks. Bob was doing it again, with even more precision: 12:05, 12:25, 4:50, 5:10.

When he finished, Miller asked him if he had received any correspondence from his cousin in California, Teresa Heatherington.

"Yeah, I got a Valentine's Day card from her," Bob replied innocently, as if he had nothing to hide.

Before he left, Bob asked Owen when he thought they'd be

through with his house. Owen apologized for any inconvenience, but said that it was taking longer than expected to complete the crime scene investigation.

"No rush," Bob said. "I just need to get some clothes for me and Gary Wayne. We'll never spend the night in that house again." Of course, he was telling Gary Wayne just the opposite.

Bob couldn't seem to stay away from Bark-n-Holler. He went out there *twice* on Friday, saying he wanted to feed the animals and get a change of clothes, and dragged Gary Wayne with him one time. When the cops escorted them inside to get their clothes, Gary Wayne saw the blood-soaked carpet where Sandra's head had been. "That's always been one of the memories that's stuck in my mind," he says.

Bob was back out at Steep Hollow at ten o'clock Saturday morning—for another change of clothes—and again at 10:53 P.M. to feed the cats. For years, Bob had complained about Sandra's animals, and had even shot a couple of cats that she brought home, but he suddenly couldn't bear for them to go hungry.

Bob had plenty of helpful hints to speed up the investigation: He volunteered that he had a complete household inventory on film; after Sandra's Ruger .22 was discovered missing, he supplied Owen with a box of ammunition for it; on another trip, he told officers that he had a "hot tip" that the tank behind the house needed to be searched with underwater metal detectors (investigators searched it and found nothing).

"It got pretty sticky there for a while, keeping control of the crime scene and keeping Bob out of there," Owen recalls. "He was nosy—he wanted to know what we were finding, what we were getting, why we were taking stuff."

•   •   •

Charlie Owen knew that he was looking for a hit man. Bob Black had a motive for murdering his wife, but he also had an alibi—he had been with Gary Wayne. So Owen was looking for someone who could have done it for Bob. Forty-eight hours after Sandra's murder, he had found *three*!

At 1:00 P.M. on Saturday Owen got a phone call from a reliable crimestoppers informant who hung out with the biker crowd.

The woman told Owen that Bob Black had paid Mark Huber $1,000 in 1981 or 1982 to kill his wife.

Owen rushed out to Steep Hollow to tell Chris Kirk about the call. Kirk had spent the morning inventorying the master bedroom, where he had discovered some alarming items in Bob's closet: a belt of M-60 machine gun ammunition, a dummy handgrenade with a live fuse, and two 4-inch blocks of C-4 military explosive.

He had then moved to the attic, where he found an ammunition box containing forty-nine love letters from Teresa to Bob and fifty-three letters from Bob to Teresa, which she had returned to him after moving back with her husband. Kirk had started reading the letters and quickly realized that Bob and Teresa were far more than kissing cousins.

Ironically, just before Owen arrived, Kirk had found an envelope with *David* Huber's name and address written on it. Inside were Bob's treasured "s-e-x" photos of him and Teresa.

Owen told Kirk about the crimestoppers call, and Kirk showed him the envelope with Huber's name. The address on the envelope was only three blocks from the Safeway store where Sandra's van had been recovered. David Huber might be their hit man!

Kirk immediately shut down his search of the house, and they returned to the sheriff's department to draft an affidavit for a search warrant. At that point, they were no longer searching the victim's house for evidence of who had killed her, they were searching for evidence *against* her husband. With Bob Black an official suspect, they needed a search warrant.

When Owen got back to his office, he received a second crimestoppers' call, from a different informant, who said that Bob had offered $1,000 to Mark Huber *and* John Gorris to kill Sandra. Owen knew Mark Huber and Gorris (in fact, he had arrested both of them: Huber for robbing a local grocery, and Gorris for stealing Harley parts). Owen contacted Gorris, who verified the story but denied any involvement in Sandra's death.

David Huber, on the other hand, was an unknown quantity, but by nightfall, Owen had found two people who knew him: Randy and Gemma Sowders, who had shared a duplex with David and Janie Huber the summer before. They told Owen that Bob had asked Huber to go to California with him to kill his girlfriend's husband; they also told him that Huber was AWOL.

The investigation was racing forward with lightning speed. The cops were worried, however. They still didn't have enough evidence to arrest Bob, and they were afraid that if he was desperate enough to have asked three local men to kill his wife—and had finally succeeded—he might be crazy enough to try to kill Marjorie Eimann too, to own the day-care business outright.

•   •   •

Bob Black was going to make Sandra's funeral the greatest show of his life. The show to end all shows. Everything had to be perfect for his Sandy.

The family visitation at the funeral parlor was scheduled for Saturday night. That afternoon, Bob nearly drove the funeral director to exasperation calling up local florists and complaining that the flowers weren't fresh enough. There were *tons* of flowers— Sandra's closed casket was surrounded by dozens of standing funeral sprays—but Bob still wasn't satisfied. He kept fussing with them, rearranging them, putting all the flowers of one color together—red carnations in front, yellow mums behind. In the center of the virginal white casket Bob placed a huge spray of red and pink roses.

Still, the flowers weren't enough. Bob hung the painting of Romal, Sandra's favorite German shepherd, on the wall behind the casket; on either side of the painting he placed a vase of yellow mums and beneath it a spray of roses. This was the dog that Sandra's family suspected Bob had poisoned.

And there was more: To the right of the casket he placed a framed color photograph of Sandra and baby Gary Wayne, sitting on the beach in Hawaii at sunset. The sky was aflame with brilliant streaks of red and gold, which backlit Sandra's face with a golden glow and showed the blond highlights in her sun-bleached hair. She looked very beautiful, and very thin.

Bob saved his crowning touch for the visitation. At the head of the casket he had placed a more recent photo of Sandra—a 12" by 14" studio portrait—on a small round table. At a momentous point, when the chapel was crowded with Sandra's family and friends, Bob and Gary Wayne marched solemnly down the aisle to the casket—Bob standing ramrod straight, shoulders back, beer belly sucked in, eyes straight ahead, with full military bearing—and placed two beautiful long-stemmed roses, one red and one yellow, in front of Sandra's picture. The roses were laid across each other, pointing toward Sandra. Between them Bob left a note that read: "You will always be in my heart."

He planned even more pomp and ceremony for the actual funeral on Sunday afternoon. He asked the Cavaliers, his Wednesday night motorcycle club, to ride in formation from the funeral home to the cemetery, leading the funeral cortege. Sunday morning, Bob called Dan Linder, the owner of Action Dogs USA, and asked to borrow his video camera (Linder videotaped his students working their dogs) so that he could videotape the Cavaliers leading the procession. When Bob came to pick up the camera, he asked Linder if *he* would mind operating it, since Bob might be too busy himself. Linder thought that the whole idea was in extremely poor taste, but reluctantly agreed.

Sandra Black's funeral was huge. Although some of her friends were still too shaken by her death, or too afraid of Bob, to attend, it was standing-room-only in the Memorial Funeral Chapel. When the guests signed the funeral book, they saw the following note from the grief-stricken husband: "Mr. Bob Black requests that memorials be made to Pct. #3 Volunteer Fire Department" (the Steep Hollow fire department).

Sandra's family was terrified that Bob might try to kill Marjorie at the funeral. A handful of plainclothes deputies—including Charlie Owen—was scattered throughout the crowd, keeping a watchful eye on Bob.

The family was seated on one side of the chapel behind a translucent curtain. Marjorie and Glen Eimann were in the front row, and Gary Wayne and Bob were seated behind them. Bob was wearing a conservative blue suit and white shirt, but he had a bright red bandana tied around his neck, cowboy style. Seated next to him was the man who had seemingly become his best friend overnight: Don Ballard, the insurance salesman. Some of Sandra's relatives didn't even know who Ballard was, and assumed that he was an undercover cop.

Just before the service started, Gary Wayne decided that he wanted to sit with Marjorie, and as they were rearranging the chairs to make room for him, Marjorie turned around; for just a second, her eyes met Bob's. He was glaring at her with pure white hatred. Suddenly, it hit her: *Bob did it.* Marjorie had been so sedated and so in shock since the murder that she was unaware of her family's suspicions about Bob, but at that moment, she *knew.*

Because of the fears about Bob, the funeral was very short. Three of Sandra's favorite hymns—"What a Friend We Have in Jesus," "Amazing Grace," and "Pearly White City"—were played, followed by a brief ceremony by Rev. William Brumlow. Throughout the service, Bob wept copiously. His wails carried all the way to the back of the chapel, and even some of his friends who did *not* suspect him thought it was a bit excessive.

The Cavaliers decided not to ride in the funeral procession, as Bob had hoped, but Dan Linder did videotape it. Bob asked Don Ballard to ride in the car with him to the cemetery. On the way, Bob pulled himself together long enough to ask: "Do you think there will be any problem with the insurance paying off?" Ballard told him no.

It was damp, cold, and raining, and the graveside service was also intentionally brief. The family whisked Marjorie away immediately afterward, for fear that Bob might try something there. As she was getting in the car to leave, she saw Gary Wayne standing all alone under an oak tree, crying his heart out. Marjorie walked over and hugged his neck, and held him while he cried.

Meanwhile, Bob was making his final grand show: before Sandra's coffin was lowered into the ground, he flung himself on top of it, kissed it, and sobbed uncontrollably.

•   •   •

That night, at 10:30 P.M., Charlie Owen and Chris Kirk paid a visit to Bob and Gary Wayne at the E-Z Travel Motor Inn. The officers asked Bob to sign a consent form to search Bark-n-Holler, which would eliminate the need for a search warrant. Bob initially signed the form, but when they also asked him to take a polygraph test, he refused—and withdrew his consent to search.

After the officers left, Gary Wayne asked his father: "How come you won't take the lie detector test?"

Bob said that polygraphs weren't always accurate, that he knew someone who had been falsely accused after failing one, and that he was afraid if he failed it, all the fingers would be pointing at him.

For the first time, Gary Wayne thought: *My dad may have something to hide.* Sandra's family had made a point to hide their suspicions from Gary Wayne, but he was thinking it on his own.

● ● ●

On Monday, Gary Wayne returned to school. Immediately after the murder, Bob had offered to let him stay out for as long as he wanted, but by Sunday he was pressuring him to go back. Gary Wayne hoped that school might get his mind off his mother's death, and he gave in to his father's desire. Bob had always wanted him to be tough, to be a little man.

So he went to school—and it was awful. His friends didn't know what to say; so most of them said nothing. His teachers were more helpful: they told him that they were sorry about his mother and not to worry about his school work.

He couldn't do his work anyway. All day long, he sat at his desk, filling sheet after sheet of paper with the same word: "Why?"

● ● ●

Gordon Matheson knew that he had to do something. He called the sheriff's department on Sunday night, then went down Monday morning and gave a written statement, detailing what Bob had asked him to do. Deputy Dick Gulledge told him that he wasn't the only person Bob had asked to kill Sandra, and Matheson agreed to testify.

● ● ●

At 6:35 P.M. Monday, Judge Carolyn Ruffino issued a search warrant for Bark-n-Holler. It was served on Bob that evening when he took Gary Wayne in to the sheriff's department to be questioned. Sheriff Miller wanted to compare Gary Wayne's version of Thursday's events to Bob's, and he assigned "nice guy" Chris Kirk to talk to him. But Gary Wayne gave the same story as Bob did, with exactly the same times. When Kirk asked him if he thought that his father had anything to do with the murder, the boy hesitated. "I thought, *Maybe I should go ahead and say yes,*" he recalls. "But I said no. I was trying to keep my dad out of trouble."

While Kirk was questioning Gary Wayne, Bob was waiting outside in his El Camino. Sheriff Miller decided that it was time to have a heart-to-heart talk with his prime suspect.

"Bob, can I talk to you for a minute?" he asked.

"Sure, Ronnie," Bob replied.

Miller eased his enormous frame into the passenger seat of the El Camino. "Bob, you could sure help us move the investigation if you'd go ahead and take a polygraph."

"I can understand that, Ronnie, but I just don't know if I can take a polygraph or not," Bob replied.

"Well, Bob, why not? If you didn't do it, then we can eliminate you and go on to the next suspect."

"I just don't know, Ronnie. They're not always accurate. I might need to talk to an attorney."

"Bob, why would you need to talk to an attorney if you're not guilty?"

"Well, Ronnie, I just would." Then Bob changed the subject. "You know, Ronnie, I've found the Lord," he said.

Miller decided to stop playing around. "That's good, Bob. You're gonna need the Lord, 'cause you've done a terrible thing."

Bob was unfazed. "Well, I can understand how you might feel that way, Ronnie. It's a terrible tragedy. But I've got my life right with the Lord."

"Well, I hope so, Bob," Miller said. "Your soul belongs to the Lord, but your ass belongs to me."

• • •

On Tuesday afternoon Charlie Owen arrested David Huber for being AWOL from the Marine Corps. Huber gave a written statement about Bob asking him to kill both Sandra *and* Ted Heatherington.* On Tuesday night Mark Huber also gave a written statement about Bob soliciting him in 1982. With the Hubers, Matheson, and Gorris, the investigators had four potential hit men, but none of them seemed to be the one.

---

* Huber was given two polygraph tests, both of which he failed. "I didn't tell them *everything,* but I told them the basics," he admits today. He spent two weeks in the county jail, and was then sent back to Camp Lejeune, where he spent two months in the brig.

. . .

On Thursday afternoon the sheriff's department released Bark-n-Holler to Bob Black, and he and Gary Wayne returned to the house. The blood-soaked carpet in the dining room had been cut out, but there was still dried blood on the dining room walls, the table legs, and the curtains (Hearn's second shot had hit several arteries in the eye, which are under so much pressure that blood had spurted seven feet in the air).

It was a ghastly sight. Instead of rushing Gary Wayne out of the house, Bob sat him down in the living room, got a bucket of hot soapy water, and let him watch while he nonchalantly scrubbed Sandra's blood off the walls. "I couldn't figure out why in the world he didn't have any tears coming out of his eyes," Gary Wayne recalls. "He just cleaned it up in a normal fashion, but I couldn't understand how he could do it."

They slept in the living room for the next few nights, with a loaded revolver on the coffee table, in case the killer returned.

4

For JOHN WAYNE HEARN, everything was starting to fall apart. He was broke, he was jobless, and he was the prime suspect in two murders. Worst of all, his affair with Debbie Banister was turning sour. Some days, Debbie was as sexy and loving as ever, but other days she seemed withdrawn, as if she were losing interest. They had gotten into several terrible arguments, but then they would go to bed and everything would be fine again—for a little while. Hearn never knew which Debbie to expect the next morning.

They decided that he needed to get out of town until the Batie and Banister investigations cooled down. Debbie said that she would join him later, after her house sold. On Saturday, February 23, Debbie helped him pack his things. It didn't take long: he just had his clothes, some dishes, a few sticks of furniture, and his pictures of Debbie.

He still had the murder weapons—the AR-7 and the Winchester 1200—but it was time to get rid of them. Hearn ran a rat-tail file down the barrel of the AR-7 to destroy the telltale "lands and grooves" that would identify the rifle's ballistics, then wiped down both guns to remove any fingerprints. He borrowed Debbie's car, and drove three miles south on U.S. 441 to an observation stand overlooking Payne's Prairie. It was pouring rain; so Hearn jumped out of the car, ran to the edge of the swamp, and heaved the guns— the AR-7 was disassembled and stored in its plastic stock, and the Winchester 1200 was in its waterproof case—as far as he could into the tangled bog of willows.

That night, after he had finished packing, he went with Debbie to the Simses' trailer to play cards, then left for Columbia the next morning. He was going home to Mama.

• • •

On Tuesday afternoon Debbie Banister had her third, and final, interview with Don Denton. He had asked her to bring in Joe Banister's guns so that they could be inspected and photographed. Debbie arrived at the sheriff's department at 2:45 P.M., where Denton was waiting for her, along with Wiley Clark, whom she had never met.

Debbie dumped the guns on Denton's desk: a .45 revolver, a .22 pistol, a 30-30 caliber hunting rifle, and a Mini-14 rifle. Denton wanted to check the guns to make sure they weren't loaded, but he couldn't figure out how to eject the magazine on the Mini-14. He handed it to Clark, who couldn't figure it out either. Debbie watched them fumble around for a few seconds, then grabbed the rifle and jacked out the magazine like an expert. Denton remembered how she had professed her ignorance of guns in their first interview, when she had described Joe's old .38 pistol as having a "little wheel" where the bullets went.

Denton asked her several times if those were all of Joe's guns, and Debbie assured him that they were. By then, Denton and Clark had learned from a neighbor that Joe had owned an AR-7, but Debbie never mentioned that gun, which was floating in Payne's Prairie.

The investigators questioned her about her job history and her marriages, but soon came around to the subject they were most interested in: John Wayne Hearn. Debbie stuck to the Cottondale story, still insisting that they had a platonic relationship and that Hearn had come to Gainesville in late December because of her father's heart attack. "That was the first time I had seen him since 1980," she said.

Wiley Clark bored in on her: Had Hearn ever phoned her before December? Had he ever called her at home? Had he ever called her at Sun Bank? No, no, no, Debbie insisted.

When they started questioning her about Joe's insurance policies, Debbie became incensed and warned that if they "harassed" her the way Farnell Cole and Charlie Sanders had been harassing

Marlene, she would sell her house, move out of Bradford County, and they would never see her again—which, according to Hearn, was exactly what she was already planning to do.

Denton and Clark asked her to come back the next day, and Debbie agreed to do so. But on Wednesday she called Denton and said that she couldn't come because one of her children was sick. They rescheduled the interview for the following day, but Iris Sims called that day and said that Debbie couldn't make it. She never came back again.

•   •   •

All of Wiley Clark's questions about phone calls must have alarmed Debbie. That evening, she called Hearn twice from a *pay phone* at the Pantry Pride in Starke. All of a sudden, Debbie was panicked about incriminating phone calls.

It was a little late. Clark and Tom Elwell had already subpoenaed long distance phone records for Hearn (from both his Riverdale and Gainesville apartments), Debbie Banister, Iris and Frank Sims, Mary Watson, and Sun Bank, among others. He had also subpoenaed Hearn and Debbie's bank records and Visa bills. In Florida, the state attorney has broad subpoena power, and Clark was gobbling up the paper trail that Hearn and Debbie had left across Florida, Georgia, and South Carolina.

On Wednesday, instead of talking to Denton and Clark, Debbie had a frantic meeting with Marlene and Pat Bouchette at the Inn-Out drive in, where she fretted about the phone calls between Hearn and herself on the night of Joe Banister's death.

At 9:22 P.M., she called Hearn from a Gainesville pay phone and told *him* to go to a pay phone and call her back. Hearn told Mary Watson, "Mom, that was Debbie. I've got to go to a pay phone and call her back."

"For what?" Mary asked.

"I don't know, I'll be back in a few minutes."

He drove to a nearby Zippy Mart and called Debbie at *her* pay phone. "There's a problem," she said anxiously. "I have to see you *now*."

"What's wrong?" he asked.

"I can't tell you on the phone. Where can we meet?"

Hearn suggested a Union 76 truck stop south of Savannah,

Georgia—approximately halfway between Gainesville and Columbia. Debbie told him that Marlene would be coming with her.

"Pack your clothes, you won't be coming back home," she
ordered.

"You're crazy as hell," Hearn replied. "I'll meet you in Savannah, but I *am* coming back home."

When he returned to his mother's house, he was as white as a
sheet. He went into his bedroom, threw some clothes in a suitcase,
and walked into the living room to say good-bye.

"Johnny, what's going on?" Mary asked frantically.

"I don't know, Mom," he said, very subdued. "Debbie just
said she had to talk to me." He handed her a thick envelope.
"Here's my insurance policy, in case something happens to me."
All of a sudden, he started crying.

"Johnny, what's going on?" Mary cried.

"I don't know," he whimpered. He pressed the envelope into
her hand and said, "I won't be going the Interstate; I'll be taking
the back way."

Mary talked to him the whole way to Savannah on the CB
radio. Hearn phoned her as soon as he arrived at the Union 76
truck stop, at 12:30 A.M. He called her again, at 1:25 A.M., when
Debbie and Marlene arrived. Hearn rented two rooms at the Roadway Inn—one for Marlene and one for Debbie and him—and they
went to bed.

The next morning Marlene and Debbie started ranting about
phone bills and tapped phone lines and the cops watching everything they did. They were so worked up, and talking in such circles,
that Hearn never understood exactly what was the problem. But he
understood the bottom line: Debbie wanted him gone. He protested that he didn't have enough money to leave, and Debbie
suggested that he borrow some from his mother. At 11:00 A.M.,
Hearn called Mary Watson—who taped the call.

"What's going on?" Mary asks.

"Uh . . . I don't want to talk about it on the phone," he says.

"Oh . . . well, is everything all right?"

"Ummm . . . yeah."

"Uh-huh."

"They've got your phone bugged," he says sternly.

"No!" Mary exclaims.

"Well, what it amounts to, I'm gonna have to pack up and get the hell out of Dodge."

"Why?" she asks.

"Why?" He snaps. "What do you think why—'cause they are gonna charge me with it. Uh, let me ask you a question. . . ."

"What?"

"Do you think y'all could borrow a thousand dollars—a short-term note—and I'd give it back to you in sixty days?"

"I doubt it," Mary says, "but I guess, I guess we could try. . . . I don't know."

Since Mary was so noncommittal about the $1,000, Debbie called Frank Sims and asked him for the money. Later that day, Frank tried to call her back but couldn't read his own writing (he had scribbled down the phone number of the Roadway Inn) and ended up calling Mary Watson at 1:22 P.M. When her telephone answering machine came on, Frank started leaving a message:

"This is Frank Sims. I need desperately to get hold of John," he says. His voice is wooden, and he sounds drugged. "He called, waking me from a sound sleep, and I did not get a number or anything to call him back. If he contacts you, it is very important that he call me so I can—"

At this point, Mary picks up the phone. "Hello, hello?"

"Hello? Uh . . . this is Frank Sims." He starts repeating his message, but Mary interrupts him.

"Uh, Mr. *Sims*?" she asks.

"Yes, ma'am."

"I don't believe I know you, sir?"

"Uh, no ma'am, you don't. I'm from Gainesville, Florida. I have never met you. And that's why if John would like to call me back, he has my number." Frank says that Hearn needed "some papers or something," but he can't read the phone number that he wrote down. He also tells her that he's recovering from a heart attack, and is on "some very heavy medication" that's got him "bouncing off the walls."

"Yes, sir, I believe your name has been mentioned here," Mary says. "Something about you having a heart attack. And you have a daughter that's had some problems?"

"Right," Frank says.

"Uh-huh . . . well, is there more problems?"

"Uh, no ma'am, not to my knowledge."

"Uh-huh."

"Because as far as I know, that is just totally died down."

"Uh-huh."

"You know, the nearest they can figure out it was a joy killing. Someone riding around that was high on drugs or alcohol."

"Mmmm," Mary says sympathetically.

"That just passed a man and shot him through the window as he passed him," Frank adds. " 'Cause the man was amiable, you know, he wasn't a real aggressive man to people that—course now I never lived with him, so don't get me wrong, you never really know anyone till you live with them."

"Right." Mary is playing along, trying to get information.

"But, uh, Debbie, uh, would be the last one to tell me if there was anything wrong, 'cause she'd be afraid that I'd get in trouble, because she knows the least I'd try to do is beat the stew out of him. Course she also knows that'd be the *most* I'd try to do."

Mary finally gets to what *she* wants to know. "Well, how do they figure John into it?"

"Uh, just through him knowing me, and knowing Deb," Frank says. Without any prompting, he suddenly launches into the Cottondale story, telling her that Debbie and Hearn had met years ago in Alabama. "It was strictly on a platonic friendship relation . . . nothing serious—just friendship. John's just really a guy to like."

That night, February 28, Frank Sims drove to Brunswick, Georgia, and met Debbie, Marlene, and Hearn at the Truck Stops of America, where he delivered $1,000 to Hearn. The exchange only took a few minutes: they sat down in the restaurant, Frank handed over ten one-hundred-dollar bills, Hearn told him "I'm leaving; it's been nice knowing you," and Frank said "Good luck to you," and drove back to Gainesville.

Hearn, Debbie, and Marlene returned to Savannah and spent the night. According to Marlene, Hearn and Debbie called Bob Black several times from the motel—to hustle him about paying the $10,000—but he wasn't home.

Friday morning, Hearn drove home to Columbia, and Debbie and Marlene returned to Gainesville. They had decided to meet the next day in Cordele, Georgia, with their children so that the kids could spend the day together before Hearn left.

Debbie called Hearn on Friday night. "Before you come down here clean out your pickup truck," she said. "You're not going to take it back home with you."

"What the hell you talking about?" he asked.

"You're gonna have something else to drive," she said.

Hearn told his mother that Debbie must be buying him a new car.

• • •

On Saturday they met in Cordele at the same Shoney's restaurant where everything had started back in November.

Hearn and his son Wayne arrived first, and then Debbie, Amanda, and John in her Oldsmobile. A few minutes later, Marlene and her son Brad pulled up in an old beat-up Dodge sedan.

"That's what you're gonna drive," Debbie announced.

"You gotta be kidding," Hearn said.

They checked into the Econo-Lodge next door to Shoney's. Marlene and the four kids were in one room, and Debbie and Hearn in another. The children swam in the motel pool and played at a nearby playground. On Saturday afternoon they went shopping in Albany. Hearn drove the old Dodge to check it out; but the rear end was squalling, and the transmission would hardly shift gears.

"You people are crazy," he told Debbie and Marlene. "I wouldn't make it a hundred miles in this thing."

That night, and again the next morning, Hearn and Debbie repeatedly called Bob Black, trying to find out about the money. On Sunday, Hearn and Wayne drove back to Columbia in his pickup truck.

Hearn started packing his clothes to leave. The week before he had made a flurry of phone calls to some of his contacts from his *Soldier of Fortune* ad, trying to arrange a way out of the country. He made seven phone calls to a man in Greenbriar, Tennessee, who claimed to be organizing a CIA-sponsored mission, code-named "Operation Golden Eagle," to fly U.S. military personnel in and out of Central America. He also made a half-dozen calls to a pilot from Ann Arbor, Michigan, trying to arrange for a flight into Canada. Debbie Banister had even called the Canadian consulate to find out what it would take for her and her kids to move there with him.

But none of it had panned out. When it came to the crunch, Hearn was just another *Soldier of Fortune* wanna-be, living in a fantasy world. Except that he had killed three people—that much was real, and inescapable.

On Monday, March 4, he called Debbie early in the morning, then called Bob Black to ask again about his money (the insurance still hadn't come through). That afternoon, he loaded his truck, told his mother that he was going to New York, and left.

* * *

That same day four Florida investigators—Don Denton, Wiley Clark, Farnell Cole, and Charlie Sanders—swept into Atlanta like William Tecumseh Sherman on his march to the sea. They were hot on the trail of John Wayne Hearn, murder suspect.

Over the next two days, they interviewed Eunice Weeks, Paul Englett, Hearn's former girlfriend Judy, his supervisors at Transus, and even his Riverdale postman. Weeks told them about Debbie Banister's weekend visit in December, which blew apart Debbie's "platonic friendship" story and her claim that she hadn't seen Hearn until *after* Frank Sims's heart attack. Judy reported that Hearn had phoned her around 1:00 P.M. on Sunday, January 6, which gave him enough time to have shot Cecil Batie and driven to Atlanta.

On Thursday, March 7, the investigators drove on to Columbia, for another shot at Mary Watson. That afternoon Mary and Elaine Hearn both went to the Richland County Sheriff's Department for questioning. Mary had picked up Wayne after school and brought him with her because there was no one to watch him at home. That would turn out to have profound consequences.

While Denton and Sanders were interviewing Elaine in one room, Clark and Cole were questioning Mary in another. Meanwhile, Wayne was sitting by himself in a back office.

Elaine Hearn was completely cooperative, and reported that Hearn had told her in November that he was going into the business of "killing people for money," and that a Florida woman had wanted to hire him to get her children back from her ex-husband.

But Mary Watson was a different story. She was determined to protect her son at all costs and was still insisting that he had been home the weekend of Joe Banister's death and that she didn't know Debbie Banister. Wiley Clark kept pounding away at her, but Mary wouldn't crack.

After forty-five minutes, she was still holding firm, and Farnell Cole was so worn out that he had to take a break. "It was just exhausting," he recalls. "I just got up and left the room, because I had heard enough of her shit."

He wandered into the back office where Wayne was sitting, and started talking to him (a good cop never misses an opportunity). In passing, Wayne mentioned that he was getting a "new sister and brother named Amanda and John," who lived "far away." Cole's ears perked up. The boy added that he had met his new sister and brother for the first time at his grandmother's house, after Christmas, and that the last time he had seen them was at a "funny apartment."

Cole pulled a photo of Debbie Banister out of his pocket and showed it to him. "Do you know this woman?" he asked.

"Yes," Wayne replied, "that's my new mama."

"Is that right?" Cole said, trying to sound nonchalant.

"Yes, I'm going to go to Disney World with her and my new brother and sister," the boy added.

"Well, that's great," Cole said. "You know, I live down there pretty close to Disney World."

Cole hurried back to the interview room, where Wiley Clark was still hammering away at Mary Watson. Cole walked up to her, called her a liar, and stuck Debbie's picture in her face (Mary had already been shown the photo, and had claimed that she didn't know the woman). "You know who your grandson just told me this is?" Cole asked.

"No, sir," she replied stubbornly.

"He said it's his new mama," Cole said.

Mary Watson went to pieces. She had held out for as long as she could, but Wayne's admission was too much for her. She broke down and started crying and had to excuse herself to go to the bathroom. When she came back out, she told them everything.

The next morning, the investigators went to her house and she gave them the photocopy of the Federal Express letter and the $1,000 cashier's check from Bob Black. Clark had frightened her into turning over the letter by saying that there were "vicious people in Florida" who might have Hearn killed. Mary thought that the letter was something *Debbie* was involved in—not *Hearn*—but had no earthly idea what it really meant. Neither did the cops.

• • •

Sheriff Ronnie Miller was pissed. Two weeks had passed since Sandra Black's murder, and he still hadn't made an arrest. It was exactly what he *didn't* need. He was already taking a beating in the press over the court challenge to his disputed election win in November, and an unsolved murder—the *first* major crime of his new administration—was his worst nightmare.

Two days after the murder, the Bryan-College Station *Eagle* had run a blaring headline, "Sheriff has no suspects in shooting," with a photo of Miller standing forlornly in front of Sandra's van in the Safeway parking lot, looking nearly as big as the van itself. The photo caption read: "A murder to solve." Yes, it was *his* murder to solve—his personal test—and he knew it.

Since then, his court problems had been splashed all over the front page of the paper, and each day that dragged by without an arrest increased the public's perception of an impotent administration. He even had the college students mad at him: his opponent's challenge was scheduled to go to court on March 11—the *first* day of A&M's Spring Break—and 240 students whose votes had been challenged were going to have to spend their vacation in court, rather than on the beach. (Miller's election was eventually upheld by the Texas courts.)

If this pressure wasn't enough, some of Sandra Black's relatives were raising hell behind the scenes and threatening to hire a private investigator because Miller wasn't moving fast enough.

So Miller was not a happy man, and as big and vociferous as he is, his deputies knew it. "We could feel it from the sheriff," one admits. "Yeah, he was under pressure, and we had to get something done."

The pressure had even created friction between Miller and Bill Turner, the district attorney. Miller thought that he had enough evidence to arrest Bob, but Turner disagreed. "We were trying to argue with the damn DA: 'God dang, Bill, what do you want, an airtight case?' " says Miller.

Turner admits that there was tension. "The sheriff was wanting to get the warrant, and wanting to get the warrant, and I was
kind of in this position of resistance," he recalls. "I was saying,
'Until we have it, until we have it, I'm not gonna do it.'"

The "it" was the hit man. They had a motive, they had a
sensational love affair, and they had four local people who claimed
that Bob Black had solicited them—but they didn't have the killer.

• • •

Sgt. Bill Bryan was stuck with a thankless job. Before Charlie
Sanders and Farnell Cole had left for Atlanta and Columbia, they
had asked Bryan, an ACSO investigator, to run down some of John
Wayne Hearn's long-distance phone tolls. All of the subpoenaed
documents—phone bills, bank statements, and credit card bills—
had been pouring into the sheriff's office and piling up. The phone
records alone were staggering: hundreds of pages of monthly
printouts, dating back to April, 1984, for Hearn, Debbie, the
Simses, Mary Watson, Sun Bank, and a half-dozen pay phones
between Palatka and Starke. Each bill had to be analyzed, each
long-distance call tracked down and identified. It was a tedious job
that in a larger department would have been done by a lower-paid
intelligence analyst, not an investigator.

Instead, Bryan got stuck with it. A burly man known to everyone as "Bear," he is an anomaly in the Alachua County Sheriff's
Department: a rabid Florida State University fan in the heart of
Gator Country, who plasters his office walls with posters and
bumper stickers touting UF's biggest rival. Bear was slowly working his way through Hearn's phone bills. For each call, he would
contact long-distance information for that area code, find out what
city the phone number corresponded to, call the local police department, and ask who the number was registered to.

On the morning of March 8, Bear Bryan came to the number
(409) 822-1603, which Hearn had called on January 2, 1985. The
long distance operator told him that it was in Bryan, Texas, and
gave him the number of the Bryan Police Department. He called it,
and was directed to Captain Gene Knowles, head of the criminal
investigation division.

Bear identified himself, explained that he was investigating
two homicides in Florida, and needed to find out who the 822-

1603 number belonged to. Knowles checked in Bryan's "reverse directory," which is indexed by phone numbers, rather than names, and told him that it was registered to a Robert V. Black, Jr.

"Have y'all had any unusual homicides out there lately?" Bear asked.

"Yeah, this guy's *wife* was just murdered two weeks ago," Knowles replied. "I need to refer you to the sheriff's department."

"I think you better," Bear said.

Bear called Charlie Owen, who told him the details of Sandra Black's murder. "I've got somebody who needs to talk to you," Bear said.

He called the sheriff's department in Columbia, and left a message for Farnell Cole to call him back ASAP. Cole and the other investigators were still at Mary Watson's house. When they returned to the sheriff's department, Cole phoned Bear.

"You ain't gonna believe this," Bear said and proceeded to fill him in on the Black case in Texas.

"Well, you ain't gonna believe *this,*" Cole responded. "Hearn's mama just gave us copies of an alibi letter and a thousand-dollar cashier's check from Bob Black."

Bear laughed. "I think you need to call the sheriff in Bryan, Texas."

"I think I will," Cole quipped.

•   •   •

At 1:30 P.M., Cole called Charlie Owen and solved Sandra Black's homicide over the phone. The whole case had just been blown wide open. They had copies of the letter and the check, they had Mary Watson's statement that Hearn had left for Texas on February 19 (supposedly to repossess a plane), and they had a homicide on the twenty-first. There still wasn't a case on Hearn in Florida, but Texas had enough to put him and Bob Black in jail.

"It sent a shock of adrenaline plumb through me," Owen recalls. "I thought, 'We've got the son of a bitch. Here's what we've been waiting for.' "

While the Texas investigators were elated, the Florida cops were furious. When Denton, Clark, Cole, and Sanders had first learned about Hearn's ad in *Soldier of Fortune,* they had tried to arrange a sting operation on him with the cooperation of the sheriff's department in Jacksonville, Florida. They were planning to call Hearn and try to arrange a "hit" in Jacksonville, as a way to get him into custody. But when they called the FBI to clear the plan, the FBI told them, "Hold off on Hearn, we have an active case on him."

In the interim, Sandra Black was killed. "That pissed us off because we felt like we could have stopped that, if we had been able to pursue [the sting]," says Cole.

That afternoon, Chris Kirk obtained a subpoena for Bob Black's bank records at Western National Bank, and was given a copy of the cashier's check and the $1,000 personal money order. He also found a teller who remembered selling them to Bob.

Finally, Sheriff Miller had what he needed for a warrant. Owen and Kirk worked until 2 A.M. drafting a probable-cause statement, then Judge Carolyn Hensarling, the same magistrate who had pronounced Sandra Black dead, issued warrants for John Wayne Hearn and Bob Black. The charge was capital murder. The warrants were teletyped all over the country, with Hearn listed as "armed and dangerous."

•   •   •

Bob and Gary Wayne had gone to Houston for the weekend, so Bob couldn't be arrested until they returned on Sunday. Miller and Owen were afraid there might be a shoot-out if they tried to arrest him at home, or perhaps even a hostage situation with Gary Wayne. So, at 2:50 P.M., Owen called Bob and told him that he could come down to the sheriff's office and pick up his guns, which had been seized under the search warrant, because the cops were finished with them.

Unmarked cars were hidden all along FM 1179, in case Bob tried to make a run. "We were really worried about him getting on the bypass and going to Houston and hopping a plane to Africa or South America," Owen recalls. "But we would have popped him if he'd tried it."

Gary Wayne was outside rototilling the garden, getting it ready for spring planting, when Bob walked up. "Kill the tractor," he said. "We've got to go pick up our guns."

They drove to the sheriff's department, where Owen and Kirk were waiting for them. Owen asked Gary Wayne to wait in the outer office and led Bob to a back room, where he read the warrant and arrested him.

"Like I said, Bob, your ass belongs to me," said a jubilant Ronnie Miller.

"Well, Ronnie, I understand," Bob said, as friendly as ever.

They brought in Gary Wayne, and Bob told him, "They've arrested me for the murder of your mother." Afterward, Miller drove Gary Wayne down to the Brazos River, where Larry Eimann was fishing. The boy cried some, but he was still fighting back his tears. More than anything, he was mad at the sheriff: his mother was dead, and now his father had been taken away too.

5

IT WOULD HAVE MADE a great television commercial. "John Wayne Hearn," the announcer would say off camera, "you've just been charged with capital murder. Where are you going now?"

"To Disney World," a beaming Hearn would reply, striding confidently through the gates of the Magic Kingdom in his Marine Corps T-shirt, with one arm wrapped around a smiling Debbie Banister.

Yes, Disney World. It seems only fitting, given the fantasy life he was living. Hearn and Debbie and her two kids left for Disney World on Friday afternoon, March 8—*before* they learned about the warrant in Texas—for one last weekend fling before Hearn hit the road.

While they were traipsing through Fantasy Land and the Haunted Mansion, all hell had broken loose on Batie Hill. Friday night, Farnell Cole stopped by the Simses' trailer and told them about the warrant for Hearn in Texas. Iris and Marlene panicked and started trying to get in touch with Debbie, to warn her about it. On Saturday afternoon Iris called Mary Watson and left an "emergency" message on her answering machine. Mary called her back at 2:38 P.M., and recorded the call.

"Hello?" Iris says, answering the phone.

"Hello, Mrs. Sims?" Mary says.

"Yes."

"This is Mary Watson, returning your call."

"Oh, yes," Iris says. "Uh, Mary, listen . . . uh . . . I was trying to reach Deb. I was trying to get a message to her, uh, to come home immediately."

"Uh-huh."

"And I didn't know if she was up there or not . . . uh, have the police talked to you, Mary?"

"No, Debbie's not here."

"Well, uh, I didn't think she was, but have the police talked to you?"

"No, were they supposed to?" Mary asks curtly.

"Well, they told us that, uh, you had said, uh, your insurance policies were gone, and that they have a warrant out for John, and all sorts of stuff, and I just didn't know. . . ."

"Uh-huh—no." Mary sounds frightened.

"You know, they said you broke down and admitted this, that, and the other, and uh. . . ."

"No!" Mary exclaims.

"Yeah, well that's what I figured all along, you know. . . ."

A few seconds later Marlene got on the phone. "Mary?" she says.

"Yes?"

"This is Debbie's sister."

"Yes?"

"And, uh, listen, there's a lot going on. The police come to our house last night and they point-blank said that there is a warrant out on John for first-degree murder."

"For what?" Mary cries. "Where?"

"The warrant went out yesterday morning, supposedly, and it's for somebody in *Texas,* and that's all that I know. Matter of fact, if this telephone is tapped, I'm in trouble *right* now. . . . Anyway, if this is true what this man said about a warrant being out for him then they're in a lot of danger."

Mary is frantic. "Why? What? What? I don't know what's going on."

"Well, I don't either," Marlene says. "All this policeman told us is that it had something to do with something in *Texas*—that a man up there said that he hired him to kill his wife."

"What?"

"In *Texas.*"

"You're kidding!"

"No," Marlene says. "Okay, so with somebody saying that, then they could put out a warrant for your son."

"Yeah."

"All right, well I know that he don't know this, and I know that Debbie don't know this. And I don't know where they're at, but I don't want no police to go storming in where the hell they're at and bullets go flying everywhere either."

"My God, no!" Mary exclaims. "Well, why should they get hurt? Who's done what?"

"Well, you gotta realize, these people—he's being accused of *murder,* so whenever the cops do find out where he's at, they're not gonna go in shaking hands."

"Well, how can he say he's wanted for murder? When? Where? How? Who?"

"They didn't tell us," Marlene says. "The men, all they said was it was last month on the twenty-first in Texas."

"Last month on the twenty-first?" Mary asks. "Well, I don't know where they're at. This doesn't pertain to Debbie's husband, or your husband, getting killed?"

"No, no," Marlene replies.

"Well, what about that mess?"

"Well, he told us that he thought that John killed Debbie's husband and killed *a guy* named Cecil Batie and then this woman up in Texas, but I don't guess they have anything, you know, no evidence on him here, but *some guy* [she says it with disgust] up in Texas said that he hired him, and that's why the warrant's out on him."

"Oh, no!" Mary gasps.

"Yeah."

"Well it sounds to me like somebody's framing up on John," Mary says. "I wish to God he had never seen the state of Florida."

"Yeah, yeah, I know exactly what you mean," Marlene agrees.

•   •   •

Hearn and Debbie returned home late Sunday night, and the Simses called them at 11:00 P.M. and broke the news. Hearn knew that the cops would be looking for him at Debbie's house, and he decided to leave that night; but a universal joint on his pickup truck was worn-out, and he couldn't get it replaced until Monday morning. Debbie dropped him off at a cheap motel in downtown Starke, where he spent the night. The next morning she came by to say good-bye. Hearn broke down and cried, but Debbie was strong.

That morning, he got the U-joint replaced at the local Chevrolet dealership and drove out of Starke. For the first time in his life, he was on the run. And he had no idea where he was going. He had told his mother that he was going to New York, so he headed in the opposite direction—west. He drove across the Florida panhandle, through Mobile, Alabama, and into Mississippi. He drove straight through to Jackson, Mississippi, 575 miles away, and checked into the Airways Inn, where Transus drivers always stayed.

He holed up there overnight. Tuesday morning he called his mother—he had her go to the Zippy Mart, and called her back there. He told her that he was in Mississippi but wouldn't say where he was going. He insisted that he had done nothing wrong but said that no one would believe him and he didn't want to be electrocuted for something he hadn't done. Then he started crying (as did Mary), told her that he was sending her his last will, and said good-bye.

In his motel room, he wrote out a two-paragraph will, designating his son Wayne as the beneficiary of his life insurance policy—with his parents overseeing the moncys until Wayne turned eighteen—and had it notarized by a notary public in Jackson.

He also wrote a "farewell" letter to Debbie Banister, which appeared to be intended to throw the cops off his trail. He began by proclaiming his innocence:

> I know that everyone is trying to convince you that I killed
> Joe. Well I want you to know this—I did *not*. I know how
> you felt about him. . . .

Then he offered a phony explanation of why he was leaving, to do a mission—code named "Operation Golden Eagle"—for World Security Group:

> WSG is an elite group of men, whom I am the commander.
> We do things for Governments, including the good old US.
> If you ever ask they well deny it, of course. I can't and

won't go into detail but we are in final phase of Golden
Eagle. I know you don't know what it is but it will hit
national and international papers before long. I realize that
I have fallen deeply in love with you and I could not leave,
knowing there is a good chance I won't make it back. I
believe in the U.S. and what it stands for. I have a chance
to at least slow down communism in another country. We
will be leaving the training area in Miss. tomorrow for New
York where we will board a freight for; best if you don't
know.

   I'm sorry Debbie, I didn't want to leave you without a
good-bye but if I don't make it back I don't want you to cry
over me. You cried enough over the man you really loved.

• • •

Tuesday afternoon, Ann McNeese, Hearn's sister in Houston,
called Mary Watson. Ann had heard from her adopted sister that
there was a murder warrant out for her brother and called to find
out the details. But Ann also knew her mother: if Hearn *were* in
trouble, Mary wouldn't want to believe it. And if Ann pushed for
details, Mary might get mad at *her*. So the conversation was a dance
of deception: they talked for twelve minutes before Mary ever
mentioned the Texas murder, another twelve minutes before she
disclosed that the victim's name was Black (even though Ann had
told her very early in the conversation that Hearn had gone to
Bryan to see a Mr. Black), and she *never* admitted that Hearn was
charged with the murder. As the truth emerged, however, Ann had
a very different reaction from Mary's to the possibility of her brother's involvement.

   This excerpt of the taped conversation begins with Ann
describing Hearn's trip to Bryan in January, supposedly to buy a
gun collection from a Mr. Black.

   "What's he need with that?" Mary asks.

   "I don't know," Ann says.

   "Boy, he can get into some crazy things, can't he?" Mary says
it as if she's talking about Dennis the Menace pulling some wacky
mischief—not a triple murder.

   "I hope he don't get himself in any kind of trouble," Ann says
later.

"Well, that makes two of us," Mary replies. "You know, other people don't care whether he's in trouble or not, and being a pilot he could go and fly here, fly there, and get into trouble *without even knowing it.* Repossessing a plane, you know . . ."

"He may be *stealing* it instead of repossessing it," Ann says.

"Well . . ." Mary sounds skeptical.

"Without *knowing* it," Ann adds, as if to placate her mother.

"Yeah, that would be my concern."

"You know, when somebody offers you ten thousand dollars to repossess a plane, there's gotta be something wrong," Ann says.

"I don't like the situation that he's gotten himself into," Mary agrees. "Uh . . . [she hesitates, as if deciding whether to tell Ann any more] the Florida police came up here and talked to us, oh, back last month and—"

"The *Florida* police?" Ann says, puzzled.

"Yeah."

"About what?"

"Uh, this girl Debbie he's talking about, her sister's husband was killed and then *her* husband, Debbie's husband, was killed."

"How was he killed?"

"Uh . . ." Mary pauses.

"Shot?"

"Yeah, both of them was shot," Mary admits.

"They think Johnny did it?" Ann asks.

"I don't know," Mary replies. "I don't believe Johnny could do anything like that. And the sister's present husband was beat up and run over with a van or something, and Debbie said that her sister did that. Did it to her own husband."

"That's terrific," Ann says sarcastically. "You don't think that she got him doing stuff like that, do you?"

"Ann, I don't know," Mary says, then she catches herself, and adds quickly: "No, I don't believe that *he's* doing it."

"Well, people do crazy things for other people."

"I know. . . ."

"You know, he may, may do it because of her—*for* her."

A few seconds later, Mary says, "Well, I don't know, honey, I just don't believe that Johnny could do anything, I really don't."

"I hope he couldn't," Ann says, "but, you know, there's always the chance."

"Yeah, well . . . being a mother, I just can't believe it."

"There hasn't been nothing come up about him being out here, has it?"

"Yeah, it sure has," Mary admits. "There was a woman killed out there."

"Where?" Ann asks.

"In Bryan . . ."

"That's where he went," Ann says suspiciously.

"There was a woman killed in Bryan, sure was."

"You don't think he come by here as an alibi, do you, if he was to do something like that?" Ann asks.

Mary doesn't want to face that possibility. "Honey, I don't believe he would do anything like that."

"Well I'd like *not* to believe it," Ann says, "but you never know what to believe."

"Well, I don't know what's happened," Mary says. "I wish I did. I'm worried, needless to say. And there's been so many telephone calls here from all over the world."

"For him?"

"Yes. People from Kansas, people from Utah, people from here, from there—you name it. And there was one today come in from North Carolina. . . . It's just like I told your dad, if Johnny *has* done anything, if he's guilty of anything, he's not in his right mind."

"No, there's something wrong," Ann says.

"And that Vietnam incident, I believe it's coming out."

"Well, you know how Johnny is when somebody tells him that somebody's hurt 'em, or something like that?" Ann suggests.

"Uh-huh."

"You know, if that gal told him that this guy *hurt* her or something, and you know, if she *pushed* him enough, and made him, you know, angry enough . . ."

"Nooo, he would never get that angry," Mary insists.

"I don't know," Ann says. "Look at the times he's hit you, and, you know, all that stuff."

"Yes, but, honey, I never will believe that that was deliberate. I think that was during the times that he was having flashbacks that none of us knew anything about."

"Yeah," Ann says, backing off.

"I really do," Mary says.

"What I'm saying though is, if she *pushes* him enough, it's possible that that happened now. You know, if she pushes him enough to get him to do these things for her, it's possible. . . ."

Later, Mary says, "So we're worried now. I've cried until I can't cry, and I don't want to start again. I never needed somebody to talk to any more in my life, and had less to talk to, if you know what I mean."

Finally, twenty-four minutes into the call, Mary tells Ann, "Well, you watch the papers."

"Well, see, I don't get the paper," Ann says. "I haven't even looked at the *Chronicle* or nothing."

"Yeah, well, I don't remember what day that woman was killed out there," Mary says. "Uh, it seems to me like they said the twenty-first. It was on a Thursday. February twenty-first. And the name was *Black.*"

"*Black?*" Ann exclaims, shocked.

"Yeah, the name was Black."

"Maybe it's a coincidence, but . . . if I remember right, that's the name he gave me of having to go and talk to about that gun collection."

"I know, that's what you said," Mary replies. There's a long pause. "Well, something's just not right, I don't know. . . ."

"I bet you she's got him mixed up in all kinds of shit," Ann says.

• • •

Later Tuesday afternoon Mary got a phone call from Wiley Clark, who wanted to know what Hearn had told her that morning. Mary argued with him that Debbie Banister was involved in the murders, to which Clark responds: "Mrs. Watson, I know why you don't want to believe it, but you're gonna have to face reality sooner or later. Your son has killed three people, at least, that I know of. He may have killed more than that."

He scolds Mary for telling Hearn details about the investigation that she shouldn't have and warns her, in brutally honest language, about what might happen if Hearn doesn't turn himself in: "What you're gonna do, if you keep on doing this stuff and keep doing it, until we have to arrest him in a bad situation, and he may not come out of that situation."

Mary is beside herself. "I have asked him to turn himself in, wherever he was at. I begged him this morning and—"

"He wouldn't do it, would he?" Clark says coldly.

Mary assures Clark that she'll cooperate. "I promise you I'll do that, I'll do anything I can to help him, or whatever, because I want him safe. I told you before, if he's guilty he needs help, and if he's innocent he still needs help."

"Well, if we have to arrest him under bad conditions then that's not our fault, okay?" Clark says. "We're doing the best we can to make it easy."

"Well, I am, too, believe me," Mary says. "I'm trying."

"Everybody knows what his reputation is," Clark adds. "If he pulls a gun on anybody, nobody that's involved in this investigation is going to hesitate to kill him. And that's a fact."

"Unnh!" Mary gasps.

"If he does that, that's what's gonna happen to him."

"Well, why would he?" Mary asks frantically.

"In his present state of mind, that's what he will probably do," Clark says. "If *you* can't convince him to turn himself in."

Once again, it is up to Mary Watson.

"You've got to keep in mind he's a very desperate person," Clark continues. "He doesn't have anything to lose."

"Yes, he's got a son to lose here, you know, he's got—"

"The point is, he doesn't have anything to lose. Killing one more person ain't gonna make any difference to him, probably."

"Well, have you inquired with Debbie as to where he is?"

"Ma'am, Debbie's not gonna tell us," Clark replies. "You can ask Debbie how old she is, and when she tells you, you have to go look it up. It doesn't do any good to ask that woman a question."

•   •   •

By late afternoon Clark's warning that Hearn might be shot had Mary Watson in a panic; and when Debbie Banister called at 6:56 P.M., Mary took out her frustrations on her. Debbie was pleasant and cordial, but Mary Watson was through with the pleasantries. She grilled Debbie for over an hour about Hearn's and her involvement in the murders, and caught Debbie in numerous contradictions. Even with old Mary Watson, Debbie couldn't keep her story straight.

Mary began by questioning her about the murders themselves:

"Okay, let me ask you something point-blank," Mary says. "And Debbie, you tell me the truth."

"Yes, ma'am," Debbie says obediently, like a little girl.

"Did *you* have anything to do with your husband's death?"

"No, ma'am, I did not."

"Did *Johnny* have anything to do with your husband's death?"

"No, ma'am, not that I know of."

"Did Johnny have anything to do with Marlena's husband's death?"

"No ma'am, not that I know of—at all."

"Did *you* have anything to do with it?"

"No, ma'am."

"Did, uh, Marlena *hire* someone to do it?"

"No, ma'am. She lives off welfare and food stamps, how could she hire anybody?"

Later in the conversation, Debbie offered her explanation of why the cops are accusing Hearn: "They're trying to find somebody to take the fall, and they're saying he would have the motive 'cause he was in love with me. Well, love is not—it may be a motive for murder, but that doesn't mean that someone's *guilty* of murder. He was not here the weekend Joe was killed, and he wasn't even in Gainesville the weekend that Cecil was killed. And he is the only common link, and that's why they're trying to say he did it."

"Well, I don't believe he did it," Mary says.

"No, no, he did not!" Debbie says. "I'll never believe that he had anything to do with it. . . . See, they're trying to say that the two [murders] had a common motive. Well, the only common thing is Marlene and I being sisters."

"And two sisters have their husbands killed," Mary says dryly.

"One's husband, and one's *ex*-husband for ten years," Debbie corrects her. "[Marlene] wasn't in town when hers was killed, and I wasn't in town when mine was. . . . But that doesn't mean that we couldn't have set it up—sure. I mean, that's what they're *saying*. They're saying we set it up, one of us set it up, or both of us set it up and that John was the one who did it. . . . And I'll swear to God he didn't have anything to do with it."

"Do you have any idea who might have?" Mary asks.

"No, ma'am, I don't have any earthly idea. I don't know any of Cecil's friends or enemies or connections. I had nothing to do with that man. And as far as Joe, Joe didn't have an enemy, not that I know of. I mean, after six years I never even heard the man raise his voice to anybody."

Later, Mary says: "Now I lied to the police at first and I told them I didn't know anything, and then I had to, I had to tell them the truth because they showed Wayne a picture of you and said, 'Do you know who this is?' 'That's going to be my new mother.' "

"Right, I know," Debbie says sympathetically.

"You *were* at my house."

"But you know, they haven't asked *me,*" Debbie protests. "And that's exactly what I'll tell them: I was *there,* I went up there that weekend. You know, I mean I have no doubt in my mind about telling them *whatever* they want to know, but they haven't asked me anything. They haven't questioned me, they haven't talked to me at all. . . . I get up in the morning and I go to work—no calls, no nothing. They go and talk to Mom and Dad—*Alachua County*—but the people here in *Bradford County* have not talked to me at all."

In fact, Don Denton had already interviewed Debbie three times, and several minutes later, she admitted it: "Well, see, I told them the last time I talked to them in Bradford County—now Alachua County, about Cecil, I've not talked to them ever—but this Bradford County bunch, I went down and I talked to them three or four times and I haven't heard a word from them since."

•   •   •

Mary also caught Debbie lying about her relationships with Hearn and Joe Banister: "I saw [Hearn] *one* time while Joe was alive," Debbie insists. "I saw him *one* time."

"Now you went to Atlanta to see him," Mary fires back. "They have records of the dates and everything."

"That's right, that's right," Debbie admits. "But see, they've never *asked* me if I went to see him. . . . they haven't asked me any of that."

Mary asks whether Hearn ever met Joe Banister.

"Yeah, he had met him twice," Debbie says. "He met him once up at the hospital, when Daddy was in the hospital . . . and then he met [Joe] also over at my Momma and Daddy's. . . . There wasn't any *problem* with them not knowing each other. Joe knew that he was a friend of mine, and that's all Joe knew. Because Joe and I were not having any type of problems—that *Joe* knew of."

Mary pounces on her. "But then you told me that he was a wife-beater!" she cries. "He beat you!"

"He *had*," Debbie whines. "But I could not *prove* that he had. So to say something that I cannot prove does not serve any purpose. . . . For everybody in the world to know him as a very quiet and passive person, would never in their dying day believe that he had ever beat me, so it's my word against his reputation, and my word would sink."

* * *

Next, Mary quizzes her about Joe's murder. Debbie claims that she can "barely remember what happened that night," but her memory is crystal clear when it comes to her own alibi: "As far as Joe, I know what happened when we left from going out to eat. I know what time I went and got the kids, and what time the highway patrolman stopped me for speeding—I know those things. Well, when they came and they told me that Joe had been shot, I don't remember anything—"

But then Mary springs a trap—ambushing Debbie with the most damning evidence against her: her phone calls to Hearn that night. "But you talked with Johnny forty-five minutes after your husband was dead," she charges.

Reeling, Debbie scrambles to come up with an answer. "I called—I may have *called* his apartment, but I didn't, I don't remember, I don't . . . I didn't *talk* to him," she sputters. "His re— he has a recorder. That recorder was on. I may have called him a couple of times . . . see, I don't know what I did. I know not long after Joe's death Momma called here one night and talked to me for thirty minutes, and I don't remember the first phone call."

"Uh-huh," Mary says skeptically.

"You know, I don't—I may have called him, but I don't remember *talking* to him."

Later, Debbie takes another stab at explaining the calls: "And if I called his house, which I'm sure I did—I called his house, but it was because out of desperation I needed to talk to somebody—and I tried to call. That doesn't mean he was there."

"Uh-huh."

"Because to the best of my knowledge, when I called that house there wasn't anybody there. All I got was his stupid machine. And I probably left a message on it each time I called."

• • •

Near the end, Mary talks about the effects this was having on Wayne. "But I cannot ease the pain that's in this child's heart and in his mind," she says. "And when he tells me, 'Grandmother, if they put my daddy in jail I just won't ever stop crying.' "

"Well, why did [Clark and Cole] talk to *him*?" Debbie asks indignantly. "What would make them want to talk to an eight-year-old?"

"I was in one office and he was in the other," Mary says. "I cannot tell you that. I do not know."

"Well, I would think that that would be *cruel*," Debbie says pitifully. "That would be cruel to do that to a child."

"Well, not necessarily," Mary retorts. "They didn't have to question him harshly—and probably didn't. I doubt seriously."

Mary also talks about the effect it's having on her: "This Rock of Gibraltar is beginning to rock, but it's not rocking the right way. I'm gonna crack up. Now I have no choice in the matter; my nerves just will not take it."

The conversation ends with Mary clarifying a comment she had made to Marlene two days before, which Hearn had thrown back in her face: "I did *not* say I was sorry Johnny met you," she says angrily. "I said, quote, 'I wish my son had never gone to the state of Florida.' "

"Yes, ma'am," Debbie says. "Well, I couldn't say that I would really blame you even if you said the other."

• • •

Tuesday night, John Wayne Hearn's world collapsed. Debbie Banister called him in Jackson after she finally managed to get off the phone with Mary Watson, and told him that she didn't want to see him again.

According to Hearn, Debbie was furious with Mary for keeping her on the phone for over an hour when she knew that Debbie's phone might be bugged. She told Hearn that the police had been to her house looking for him, and knew his license plate number and the color of his truck.

"I'm not going to lose my kids over you or anybody else!" Debbie cried. Hearn tried to reassure her that everything would work out, but Debbie was raging and inconsolable. Her anger kept building, until she delivered the final blow: "As far as I'm concerned, you can *drop dead*!" she told him, and hung up.

Hearn slumped on the bed and cried. Alone in a fifteen-dollar motel room in Jackson, Mississippi—the kind of cheap motel in which he had wasted his adult life—he was devastated. He had killed three people for Debbie Banister, and she had just told him to drop dead.

· · ·

Early Wednesday morning, Hearn climbed in his truck and drove out of Jackson. He still had no idea where he was going, and his options were shrinking quickly. After Debbie's phone call, he knew that he only had two choices: to turn himself in or to leave the country. There was no going back to Gainesville—or to Debbie.

He could try to make it to Canada, but Canada would be no safe haven with a murder warrant on his head. Mexico was closer, but to get there he would have to drive across Texas—and he was certain to get picked up. To make matters worse, he was almost broke. After the weekend at Disney World, Frank Sims' $1,000 was nearly gone.

So Hearn continued driving west. He thought the cops would be expecting him to go east—toward New York, where he had told his mother he was going (he didn't realize that Mary had already told Wiley Clark that Hearn was in Mississippi).

On impulse, he headed for Denver, 1,200 miles away. There was a big Union 76 truck stop outside of Denver, where Hearn used to stop and hire "swappers" to unload his truck for forty dollars a load. He figured that he could hide out at the truck stop and work as a swapper until he could plan an escape.

All day long he drove westward—through the Ozark Mountains of Arkansas and the foothills of Oklahoma, across the Kansas plains. He had driven crosscountry many times, but he had never felt so alone. He stayed on the backroads, avoiding the interstates, and kept glancing nervously in the rear-view mirror, expecting any moment to be pulled over and arrested—or shot.

As the miles rolled by, his idea about the Union 76 truck stop seemed more and more impractical. How long could he expect to hide there without being arrested? And how many trucks could he unload, at forty dollars a pop, before his knees gave out? To get out of the country and start a new life, he needed a lot of money— and quickly. He had killed three people, but he was no bank robber, no thief. There was only one thing that he knew how to do that could earn him any fast money: flying.

Gradually, a plan hatched in his mind. Twenty-six miles north of Denver is Boulder, the home of *Soldier of Fortune* magazine. Robert K. Brown was offering a $100,000 reward to any Russian or Nicaraguan pilot who defected with a Soviet Mi-24 attack helicopter, which was the backbone of the Sandinista air force. Hearn knew nothing about the Mi-24, but he had flown Hueys in Vietnam (it was against regulations, but sometimes one of his pilots would let him take the controls). *Aren't all helicopters basically the same?* he thought naively.

That was it. He would go to Boulder and talk to Robert K. Brown. The reward offer specified: "Does not apply to U.S. citizens," but Hearn would talk man-to-man with Col. Bob. *Colonel* to *Colonel.* "How badly do you want one of those babies?" he would ask. If Brown agreed to pay him, he would go to Nicaragua, steal an Mi-24, and fly it out. *Soldier of Fortune* magazine had gotten him started in this game, perhaps it could get him out.

It would be the ultimate mission. He would sneak into Nicaragua and steal an Mi-24 right out from under Daniel Ortega's nose. He would put together a team of kick-ass commandos from the portfolio of resumés that he was still carrying around in his briefcase; he would show the world that the Sandinista army and their Soviet advisors were no match for a handful of aging ex-marines. *Semper Fi!* He'd spit in Ivan's eye.

Of course, he also knew that it would probably be his *last* mission. The Sandinistas had ten Mi-24s; he would have to steal one and blow up the rest. Once he made it to the helicopter, all he knew to do was flip every switch until he found the igniter, then try to fly it into Honduras. He figured that he had an eighty percent chance of dying. But at least he'd die a hero. Just like his daddy. Just like John Wayne, in the movies. People might even forget that he had killed three people.

And what difference would it make if he died, anyway? Without Debbie Banister, he had no reason to live. He couldn't get her off his mind. His truck was a shrine to Debbie: He had a framed album of photos of Debbie and her children lying on the seat beside him so that he could look at her while he drove.

The more heartsick he became over Debbie, the madder he got at his mother. All his life, he had chosen between his mother and the women he loved, and his mother had always won. Debra had left, Elaine had left, the others had all left. But Debbie Banister was different. He would show his mother just how different.

Late Wednesday afternoon he pulled off the highway and called Mary Watson. He ordered her to go to the Zippy Mart, which Mary did, although she carried with her a new Radio Shack microcassette recorder and a stick-on phone mike, which she had bought to record his calls for Wiley Clark.

Hearn lashed out at his mother like he had never done before. He cursed her for keeping Debbie on the phone so long and blamed her for losing the only woman that he'd ever loved. Mary pleaded with him to turn himself in, but Hearn told her that if he did he would be killed by the "big organization" that he'd been working for, which had people all over the world—even in jail.

"We can get you a lawyer," Mary told him. "We'll sell the house. We'll prove you didn't do it."

"Yeah, you'll be saying that right up until the day they electrocute me," he said scornfully.

Mary begged him to come home, but he said that he was never coming back, that he was going to be involved in a government-sponsored operation in Central America. "You'll read about it in the papers," he said. "I love my country."

At the end, he was crying. "Tell Wayne I love him," he sobbed. "I love you, I love Wayne, I love Dad. . . . but I love Debbie and Amanda and John above everything in the world."

He had finally broken with his mother, but it was too late. Debbie Banister was already gone. He climbed back in his truck, and drove on toward Boulder.

• • •

That same day Ann McNeese called Chris Kirk at the Brazos County Sheriff's Department, identified herself as John Wayne Hearn's sister, and offered to help get Hearn into custody.

The next morning Ann called Debbie Banister, who said that Hearn had called her from a motel in Hugo, Colorado, eighty-five miles southeast of Denver. Ann called Hearn at the motel and persuaded him to talk to Kirk, who promised not to trace the call. Eventually, Kirk talked him into turning himself in.

One factor was that Hearn knew he would never see his son again if he left the country. Another, perhaps more significant, factor was that he was afraid of dying—either on a bumbling suicide mission to Nicaragua or on some lonesome Colorado highway. Kirk convinced him that until he was in custody, he was fair game for every hotheaded cop in the country. Ultimately, Hearn was more mama's boy than he was John Wayne; he didn't want to die.

Hearn refused to turn himself in in Colorado, but agreed to drive back to Texas and turn himself in there. Kirk promised not to make a big show out of the arrest: no handcuffs, no drawn guns, no sirens or flashing lights.

Sheriff Ronnie Miller bet Kirk a steak dinner that Hearn wouldn't do it. "That son of a bitch ain't gonna drive 800 miles to turn himself in—not facing the death penalty," Miller said. "Ain't no way."

• • •

Miller lost the bet. On Friday, March 15, 1985, in Huntsville, Texas, Hearn turned himself in. The arrest took place in the parking lot of the Bonanza Steak House, off Interstate 45, right across the street from the Texas State Penitentiary.

Kirk, the compulsive organizer, tape-recorded the event. He had agreed to give Ann a few moments alone with Hearn before he was arrested. At 1:30 P.M., Hearn pulled into the parking lot. He got out of his truck, crying, and hugged Ann. "I didn't do it," he bawled.

"Don't worry, we'll get an attorney and prove it," she replied.

Kirk gave them about thirty seconds, then walked over. Hearn was still crying. "Get it together, Johnny," Ann said softly.

"John," Kirk said, offering his hand.

"This is Mr. Kirk," Ann said.

"Hello." Hearn whimpered.

"I'm glad you came in," Kirk said. "You're doing the right thing. Is everything okay right now?"

"Yes, sir," Hearn replied, still crying.

"Okay," Kirk said.

"Settle down, bud, it's okay," Ann said.

Hearn handed Kirk the portfolio that he'd been carrying in his briefcase, with his World Security Group resumes. "I want to give you this stuff and I want to tell you something," he sobbed. "When you open this and start going through it my whole family's life's gonna be in danger, and *my* life's gonna be in danger when you start reading stuff that's in it."

"Settle down, babe, okay?" Ann said.

Kirk didn't want to accept the portfolio until after the arrest. "Just hold on to that and we'll talk shortly," he said.

The warrant was read, and Hearn was mirandized. Then Kirk asked him about the papers.

"They have to do with World Security Group," Hearn said.

"World Security Group?"

"Yes."

"And you're turning those over to me at this time?"

"Yes."

"Okay," Kirk said. "They're consisting of an envelope, a file folder, and two spiral notebooks. Okay . . . I'll guard these with my life."

6

JOHN WAYNE HEARN was not what Sheriff Ronnie Miller was expecting. He was expecting a *bad boy*—a gun-for-hire mercenary who had already killed three people. Hearn was certainly big enough for the part, but Miller wasn't sure what to make of him when he spent the drive from Huntsville to Bryan whimpering in the backseat of the squad car. *This guy is a mercenary?* Miller thought to himself. *This guy killed three people?*

He was even less sure when they got Hearn back to Bryan, where Miller and Chris Kirk decided to try the classic "good cop-bad cop" routine on him. Miller, all 300 pounds of him, played the bad cop; while Kirk, the college boy with the "trust me" face, played the good cop.

Miller handcuffed Hearn to a chair, then leaned over him, with his beefy forearms imprisoning Hearn in the chair, his mammoth belly almost touching him, his face only inches away. Miller started yelling at him: "We're gonna get the goddamn truth out of you, one way or another! You come down here and kill some girl you don't even know!"

Hearn protested that he hadn't done anything.

"You sorry scumbag!" Miller yelled. "We know about the alibi letter Bob Black sent you."

"I've never seen that letter," Hearn whined.

Miller called him a liar and threatened to get the fingerprints off the letter and prove that he had. Hearn asked him to please get the fingerprints off it, which would prove that he had never seen it

(Hearn maintains that he pulled the $1,000 cashier's check out of the envelope, but not the letter).

"You think you're a badass, don't you, boy?" Miller said. "We'll pull the goddamn cuffs off you and see how bad you are!"

At that, Hearn broke down completely and started blubbering like a baby. He cried so hard and so long that snot was running out of his nose and dripping onto the floor.

Miller backed up and stared at him, flabbergasted. "After ten years of investigations, I had never seen a mercenary with snot coming out of his nose," he recalls. Finally, Miller walked out in the hall and told Kirk and Owen, "I dunno, boys, any guy that slings snot can't be *bad*."

• • •

Chris Kirk put Hearn back together after the snot-slinging episode —fed him supper and let him take a nap—and started interviewing him at 9:25 P.M. Kirk, the good guy, went strictly by the book: He tape-recorded the statement (as required by Texas law) and re-mirandized Hearn before he started. There was no yelling this time, but Hearn still started bawling three minutes into the interview (the first time he mentioned his mother and his son) and cried repeatedly throughout.

Hearn had no idea of all the evidence they already had on him in Texas. Miller had told him about the Federal Express letter but he didn't know that Kirk also had copies of his motel registrations, rental car receipts, and airline tickets from both trips to Texas, plus copies of the $1,000 cashier's check and the personal money order.

Mary Watson might have put the final nail in her son's coffin by turning over the letter and cashier's check, but Hearn pounded it home himself: When Deputy M.L. Maddox searched Hearn's briefcase he found a leather pouch containing a gold pendant with ten small diamonds and three blue sapphires, which had been positively identified as having belonged to Sandra Black.

Not knowing any of this, Hearn had to wing it with Kirk, making up his story as he went along and adapting it according to Kirk's reactions and the new information that he learned. Hearn may have been a snot-slinging mercenary, but he was one hell of a liar, and as the interview went on, his confidence soared.

He spun a wild tale, claiming that he was being set up by

powerful operatives within World Security Group. With his life on
the line, he was no longer *Colonel* Hearn, the *commander* of World
Security Group, but a lowly peon who had only done as he was told
and had answered to anonymous bosses who communicated with
him solely through Message World.

He showed Kirk the letter from L.C. Mitchell in Toronto
about overthrowing the government of "French Guiana"—as
Hearn mistakenly calls Guyana. Hearn described how in late November, 1984, he had piloted a single-engine Cessna 206 loaded
with four armed men—one of three such planes allegedly involved
in the mission—from an abandoned air force base in South Carolina to Kerrville, Texas, for refueling, and then on to "French
Guiana." Halfway across the Caribbean, Hearn said, he had gotten
cold feet, had intentionally overheated the engine, and had
aborted the mission.

Because of that, he said, he had cost World Security Group
hundreds of thousands of dollars, and the organization's leaders
were now framing him for Sandra Black's murder.

Kirk was skeptical. He asked Hearn to explain where he had
gotten the gold pendant set that had been found in his briefcase.
Hearn claimed that his World Security Group masters had left it for
him in a locker at the Atlanta bus station several months before.

Kirk didn't buy it. "John, I am going to tell you that that piece
of jewelry has been positively identified as a piece of jewelry that
was stolen in the burglary that occurred at the time of Sandra
Black's death. What do you have to say about that?"

"There is nothing I can say about it," Hearn replied glumly.

Kirk pressed him. "It is in your possession. We have to have
some type of explanation for it other than the vague one we have
got."

Listening to the interview tape, one can almost smell the
sawdust burning as Hearn scrambled for an answer. "It's all falling
into place," he said at last, in a conspiratorial whisper.

"What's falling into place?" Kirk asked.

"They set me up," Hearn said. "The motherfuckers set me
up."

He nearly pulled it off. By the time he showed Kirk all of the
letters in his portfolio file and described the other "missions" that
he claimed to have done—two gun-running flights from New

Jersey to Brownsville, Texas, delivering weapons intended for the *contras;* brokering the sale of 600 weapons left in Honduras by the U.S. Army after a training exercise; and the upcoming "Operation Golden Eagle," which Hearn claimed would be flying military personnel in and out of Central America, allegedly with the CIA's backing—Kirk's head was spinning.

"This thing goes deep," Hearn said. "I told you that in the car."

"I'm starting to believe you," Kirk replied, obviously mesmerized by the tales of overseas intrigue.

When the interview finally ended, at ten minutes after midnight, Kirk came out and told Sheriff Miller, "I think someone else may be involved."

Seeing a chance to win back his steak dinner, Miller responded, "You wanna bet?"

• • •

Saturday morning, Don Denton, Wiley Clark, and Farnell Cole were on the first plane to Bryan, Texas. Denton had been gone so much in the past month (after two trips to Columbia, one to Atlanta, and almost-daily jaunts to Gainesville) that it had become a sore point at home. When he called his wife to tell her that Hearn was in custody, he tried to make a joke: "Honey, you're not going to believe where we have to go now—*Anchorage, Alaska!*"

She didn't laugh. "Well, you might as well go to hell," Dot Denton responded, "you've been everywhere else in the past month." For the wife of a Methodist minister, those were strong words.

Before leaving for Texas, Wiley Clark went to see his boss, Johnny Yardborough, the chief investigator for the state attorney's office. "Don't send me out there without telling me what I can give him and what I can't," Clark said. "I don't want to have to run back and forth to a phone like an idiot when I'm talking to a man about two or three murders."

Yardborough consulted with Eugene Whitworth, the state attorney for the six-county district. They agreed that, if necessary, Clark could offer Hearn a deal on the death penalty—provided that he confessed and testified against everyone who had hired him, both in Florida and Texas. "I had to have that, or there wasn't any sense in me going out there," Clark says.

•   •   •

Denton, Clark, and Cole arrived in Bryan at three-thirty on Saturday afternoon. First, Clark met with Bill Turner, the Brazos County district attorney, and briefed him on the Florida cases. Without Hearn's testimony, Clark said, Debbie, Marlene, Iris, and Frank Sims would all go free. Florida was willing to make a deal with Hearn to give up the death penalty, but that would only work if Texas did likewise.

Texas didn't need to make a deal with Hearn. With the Federal Express letter and cashier's check, the gold pendant, and the paper trail that placed Hearn in Bryan on February 21, Turner had an airtight case on him. And he didn't really need Hearn's testimony to convict Bob Black. But it was also clear that the Florida investigators were the ones who had broken the case—and without Hearn's testimony, Florida had no chance of getting a conviction on the Sims family.

Given all of that, Turner agreed to waive the death penalty, provided Hearn pled guilty and testified truthfully in *both* states. It was a stranglehold deal: If he didn't testify in Florida, then Texas would give him the needle (execution is by lethal injection), and if he didn't testify in Texas, then Florida would electrocute him. Hearn couldn't have picked two worse states in which to be charged with capital murder: Florida and Texas are the two leading death-penalty states in the country.

First, however, Hearn had to talk.

Denton, Clark, and Cole got their shot at him at five-thirty that afternoon. They decided to tag-team him: Clark and Cole would be the first team, Denton and Chris Kirk the second, and Sheriff Miller and Charlie Owen would freelance in and out.

Hearn was led into the interview room handcuffed and shackled. "Hello, Mr. Clark," he said politely.

"Hello, John," replied Clark, who was itching to begin.

After his interview with Chris Kirk the night before, Hearn must have been feeling confident. Kirk had told the Florida investigators about Hearn's World Security Group escapades, but they completely discounted his stories and thought that Kirk was wet behind the ears for believing them. Clark, Denton, and Cole couldn't have cared less about what Hearn had done or not done in Central America or Guyana. They were only interested in one thing: Had he killed Cecil Batie and Joe Banister?

Once the interview began, it didn't end for seven hours. Hearn started out repeating the story that he'd concocted the night before about World Security Group setting him up, but Clark and Cole didn't buy it, and told him so. Clark started laying his cards on the table a little at a time (in case Hearn refused to cooperate), telling him what they had on him in Florida—his telephone calls to Debbie, her trip to Atlanta, the paper trail across Florida, Georgia, and South Carolina. Faced with this barrage of evidence, Hearn clammed up and stared at the floor.

"As long as you let him tell his story, it was semibelievable," Farnell Cole recalls. "If you confronted him with something, then he would just pout and look at the floor." It was a technique that Hearn had practiced for years: "pouting for Mama," Elaine Hearn calls it.

Wiley Clark began yelling at him, trying to get a response. "I'd say 'John! John!' I'd have to ask him a question three or four times to get any response," Clark recalls.

Today, Hearn claims that Clark gave him vivid descriptions of being electrocuted, a charge that Clark and Cole deny. However, Cole admits that they hammered away at the death penalty: "We pounded him with the fact that we had three chances to see him go to the chair—between Texas and the two Florida cases—and we'd take those odds any day of the week. At least one time he'd sit, and we really didn't care about the other two."

At one point, Hearn told them that he wanted to talk to a lawyer, and Clark stood up and threw his papers on the desk. "That's fine, I can't talk to you anymore," he said angrily. "If you get a lawyer, he's going to tell you not to talk to us, and that's the end of this conversation. I can't help you, I can't do anything for you, you're gonna get the death penalty out here, and we're gonna do our damnedest to get you the death penalty in Florida." When Clark and Cole started walking out of the room, Hearn changed his mind and agreed to keep talking.

Hour after hour, the interview dragged on, with Clark yelling and Hearn staring at the floor or giving one-word replies. Clark kept telling him that they knew Debbie was involved, and that she didn't love him, but Hearn still refused to admit anything.

Three or four hours into it, Denton and Kirk came in and tried the good-cop approach, but they were no more successful. By then, Hearn was so pent up that when Kirk reached out and touched his arm, he reared up, threw himself against the wall, and screamed: "Don't shoot me!! Don't shoot me!!" He started crying and actually foaming at the mouth.

Wiley Clark was afraid that Hearn was flipping out and he yelled at Farnell Cole, "Get witnesses!" Cole threw open the door and hollered, "Everybody come in here—now!" Hearn calmed down after about thirty seconds, but not before scaring Charlie Owen half to death. "Scared the hell out of me," he recalls. "Hearn's a pretty big boy, and I wasn't sure what he was going to try."

At another point, Hearn allegedly started speaking in other voices—as "Skippy." Ironically, Skippy didn't exist. Bob Black had addressed his Federal Express letter to "Skipper" (his nickname for Hearn), but after three generations of photocopies, the word looked like "Skippy." The night before, Chris Kirk had asked Hearn, "Who is Skippy?" At that time, Hearn said he didn't know, but twenty-four hours later, he *became* Skippy. "He was trying to con us with the old split-personality thing," says Denton.

Finally, around midnight, Hearn admitted killing Cecil Batie and Joe Banister. He had gotten angry at Wiley Clark, so Clark and Cole had left the room to give Denton and Kirk—the good guys— one last shot. Hearn told them that he didn't mean to kill anybody, that he only meant to "scare the people." He said that he wanted to scare Cecil Batie because he was hurting Marlene and her children and that he fired one shot and the shotgun jumped out of his hand and fired itself the second time. He said that he wanted to scare Joe Banister because he was beating Debbie, and drove alongside him, fired two shots, and kept driving.

Today, Wiley Clark believes that fear of dying was what finally made Hearn confess. "If we hadn't been able to get him out of the death penalty in Florida, I don't think he would have ever talked to us," Clark says. "Yeah, he was scared of dying."

•   •   •

Sunday morning, the Florida investigators had a big problem: they knew that Hearn's late-night confession would never stand up in court. Verbal confessions are admissible in Florida, but any good defense attorney would argue that the confession had been coerced. Given the length of the interview, Clark's yelling, and the investigator's tag-teaming of Hearn, a trial judge would probably agree.

However, they were also aware of a recent U.S. Supreme Court ruling (in *Oregon* v. *Elstad)* that had given law enforcement officers more leeway to "clean up" a dirty confession. They felt that if they could get Hearn to repeat his confession on Sunday morning—after a night's sleep and breakfast—*that* statement would be admissible.

Which is exactly what they did. Hearn was brought in and mirandized by Clark and Cole (Chris Kirk had already mirandized him twice). Then Hearn repeated his story, without hesitation: he had killed Cecil Batie and Joe Banister by accident. This time, Denton took extensive notes.

When they tried to get Hearn to say any more, he went back to pouting and staring at the floor, but little by little, they pulled out the details: Hearn told them about buying the Winchester 1200, about stealing the shotgun shells from Frank Sims, and about tossing both guns in Payne's Prairie. When he admitted the latter, Wiley Clark was kneeling on the floor, looking up at him. "It was ridiculous, but the son of a bitch wouldn't look at you," Clark says. Hearn was adamant that Debbie Banister had not been involved in either murder and said that he had *stolen* the AR-7 from her house without her knowledge.

While he was confessing, Hearn also admitted to Charlie Owen that he had killed Sandra Black. Once again, it was "an accident." He said that he had wanted to leave Steep Hollow but couldn't, because of the dogs, and that when Sandra came home she saw him and started screaming, and he got scared and shot her.

He also told Owen about tossing the Ruger .22 off the bridge at Lake Conroe. On Sunday afternoon he directed Owen and Kirk to the spot, but the gun was never recovered. (Owen suspects that it landed on the bank and was picked up by a local fisherman.)

Sunday evening, the Florida investigators left Bryan. They had gotten only part of what they had come for: They had an indictable case against John Wayne Hearn but only circumstantial evidence against Debbie Banister, and nothing on Marlene or the Simses.

•   •   •

Bob Black wasn't talking to anyone except his lawyer.

He *was* writing to Gary Wayne almost every day. He rarely mentioned the reason that he was in jail, and instead, tried to come across like a typical loving dad: he told Gary Wayne that he was proud of him, asked him about school, and reminded him to do his chores. When he did mention Sandra's murder in one letter, he told Gary Wayne that he had "some fortune" in "becoming a man so early in life."

In fact, Gary Wayne *was* trying to be a man, the way his father wanted him to be. He started going to counseling shortly after Bob's arrest, and the counselor described him this way:

> He was very positive—almost too much. He acted as though everything was fine. One would never know within the last three weeks his mother was murdered, he found the body and his father was arrested for hiring the hit man to kill his mother. Gary stated he was fine, it did no good to worry or think about all this so he didn't. He maintained a pleasant look on his face and laughed throughout. He stated his father did not do this.

Despite what he told the counselor, Gary Wayne was a terribly confused and frightened fifteen-year-old. He was afraid to go outside, afraid to be alone in the house, and terrified that someone might kill *him*—just like his mother. Marjorie Eimann had to sleep in the same bed with him, but he still had nightmares almost every night and numbing headaches at school, where his grades had plummeted.

Gary Wayne was most confused about his father. He had visited Bob in jail the first two Saturdays after he was arrested but didn't go back again and seldom wrote, despite Bob's pleadings.

Marjorie decided that Bob's letters were going to drive Gary Wayne over the edge and started dumping them in the trash unopened. She fell back on the technique that Henry Arnold had used with her many years before: fishing. "I carried him to every tank in Brazos County," she says, "trying to help him get better."

With Bob unable to get to Gary Wayne, he started working on his best friends: Lance Basham and Butch White. Bob wrote to them, phoned them, and eventually convinced them to visit him in jail. When they did, he sent Lance out to the cemetery to put flowers on Sandra's grave.

7

Florida Slaying Cases 'Like a Television Script'

Starke—A self-proclaimed mercenary, pilot, businessman, truck driver, former marine and freelance photographer has admitted killing three people in two states, including two men in Alachua and Bradford counties, Bradford County investigators said yesterday.

"It reads just like a television script," Bradford County Sheriff Dolph Reddish said. . . . "The investigation is continuing. We do expect other arrests."

—Florida *Times-Union*
March 19, 1985

Debbie,

I am so mixed up at this time. . . . They just kept asking hundreds of questions, I don't even remember answering most of them. At one time I didn't even remember where I was at. . . .

Debbie, I don't know what's going on, they are trying to prove I did something that I didn't. I have your pictures and I cry a lot each day that goes by. I love you more now than I ever did. . . . I am so depressed that I only want to die at times. I miss you and I do need your love.

Yours forever,
Johnny

My Darling Debbie,

    Please don't abandon me now. You are all that I
continue to live for. I love you so much and hope you will
help me as you said. . . . They were going to arrest your
dad for Cecil and you for Joe. They just kept baddgering
[sic] me for 2 days. . . . I think there is a name for it
called mind conditioning. . . . Write me please!!!!!

Loving you is right

On Saturday, March 23, Mary Watson arrived in Bryan with
Tom and Wayne to visit Hearn. She bought him a TV set for his jail
cell and had pictures taken of all of them together. Hearn's eyes
were blurry and red-rimmed from crying. On Sunday Mary returned home to Columbia.

On Monday Hearn suddenly changed his story. He gave Chris
Kirk an eight-page handwritten statement in which he stated that
he had picked up a man named "Doug" at the Goodyear blimp, on
orders from World Security Group. Hearn claimed that Doug had
killed Sandra Black, and *he* had only burglarized the house, at Bob
Black's direction.

Today, Hearn admits that the statement was a reaction to his
mother's visit. She didn't want to believe that he was guilty, so he
made up a story to satisfy her. Kirk paid no attention to it.

Saturday morning [March 30]

My Beautiful Lady,

    No one can make me believe you don't care. It sure
seems that way. . . . not even one single letter from you.
. . . I feel as though I have been abandoned by every one.
To take this alone. I'm trying very hard to be strong but
without word from you it is very hard for me to do. . . .
By now I'm quite sure things are starting to fall in place for
you. Debra, you promised me you would stand beside me. I
believed your promise. Please don't let me down now.
After all, how long does it take to write a letter to me.

Loving you forever,
Me!

Saturday night [March 30]

My Beautiful young Lady,

. . . You answered the most important question of my life
once before with a yes. I hope you still mean that. I want
that more than anything in the world. I'm sure you know.
  Will you marry me?
  Will you marry me?
  Will you marry me?
  Will you marry me?
  Will you marry me?
  Will you marry me?
My only reason for living . . .

Forever yours,
Me

Widow Says She Is Asked to Prove Her Innocence in Killing

By Bill Shields
Sun staff writer

Starke—"Whatever happened to the idea of being innocent
until proven guilty?" That's the question being asked by Debra
Banister. Her husband, Joe Banister, 41, of Starke was shot
and killed on Feb. 2. . . .

  Mrs. Banister said she had nothing to do with the death of
her husband and did not hire or make a deal of any kind with
Hearn or anyone else to kill him. "I loved my husband very
much," she said. . . .

  Mrs. Banister said she didn't suspect that Hearn had shot
her husband until she read about it in the paper . . . [she]
said Hearn had never been in her home in Starke and she
didn't know how he might have gotten one of her husband's
guns. . . .

  "The only other thing I've done physically is that I had a
perm put in my hair that I call my 'jail cell curls' so I wouldn't
look all shaggy or whatever if I went before the judge," she
said. . . . "I cry a lot, but I look into my little boy's big blue
eyes and I look at my little girl and I know that I have to fight
back for them. My name and my reputation has gone to hell in

a hand-basket, so they say. So all I have got left to fight for are my children."

—Gainesville *Sun*
Sunday, March 31, 1985

Monday afternoon [April 1, 1985]

My Beautiful Lady,

Why Debra, why haven't you written to me? . . . Stop hurting me please! . . . I can't believe you are doing it intentionally. I know you care. . . . There was a wedding on TV today and I cried so much over us. You are very strong. I found out a lot stronger than me. . . . I am getting the strangest feeling though. 3 weeks and no word from the woman who really convinced me she loved me so much . . . I realize I can't take much more on my own now. . . .

Forever yours,
Me

P.S. Don't forget W.Y.M.M.

Tuesday morning, April 2

My Beautiful Lady,

Okay Butthole, don't you think its about time you wrote to me. . . . I look each day for word from the person I love . . . I just can't believe you don't love me. . . .

Listen Butthole, take care of our kids . . . Please love me, Don't ever stop—I need it so bad.

Forever yours,
Johnny

In Starke, Don Denton, Wiley Clark, and assistant state attorney Tom Elwell were preparing to go before a Bradford County grand jury on the Joe Banister case. Their evidence was increasing daily: on March 22, after a four-day search of Payne's Prairie, a team of divers had recovered three pieces of an AR-7 survival rifle

—the butt, the butt plate (the cap on the end of the butt), and an ammunition clip—near the observation platform where John Wayne Hearn said that he had thrown it. They did not find the barrel of the AR-7 (which made it impossible to match the ballistics of the gun with the bullet fragments removed from Joe Banister's head), nor did they find the Winchester 1200. Nonetheless, they had found an AR-7 right where Hearn had said it would be.

Mary Watson, who still believed that her son was innocent, was frantically searching for evidence *against* Debbie Banister. She went through Hearn's belongings and found two letters that Debbie had written to him (on December 19, 1984, and January 9, 1985). The letters made it clear that Hearn and Debbie were having an affair before Joe Banister's death. She also found a napkin with the floor plan of a house drawn on it—which turned out to be Cecil Batie's. Mary sent the letters and the napkin to Elwell.

Still, Denton, Clark, and Elwell had a major problem. They had a solid case against Hearn but only circumstantial evidence against Debbie. They could prove a gigantic love affair, and had the highly suspicious phone calls that she and Hearn made on the night of Joe's murder, but that was it. Hearn had not implicated her, and they had no other testimony or physical evidence to link her to the murder.

There was reportedly some reluctance from higher-ups in the state attorney's office about even trying to indict her, since there was insufficient evidence to get a conviction. But Denton and Clark argued that the only way to get Hearn to implicate Debbie was to first put her in jail. He was still too much in love with her to *send* her to jail himself, but he might talk if she were already there. "We had to take that pressure off him," Clark says.

The grand jury was scheduled to convene on Thursday, April 11. Hearn got wind of it on April 3, and immediately wrote to Debbie.

Wed. morning [April 3]

My Beautiful Lady,

I don't know if you know whats going on there or not but I just found out. They are going before grand jury to try to indict both of us. Debra you had nothing to do with any thing but they are trying to say you are. They are bringing Eunice from Atlanta, they talked to her again, they have supenad [sic] my mother and they have phone records from bank where we used to talk. I saw you in so much pain and saw you suffer so much. . . . I know how he use to hit on you all the time. How he use to abuse you. You don't know anything. there is more I want to say but I need to tell your attorney and you face to face. Not in a letter.

Debbie no matter what happens in the end please keep in touch with me. Please don't hate me when this is all over. All I ever wanted was you to be safe.

Well, I'll call later on tonight and talk to you. I know about article in newspaper and other things. I know why also. . . .

> Forever yours,
> Johnny

P.S. You can show this letter to Val [Val Bates, Debbie's attorney]. It will help him some. The other I need to tell him not in a letter or phone. Couldn't stand to see you hurt or abused anymore. Didn't mean to hurt anyone especially you. Please don't hate me. Only wanted to scare him.

I hope this will help Val. Please don't hate me, I saw you hurt and beat on too much. Debbie it was an accident, only meant to scare, I'm sorry. I'm sorry. Forgive me please. I lost my head.

It was the first time, in print, that Hearn had admitted killing Joe Banister, but his crude attempts at protecting Debbie were all too obvious (". . . show this letter to Val. It will help him some."). However, Debbie wouldn't receive the letter for two weeks. In what appears highly suspicious, this letter, along with the next *nine* letters that Hearn wrote to her—in which he denies her involvement in the murders—were not postmarked from Bryan until April 16, the day after Debbie was arrested. The sheriff's department apparently didn't mail the letters until after Debbie was in custody.

Thursday morning, [April 4]

My Beautiful Baby,

. . . Baby, through all of this please don't cast me aside
. . . I do need you so bad. Baby, the other day I got so
depressed. I had electric cord in hand fixing to stick it into
toilet. All of a sudden it was like I heard you calling out to
me "Johnny please don't I love you." It was so hard to
stop myself. . . . Have been having bad nightmares or
flashbacks to Vietnam . . . I have ask to see head doctor
but no one yet. . . .

On Friday, April 5, Hearn received the first of two letters that
Debbie would write him, and his spirits soared. He wrote her a
flurry of letters, accusing the Florida investigators of making up
lies about him (these letters weren't postmarked until April 16).

Friday afternoon [April 5]

My Beautiful Lady,

Received two letters from you today. . . . Thank you,
Debra, thank you for standing behind me. You know I need
your support. I am so sorry that you are going through
what you have. I did not say I did anything for money in
Florida. That is a lie. . . . I have found out that the police
have really said a bunch of lies to everyone. . . . I know
they are not true. . . .

Always,
John

Saturday night [April 6]

Beautiful Debra Ann,

I don't even know if you are getting my letters now. I
am so scared something has happened to you. . . . You
have done nothing, Debra, nothing. I have been tricked
into lies by corrupt police who have an ego problem . . .
They refused to let me have attorney and made up their

own stories when they came here. Wiley Clark would lie
about his own mother to take care of his ego. . . .

Within a few days, however, Hearn's doubts had resurfaced,
and by April 10, after no further word from Debbie, he was about
to crack.

> Thursday night [April 11]
>
> My Beautiful Baby,
>
> . . . All I do is think of you all the time. I wonder if I
> could erase myself out of the picture if it would help you. I
> get so depressed when I start to think about it . . . I
> would give my life for you anytime. . . . I need you so
> bad, baby . . . No matter what happens you will always be
> my life. . . . You will always be there until my death. I
> need you, I need you my darling. Please don't ever cast me
> aside, I could not live without that. . . .
>
> Forever yours,
> *Me!*

That night, alone and depressed but still desperately in love,
he wrote to his mother and said that he was through writing to
Debbie. He never wrote her again.

• • •

On Monday, April 15, Debbie Banister and John Wayne Hearn
were indicted by a Bradford County grand jury for the first-degree
murder of Joe Banister. One hour after the indictment, Debbie was
arrested in front of Marlene's trailer by Don Denton, Wiley Clark,
and Farnell Cole. A local television camera crew filmed the arrest,
which was broadcast on the evening news.

It was Debbie's first starring role on local TV, and she played
it to the hilt. She refused to turn over her children to two female
HRS caseworkers but stood defiantly in the yard, clutching
Amanda to her breast. Marlene was right beside her, carrying John,
while Iris Sims stood protectively between them.

The children were wailing pathetically, and Cole tried to hustle Debbie along. "Come on, Debbie," he said, "you're under

arrest, okay—we're fixing to take you to the jail." He pointed to Amanda. "You're gonna have to put her down."

Debbie finally handed Amanda to her mother. The girl reached out to Debbie and cried even louder. Cole, looking uncomfortable in a shirt and tie, gave Debbie a gentle prod with one finger, and steered her toward his car.

"No! No! I want to stay with her!" Amanda screamed, as one of the HRS workers put her in another car.

Marlene gave Debbie a good-bye hug (by then both of them were crying). Debbie removed her gold necklace and handed it to Marlene. Cole handcuffed Debbie and opened the passenger door of the car. At the last moment, Debbie turned to the camera and said tearfully, "I just want my kids, and I'm not guilty."

•   •   •

On April 29, Don Denton and Wiley Clark flew back to Texas to talk to Hearn one more time. They had Debbie in jail where they wanted her (her bail had been set at $250,000), but they still had a weak case against her. Denton and Clark had been trying to convince Mary Watson and Ann McNeese that Hearn needed to tell the truth to avoid the death penalty. In turn, Mary and Ann had been working on Hearn.

They weren't the only ones working on him: Iris Sims had also developed a sudden interest in Hearn's welfare. She hadn't written him at all during his first month in prison, but after Debbie's arrest she fired off three quick letters—on April 25, April 30, and May 6. Iris enclosed copies of newspaper articles about Debbie's bond hearing (at which Mary Watson had testified), along with the snide remark: "Your mother is doing everything she can to discredit Deb." She described Debbie's plight in jail in great detail, reassured him that Debbie loved him, and urged him to hold the fort, saying, "We *all* care."

But Hearn had already turned against the Simses. On April 29, after several hours of questioning (this time with his court-appointed attorney present), he gave Denton and Clark a written statement in which he said that he had received a phone call in October, 1984, from "a female," asking him to get her sister's kids back. He went on to say that after subsequent conversations, Frank Sims had "agreed to pay me ten thousand dollars to kill Cecil

Batie," and that Debbie Banister had brought him a sealed envelope with the money but added, "She did not know what was in the
envelope."

The next day he gave them Debbie too. He identified her as
"the female" who had called him (although he still stuck to the
Cottondale story about meeting her years before), and said: "It
was understood through the conversations with Debbie Banister,
Frank Sims, and Iris Sims that I would receive ten thousand dollars
to kill Cecil Batie." He added a disclaimer at the end about his
earlier statement: "In previous conversations with law enforcement officers . . . I did not tell them the whole truth and pur-
posely did not tell them about Debbie Banister's part in the death
of Cecil Batie because I loved her and did not want to get her into
any trouble."

•   •   •

Denton and Clark returned to Florida the next day, still feeling
somewhat frustrated. True, Hearn had finally linked Debbie,
Frank, and Iris to the crimes for the first time, but there were
problems with his statements: they only dealt with Cecil Batie, not
Joe Banister; and the two statements were contradictory, which
undermined their credibility. They still didn't have what they
needed.

8

On June 7, 1985, John Wayne Hearn appeared as a State's witness in front of an Alachua County grand jury that was hearing testimony on the Cecil Batie case. He agreed to testify as part of a plea-bargain worked out the night before, after a marathon thirteen-hour negotiating session between Hearn, his lawyers, and the state attorney's office. Hearn agreed to plead guilty to all three murders and to testify in Florida and in Texas, in exchange for three life sentences.

That afternoon, indictments were returned against Hearn, Debbie Banister, Marlene Sims Watson, Frank Sims, and Iris Sims for the murder of Cecil Batie. All five were charged with first-degree murder and conspiracy to commit murder.

Marlene was arrested that evening while eating dinner at a Western Sizzlin' Steak house, and Frank and Iris were picked up at home. Eugene Whitworth, the state attorney, held a press conference that night and declared: "I think everyone here will tell you this is the most bizarre, complex case they've dealt with in their life. If you had the movie rights to it, you'd probably make a million dollars."

•   •   •

Mary Watson still didn't want to believe that her son was guilty. Someone else had to be at fault. That someone, in Mary Watson's mind, was Debbie Banister. So, just as she had done in the past—at Parris Island, in Vietnam, in the custody battle for Hearn's son— Mary decided to take matters into her own hands.

The weekend after the Alachua County indictments, she hauled out her box of tapes of recorded phone conversations and started going through it. There were dozens of tapes, going back to 1982, but Mary worked resolutely, stubbornly—searching for something to clear her son.

Finally, on Monday afternoon, she found the January 27 phone calls between Hearn and Debbie, in which they were plotting the murder of Joe Banister. "Praise God," Mary said, "let this be the one."

She called Ken Roach, an investigator in the public defender's office in Gainesville, and played the conversations for him over the phone. He told her to take the tape out of the recorder and not touch it. The next morning, Wiley Clark flew to Columbia and picked up the tape. He finally had what he needed.

Mary Watson had done all that she could: She had given them the Federal Express letter and cashier's check from Bob Black, the letters from Debbie to Hearn, the napkin with the floor plan, and now the tape. She had done it all out of love for her son, hoping to somehow set him free. In reality, the evidence she supplied did just the opposite. "She put her son in the electric chair," says Lloyd Vipperman, a Gainesville defense attorney. "She literally strapped the anklets on him."

•   •   •

On June 13, 1985, John Wayne Hearn pleaded guilty to the first-degree murder of Joe Banister, and was given a life sentence with a mandatory twenty-five-year term. When Judge R.A. "Buzzy" Green asked him, "Why did you do such a thing?" Hearn bowed his head and cried.

•   •   •

On June 18, 1985, Hearn pleaded guilty to first-degree murder and conspiracy to commit murder in the death of Cecil Batie. Sentencing was withheld until after he testified against his four coconspirators: Debbie, Marlene, Frank, and Iris.

Assistant state attorney Ken Hebert, the prosecutor in the Batie case, agreed to not seek the death penalty against Hearn, but there was no deal on whether his life sentence would be consecutive or concurrent with his sentence in the Banister case.

Debra Banister's Relatives Won't Testify for Her

Starke—The trial of Debra Banister for the murder of her husband remained on schedule after a hearing here Friday, but her sister and parents have refused to testify in her behalf. . . ."

—Gainesville *Sun*
August 10, 1985

Ten days after the above newspaper article appeared, Marlene requested a transfer from the Alachua County jail, where she was sharing a cell with her sister. Marlene claimed that Debbie had became "argumentative and threatening" toward her because she wouldn't testify. That same day, Marlene was transferred to the Levy County jail.

The Sims family had started out fiercely protective—"the family that slays together, stays together" could have been their motto—but as the noose drew tighter around them, Debbie was left to face the threat of the electric chair alone.

• • •

On Monday, August 19, 1985, Debbie Banister went on trial for the murder of her husband. During the week-long trial, Tom Elwell called fifteen witnesses, leading up to the main attraction: John Wayne Hearn. It was standing-room-only when Hearn testified on Thursday. This was the most publicized murder trial in Starke in a decade. "It's like a daytime soap opera, only this is real life," one observer remarked.

Elwell's main objective was to bring out Hearn's true personality on the stand, to dispel the jury's preconceptions about a triple murderer. "We must make Hearn look like a teddy bear on the stand," he told Don Denton.

It worked. When he took the stand, Hearn politely answered Elwell's questions with a "Yes, sir" or "No, sir," and started crying eight minutes into his testimony, describing Debbie Banister's first kiss on the end of his nose.

He spoke so softly that Judge Green and Elwell asked him repeatedly to speak up, and Green eventually called a recess to have a lavaliere mike attached to his shirt. As Hearn was being led from the courtroom, he had to pass Debbie Banister, who was seated at the defense table. As he walked past, Debbie raised her hand to her mouth—so that Hearn could see she was still wearing his ring.

Hearn went to pieces. Elwell hurried him into his office and sat him down. "What's wrong?" he demanded.

"Did you see what she did?" Hearn blubbered.

"Yeah, I saw," Elwell said. "And when I take you back in there, I want you to tell the jury about it."

After the recess, Hearn recounted what Debbie had done with the ring. "That had a real impact [on the jury]," Elwell says. "From then on, they watched her during the trial."

During cross-examination of Hearn, Debbie's attorney, Clifford Davis, raised doubts about various parts of Hearn's story and grilled him about why he had waited until he had a deal on the death penalty to implicate Debbie. But what Davis couldn't discredit was *the tape* of the January 27 phone calls, which Judge Green had allowed into evidence.*

The tape was Elwell's star witness. He played it right after Hearn's testimony and had a transcript prepared so that jurors could follow along. "No question about it, the tape was the most significant piece of evidence in the case," he says. "In the end, it wasn't Hearn against Debbie—it was the tape."

When Debbie took the stand on Friday morning in her own defense, she finally admitted to having had an affair with Hearn but claimed that she had broken it off the day of Joe Banister's murder and that Hearn had killed Joe in a fit of jealous rage. On cross-examination, Elwell questioned her about this supposed breakup.

"I tried and was trying everything I could to salvage the marriage I had," Debbie insisted.

"Okay, I see," Elwell said sarcastically. "And by trying, you were going out of town, visiting another man—your lover. . . . You were seeing him—I was going to say 'morning, noon, and night,' but that's not true; you were just seeing him noon and night, after work, and you were telephoning him some seventy-five

---

* Florida law prohibits recording phone calls without both parties' agreement, but South Carolina law does not. Elwell argued successfully that since the recording was made in South Carolina, Florida's law did not apply, and *federal* law— which does not prohibit recordings—should take precedence.

to eighty times—all at the same time you were trying to *work things out* with your husband?"

"Yes, I did talk to him a lot," she answered. "I did go by and see him. But that does not mean that I was not trying to work out things with Joe. If I did not want to work out things with Joe, then I would have been asking legal counsel what I had to do. But I never talked about it. I tried everything I could to avoid it."

"Isn't it a fact, Mrs. Banister," Elwell fired back, "you found *another way* to get a divorce?"

"No, sir, that's not true," Debbie replied.

On several occasions when Elwell pressed her too hard, Debbie began to cry. "She walked me around the courtroom like I was a pony at a circus," he recalls. "I have cross-examined hardened killers—even Ted Bundy—and there has never been *anybody* that was more elusive than this woman."

The jury convicted her anyway. After three hours of deliberation, the jury returned a verdict of *second*-degree murder. Eleven jurors voted for first degree, but one held out for second, and rather than declare a mistrial, the other eleven changed their votes.

Fifteen minutes after the verdict, Judge Green sentenced Debbie to seventeen years in prison, the maximum under Florida's sentencing guidelines for that offense. She showed no reaction to the verdict or the sentence and was led from the courtroom and returned to the Alachua County jail.

In the final analysis, Mary Watson had won the war. She may have "strapped the anklets" on her son, but she also sent Debbie Banister to jail.

• • •

On February 24, 1986, one year and three days after Sandra Black's death, Bob Black was convicted of capital murder by a Brazos County jury. The trial itself was anticlimactic, compared to several events that happened prior to it.

The first was Bob's attempt to convince Gary Wayne of his innocence. Bob wrote numerous letters to him in the months preceding the trial, although the boy seldom wrote back. Bob stepped up his efforts as the trial approached. On January 5, two weeks before jury selection, he sent a rambling eight-page letter to Gary

Wayne, in which he invoked Sandra's memory to try to win the boy's sympathy.

In the letter, Bob went to great lengths to profess his love for Sandra: he told Gary Wayne that she was the "finest woman" he knew and that he was certain Sandra was looking down on him and was happy about the positive changes he had made in his life since he had been in jail. Bob reminded Gary Wayne of how well he and Sandra had been getting along before Christmas and said how proud he was of her for losing weight and offering to pay for him to go back to school. He recounted the ways he had tried to show his love: the diamond he had bought her for Christmas, the horse barn he had built, and the new van—and bemoaned the fact that "it ended" just as he was "ready to try again."

After assuring Gary Wayne that Sandra loved him so much that she would do anything for him, he added: "You know, if I would have ever been in jail for anything before—even if I were wrong in what I did to go to jail—there is no doubt whatsoever in my mind that she would be fighting for me any way and every way to get me out once she was over being mad!"

Bob told Gary Wayne that Sandra was his "lady," that she would have even fought the "devil in hell" on his behalf, and that if they could just be together for one day, he would have a celebration and remarry her. Finally, he ended with a plea to Gary Wayne:

> Without her, there is no one to carry the torch on my behalf; no one who is a faithful friend, no one who cares that my life may be nearing its end unless it is her own son—and mine; you.
>   Would you consider becoming the champion your mother always was? . . . is there enough of your Mother in you to have courage like she did to fight any and all odds for me once? Please."

Three days later, on January 8, Bob cut his wrists with a serrated kitchen knife, and was found bleeding in his cell by a jailer. He was taken to St. Joseph's Hospital, where he was stitched up and kept overnight for observation. The cuts were superficial, and Brazos County authorities suspected that the suicide attempt was actually part of an escape plot.

Several weeks earlier, during a routine shakedown of Bob's cell, jailers found two handwritten maps: one was a detailed floor plan of the jail (with a dot marking Bob's cell) and the other was a map of downtown Bryan, within a two-block radius of the jail. A fellow inmate reported that Bob had been talking about escaping, had offered "good money" to anyone who would help him, and one of his schemes was to slip away while being transported outside the jail to receive medication.

The suicide attempt did raise doubts about Bob's mental competency, and Judge W.T. McDonald ordered a psychiatric examination. On January 17, Dr. John Talmadge reported that Bob *was* mentally ill but competent to stand trial. "It is possible to be legally sane and at the same time suffer from a variety of mental disorders, such as anxiety and depression," Talmadge said. "Mr. Black suffers from a depressive disorder that has been treated in the past by other psychiatrists." He claimed that the disorder did not impair Bob's ability to determine right from wrong—the standard for an insanity defense in Texas.

Earlier, Bob's defense attorney, Robert R. Scott, had considered using post-traumatic stress disorder as the basis for an insanity defense (which has been successful in several cases), but dropped the idea after a psychiatrist told him that the crime didn't fit the PTSD profile. "If he had killed her himself, or had a flashback or something, that might have fit," Scott recalls. "But [Sandra's murder] was at least one step removed from that."

Scott had also approached district attorney Bill Turner about a deal on the death penalty. "I thought all along that Hearn was the one they were going to try to kill, instead of Bob," says Scott. "But then Florida cut Hearn such a good deal that it became a question of having to get somebody, and they decided to get Bob."

When the trial began on February 18, the Bryan courtroom was packed to capacity. Bob was clean-shaven and dressed in a dark business suit. Always a charmer with the ladies, he reportedly turned to a group of women sitting behind him, smiled, and said, "I want to thank y'all for coming to my trial."

Over the next four days, Bill Turner and assistant DA Margaret Lalk paraded twenty-eight witnesses to the stand, including Gary Wayne Black, Marjorie Eimann, Teresa Heatherington, David

Huber, Gordon Matheson, and the state's star witness: John Wayne Hearn.

On cross-examination Scott caught Hearn in a number of contradictions in his story, but with the testimony of the others—plus the Federal Express letter and cashier's check supplied by Mary Watson—Bob's conviction was a foregone conclusion. In fact, Scott didn't call any defense witnesses and concentrated instead on avoiding the death penalty. It took the jury only two hours to return a guilty verdict.

In Texas, there are separate guilt and punishment phases of a criminal trial. To justify the death penalty, the state must show beyond a reasonable doubt that there is a "probability" that the defendant would commit "criminal acts of violence that would constitute a continuing threat to society." To make their case, Turner and Lalk introduced evidence about Bob's solicitations to kill Ted Heatherington and Marjorie Eimann, his 1982 solicitation to kill Sandra, and his past acts of violence.

In Bob's defense, Scott called sixteen character witnesses to the stand. Prior to trial, Bob had written to John Blackman (his pilot in Vietnam) and to several of his old classmates from Haskell, asking them to testify, but none of them did. Ironically, his defense ended up resting primarily on his accomplishments in the Boy Scouts: three of the sixteen witnesses were old friends of his parents from Haskell, who told about his exploits as an Eagle Scout, and five others were men who had worked with him more recently as an adult scout leader.

Scott also made a tactical decision to not introduce Bob's history of psychiatric treatment, for fear of a backlash from the jury. "It can end up creating a 'rabid dog' mentality," he explains. "The jury starts thinking 'He'll never get better, what are we gonna do?' and it ends up being the ASPCA." In other words, if jurors think that the defendant is a "crazed killer," they may decide that their only option is put him to sleep.

Bob's parents, his younger brother, Gary, and one aunt also testified. Vannoy Black's testimony brought tears to the eyes of some jurors and spectators, as he spoke proudly of Bob's achievements as an Eagle Scout and a Marine Corps officer.

"Do you love him?" Scott asked him at the end.

"I'll show you that I do if you let me," Vannoy replied. "I'll come over there and kiss him on the cheek and hug his neck just right now." After being excused from the witness stand, Vannoy stopped in front of Bob and saluted him; Bob rose and embraced his father, and they kissed each other on the cheek.

The jury deliberated for approximately seven hours before returning their verdict: the death penalty. Judge McDonald sentenced Bob to die by lethal injection, and also gave John Wayne Hearn a second life sentence in exchange for his testimony.

•   •   •

Immediately after the sentencing, Sheriff Ronnie Miller allowed Bob's parents, his brother, and Gary Wayne to visit with him before Bob was taken to Death Row in Huntsville. While Miller, Chris Kirk, and Charlie Owen kept a respectful distance, Bob talked with his family for a few minutes. He wanted to have some photos taken; so a deputy obliged and took one snapshot of the entire family and a second of just Bob and Gary Wayne.

It was a terribly sad moment: Bob was dressed in an orange prison jumpsuit, and in another few minutes he would be on his way to Death Row. Yet you would never know it from the photos: Bob is standing in the center, his arms wrapped around the others, grinning proudly. In fact, *everyone* is smiling, as if Bob had just been chosen a NASA astronaut instead of being condemned to death.

Gary Wayne had been crying after the verdict, but even he is grinning. "I guarantee you I didn't *feel* like smiling," he says, "but my dad wanted us to take a good picture."

After the photo, Vannoy and Bob enacted a ceremony that they had been preparing for all of their lives—a hollow ritual that symbolized all of the misplaced values, phony images, and empty allegiances that had led Bob to that place. According to Sheriff Miller, Vannoy stood up and said, "Son, I'm going to salute you one last time." Then he and Bob snapped to attention, and they solemnly repeated a Boy Scout oath!

Ronnie Miller had never seen anything like it. "I said to myself, '*Goddamn!*'" he recalls, shaking his head. "And that's when I left."

"Oh, it was a mess," Chris Kirk agrees.

Bob was on his way to Death Row, yet he was still promising to uphold his Boy Scout's honor.

• • •

On October 29, 1986, Marlene Sims Watson pleaded guilty to conspiracy to commit first-degree murder and to a second charge of burning to defraud an insurer. As part of a plea-bargain deal with the state, she agreed to testify against her parents and her sister, Debbie Banister. In return, assistant state attorney Ken Hebert agreed to drop the first-degree murder charge against her.

After seventeen months in jail, Marlene had finally agreed to talk. The state's strategy all along was to wait her out. "Trying to get family to 'rat out' family is almost impossible," Charlie Sanders explains. "But we figured that one of the girls—either Debbie or Marlene—was going to talk to us."

Ken Hebert felt that he had no choice but to make a deal with one of the Sims sisters in order to convict the rest of the family. John Wayne Hearn could testify about *Debbie's* involvement in Cecil's murder, but most of what he knew about the other family members was hearsay.

In September, 1986, Hebert approached Marlene's attorney, Thomas Farkash, with an offer to drop the murder charge and release Marlene from jail in exchange for her guilty pleas on the other two counts, a "complete and truthful statement" about the crimes, her testimony in all trials and hearings, and full cooperation in the investigation, including taking polygraph tests.

Over the next few weeks, Hebert and Farnell Cole made repeated trips to the Levy County jail, where Marlene was imprisoned. Farkash would bring her out, and she would say, "This is the whole story, Mr. Hebert, I promise," and give him a new version of events. Hebert would say, "No deal, she's lying," and put her back in jail.

That went on for over a month—statement after statement, failed polygraph after failed polygraph. For example, on October 9, 1986, Marlene was asked three questions by Jesse E. Blitch, a certified polygraph examiner: 1. Did you ask anyone in your family to have Cecil Batie killed? 2. Did you see John Hearn receive that map of Cecil Batie's home at the skating rink on January 5, 1985? 3. Prior to picking up your kids on January 4, 1985, did you know that Cecil Batie was going to be killed on the weekend of January 5 to 6, 1985? Marlene answered no to each question, but Blitch concluded that in his opinion, she wasn't telling the truth on questions 1 and 3, and her answer on 2 was inconclusive.

A few minutes later, he asked her three additional questions: 1. Did Debbie tell you that Val Bates or Cliff Davis had possession of that shotgun after Cecil Batie's death? 2. The morning of Cecil Batie's death, did Debbie tell you that Cecil Batie had been shot twice with a shotgun? 3. Have you told the whole truth to the state attorney about this case now? Marlene answered yes to each question, and Blitch said that he didn't believe she was telling the truth on any of them.

Hebert, a "full-blood" Cajun from New Iberia, Louisiana, doesn't believe that Marlene ever told him the whole truth. "I yelled at that woman, I walked out of the room, I screamed at her, I threw things down, I called her a liar, I turned off the deal three or four times—and in the end I never could get a statement that I totally believed in," he says.

On October 23, 1986, she gave her final version of the story: an eighteen-page sworn statement, which was tape recorded. Finally, Hebert agreed to the plea bargain. "We felt like the *essence* of what she was saying was believable," he says. "There was enough credibility for us to list her as a state witness, and say to the other defendants, 'Now the ball's in your court.' "

•   •   •

The Cecil Batie case finally came to an end on February 6, 1987, when John Wayne Hearn, Debbie Banister, Marlene, Frank, and Iris Sims were sentenced by Judge Elzie Sanders.

Hearn's public defender, Johnny Kearns, pleaded with Sanders to make Hearn's life sentence *concurrent* with his two earlier life sentences, rather than consecutive. He cited Hearn's three tours in Vietnam, his testimony in the other cases, the theology courses that he was taking in prison, and his "seduction" by Debbie Banister.

However, Ken Hebert argued for a consecutive sentence. Looking at Hearn, he said, "Debbie Banister was not there when you pulled the trigger. . . . In at least two of those cases, you did it for money; not love—money." Sanders agreed with Hebert, and imposed a consecutive life sentence with a mandatory twenty-five years.

For her earlier guilty pleas Marlene was sentenced to five and a half years in prison and five years probation. She was returned to prison, with credit for 510 days that she had already served.

As Hebert had hoped, Marlene's guilty plea was the catalyst for the other family members to plead as well. Frank and Iris Sims pleaded *nolo contendere* to being accessories after the fact to first-degree murder, and were fined $5,000 apiece, and given five years probation.

Debbie Banister pleaded *nolo contendere* to conspiracy to commit first-degree murder, and, in exchange, the state dropped her first-degree murder charge. Judge Sanders exceeded the sentencing guidelines and gave Debbie thirty years, to be served concurrently with her seventeen-year-sentence for Joe Banister's murder. With gain time and good behavior, she could be out in twelve to fifteen years.*

Debbie's attorney, Lloyd Vipperman, was surprised that the state offered her a deal instead of going to trial, but Hebert defends that decision. "My whole credibility in front of a jury is based on my belief that what I'm saying is true," he says. "In the end, I was left with whether I believed Marlene."

Even though he is a defense attorney, Lloyd Vipperman can sympathize with Hebert. "This whole family seems to be a scurrilous bunch of liars," he says.

---

* Because of prison overcrowding, Florida inmates automatically get ten days of *statutory* gain time per month, and may also receive *earned* gain time of up to twenty days per month. Currently, inmates doing time for violent crimes are serving about forty-eight percent of their sentences.

Part Seven

GRAVEN IMAGES

Thou shalt not make unto thee any graven image, or any likeness of any thing that is in heaven above, or that is in the earth beneath, or that is in the water under the earth:

Thou shalt not bow down thyself to them, nor serve them: for I the Lord thy God am a jealous God, visiting the iniquity of the fathers upon the children unto the third and fourth generation of them that hate me;

And shewing mercy unto thousands of them that love me, and keep my commandments.

—Exodus 20:4–6

1

THE STORY should have been over.

The trials had ended. The good guys had won. The bad guys had gone to jail, in most cases. The families of the victims were putting their lives back together—trying to get on with life.

Except that they would never really "get on with life," not completely. And one woman couldn't let the story end. Not yet.

Marjorie Eimann still couldn't believe that in Bryan, Texas, a man could hire a hit man out of a magazine to come to town and kill his wife. *His* wife; *her* daughter. Marjorie Eimann is not a legal scholar. She is a very simple, straightforward woman, and she kept asking what to her seemed like a very simple, straightforward question: "How could *Soldier of Fortune* magazine run ads for hit men?"

In December, 1986, one of her sisters, Margaret Ann Mauro, was talking to a customer in her jewelry store. "Has Marjorie thought about suing that magazine?" the customer asked. Mauro relayed the question to Marjorie.

"Well, I don't know," Marjorie replied. "Could I?"

"I'll ask Travis Bryan," Mauro suggested. "He'll know."

Mauro met with Bryan, a former Brazos County district attorney, who said that he thought Marjorie could file a wrongful death suit against *Soldier of Fortune*—but she would have to hurry: the two-year statute of limitations on Sandra's death would run out on February 21, 1987.

Marjorie asked Gary Wayne how he felt about going back to court. "Go ahead," he said. "It's just one more hurdle to cross."

On December 20, 1986, Marjorie, Gary Wayne, and Glen Eimann signed a contract with Travis Bryan's firm—on a forty-percent contingency fee—to represent them in a lawsuit against *Soldier of Fortune.*

Bryan decided to file the suit in federal court in Houston. Since he is primarily a criminal trial lawyer, he wanted to find a topnotch civil lawyer to take the case. He called several lawyers he knew in Houston, got some recommendations, and interviewed a few civil trial lawyers. None seemed right for the case.

Finally, he called a former Houston prosecutor, Mike Hinton, who told him: "I know the perfect guy—Ron Franklin." Hinton arranged a meeting between the two men on January 5, 1987. Bryan laid out the facts and showed Franklin the September, 1984, issue of *Soldier of Fortune* with John Wayne Hearn's ad.

"Is there a civil case here?" Bryan asked.

Franklin had never seen the magazine before and was appalled by some of the ads. "If I can get this *one* issue in front of a jury, I have no doubt that we'll win—and win big," he replied.

He cautioned Bryan that trying to hold a magazine liable for the content of its ads would raise unprecedented First Amendment issues,* but added, "I refuse to believe that the First Amendment would allow a publisher to knowingly publish ads for hit men. We'll take the magazine off the racks for this."

Travis Bryan had found his man.

•   •   •

Ron Franklin is a volcano attorney—literally.

In 1985 he represented the families of seventeen victims of the Mount St. Helens eruption in a suit against the Weyerhauser Company (the suit was settled out of court). His law partner, Graham Hill, calls him "the king of the exotic case," and Franklin has a reputation for taking—and winning—unusual cases. Together with Hill (the two men try their lawsuits together), he won $3.5 million for a Lubbock man crushed by a cotton stripper, $4.5 million for a

---

* Simply stated, under the First Amendment courts give utmost protection to "core" speech, but less protection to "commercial" speech, such as advertisements. Courts have ruled that publishers may not *knowingly* advertise illegal products or services. As an example, a publisher may run an ad that says "Legalize Marijuana Now!" but not one that says "Marijuana for Sale, $30 an ounce."

longshoreman paralyzed by a falling hundred-pound bag of rice, and $140 million for 1,100 employees in a class-action suit against El Paso Products.

He also has a reputation for theatrical flair in the courtroom. When he sued General Motors on behalf of a woman who was paralyzed when her Pontiac TransAm flipped and the roof collapsed, Franklin asked the jury: "If I turned a TransAm upside down and dropped it, how high off the ground would it have to be for the roof to be crushed flat as a pancake?"

The correct answer, according to his experts, was nine inches. To prove it, Franklin and Hill bought a TransAm, raised it upside down with a crane, turned on a video camera, and dropped it nine inches. It went flat as a pancake; they won the case.

At thirty-nine, Franklin is tall, slender, and boyishly handsome. He has a reserved confidence: he is sure of himself and in control of his emotions. His success as a trial lawyer has brought him wealth—a blue Ferrari and a River Oaks mansion—far beyond his modest upbringing in Houston.

Franklin and Hill, the son of John Hill, a former chief justice of the Texas Supreme Court, specialize in personal injury lawsuits. At the offices of Hill, Parker, Franklin, Cardwell, and Jones, a fifteen-member firm, Ron Franklin is legendary for his obsessive-compulsive behavior during trials (he gets so intense that he has been known to walk right past his own clients without seeing them) and for his extremely careful preparation. "Ron's preparation level is unmatched," says Hill. "He plans out *exactly* what he's going to do."

Franklin also brings a heavy dose of righteous indignation to the courtroom. His school-boy good looks belie the aggressive, "in-your-face" cross-examination style that he uses on defense witnesses. "Every case comes down to the good guys versus the bad guys, and we try to represent the good guys," he says.

In the *Soldier of Fortune* case, he never had any doubts.

·   ·   ·

On January 7, 1987, Franklin filed a $107 million negligence suit in U.S. District Court in Houston against Soldier of Fortune Magazine, Inc. and its parent company, Omega Group, LTD. The complaint alleged that John Wayne Hearn's ad, and other personal-service ads, were "thinly disguised offers of guns for hire," and that by publishing such ads, *Soldier of Fortune* provided its readers with "lists of hit men," and "knew or should have foreseen that such professional killers would be retained to commit the ultimate crime of murder." Franklin charged that *Soldier of Fortune,* by its "wrongful conduct and negligence," was a "proximate cause" of Sandra Black's death.

That night, the story went out on the AP and UPI wire services. CBS News called the next day about an interview. Already, Marjorie Eimann's simple, straightforward question had become a national news story.

• • •

It had been a rough two years for *Soldier of Fortune* magazine. Throughout 1986 and 1987, there had been a tidal wave of news stories about crimes linked to SOF classified ads. On March 6, 1986—one week after Bob Black's murder conviction—the magazine had announced that it would no longer carry personal-services ads, but that did nothing to slow the tide of bad publicity.

At that time, SOF editor James L. Pate claimed that pulling the ads had nothing to do with Black's conviction and was "just coincidence." However, SOF's staff had been in turmoil for months over the ads. On January 24, 1986, Pate had sent the following "confidential" memo to publisher Robert K. Brown:

Confidential
24 Jan 86

To: RKB

From: JLP

Re: Classified ads, specifically the following:

1. Need a real professional? Need quick confidential action? Contact this operative by phone or mail. Work alone or can provide team, short or long term, all considered. Absolute discretion given and expected. Dusty, Palmerdale, Ala.

2. Gun for hire: Nam sniper, instructor, SWAT, pistol, rifle, security specialist, bodyguard, courier, plus. All jobs considered. Privacy guaranteed. Mike

3. Financial and personal assistance requested for merc operation—low risk, VERY high return; needed immediately in San Francisco area (or able to get here) call

These three classifieds have come to my attention in the past week because of criminal charges that have either been filed or are pending. . . . All the hard work we have done in the past year to gain wider acceptance for Soldier of Fortune and enhance our credibility and respectability could easily go down the drain with a single $20 classified. My personal suggestion is that we cut out these types of ads all together; they certainly are not worth the small revenue they produce when compared with the potential public relations damage they can do when reported in the news. . . .

Pate went on to say that "Dusty" in the first ad, was an Alabama man who had been charged with capital murder for the contract killing of a man's wife. "Mike" in the second ad was facing multiple charges, including murder. The third ad was placed by a man who had been the subject of an earlier staff memo from SOF senior editor John Coleman:

This ad is running in the February '86 SOF (page 144). If you get any queries about it, please refer them to me.

The guy who ran the ad is a certifiable fruit cake; he, and the ad, have come to the attention of the San Francisco Police Intelligence Division and the District Attorney's office. The DA has disconnected his phone, so we may get some questions directed our way about the ad.

Coleman

Over the next few months, *Soldier of Fortune* was inundated by reports of other crimes commissioned out of its back pages:

• On March 3, 1986, Indiana police arrested eight heavily armed men who were preparing to storm a courtroom and free Roger Jaske, a convicted murderer. The men had responded to Jaske's SOF ad:

MERCENARY LOOKING FOR MALE CAUCASIAN PART-
NER age 18–25 willing to accept risk. Must have guts, be able
to travel and start work immediately. No special skills required. High pay guaranteed. Ask for SUNDANCE

• On April 4, 1986, Doug Norwood, a University of Arkansas law
student, filed a $4 million lawsuit against *Soldier of Fortune* and
seven individuals, after four separate murder attempts on his life.
Norwood had been shot twice, his car had been fire-bombed, and
he had escaped two other bungled murder attempts before his
assailants were arrested in January, 1986.

The bungling hit men were part of a murder ring operating
out of a sleazy strip-joint in Knoxville, Tennessee. Their leader,
Richard "Doc" Savage, had run this ad in *Soldier of Fortune:*

GUN FOR HIRE, 37-year old professional mercenary desires
jobs. Vietnam veteran. Discreet and very private. Bodyguard,
courier, and other special skills. All jobs considered.

After his arrest, Savage told reporters: "I couldn't believe it,
nearly everybody wanted someone killed. They wanted me to kill
their wives, mothers, fathers, and girlfriends." Savage had so many
job offers that he hired several other men, including Sean Doutre
and William Buckley. Over the next few weeks, a staggering record
of crimes committed—or attempted—by members of the Savage
gang came to light:

• In June, 1985, two gang members blew up the Keough Poultry
Company in Fertile, Iowa (no one was injured).

• In August, 1985, Alice Brado paid Savage $20,000 to kill her
ex-boyfriend, Dana Free. Buckley and another gang member wired
two grenades to the bottom of Free's car, but one fell off and rolled
out on the driveway. Free saw it and leaped to safety.

• One week later, some of the Savage gang members made three
successive attempts to blow up a bar in St. Paul, Minnesota (they
were hired by a competing bar owner), but the bombs failed to
explode.

• Sean Doutre had more success on August 26, 1985, when he gunned down Richard Braun, an Atlanta businessman, in his driveway. Braun's sixteen-year-old son was also wounded, and watched his father bleed to death. Savage had been paid $10,000 by Bruce Gastwirth, Braun's business associate.

• In early October, Savage dispatched Buckley and two other men to Louisville, Kentucky, to kill Victoria Barshear, but the men balked because she was too pretty. Savage had been hired by Barshear's husband's ex-wife.

• On October 12, Buckley tried again to kill Dana Free, by tossing two grenades into the home of his ex-wife and daughter. Free wasn't there, and the women were uninjured in the blast.

• On October 30, a bomb exploded in the luggage compartment of an American Airlines jetliner shortly after it landed at Dallas-Fort Worth. Albert Thielman, a Texas man, had allegedly bought the bomb from William Buckley, hoping to kill his wife and collect $2.6 million in insurance. None of the 154 passengers or crew members were injured.

• On November 16, Sean Doutre bludgeoned to death Anita Spearman, a West Palm Beach, Florida, woman, while she was asleep in her bed. Savage had been paid $20,000 by her husband, Robert Spearman.

In the initial onslaught of publicity about the Norwood lawsuit and the Doc Savage gang, SOF publisher Robert K. Brown had laid low, refusing comment. But after the Eimann suit was filed in January, 1987, he launched a counterattack in typically swaggering style. In his August, 1987, Command Guidance editorial, Brown issued a resounding denial to charges of SOF complicity in the crimes and, for good measure, threw a jab at the news media:

Just the Facts—Please

I know many of you have seen and heard news stories during the last several months concerning certain classified ads that have appeared in *Soldier of Fortune* magazine in the past, and about the lawsuit against us in Fayetteville, Arkansas.

I've decided to address this issue right now, because the media persists in portraying it in its typically sensational and inaccurate manner. However, because of the pending lawsuit, I must keep some of my more acid comments necessarily restricted. For now, at least. . . .

For years, certain segments of the media have enjoyed dropping the hatchet on SOF as we actively and vocally support causes they oppose. . . . And now that they've got the golden opportunity to distort the truth and misrepresent the facts concerning our classified advertising, they're jumping on the ratings bandwagon with vindictive glee.

Let me state once again in the strongest terms that we have never knowingly permitted our advertising to be used as a conduit for an illegal activity. If the thought that personal services ads might be used for an illegal purpose had ever crossed our minds here at the magazine, then those ads would never have seen our printer's ink, much less the light of day.

•   •   •

Ron Franklin had found the basis for his case. With his own words, Robert K. Brown had drawn a line in the sand: *If the thought . . . had ever crossed our minds.* Franklin would spend the next six months trying to prove that the thought of the ads being used for illegal purposes had indeed crossed Brown's mind, but he had wantonly ignored it.

•   •   •

One day after filing the Eimann lawsuit, Franklin found an expert witness to testify on his client's behalf: Dr. Park Elliot Dietz, a forensic psychiatrist and criminologist at the University of Virginia. Dietz had been quoted in a July 20, 1984, Philadelphia *Daily News* article about James Oliver Huberty (who had killed twenty-six people in a McDonald's restaurant in San Ysidro, California), saying that Huberty fit the profile of a "Soldier of Fortune killer," and that *Soldier of Fortune* magazine carried "ads for hit men."

Franklin phoned Dietz on January 8, 1987, and explained the Eimann lawsuit. Dietz told him that he considered *Soldier of Fortune* to be the "flagship of the violence industry in America." Franklin mailed a $2,500 retainer check to Dietz that same day.

Dietz's credentials were impressive: he had both an M.D. and a Ph.D. in sociology (focusing on criminal behavior), had been the lead psychiatrist for the U.S. government in the John Hinckley trial, and had also served on Attorney General Edwin Meese's pornography commission.

Franklin asked Dietz to do two things: first, analyze every personal-services ad ever published in *Soldier of Fortune;* and second, identify all crimes commissioned through the magazine and the dates that they were first reported in the press. It was a difficult task just to locate back issues of the magazine, since SOF had stopped selling them in May, 1986, and the magazine is frequently stolen from public libraries.*

Eventually, Dietz was able to acquire a complete set of the classified ads, and he and a team of graduate students spent the next five months analyzing, categorizing, and cross-referencing all 18,860 classified ads—including 2,000 personal-services ads—that had appeared in SOF from its first issue through July, 1986, when the last personal-services ads were run.

•   •   •

Despite Bob Brown's fierce denial of any wrongdoing, in May, 1987, SOF settled out of court with Doug Norwood (for an undisclosed amount) just prior to trial. But Norwood had only sued for $4 million; the Eimanns were asking for $107 million!

In January, 1987, the Lexington Insurance Company, which underwrote the magazine's $500,000 liability policy, had hired Larry D. Thompson, of the Houston firm of Lorance and Thompson, to represent the magazine in the Eimann case.

Thompson, fifty, is a big-boned, affable family man (he has

---

* In March, 1990, I went to the Library of Congress to examine its collection of *Soldier of Fortunes*. After a two-hour search by three different departments, I was told that the Library of Congress no longer has *any* back issues of the magazine. "You know, urban guerrillas like to steal it," one librarian told me. He suggested that I try the Pentagon Library. I managed to get in there, and found about forty loose issues, but no bound volumes. "We have the same problem as the Library of Congress," a reference librarian said. "We can't keep them on the shelf long enough to bind them." Is not even the Pentagon safe from urban guerrillas, I wondered?

three teen-age children and coaches soccer in his spare time) who seems too unpretentious to be a high-dollar attorney. The bulk of his practice is defending doctors or insurance companies, but SOF hired him because of his experience in libel cases. He is the younger brother of Thomas Thompson, the author of *Blood and Money,* the celebrated 1976 true-crime book about murder among Houston's super rich. Larry Thompson successfully defended his brother (who died in 1982) in three libel suits spawned by *Blood and Money*—winning two in trial and getting the third dismissed.

Thompson was hoping that the Eimann case would never go to trial. His hopes for a dismissal were riding on the First Amendment. "We really thought we'd never try the case," Thompson says. "We knew that if we did we were going to have a tough row to hoe, frankly, because of [Sandra Black's] death. So we were working very hard . . . on our motion for summary judgment."

•   •   •

On May 8, 1987, Ron Franklin and Larry Thompson had their first conference with David Hittner, the federal judge who had been selected, by random drawing, to handle the Eimann lawsuit. Hittner, forty-eight, was a recent Reagan appointee to the federal bench, who had previously served nine years as a Texas district court judge. A former army infantry captain and paratrooper, he had a reputation as a hard-working, no-nonsense judge who ran a tight ship.

The Houston federal courts were so backlogged with criminal cases, which took precedence over civil cases, that it could have easily been four or five years before the Eimann suit was put on the docket. But Hittner was intrigued by the case. "You're lucky this is an interesting case," he told the attorneys. "How about a February, 1988, trial date?"

•   •   •

On June 27, 1987, Park Dietz sent a preliminary report to Ron Franklin on his study of SOF's classified ads. His conclusions were startling: Out of approximately 2,000 personal-services ads published in the magazine, Dietz estimated that over half suggested the advertiser's "willingness to engage in criminal conduct or activities." Included among his many examples were the following:

GENTLEMAN THAT IS BORED in peace is looking for a bit of excitement. Within the boundaries of law if possible; has nothing against "crime" if sufficiently entertaining. May accept permanent employment if it suits my taste. . . . Gentleman Peter.

RETIRED ESPIONAGE AGENT Spanish-speaking, flyer, seeks well paid venture one man operations, legal or not.

DEVIOUS, young, American man wants action, high risk dirty work. Does anything, travels anywhere, anytime.

MERC FOR HIRE. Anything, anywhere if the price is right.

EX-MARINE, Vietnam vet, with devious, discreet mind, seeks dirty work. Anything, anywhere.

MR. EMPLOYER: Ex-Ranger, 3 years Vietnam, will do anything for money, from bodyguard to ?

FORMER SOG GROUPIE AVAILABLE . . . WM, 6', 202 lbs., 38. Physically and mentally outrageous, morally questionable, philosophically strong. Will accept some Red, White and Blue work, domestic civilian/military, whatever. Usual disclaimer of no illegal work. Usual fees. Gavin.

EX-INTELLIGENCE TYPE wants high risk, cash only contracts. Will do anything in the U.S. Satisfaction guaranteed. Courier also.

MERC FOR HIRE. Anything, anywhere. Expert in small arms, demo, ambush, espionage. Anonymous, discreet, thorough. Money right, no questions asked.

MERC FOR HIRE. Anything, anywhere. Don't get mad, get even. Work alone, short term, discreet, confidential, SKIPPER.

VIETNAM COMBAT MARINE seeking short-term work. Nothing too dirty, just ask. Contact THE ANT.

Dietz had also identified more than two dozen criminal acts linked to SOF personal-services ads, which, assuming that other crimes had gone undetected, he called "merely the tip of the iceberg." These included five murders, nine attempted murders, eight murder plots, three attempted jailbreaks, and two attempted bombings.

He compiled the list by doing a computer search of AP and UPI news releases, using a computerized data base called NEXIS. In addition to the well-publicized crimes committed by John Wayne Hearn and the Doc Savage gang, Dietz found many other incidents, including:

• In May, 1979, a Florida man, Raymond G. Miller contacted Jerry Baker, an SOF advertiser, and asked him to kill his wife. Baker turned Miller in to authorities.

• In February, 1980, Robert Eugene Cotner ran an ad that began "NOW HIRING for exciting high-risk, undercover, stateside work." Cotner instructed two respondents to "terminate" an Oklahoma City man, and promised a $2,000 reward. The men reported Cotner to the FBI, and he was arrested and convicted of sending a threatening communication through the mail.

• In 1981, Curtis Terry, who advertised in SOF under the alias "Swamp Rat," was secretly filmed by a Chicago television reporter offering to kill anyone, except the President, "if somebody pays me enough money." The reporter aired the tape, and Terry resigned his job as police chief of Bells, Texas, which he had only held for one day.

• In 1981, LaMoine Meyer, from Nebraska, allegedly offered $10,000 to an SOF advertiser to kill Raymond Burgland. The advertiser warned Burgland of the plot, and Meyer was arrested and charged with conspiracy to commit murder. Ultimately, he pleaded guilty to a lesser charge.

• In 1982, a California man was indicted for attempted murder after he responded to an SOF ad that read "MERC WILL DO ANYTHING." The man wrote a letter asking to have his wife "eliminated," but apparently mailed it to the wrong address, and was arrested.

• In August, 1986, a woman from Spokane was indicted for conspiring with James Dickerson to kill her husband. Dickerson had run an ad in SOF that read, in part: "HAVE GUN WILL TRAVEL:

guns for hire. All jobs considered." Dickerson pleaded guilty to conspiracy, and the woman was hospitalized for observation.

• In July, 1986, FBI agents foiled an attempted jailbreak at Lewisburg federal prison, led by this same James Dickerson, which was intended to free a reputed Philadelphia mobster. Dickerson pleaded guilty and was given twenty-five years, and the man who hired him received a five year sentence.

• In April, 1986, Lucinda Leigh, 41, sent letters to eight different SOF advertisers, asking them to kill the wife of her ex-lover. One of the advertisers turned her in, she pleaded guilty, and was sentenced to ten years in prison.

Dietz concluded his report by stating "to the knowledgeable reader of *Soldier of Fortune* and in the context in which it appeared," Hearn's ad for "high-risk assignments" expressed "among other things—a willingness to murder for hire."

• • •

Armed with Dietz's damning report, Ron Franklin set out to line up the one witness he thought he had to have to win the case: John Wayne Hearn. On August 7, 1987, he mailed a letter to Hearn, imprisoned at the Receiving and Medical Center (RMC) in Lake Butler, Florida, asking to take his deposition.

Hearn refused. He wrote back on August 12, stating that he didn't want his family "drug into the public eye again" (in its July 6 issue, 1987 *People* magazine had run a long article on the Batie and Banister cases). He added: "Why can't Mrs. Black's parents and son let Sandra rest in peace instead of trying to capitalize on her death and get rich quick?" and asked why he should "help the Eimanns get rich" when his son Wayne "has to live and grow up with absolutely nothing in his life?"

Hearn had been angry about the Eimann suit ever since it was filed. On January 13, 1987, he had written an unsolicited letter to Robert K. Brown saying: "At '*NO*' time did I advertise in your publication for 'Murder for Hire.' " Hearn had offered to talk to Brown or his attorneys about the case, but no one at SOF contacted him for months.

In the meantime, Ron Franklin went to work on him. He composed a handwritten letter (from then on, all of his letters to Hearn would be handwritten, giving them a personal touch), requesting a meeting to discuss "the questions raised in [your] letter." Hearn agreed—with "no tapes, no notes, no one else present."

Franklin flew to Florida on September 14, and told Hearn: "If you feel any remorse for what you did, and want to help Gary Wayne, you need to testify." Hearn was more interested in his own reputation (he wanted the world to know that he hadn't intended to advertise for murder for hire), but nonetheless agreed. The deposition was scheduled for October 13.

At that, Hearn testified that he had received fifteen to twenty phone calls per day on his ad, ninety percent of which were requests for illegal activities. Those included an estimated three to five calls per day asking him to murder people, and "frequent" calls for assaults, bombings, jailbreaks, political assassinations, and delivering illegal guns or drugs.

"Did the *Soldier of Fortune* personal-service classified advertisements make your professional life possible?" Franklin asked.

"Yes," Hearn replied.

"Would you characterize virtually all of the activities we'd discussed today as, quote, high-risk assignments?"

"Yes," Hearn said.

"All the way from political assassination to jailbreaks to murder?"

"Yes."

On cross-examination, Larry Thompson got Hearn to restate that he had never intended to advertise for criminal activities. Then he tried to steer Hearn toward one of the main pillars of SOF's defense: that Bob Black and Hearn were the "proximate causes" of Sandra Black's death, not *Soldier of Fortune* magazine. First, he tossed Hearn a warm-up question: "If you had never met Debbie Banister, would you have done any of these murders?"

"No, sir," Hearn replied.

Then Thompson pitched a home run ball, hoping that Hearn would knock it out of the park: "Did *Soldier of Fortune* or Bob Brown have anything to do with any of these murders, as far as you're concerned?"

"What do you mean, 'have anything to do with'?" Hearn asked.

At this point, Thompson violated a cardinal rule of trial lawyering—*Never ask a question to which you don't already know the answer*—and the result was Hearn's most damaging reply of the day. "Were they responsible in any way, in your opinion?" Thompson asked.

Hearn thought for a moment, then said: "If I had never run an ad in *Soldier of Fortune*, Debbie Banister would have never gotten in touch with me, and I would have never killed anyone."

•   •   •

On September 23, Franklin and Thompson flew to Boulder to take the deposition of SOF publisher Robert K. Brown. The deposition was video-taped, and lasted all day. Brown set the tone by refusing to shake Franklin's hand, and it was open warfare from then on.

The mental skirmishing started *before* the first question. Trying to make Brown nervous, Franklin made him wait a full forty seconds before asking a question. Meanwhile, Brown was doing a pretty good impression of Sonny Liston staring down his opponent before the opening bell: he glared at Franklin, pursed his lips as if to spit (Brown chews Skoal and is a notoriously indiscriminate spitter), flared his nostrils, and, finally, let out a big lazy yawn, as if he was so bored that he might fall asleep.

At last, Franklin said: "Mr. Brown, I understand that you're the 'senior statesman of the popular paramilitary business in the United States'—is that right?" He had been preparing the question for days, hoping to immediately put Brown on the defensive.

Brown gave a gruff laugh. "Well, who says that?" he replied in a kiss-my-ass tone of voice.

"Well, *you* do," Franklin retorted, and handed him a 1985 Command Guidance editorial, under Brown's byline, which described him in those very words.

Brown scanned the editorial, then said, "To the best of my knowledge, counselor, this is one of the articles that was written—or I should say, one of the editorials that was authored by one of my staff—which is not an unusual situation."

"Oh, so you don't even write your own editorials?" Franklin asked, with a thick layer of sarcasm.

"That's kind of a leading question, isn't it, counselor?" Brown responded, setting his jaw.

"Yes, sir, it is. I'm entitled to do that," Franklin fired back. "We need to get one thing straight before we get any further," he added, and proceeded to lecture Brown on deposition protocol. If Brown had thought that he could intimidate Franklin with tough-guy posturing, he was mistaken.

With his readers, Brown shamelessly promoted himself as a "take-no-prisoners" macho warrior, and even for mainstream press interviews he was fond of being photographed behind his desk, holding an assault rifle and wearing a T-shirt that read "Kill 'em all, let God sort 'em out." On the witness stand, however, he became strangely dissembling. When Franklin asked him to define the "popular paramilitary business in the United States," Brown said that he couldn't, even though his editorial stated that he was its senior statesman.

"You're going to tell me today that you are not part of that paramilitary business?" Franklin asked.

"I would say no, I'm not part of—I don't know what paramilitary business is, counselor."

"But whatever it is, you're not part of it?"

"I don't know what it is," Brown replied. "Maybe I am, maybe I'm not. It depends. It's all in the eyes of the beholder."

"Is it your opinion that *Soldier of Fortune* magazine is part of the paramilitary business?" Franklin asked.

"My answer would be the same, counselor—I don't know."

"You just don't know?" asked Franklin, incredulous.

"I don't know what the individual is talking about when they talk about the paramilitary business," Brown replied.

"Even if that individual happens to be *you*—in your Command Guidance editorial?"

"That's correct," Brown said.

•   •   •

It went downhill from there. When the deposition ended, Franklin was convinced that Brown would be the Eimanns' best witness.

•   •   •

In the depositions that followed, *Soldier of Fortune*'s current and former staffers supported Brown's contention that no one at the magazine had suspected any criminal activities related to the personal-services ads. However, Bill Guthrie, a former editor, testified that he (and almost everyone else on the staff, *except* Bob Brown) had wanted to drop the ads for years—not because of fears of illegal activities but because of the "degrading image" the ads gave to the magazine. But Brown liked the "mystique" of the ads, so they remained.

The closest thing to a break in the ranks came from Dale A. Dye, a retired Marine Corps captain, who was the executive editor of *Soldier of Fortune* from June, 1984, to June, 1985. Dye's first exposure to SOF's readership came at the 1984 annual convention in Las Vegas, and he returned from that with concerns about readers who were "living and dying" by the magazine. "My opinion, when I got home from that convention . . . was that we had some people out there who were weird," he said. "People who held beliefs and feelings that I thought were contrary to what a rational human being would hold."

After the convention, he began to worry that the personal-services ads might "splash mud" on the reputation of the magazine. "I kept having images of guys getting a job somehow as a dope runner or a bag man or a bodyguard for somebody who was unsavory," he said. He talked to Bob Brown on several occasions, trying to get him to drop the ads, with no success.

•   •   •

As the February trial date drew closer, Ron Franklin entered his obsessive phase. His secretary, Karen Heck, and his law partners recognized the familiar glassy-eyed stare, and knew to stay away from him. What he was most obsessed with was trying to find irrefutable proof that *Soldier of Fortune* had had *actual knowledge* of crimes being committed from its ads. He had found some evidence: a New Jersey state trooper, Edward M. McCabe, said that he had phoned SOF ad manager Joan Steele in April, 1984, about a criminal investigation he was conducting on G. Nicholas Geyer, an SOF advertiser.

More significantly, Franklin had also found two dozen newspaper articles from the Denver *Post* and the *Rocky Mountain News* on the August, 1984, trials of Robert Konitski and five co-conspirators, who had kidnapped Dr. Michael Roark, a Thornton, Colorado, pathologist, at gunpoint and extorted $280,000 from him. Konitski had run an ad in SOF that read: "RECOVERY AND COLLECTION! International agents guarantee results on any type of recovery." He had been hired by Bruce Richardson, a founder of the Sons of Silence motorcycle gang, whose wife claimed that Roark owed her money.

Konitski, Richardson, and his wife were tried in Denver in 1984, and the trials were covered regularly by the Denver *Post* and the *Rocky Mountain News*—the two largest newspapers in the state. Denver is only twenty-six miles from Boulder, the home of *Soldier of Fortune* magazine, and both papers are sold on street corner news racks. Surely Bob Brown must have known, Franklin thought.

It was damaging evidence, but Franklin was still looking for a smoking gun.

• • •

On February 8, 1988, Judge David Hittner denied *Soldier of Fortune*'s motion for summary judgment. He rejected SOF's claim that since John Wayne Hearn's ad did not propose illegal activity "on its face," its publication was protected by the First Amendment.

Hittner emphasized the "narrowness" of his ruling on the First Amendment, saying that it was meant to apply only to commercial speech, and not to core speech. While allowing that the publication of Hearn's ad in a typical city newspaper might not be unreasonable, Hittner declared that given the "nature of the magazine [SOF] and its readership" and the fact that many other personal-services ads "expressly offered criminal services," the reasonableness of SOF's decision to publish it was a question for a jury.

Similarly, he ruled that the question of foreseeability—of whether *Soldier of Fortune* knew or should have known that criminal conduct might ensue—"rests with the jury."

Eimann v. *Soldier of Fortune Magazine, Inc.* was going to trial.

2

MARJORIE AND GARY WAYNE arrived in Houston on Monday, February 15, 1988, the day before trial, and checked into the Holiday Inn, where they would spend most of the next three weeks. They were not strangers to Houston, with its sprawling growth and stampeding traffic. They came to Houston at least once a year, for the Houston Fatstock Show and Rodeo at the Astrodome.

This time, however, *they* were the show. When they arrived at the federal courthouse on Tuesday morning—Marjorie dressed in a blue dress with a white scarf, and Gary Wayne in a brown sport coat and light maroon tie—a herd of reporters and camera crews was waiting for them. All of the Houston media were there, plus reporters from CBS News, *The New York Times,* and other national media.

Ron Franklin had instructed Marjorie and Gary Wayne not to talk to reporters, but Robert K. Brown was not quite so reticent. When he marched up to the courthouse with his team of lawyers, he grinned at the cameras and gave a thumbs-up sign.

"Feeling confident about this case?" one reporter asked.

"You bet!" Brown replied feistily. "The Christians are in good shape."

• • •

Before jury selection began, Judge Hittner made a number of critical rulings that would define the nature of the trial. Larry Thompson had asked that only John Wayne Hearn's ad be allowed into evidence, and only the September, 1984, issue of *Soldier of Fortune* (in which Hearn's ad had appeared for the first time). For his part, Ron Franklin wanted all of the issues of the magazine, and all of the classified ads, in the trial.

Hittner steered a middle course: He ruled that all issues (and all classified ads) prior to, and including, the September '84 issue were allowed, but none thereafter. That opened the door to testimony about criminal acts committed prior to Hearn's ad but eliminated any later crimes, such as those committed by the Doc Savage gang.

Over Thompson's objection, Hittner also ruled that Park Dietz could testify as an expert witness (Thompson objected that he was not a *publishing* expert) and that defense witnesses could not testify about the magazine's "good works" (refugee relief efforts, POW-MIA projects, assistance to earthquake victims, etc.).

• • •

In a quick process, a jury of five men and three women (which included two alternates) was chosen. Interestingly, one of the men, a black Veterans Administration employee, was a former Marine Corps weapons specialist.

One year and ten days after the case was filed, the trial was ready to begin.

• • •

In his opening statement, Ron Franklin immediately drew the line in the sand upon which he planned to try the case—Bob Brown's claim that thoughts of criminal activity from the ads had "never crossed his mind." Franklin told the jury that he would prove that Brown knew, or should have known, that crimes were being committed, but ran the ads anyway—using their sensationalism to sell magazines.

In rebuttal, Thompson redrew the line on much narrower terms: He urged jurors to focus only on the wording of John Wayne Hearn's ad. "Mr. Franklin wants you to focus on everything except the ad in question," he said, and reiterated that no one at *Soldier of Fortune* suspected any criminal wrongdoing.

The first witness of the trial was John Wayne Hearn—by deposition. With Franklin reading the questions, and Graham Hill reading Hearn's replies, the jurors listened intently as Hearn described how he had waited for Sandra Black in her living room and shot her twice in the head, and told about the ten to twenty phone calls he received every day and the multitude of crimes that he was asked to commit.

"Did *Soldier of Fortune* magazine make your professional life possible?" Franklin asked.

"Yes, sir," Hearn replied.

"Can you think of any illegal act that was not requested of you as a result of placing that advertisement in *Soldier of Fortune*?"

"No, sir."

• • •

Next, Franklin called Robert K. Brown as an adverse witness. Larry Thompson had spent hours working with Brown, trying to improve on his performance at his October deposition, hoping to soften his garrulous image and make him more sympathetic to the jury. But Thompson's efforts went down the tubes on the second question.

"You heard Mr. Hearn testify that *Soldier of Fortune* made his professional life possible—do you recall that testimony?" Franklin asked.

"Yes, I did," Brown replied.

"Mr. Brown, given Mr. Hearn's testimony that you heard today for the first time, is there any doubt in your mind that *Soldier of Fortune* magazine facilitated the murder of Sandra Black?"

"No, there is not."

Franklin was stunned. He had hoped to force that admission after twenty minutes of questioning, but Brown had handed it to him after twenty seconds. With that point won, Franklin flipped three pages in his legal pad.

He questioned Brown about his familiarity with standards of publishing in the industry. Brown testified that he had never made any efforts to find out about publishing standards, that he had never heard of the Magazine Publishers Association of America, and that he had developed his own standards as he went along.

Then Franklin moved to the personal-services ads: "Mr. Brown, your testimony is that, of course, before September of

1984, never in your wildest dreams did you think that these personal-services ads might relate to illegal activities, correct?"

"That is correct." Brown explained that he had run the ads to give Vietnam vets the opportunity to "use their talents they learned in the military."

Using an overhead projector, Franklin displayed a series of ads, one at a time, and questioned Brown about them.

> COURIER, special services, will deliver or do job (anything, anywhere) . . . any offer, $20,000 or more. . . .

"Is it your testimony that in your wildest dreams you would not foresee that a person advertising to do 'anything, anywhere' as a courier for $20,000 or more might—*just might*—be willing to engage in illegal activities?" Franklin asked.

"I did not have wild dreams, Mr. Franklin," Brown replied.

"Well, I don't want to argue that point with you."

"I did not—the answer is no, I did not."

> MR. EMPLOYER: Ex-Ranger, 3 years Vietnam, will do anything for money, from bodyguard to ? Call Earl. . . .

"Mr. Brown, is it your testimony that it's not foreseeable that a person advertising in *Soldier of Fortune* magazine expressly stating, quote, 'will do anything for money, from bodyguard to ?'—it's not foreseeable that that person would be willing to engage in domestic criminal acts?"

Brown gave the answer that he would repeat throughout the trial: "I never expected, Mr. Franklin, that anybody would be so stupid to advertise in *Soldier of Fortune* magazine the intent that they would . . . commit a criminal act. It boggles my mind that anybody would be so stupid to do that, and I did not think that that particular ad would."

> COURIER, escort and delivery functions provided. Anywhere, anything, anytime. No questions asked.

"Again, Mr. Brown, your testimony—you could not foresee that that ad might relate to illegal activities in the United States?"

Brown tried to make a joke: "My crystal ball is very cloudy," he said. "No, I could not."

"Mr. Brown, let me ask you this: Did you ever *look* in your crystal ball, cloudy or not?" Franklin shot back.

"Often . . ." Brown replied.

"Mr. Brown, did you or did you not even make an effort to consider—to stop and think—before September of '84, whether an ad like this could result in domestic illegal activities?"

"I saw no reason to."

"So the answer is no?"

"The answer is no. Yes, sir."

The examination took on a singsong quality, as Franklin showed Brown over twenty different ads, leading up to Hearn's ad in the September, 1984, issue:

MERC FOR HIRE, high risk, no bullshit, don't contact unless you mean business . . .

"Never crossed your mind?"

"That is correct."

MERC FOR HIRE. Anything, anywhere. . . . no questions asked.

"Not foreseeable?"

"Did not appear to be a problem to me, no."

VIETNAM COMBAT MARINE seeking short-term work. Nothing too dirty, just ask. Contact THE ANT.

"Mr. Brown, are you really going to let this courtroom reflect that by your publishing an ad by a Vietnam marine vet saying 'seeking short-term work, nothing too dirty' that that's doing some benefit or service to Vietnam veterans?" Franklin asked.

"It's certainly giving them an opportunity to seek work," Brown replied.

"And, of course," Franklin added sarcastically, "I should get it clear on the record that it never crossed your mind that that particular person might be willing to engage in domestic illegal activities?"

"That is correct; it did not."

"If it had, you would have, I'm sure, done what?"

"I would have stopped everything—stopped all the ads."

Finally, Franklin read the "Gentleman Peter" ad, perhaps the most explicit ad in the magazine's history, which would come up again and again during the trial:

> GENTLEMAN THAT IS BORED in peace is looking for a bit of excitement. Within the boundaries of law if possible; has nothing against "crime" if sufficiently entertaining. . . . Gentleman Peter.

"Doesn't that give you a clue, Mr. Brown?" Franklin asked.

Brown reacted to this one. "If I had seen that ad," he said, "I would not have allowed it to run."

"Mr. Brown, I'm not asking whether or not you would have *allowed* it to run. We *know* you allowed it to run."

"Yes," Brown admitted.

"My question is . . . doesn't that ad say *on its face* that this person is using the personal-service classified ads of your magazine to offer his services to perform criminal activity? Isn't that what it says?"

"On face value, it appears to say that."

"Well, what do you mean 'on face value?' " Franklin asked.

"Well, simply because . . . the word says 'crime' does not, *ipso facto*, mean that that gentleman is going to go out and commit a crime."

At that point, Judge Hittner asked a question from the bench, which he would do throughout the trial. "Well, what else does he have to say, sir? What else does he have to say in order for you to think that he might go out and commit a crime?"

"Well, your honor, what I'm saying is simply because he says it does not mean that he's going to do it—although, certainly, there is that possibility," Brown responded.

Franklin jumped back in. "Yes, sir—and if you would have read that ad, you would have known that at least this one person was utilizing your magazine for the purpose of advertising the commission of crimes, correct?"

"That is correct," Brown replied.

Judge Hittner spoke up again. "Do you read your magazine?"

"Sometimes I do not, your honor," Brown replied. "If I'm out of the country for extended periods of time or when I have editorial, when . . . if I might enlighten you, sir."

"No, just answer the question," Hittner said gruffly.

"Okay, sometimes I do not."

"Did you read that one?" the judge asked.

"I cannot answer that question," Brown said.

When Franklin finally got to Hearn's ad, Brown testified that he had no idea how to define "high-risk assignments."

"You simply had no idea how a *Soldier of Fortune* reader might interpret the phrase 'high-risk assignment'?" Franklin asked.

"Well, that's very true," Brown replied.

The first day of trial ended with Brown still on the stand. Larry Thompson felt so emasculated by Judge Hittner's earlier rulings, and so discouraged by the direction the trial was taking, that he warned Bob Brown: "We're trying this case for appeal."

The next morning, Franklin led Brown through the list of crimes that had been reported by AP or UPI prior to September, 1984:* Robert Cotner, Curtis Terry (alias "Swamprat"), Lamoine Meyer, Margaret Sexton, Robert Konitksi, and others. Brown swore that he had never heard of or read about any of them, prior to September, 1984.

The Konitski case, which was tried in Brown's backyard, was Franklin's strongest evidence. He introduced four articles from the *Rocky Mountain News* and two articles from the *Denver Post* about Konitski's trial, all of which mentioned his ad in *Soldier of Fortune*.

"You didn't know about that?" Franklin asked.

"That is correct," Brown replied. He offered the excuse that he had been out of town during much of that time period.

Judge Hittner spoke up again from the bench: "Let me ask

---

* Judge Hittner refused to let Franklin introduce the NEXIS computer printouts into evidence, since there was no proof of which newspapers, if any, had published the AP and UPI releases. However, Hittner did allow him to question Brown about the incidents, after instructing the jury to give the testimony "whatever weight you choose."

you this, are you also saying that your staff people are out of town?"

"Well, some people are in, and some aren't, sir," Brown said.

Finally, Ron Franklin asked Brown about the new ad-rejection form that his staff had developed in early 1984, and why offers to "go anywhere, do anything" were disallowed if Brown hadn't suspected criminal activity.

"Well, one reason—the main reason—it sounds *silly*," Brown replied. "Obviously, nobody will 'do anything or go anywhere.' Otherwise, you'd have somebody practicing homosexual prostitution on the North Pole, which just is unreasonable. So, it does sound silly, and once again, the whole motive of this thing was to upgrade the image of the advertising."

Franklin asked why he had allowed an ad to run in the October, 1984, issue—*after* the new policy was in effect—that said "high-risk contracts, national and international assignments."

"I do not consider it to sound as silly as 'will do anything or go anywhere,' " Brown replied.

Franklin was incredulous. "Is 'sound silly' the test on whether or not you would run the advertisements?"

Brown was puzzled. "I'm sorry, I don't understand—*the test*?"

"Yes, sir," Franklin said. "The standard, the decision—what causes you to make a decision is how *silly* it sounds?"

"Well, once again, we struck . . . those phrases out of the ads because we thought that . . . they sounded silly," Brown said.

Mercifully, Franklin ended his interrogation on Wednesday afternoon. Thompson chose to reserve his questions until the defense presented its case; so Brown was allowed to step down. After taking his deposition in October, Franklin had felt that Bob Brown would be the Eimanns' best witness at trial—and Brown had done nothing to change his mind.

•   •   •

Franklin asked his next witness, Dr. Park Dietz, to characterize *Soldier of Fortune*'s readers, based on his study of the classified ads.

"While the readership includes people of many kinds," Dietz said, "in my opinion, [it] includes a higher proportion than you would find for most publications of people whom I would describe as paranoid."

"Why would they be attracted to a magazine like *Soldier of Fortune*?" Franklin asked.

"*Soldier of Fortune* magazine, especially in its advertisements, tells such people what it is that they want to hear," Dietz replied.

In discussing Hearn's ad, Dietz said that the *context* of *Soldier of Fortune* magazine—its articles, its readers, and particularly its ads for items such as *The Hit Man's Manual* and *How To Kill, Vols. 1–5*—gave the phrase "high-risk assignments" a special meaning. While publishing Hearn's ad in *Esquire* or *Reader's Digest* might not be a problem, to the readers of *Soldier of Fortune,* it was an offer to kill.

"It's not *Vanity Fair* magazine, is it, Dr. Dietz?" Franklin asked.

"No, it isn't," he replied.

"Makes a difference, doesn't it?"

"Makes all the difference," Dietz responded.

On cross-examination, Larry Thompson grilled Dietz about why he hadn't contacted law enforcement authorities—or Bob Brown—if he had suspected since 1980, as he had testified, that SOF was running ads for hit men. Thompson even laid some of the responsibility for Sandra Black's death at Dietz' feet. "If you had bothered to pick up the phone and call Bob Brown or *Soldier of Fortune* during that time frame, these ads would have stopped, wouldn't they?"

"They didn't stop when his own staff told him," Dietz retorted. "I don't see why they would stop when I called him."

•   •   •

On Monday, February 22, exactly three years and one day after Sandra Black's murder, Marjorie and Gary Wayne took the stand. Graham Hill handled their testimony. While Ron Franklin's lawyering style was combative, incisive, and morally indignant, Hill used a gentler, more empathetic approach. His job was to present the emotional component of the case.

He had Marjorie take the jury on a photo journey through Sandra Black's life: showing pictures of her as a little girl with her dogs, as a young bride, and as a proud mother.

"This little baby right here," Hill asked, pointing to one photo, "is that guy right over there in the blue tie?"

"That's Gary," Marjorie replied, "my pride and joy."

She painted beautiful word images of Sandra and herself can-

ning peas from the garden, sitting on the porch swing at Steep
Hollow on Saturday afternoons, drinking iced tea and throwing
sticks into the tank for the dogs to chase.

Then it was Gary Wayne's turn. All of the attorneys—Franklin,
Hill, and Travis Bryan—had been worried about how he would do
on the stand. Three years after his mother's death, Gary Wayne still
hadn't really opened up to anyone about the murder, or about his
father's conviction. He was eighteen years old, a senior in high
school, and a 125-pound cornerback on the football team—a
tough little Aggie. Serious-minded and painfully shy, he was given
to one-word answers. His first real girlfriend, Kathy Martin, who
was almost as shy as he, was sitting in the courtroom.

Now, in front of a jury, a crowded courtroom, and a gaggle of
reporters, he was going to have to confront the demons of his past
—his father having his mother killed and sending him in to find the
body—and explain how all of that had affected him.

Graham Hill had talked with him about his testimony before-
hand, but only briefly, so Gary Wayne wouldn't leave the emotions
behind in the conference room.

"What kind of person was Sandra Black, your mother?" Hill
asked.

"She always looked after my every need," Gary Wayne replied. "If I needed something, she'd get it for me. She was the one
that would take me to the doctor if I was sick. She took me to
school. She was the one that woke me up, and she just—she was the
worst person I could lose."

On cross-examination, Larry Thompson knew to go easy on
the boy so as to not alienate the jury. But he did want to make one
point, the same point that he had tried to make with John Wayne
Hearn—that *Soldier of Fortune* was not responsible for Sandra's
death. "Have you finally now accepted the fact that it was your
father that killed your mother?" he asked.

"It wasn't my father that pulled the trigger that killed my
mother," Gary Wayne replied.

"All right. That *had* your mother killed?"

But just like Hearn, Gary Wayne didn't give him the answer he
wanted. "It was *Soldier of Fortune* that gave my dad the way to do
this," he said.

On redirect, Graham Hill asked him about his fears of his

father. "Gary Wayne, why would you be afraid of your father if he was in jail?"

"Because if he could hire somebody out of *Soldier of Fortune* magazine to kill my mother, he could hire somebody out of *Soldier of Fortune* magazine to kill me too," Gary Wayne replied.

Hill had only one question left. He wanted to try to break through Gary Wayne's defenses, to let the jury see his vulnerability, his pain. He walked over to Marjorie's photo album and picked up a picture of Sandra, taken several years before her death. He held it up and asked, "Gary Wayne, what are you going to miss the most about this lady being gone?"

The photo caught Gary Wayne by surprise. His eyes filled with tears, and, suddenly, he was no longer a tough Aggie, but a little boy who had lost his mom. "Everything," he sobbed.

"Pass the witness," Hill said.

On that note, Franklin and Hill rested their case.

•   •   •

That afternoon, Larry Thompson began presenting his defense. Drawing on Bob Brown's contacts in the military and intelligence communities, he had assembled a star-studded cast of "image witnesses," all of whom testified that they were regular readers of *Soldier of Fortune* and had never suspected that the personal-services ads were solicitations for crime.

The most famous of these was retired Col. Charlie Beckwith, the founder of the U.S. Army's Delta Force, who had led the failed attempt to rescue the American hostages in Iran. When "Chargin' Charlie" took the stand, he was the living incarnation of the American hero—a real-life John Wayne. Grizzled, ruddy-faced, and rotund, Beckwith was a twenty-nine-year army veteran, a recipient of two Silver Stars, a Purple Heart, and a Distinguished Service Medal.

"I'm an army man, goddammit," he said proudly, recounting his career. "I'm very proud of that, Judge. I'm very proud of the fact that I served my country in uniform."

A collector of guns and knives, Beckwith testified that he read *Soldier of Fortune* mostly for its gun and knife reviews. He rarely looked at the personal-services ads, and had never suspected any criminal intent. "You read one of these, it sounds so macho-ish," he said. "It just didn't make my heart beat fast, so I'd go on to something else that did, that caught my attention."

With a former Marine weapons specialist on the jury, Ron Franklin felt that he had to dismantle Beckwith's heroic stature. On cross-examination, he asked, "You're not here today to defend *all* the words that Bob Brown has published for money over the past many years, are you?"

"Yes, I am," Beckwith replied. "I'm here to defend Bob Brown."

"So, I can pull out *any* ad—any classified ad out of this magazine published by Bob Brown—and you'd stand behind it?"

"Bob's my friend," Beckwith said.

The former Marine on the jury was black—as was another juror—so Franklin selected a racist ad from a 1979 issue (SOF had reportedly stopped publishing such ads in the early 1980s). "How about this one," he said. "'Revisionist and racial books, exposing the myth of World War II gas chambers, myth of racial equality.' Would you stand behind that one?"

"I don't have any problems with it," Beckwith replied.

"How about this one, 'Nazi, KKK, and extreme right-wing mailing addresses. Sixty organizations current in the United States, Canada, Britain, Ireland, and Australia.' Do you have any problem with that?"

"Yeah, a little bit," Beckwith replied.

"A *little* bit?"

"Yeah. I'd have to know more about it, but that—the Ireland part bothers me a little bit here."

"Just the Ireland part?" Franklin asked.

"Yes, sir."

"How about 'British racism magazine and catalog, $1.00, post paid from Tulsa.' No problem with that?"

"Sounds like a lie, frankly—British racist."

"Do you have any personal problem with it?"

"No."

Franklin tried another one, from the May, 1979, issue: "'Revisionist books, white pride books, send self-addressed stamped envelope. . . .' Have any problem with that?"

"What is it?" Beckwith asked.

"'White pride books' has no meaning to you?"

"Not really, no, because I don't know what he's talking about. I'd have to see the substance."

"Do you want this federal court record to reflect your personal support for a publication that accepts money in exchange for running classified ads dealing with white supremacist literature? Could you answer please?"

"I'll try," Beckwith said. "I wish I knew what all the substance was. . . . In some cases, yes, and in some cases, no. It's a double-barreled question as far as I'm concerned."

Franklin had made his point. In conclusion, he asked Beckwith if he knew who Gary Wayne Black was.

"Did he—was he supposed to work for me, or something?" Beckwith asked.

"No, sir."

"Oh, okay. Then, if I knew him, I'd tell you. I'm not good on names, but if they worked for me in the service, I—"

"But *whoever* they are, you're here to help out your friend, Bob Brown?"

"Yes, he's my friend," Beckwith replied.

"Yes, sir," Franklin said. "Thank you, Colonel."

• • •

Soldier of Fortune's other image witnesses included: *

• Neil C. Livingstone, a controversial author and terrorism consultant, who had advocated the assassination of the Ayatollah Khomeini and Muammar Qaddafi. Livingstone testified that the "Gentleman Peter" ad, and others like it, had a "strong dimension of unreality" about them, and were the "work of posturers and Walter Mittys, people trying to impress their girlfriend."

• Carlos C. Campbell, a former assistant secretary of Commerce, who had been one of the highest-ranking blacks in the Reagan administration until his ouster in January, 1984. Campbell called Bob Brown "a friend, a gentleman I have . . . a lot of respect

* Thompson had also planned to call retired Maj. Gen. John K. Singlaub, retired Brig. Gen. Heine Aderholt, and Dr. Lewis Tambs, former U.S. ambassador to Costa Rica—but decided against it after their names surfaced in connection with the Iran-Contra affair.

for," and said that he had never perceived SOF to be racist. However, on cross-examination, he admitted that some of the advertisers in the magazine "appeared to be crazies."

• William Askins, a retired CIA agent, who said that SOF was "widely read in certain circles of the agency."

• William G. Tidyman, an FBI agent in Boulder from 1973–1983, who said that he was not aware of any criminal activities linked to the ads (he had left Colorado prior to the Konitski trial).

• Dr. Lewis Duprees, an anthropology professor at Duke University, who specialized in the history of warfare. Duprees testified that SOF "gave me information I could not get elsewhere," and said that he used the magazine regularly in his lectures.

•   •   •

Thompson also called a half-dozen current and former SOF staffers, who echoed Bob Brown's position that no one at the magazine had suspected any wrongdoing. They also said that none of them were aware of the Konitski case, even though SOF subscribed to the *Rocky Mountain News.*

Joan Steele, the ad manager from 1984–1987, testified that she assumed people running gun-for-hire ads were "good guys"—like "the Equalizer." When Ron Franklin asked how she could tell the difference between the good guys and the bad guys, Steele replied: "I wasn't trying to make a distinction between good guys and bad guys. I didn't assume that they were bad guys."

However, Steele did admit that there was a special jargon in *Soldier of Fortune,* and that "high-risk assignments" was part of it.

"The word 'high-risk assignment' has a special meaning in the context of *Soldier of Fortune?*" Franklin asked.

"Yes," Steele replied.

"Essentially means hired gun?"

"To me, yes."

"To *you?* And you're the ad manager?"

"Right."

•   •   •

Ron Franklin and Graham Hill were still looking for a smoking gun —to prove beyond any doubt that *Soldier of Fortune* had known that crimes were being committed. Bob Brown and the SOF staffers claimed that they had never seen the Konitski articles, and Joan Steele testified that she didn't remember the phone call from Trooper McCabe. Franklin and Hill still needed irrefutable proof.

On January 29, two weeks before trial, Franklin had called Jim Lavine, a former Houston prosecutor who had tried the William Chanslor case in 1982. Chanslor was a former president of the Houston Trial Lawyers Association who had been charged with soliciting the murder of his bedridden wife. He had run this ad in the November and December 1981 issues of *Soldier of Fortune:*

> WANTED: Experts in poisons and chemical agents with access to same for lectures to civic groups. Excellent pay and expenses. Write to: John G. Thompson.

Chanslor had then called John Minnery, the author of the *How To Kill* books advertised in *Soldier of Fortune,* and asked him how to obtain poisons. Minnery, who referred to himself as "Dr. Death," had eventually reported Chanslor to authorities. Chanslor was convicted in August, 1982, and sentenced to three years in prison. His conviction was reversed in 1985, and, according to newspaper reports, he later pleaded no contest to solicitation of murder.

When Franklin called Lavine, who had left the DA's office to go into private practice, he had asked him: "Do you remember whether you contacted *Soldier of Fortune* magazine about that case?"

Lavine had said that he knew *Soldier of Fortune* was *involved* in the case because of Chanslor's ad, but he couldn't remember whether there had been actual contact with the magazine without looking at his case file.

"I'll try to get your file," Franklin had said—and moved on.

Now, with only three days left in the trial, Franklin and Hill returned to the Chanslor case. It might be their last hope to prove that *Soldier of Fortune* had direct knowledge of other crimes. On Wednesday, February 24, Graham Hill sent his secretary, Jaye Wright, to the Harris County District Attorney's office and told her, "If you have to sit there all day long, don't leave without seeing the Chanslor file."

When she got there, an assistant DA told her, "We can't find the file. I'd suggest you call Jim Lavine."

Wright called Lavine, but he didn't know where the file was either. "I think you're on a wild goose chase," he said. "I don't think *Soldier of Fortune* was ever contacted."

Wright went back to see the assistant DA, who told her, peevishly, that the file was "missing in action." Determined not to give up, Wright struck up a conversation with one of the office secretaries and explained what she was looking for.

"Oh, I think I know where that file is," the woman said. She made a few phone calls, and located *half* of the file in a warehouse for consumer fraud cases.

Wright spent several hours going through the thick folder, page by page. Near the bottom, she came across an empty envelope addressed to Robert Petty, an investigator for the DA's office. The return address on the envelope was *Soldier of Fortune* magazine!

They were contacted! Wright thought. Anxiously, she kept digging, and discovered a sworn affidavit, dated June 9, 1982, from James C. Graves, SOF's managing editor. At the top, it said *State of Texas* v. *William A. Chanslor.*

Wright, a petite and striking woman, started waving her hands and screaming, right in the middle of the DA's office: "I got it! I got it! They did know!"

Attached to the affidavit were copies of Chanslor's original letter placing his ad (under the alias John G. Thompson), a return letter from SOF's ad department, and a copy of the October, 1981, issue of the magazine.

Wright made a copy of the affidavit, rushed back to the courthouse, and showed it to Franklin. "This is all we need," he said gleefully.

At six-thirty that evening, Wright finally tracked down Robert Petty, the investigator on the Chanslor case, who was on a drug stakeout in Angleton, forty miles south of Houston. He told her that he remembered the case, but wasn't sure what other information he had in his files. Wright convinced Petty to meet her at his office at eight o'clock Wednesday night.

Wright, Franklin, Hill, and Travis Bryan all gathered eagerly at Petty's office that night. He went through his files and found a second affidavit from Graves (there had been an error on the first one). He also had the August 16, 1982, issues of *Time* and *Newsweek*, which contained full-page articles on Chanslor's trial—and mentioned his *Soldier of Fortune* ad. Petty remembered calling the magazine and was certain that he had told them he was investigating a murder solicitation. He still had his original notes, listing the names and phone numbers of the people he had called. One name on his list was Robert K. Brown.

They had found their smoking gun.

•   •   •

On Thursday morning, while Larry Thompson continued with his image witnesses, Franklin and Hill were trying frantically to find Jim Graves. Graves had been in Houston since the start of the trial and had been a visible member of Bob Brown's entourage.

Franklin and Hill hired a private investigator, Brook Todd, to serve Graves with a subpoena. Todd looked for him at the courthouse; at the Intercontinental Hotel, where Brown's party was staying; at Larry Thompson's law offices—but Graves was nowhere to be found.

That afternoon, Franklin began sprinkling Graves's name into the testimony so that the jury would know who he was. He asked David Graham, SOF's former chief executive officer, "Do you know of anybody on the magazine staff closer to Mr. Brown in terms of being able to influence him than Jim Graves?"

"No," Graham said.

"When is the last time you saw Mr. Graves?"

"I saw him at lunchtime today," Graham replied.

Brook Todd found out that a Jim Graves was listed as a passenger on a flight to Denver. He raced to the Houston airport, but the plane was already taxiing down the runway. Jim Graves was gone.

Franklin and Hill began to wonder: were their offices bugged?

Even without Graves, however, they still had his sworn affidavits. And they also had Jim Lavine and Robert Petty. Lavine's review of the Chanslor file had refreshed his memory, and with Petty tied up on a drug stakeout, Lavine agreed to testify. He would be a rebuttal witness on Friday, after *Soldier of Fortune* had rested its case.

• • •

Ultimately, Larry Thompson's defense fell squarely on the shoulders of Robert K. Brown. The image witnesses had portrayed *Soldier of Fortune* magazine as a legitimate, respected military journal, but it was Brown's own credibility that was on trial with the jury. On Friday morning, Thompson put him back on the stand to try and salvage the case.

For over four hours, Brown talked about himself and his magazine. He talked about his military career, his tour in Vietnam, and the early days of *Soldier of Fortune* magazine and Paladin Press. He described SOF's annual conventions, and the results of SOF readership surveys. Using an overhead projector, he talked his way through several issues of the magazine, summarizing articles about medical relief efforts in Peru, aiding earthquake victims in Nicaragua, and stealing Soviet weapons out of Afghanistan.

Judge Hittner's ruling that image witnesses could not testify about the "good works" of the magazine had forced Brown to carry that load himself, but it's always more difficult to trumpet your own accomplishments. By Friday afternoon, the jurors were tired, and several had trouble staying awake when the lights were dimmed for the overhead projector.

At the end, Brown tried to pull back from the line that he had drawn in the sand months before, in his Command Guidance editorial. In that, and in his earlier testimony, Brown had insisted that he would have pulled *all* of the ads "if it had ever crossed his mind" that any illegal acts were occurring. Now, he testified that even if he had seen the news articles about the Konitski trial, he would have investigated that *particular* ad but would not have necessarily pulled all of the ads.

On cross-examination, Ron Franklin came out firing. "Now, Mr. Brown, I think I may have detected a little shift in the wind here." He reminded Brown of his earlier testimony. "Has something happened in the last two weeks that may have changed your views about this issue?"

"Oh, I'm sure what I meant when I testified two weeks ago is it would be predicated upon a situation," Brown replied. "Certainly, if I did know . . . that they were going to be used for horrendous crimes—in the nature of murder—I would have canceled them."

"Oh, *horrendous crimes?*" Franklin said.

"I would consider murder horrendous, yes, sir."

Franklin reread the last paragraph of Brown's Command Guidance editorial, and asked him if he still agreed with it.

"In retrospect, I would have qualified that," Brown said.

"Oh, in retrospect of the last two weeks of evidence?"

"No, no, sir."

"In retrospect of having seen article after article putting your magazine on notice?"

"Well, that's assuming somebody saw them."

"And we know *you* didn't?" Franklin said sarcastically.

"That's correct."

Then Franklin started building toward his surprise witness and the Jim Graves affidavits. He asked Brown again about the Konitski articles: "Assume hypothetically that Jim Graves came rushing in with this information, Mr. Brown, and said, 'Boy, look at this: kidnapping, extortion, related to our back pages.' Would that have motivated—would that have been sufficient for you to pull these ads?"

Brown retreated to his new line of defense: He said that he would have run an investigation, would have gotten input from law enforcement officials, and then "based on the information I obtained, I would probably have stopped them. But then again, I can't speculate what I would have done four years ago."

Franklin edged a step closer to the Chanslor trial: He asked Brown if he would have pulled the ads if he had known that people were soliciting contract killers.

"If I knew that for certain, yes, sir," Brown replied.

"All right. We can rely on that big broad line?"

"That's correct."

"Because it would have been unconscionable for any publisher with *that* knowledge to keep accepting money in exchange for advertisements that could result in people getting murdered, true?"

"That is correct."

Franklin baited the trap. "Was Jim Graves your managing editor in the summer of 1982, to your general recollection?"

"I believe he was."

Franklin reminded Brown about the facts of the Chanslor

case, which Park Dietz had testified about earlier. "And your testimony, of course, is that you didn't know about this on or about the time these events were ongoing?" he asked.

"That's certainly true, sir," Brown said.

Franklin asked if he would have pulled the ads, had he known that Chanslor was soliciting a contract killer.

"Yes, I would have—I would have stopped the ads."

"Okay. If you had learned from some source, any source, that this man was using your magazine's ads to solicit contract killers, we know you would have acted?"

"Not just from *any* source," Brown replied. "I would have to have it from a good source, or several sources. If somebody just simply called me and said 'Somebody is trying to do a contract killing through a classified,' obviously, I would have questioned that."

"Fine—a *reliable* source," Franklin said. He asked Brown whether *Time* magazine qualified as a reliable source.

"I consider it, yes," Brown replied.

"Newsweek?"

"Not all the time, but generally so, yes."

Then Franklin sprang the trap: He handed Brown copies of the full-page articles in *Time* and *Newsweek* on the Chanslor trial and also brought out four-foot-tall blowups of the articles for the jury to read. "Again, you had no knowledge of that?" he asked.

"That's correct."

"Never heard of this case?"

"I was in Bangkok," Brown protested.

Franklin kept pushing Brown farther out on a limb, which he knew Jim Lavine would chop off. "You never heard about it?"

"That is correct."

"No one on your staff reported it to you?"

"No."

"You're positive of that?"

Judge Hittner got impatient and broke in: "That's what he said."

"That's what I said," Brown repeated.

"All right, sir," Franklin said. "Thank you, Mr. Brown. Pass the witness."

On redirect, Larry Thompson tried to steer Brown back to his narrow line of defense. Pointing out the "bizarre" circumstances of the Chanslor case and the innocuous language of his ad, Thompson asked, "Well, is there anything about this article, as you've seen in these exhibits, that suggests that Mr. Chanslor was offering to commit criminal services for money?"

"Not as I read it," Brown replied.

But Franklin came charging back on recross. "Your staff knew about this, Mr. Brown, didn't it?"

"Not to my knowledge."

"Your own managing editor knew about it, didn't he?"

"Not to my knowledge."

"Is Jim Graves still in Houston?"

"Pardon?"

"Is Jim Graves still in Houston?"

"I'm not certain where he is."

"Well, we heard yesterday that some of the witnesses, including David Graham, had lunch with him."

"That's correct."

"Where is he?"

"I don't know."

"Where was he spending the night?"

"I do not know."

"When was the last time you saw Mr. Graves?"

"A couple of days ago."

"Where?"

"At the hotel."

"What hotel?"

"Intercontinental Hotel."

"And what's your best knowledge of when Mr. Graves left [Houston]?"

"I have no knowledge. Obviously, after—a day or so ago; and I don't know whether he's left."

"You don't know if he's in town or not?"

"That is correct."

Thompson objected to the questions as repetitious and not relevant, and Hittner sustained it.

"To your knowledge, is Mr. Graves now in Boulder?" Franklin asked.

"I do not know where he is, sir."

"Thank you, Mr. Brown."

Thompson rested his case, and Franklin called Jim Lavine as a rebuttal witness. He testified about his prosecution of the Chanslor case in 1982 and about how Robert Petty had contacted *Soldier of Fortune* on at least two occasions to provide an affidavit verifying that Chanslor had placed the ad.

Throughout the trial, Judge Hittner had asked many questions from the bench, but at this point he asked the most important question of the entire trial: "Did they know this was concerning an ongoing investigation relative to a murder trial?"

"They did, your honor," Lavine replied.

Larry Thompson, who would have objected to the question if Franklin had asked it—on the grounds that it called for a conclusion that Lavine had no way of knowing—turned to his cohorts and whispered, "How do you object to the judge's question?"

The case was over.

•   •   •

The closing arguments on Tuesday, March 1, were divided into three segments: Graham Hill went first, followed by Thompson, then Franklin.

Hill immediately established the plaintiff's broad line—by reading Brown's Command Guidance editorial once again—and then zeroed in on Jim Graves's affidavits. "Mr. Graves's sudden departure from Houston was no coincidence, because it was time for *Soldier of Fortune* to pack its bags and get out of town," he said.

Recounting the various crimes, he said mockingly: "If anybody at the magazine had known . . . if only we had known." He pointed at Bob Brown. "You believe that he didn't hear a whisper from his number-two man who filed an affidavit in the case? They knew! They knew! Not only did they know about it, they came in here and tried to lie to you about it, and that makes me mad, and it ought to make you mad. It ought to be insulting to you."

Then, he addressed the issue of damages. He talked first about damages for Gary Wayne: "The question is, how do you arrive at a fair sum not only for what he's been through in the past but for the fact that when he walks up to get that diploma in a couple of months, his mama is not going to be there to enjoy that moment with him. . . . There may be those who say, 'Well, she wasn't anything special, she was just another Texas housewife.' But I tell you this," he said, pointing to Marjorie and Gary Wayne, "she was special to these two people right here."

Finally, he talked about damages for Marjorie: "Can you imagine anything worse, anything more horrible, than burying your own child? To bury your only daughter? Not only a daughter, but probably your closest friend?"

And from the plaintiff's table, loud enough for the court reporter to hear it, Marjorie Eimann said softly: "She was."

•   •   •

In his closing, Larry Thompson addressed one of the main legal questions that the jury would have to decide: Was *Soldier of Fortune* a "proximate cause" of Sandra Black's death. *"Soldier of Fortune* did not murder Sandra Black," he declared. "John Wayne Hearn did. *Soldier of Fortune* did not solicit the murder of Sandra Black. Robert Black did. . . . The blame doesn't rest with anybody else but those two men who have been tried, who have been convicted, and who are both now being punished."

He argued that *Soldier of Fortune* had no more "facilitated" the murder of Sandra Black than had the person who had sold Bob Black the gun, or the company that had rented John Wayne Hearn the car. "All of those things, of course, *facilitated* the murder, but did they *cause* the murder of Sandra Black?" he asked. "Were they the proximate causes of Sandra Black's murder? No more so than the ad placed by John Wayne Hearn."

He claimed that Hearn and Bob Black were ninety-nine percent responsible for the murder, but that others bore some responsibility as well: Mark Huber, John Gorris, David Huber, Gordon Matheson, Marilyn Soffar, and even Park Dietz—who had sat back and done nothing. "It gets down to such a minute thin thread to tie in *Soldier of Fortune* to this tragic event . . . that the thread just about disappears," he argued. "And we submit to you that it broke a long time ago."

Pointing out the four-month gap between the time that Bob Black first contacted Hearn and the murder, Thompson said, "At some point in time that you can't blame *Soldier of Fortune* forever just because John Wayne Hearn met Bob Black through a classified ad in the magazine."

He ran through a list of the various crimes. "So what do we have with regard to knowledge?" he asked. "We have Trooper McCabe. We have Bill Chanslor. And you have a list of other things that there is no evidence in the case that anybody at *Soldier of Fortune* knew about any of them. And I would say to you further, that if they had known about some of these things—one or two or even all of them—would it have risen to the level that you would, as an ordinary publisher, have said 'We've got a problem with regard to these classified ads, and we've got to stop the personal-services ads?' No, the answer is no."

Finally, he talked about Bob Brown. Quoting from an SOF article, Thompson described Brown as the kind of man who "believes in taking risks and undergoing hardships for a worthy cause, and receives satisfaction from doing well what most men would fear even to attempt."

"That's what *Soldier of Fortune* is about," he concluded. "It is not about the classified ads. It's not about a bunch of paranoids that Park Dietz is talking about. . . . and even though you may disagree with [Brown's] beliefs, you got to respect a man like that."

• • •

Ron Franklin had the final word. "I know you're sick of lawyers," he began. "I know you're sick of all this talking. It's going to be over in just a minute, but you got to give me my day in the sunshine here. I've worked hard. I believe in this case."

First, he attacked Thompson's arguments on proximate cause. "There are *several* proximate causes in this case," he said. "One of them is Robert Black. One of them is John Wayne Hearn. . . . But we're here . . . because of the role of another player. [Black and Hearn] have been judged. We are here about *Soldier of Fortune*'s conduct. *Soldier of Fortune*'s arrogance is why we're here today."

He ridiculed Thompson's doling out of responsibility for the murder. "Larry came up with this pie-chart concept," Franklin said. "Let's put up a long list of who could be responsible. . . . And this is the part I liked: he said, 'Gosh, how about the rental car agency. You know, what if they sued the rental car agency?' Well, let me explain the difference. . . . Everybody knows how to go out and rent a car . . . but thanks to Robert K. Brown and his magazine, he taught his readership how to do something that I, at least, wouldn't know how to do, and that is: Contact and hire a professional killer."

Franklin turned and looked directly at Bob Brown. "Thank you, Mr. Brown," he said.

Then he read from Hearn's deposition, where he described shooting Sandra Black twice in the head. He looked over again at Bob Brown. "Thank you, Mr. Brown," he repeated. "What some of their people describe as 'nonsense,' believe me, became a stark reality to Sandra Black and a stark reality to this fellow sitting right here," he said, pointing to Gary Wayne. "So, now we know how to do it. We could find a professional killer and a professional hit man. Thank you, Mr. Brown."

On an easel in front of the jury were the blowups of the Konitski articles, Jim Graves's affidavits, the *Time* and *Newsweek* stories, and other ads that Park Dietz had connected with earlier crimes. One by one, Franklin picked them up and threw them on the floor. "So, let's see, Mr. Thompson's argument, we need to put this evidence over here because he never saw that. Let's see, we take this and get it out of the way. Never saw that. Mr. Graves never talked to him."

It was Franklin at his theatrical best: outraged, indignant, and totally under control. When the jurors seemed to respond favorably, he kept going: "Let's see, what else I can find here? Oh, *Time* and *Newsweek* or Trooper McCabe. Yep, never saw that. Let's get it out of the way." He dug through the stack of posters. "Let's see, got to be some more back here. Oh, here's another Graves affidavit. Oh, there's another newspaper article. Yep, we never saw that. Let's get that out of the way." He threw that blowup on the floor too. The posters were piling up on the courtroom floor. "Let's see, what else is there? Yeah, we better take the ads too because we didn't know what the ads meant—we'll move them over here. Yeah, here we go."

When the easel was finally empty he said, "Let's see, that ought to do it. We can get the jury to buy that—and maybe if they're as blind to the evidence as Robert Brown was, maybe we got a chance, maybe we got a chance."

He was building toward a climax. "Ladies and gentlemen, I have too much faith in our system," he said. "I have too much faith in our process to know that's not what is going to happen—because you heard that evidence." He picked up a copy of the magazine and opened it to the classified section. "And it's about time to open this magazine—they can say all they want about Nicaragua, but in the back, get those out of here!" With one motion, Franklin ripped the classified ads out of the magazine. "And let's get rid of them and say the case is over, boys. The charade is over. Say anything you want in the front. I've not attacked the editorial policy of this magazine in one question, but it's time that the ads stay out of the back."

He concluded by talking about the plaintiffs' request for $20 million in punitive damages. Franklin admitted that it was a lot of money, but told jurors: "You're going to have the choice as a jury: are we going to shout or are we going to whisper?"

Awarding only $1 million, he said, would send the wrong message to *Soldier of Fortune,* which would be: "Boy, we skated that one; I thought we were in trouble for a minute." And if the jury did that, Franklin warned, "I guarantee you, the champagne is going to be popping tonight."

•   •   •

The jurors retired at 2:15 P.M. on Tuesday. They deliberated four hours that day, all day Wednesday, and four hours on Thursday. At 2:15 P.M. Thursday, March 3, they returned with their verdict.

"Has the jury reached a verdict?" Judge Hittner asked.

"Yes, they have your honor," replied Herman Castex, the foreman.

"Is it a unanimous verdict?"

"Yes, it is."

"Thank you. Would you please hand it to the marshal."

The judge read the verdict: The jury found against *Soldier of Fortune* on every issue. The jurors awarded $1.5 million to Gary Wayne Black in actual damages; $400,000 to Marjorie Eimann for actual damages; and $7.5 million to both of them for punitive damages. The total was an astounding $9.4 million.

Later, outside the courthouse, Robert K. Brown faced a sea of reporters. "Please understand," he told them, "that this was a terrible tragedy and a grievous crime was committed, and certainly we have a great deal of empathy for Mrs. Eimann and the son—but *we* didn't do it. John Wayne Hearn and Robert Black did it. And why should an innocent party be punished?"

Defense attorney Larry Thompson predicted that the case would be overturned on appeal. "You eliminate the emotions and the prejudice involved with the death, and the appellate courts are going to address just the First Amendment," he said.

As members of the jury straggled out, several stopped to talk to reporters. Jury foreman Herman Castex commented: "We wanted to arrive at a total that would set an example for other publications." And Larry Ganey, the ex-Marine weapons specialist, said: "We felt that the publisher was negligent—of knowing everything that's going on. He knew, or even if he didn't know, somebody on his staff knew what was going on. We wanted to let the country know, this stuff has to stop."

A few feet away, Marjorie and Gary Wayne were surrounded by reporters in front of the courthouse door. Ron Franklin and Graham Hill were standing behind them, smiling broadly. "We brought this case to get *Soldier of Fortune* off the magazine rack," Franklin said, "and I hope we've done that."

"We're very happy," Marjorie said. "I lost a daughter and he lost a mother, and we felt that something had to be done to stop the magazine and save other people's lives. We feel that justice has been done."

A reporter asked Gary Wayne for his reaction to the verdict. "I feel great about it," he said. "It's like my grandmother said, justice has been done."

3

ON AUGUST 17, 1989, the 5th U.S. Circuit Court of Appeals overturned the $9.4 million jury verdict in *Eimann* v. *Soldier of Fortune Magazine, Inc.* In a 3–0 ruling, the court declared that *Soldier of Fortune* "owed no duty to refrain from publishing a facially innocuous classified advertisement when the ad's context—at most—made its message ambiguous."

"Standing alone," the court stated, "the phrase 'high-risk assignments' plausibly encompassed Hearn's professed goal of recruiting candidates for bodyguard jobs. . . . Its bare terms reveal no identifiable offer to commit crimes, just as a locksmith's ad in the telephone directory reveals nothing about that particular advertiser's willingness to commit burglaries or steal cars. This ambiguity persists even if we assume that SOF knew other ads had been tied to criminal plots. No evidence linked the other ads and crimes to Hearn."

The court did not address the First Amendment issues in the case, and overturned it strictly on its interpretation of Texas negligence law.

•   •   •

In Boulder, *Soldier of Fortune*'s telephone-answering machine played a message saying that the office was closed "to celebrate our illustrious victory over the forces of evil. We just won our court appeal. . . . Thank you for calling, and Allah Akbar [God is Great]." One employee reported that the staff was out partying.

•   •   •

The 5th Circuit Court had done what Bob Brown and Larry Thompson could not do in trial: Focus the case solely on John Wayne Hearn's ad. Regardless of the evidence about SOF's knowledge of other crimes, or the explicitness of other ads, the court ruled that Hearn's ad was too ambiguous to assign liability to the magazine.

Thirteen publishing groups, citing the "potentially devastating" effects of the Eimanns' court victory on classified advertising, had filed *amici curiae* briefs on *Soldier of Fortune*'s behalf. These included the American Newspaper Publishers Association, Magazine Publishers of America, Inc., The Hearst Corporation, Scripps Howard Inc., and Time Inc.

Around the country, newspaper editorialists (including the Los Angeles *Times* and the Houston *Post)* and First Amendment scholars had rallied to *Soldier of Fortune*'s defense. "Distasteful as it seems, now is the time for all good media people to come to the aid of *Soldier of Fortune,"* wrote media critic Ron Dorfman.

On his own behalf, Robert K. Brown had hired a noted First Amendment lawyer, E. Barrett Prettyman, Jr. of the Washington D.C. firm of Hogan & Hartson, to handle the appeal. He also told his readers, in a June, 1988, Command Guidance editorial, that Ron Franklin's motivation in bringing the suit "related primarily to his or his clients' own political/social agenda" (he cited Franklin's statement about "taking *Soldier of Fortune* off the rack"), and issued a call to readers to contribute to the Omega First Amendment Legal Defense Fund.

Loyal readers responded by the hundreds—with contributions and letters of support. One wrote: "Looking at the plaintiffs in the photo [taken after the announcement of the jury's verdict] . . . it appears they have gotten over the death of their family member quite well. I think they have dollar signs buzzing around in their brains." Another wrote, "Keep the faith against the sorry bastards!"

•   •   •

The celebration over the 5th Circuit Court's reversal of the Eimann case was still going strong at *Soldier of Fortune*'s 1989 annual convention, held September 20–23 at the Sahara Hotel in Las Vegas. Over 400 SOF conventioneers—probably half of them dressed in cammies—wandered past the Sahara's blackjack tables and roulette wheels on their way to seminars on "Wound Ballistics" and the "History of the Assault Rifle," or to the poolside bar for the evening's pugil-stick competition.

Anywhere else, such a ragtag collection of aging camouflaged warriors and wanna-be shoe-salesmen from Iowa wearing authentic U.S. Army Ranger wings purchased at the SOF Expo upstairs (where you could also buy a Camo Condom for $1.50—"Don't let them see you coming!") would at least draw stares—and perhaps a few squad cars—but in Las Vegas, where *nothing* is surprising, *Soldier of Fortune* has found a home.

Robert K. Brown made more costume changes during the four-day affair than Ann-Margret, alternating between various shades of cammies, a black SWAT-team jumpsuit, and green khaki shorts with black knee socks that made him look like an overgrown Boy Scout. He was cheered lustily when he reported on the Eimann reversal on the first day of the convention.

"Well, the first thing is, we won the son of a bitch," he announced, to resounding applause. "Basically, we felt that these guys were just butt-suckers and were trying to get in our pants pockets. . . . You know, I have great empathy for [the grandmother] and her grandson. I think there's no question that they were manipulated by these attorneys."

The conventioneers were eager to talk to me about the Eimann case. "It's the biggest bullshit I've ever seen," said a short, chubby, bald-headed paramedic from California, who was attending his fourth convention. "Bob Brown's the kind of guy who would have immediately called the cops if he'd suspected anything illegal; and if they hadn't responded, he would be out in front of that house with a gun and killed the guy himself."

"All the ad said was 'high-risk assignments'—you can't blame the magazine for running that," was another typical reaction. The conventioneers were blithely unaware of other ads or other crimes connected to *Soldier of Fortune*. They have listened to what Bob Brown has told them, and believe him: The lawsuit was concocted by "butt-sucking" lawyers, out to destroy *Soldier of Fortune* because of their own political agenda.

The possibility that a sixty-five-year-old conservative God-fearing grandmother from Texas filed the suit because she couldn't believe that her daughter was killed by a hit man hired out of the magazine was incomprehensible. The lawsuit—and, more disturbingly, the *world*—was absolutely black-and-white.

One SOF staffer bristled at the suggestion that whatever enemies SOF may have in the press, Marjorie Eimann did not have a political ax to grind. "That's *your* opinion," he snapped, jabbing his finger in my face, "but I don't buy it"—and stomped off in a huff.

Included among the 400 delegates were dozens of law-enforcement officers and active-duty servicemen (many of whom were contestants in the SOF World Championship Three-Gun Match) and middle-American gun collectors and enthusiasts ("I just love old machine guns," said a United Airlines mechanic. "Shooting one's the most fun you can have with your pants on."). I also met a retired World War II signal corpsman who attends every year ("My daughter thinks we're all a bunch of wackos," he chuckled); a Portland man who came strictly for the Filipino martial arts class; and a sprinkling of survivalists, Walter Mittys, and a few truly scary kooks. As SOF's defense attorney, Larry Thompson, described them, "There were some people there who I guarantee you I wouldn't want on *my* side in a fight."

The cultural tone of the convention was set by the dozens of Vietnam vets, who played their Steppenwolf tapes around poolside (while some of their wives lounged in cammie bikinis), got shitfaced and reminisced about the war, and howled at younger, more foolhardy participants in the nightly pugil-stick competition (football-helmeted combatants bobbed around the pool in inner tubes and tried to knock their adversaries overboard).

The most excitement of the week was generated on Friday night when porno-movie queen Seka and "Bo," a huge-breasted woman with a propensity for pulling up her shirt for the crowd, battled it out to raise money for the Omega Legal Defense Fund. Each day, at the nearby "Survival Store," conventioneers could pay twenty-five-dollars and have their picture taken with Seka and Bo, topless, in front of a fake magazine cover.

"Seka looks all worn out," a navy man quipped before the pugil-stick showdown began.

"Well, it's not the years, it's the miles," his buddy replied.

At the awards banquet on Saturday night, E. Barrett Prettyman, the First Amendment lawyer who had won the Eimann appeal, was given a standing ovation and an SOF nylon jacket with "Top Gun" emblazoned across the pocket. Prettyman reciprocated the gesture by paying $700 for a Soviet Red Army sable hat (which Bob Brown had been modeling all day) at the end-of-the-banquet auction, with all proceeds going to the Omega Legal Defense Fund.

Talking about the Eimann case, Brown recounted his appearance on a talk show with Ron Franklin, where he had challenged him to a fist fight. "Seeing how Mr. Franklin called me a liar in the courtroom," Brown said, "[I told him]I would appreciate the opportunity for him to repeat that in the boxing ring or on the street corner."

The audience howled.

• • •

On January 8, 1990, the U.S. Supreme Court refused to hear *Eimann* v. *Soldier of Fortune Magazine, Inc.,* denying the writ of certiorari filed by Ron Franklin and Graham Hill on November 15, 1989.

Since the 5th Circuit Court had reversed the case without addressing the First Amendment implications (and had overturned it purely on Texas negligence law), there were no federal issues in the case.

Marjorie Eimann and Gary Wayne Black's lawsuit was dead.

• • •

Soldier of Fortune magazine is still not out of the woods, however. On June 22, 1990, a U.S. district court judge in Montgomery, Alabama, denied the magazine's motion for summary judgment in a lawsuit brought by the surviving sons of Richard Braun, the Atlanta businessman who was gunned down in August, 1985, by Sean Doutre, of the Doc Savage gang.

Savage's advertisement read, in part: "GUN FOR HIRE: 37-year-old professional mercenary desires jobs. . . . Discreet and very private. Bodyguard, courier, and other special skills. All jobs considered. . . ."

After the reversal of the Eimann case, *Soldier of Fortune* had asked that the Braun case be thrown out, because "gun for hire" was at best ambiguous.

Judge Truman Hobbs denied the motion, stating that the Savage ad "on its face, implies that the advertiser is available to kill others" and that "the publisher could recognize the offer of criminal activity as readily as its readers obviously did."

The Braun case was scheduled to go to trial in December, 1990.

When a reporter from *Forbes* magazine asked Robert K. Brown what he would do if he lost the Braun case, he replied that he might have to file bankruptcy under Chapter 11 or Chapter 7. "The plaintiffs will get a lot of old office furniture and stuff hanging on the walls," Brown said, "and I'll go across the street and start a new magazine."

• • •

Today, Debbie Banister is imprisoned in the Broward Correctional Institution in Pembroke Pines, Florida. She is serving a seventeen-year sentence for the murder of her husband, and a concurrent thirty-year sentence for conspiracy to murder Cecil Batie. She never responded to my requests for an interview.

Prison overcrowding in Florida has led to almost yearly changes in the rate of accumulated gain time, but under current statutes, she can expect to serve approximately fifteen years, and could get out of prison as early as 2004. She would be forty-eight years old.

On January 5, 1988, Debbie appealed for a reduction of sentence in the Batie case. In her handwritten appeal, she stated: "Sir, I was misled during my plea bargain negotiations, and under extreme pressure by my family who were co-defendants in this case. . . . I wish with all my heart to be reunited with my two babies. Please reconsider my sentence."

Her sentence was affirmed on February 12, 1988. Earlier, her conviction in the Joe Banister case was also affirmed on appeal. Her two children are now in the permanent custody of a relative of Joe Banister.

A psychological examination of Debbie in prison described her as having "a pathological intense need to present a favorable image to others whom she may wish to impress. Accepts little responsibility for offense and shows no remorse. [Has] a slightly arrogant attitude." Her occupational goals were listed as: cosmetology and a clerical position. "Inmate wants cosmetology bad," the report stated.

The prosecutor who sent her to jail in the Batie case, Ken Hebert, isn't worried that she won't serve her full term. "I have no regrets about the way this case came down," he says. "With the witnesses we had to work with, in the judgment of a bunch of redneck sheriffs and a Cajun prosecutor, it was the best we could do. Ask Debbie what she thinks of that sentence after fifteen years in prison. Tell me if she still thinks it was a good deal."

The attorney who defended her, Lloyd Vipperman, is also pleased. "This case was everybody's albatross, but I'm pleased with the outcome," he says. "Debbie, obviously, is not pleased— she's doing time. She'd like to see it all go away, but it doesn't work that way."

Vipperman, a huge bear of a man, believes that the plea bargain he negotiated for Debbie was one of the best deals he has ever gotten for a client. "I'm a defense attorney, I don't care about the truth," he says, laughing. "Here's a woman who committed two first-degree murders—or at least one first degree and one second—who will do a total of twelve to fifteen years in prison and be free. That is an exceptionally fine deal in a murder case."

He is, however, still troubled by the crimes themselves. "The thing that bothered me the most about the case was that I thought the murders were fairly obnoxious. It's one thing to want to kill your husband, and get mad and pull out the knife and stab him in the chest, or go get the .45 or the shotgun and shoot him. It's another to systematically plan the assassination of two human beings."

Wiley Clark and Don Denton, two of the investigators who arrested Debbie Banister, have not forgotten about her. Above Clark's desk is a framed photograph of Debbie standing over Joe Banister's grave, holding a red rose. The picture was taken by John Wayne Hearn.

And Don Denton, the Methodist preacher-turned-cop, sums up this woman—and the most fascinating case of his career—with a biblical analogy: "When you sit down with Debbie Banister, you can picture the horns and the tail. You think you're talking to the devil herself."

• • •

In December, 1988, Marlene Sims got out of jail after serving approximately three years of her five-and-a-half-year sentence. She will remain on probation until 1993. Shortly after getting out, she was able to regain custody of her two sons, Adam and Brad Batie, who had been placed in temporary guardianship while she was in prison. On the heels of the Eimanns' $9.4 million judgment against *Soldier of Fortune*, Marlene had her attorney contact Ron Franklin and ask him to file suit against the magazine on behalf of Brad and Adam. Since Marlene again had custody of the boys, Franklin refused.

Marlene and Frank and Iris Sims have moved from Gainesville back to Santa Rosa Beach, where Iris' family is from. They live off Mack Bayou Road, close to where Ivory Williams' house once stood, before Marlene and Debbie burned it down.

In November, 1989, I received a surprise phone call from Iris Sims, several days after I had sent a letter to Marlene's attorney requesting an interview with her. I talked to Iris for an hour that day, and again four days later. She was full of pithy comments about other people involved in the Banister and Batie cases. "You have to excuse me," she explained, "I have a weird sense of humor."

About Don Denton, she remarked: "At that time he was a lay preacher. I wanted to ask him—I wondered who he laid last."

On Wiley Clark: "Yeah, old Wiley Coyote."

On John Wayne Hearn: "John can't spell the word truth, let alone know what it is. If I were a psychiatrist, I guess I'd call him a pathological liar."

On Mary Watson: "She's a dingbat."

When I asked her about Marlene's guilty plea and confession, she claimed that Marlene had done that "to save her father's life" —and "it had cost her three years of her life."

She refused to agree to a formal interview without being paid. "After everything we've been through, the information would not be given away freely," she said. "We have paid a great price."

Not as much as Cecil Batie and Joe Banister, I thought to

myself. I explained that I didn't pay for interviews and that it was
also illegal under Florida's "Son of Sam" statute, which prevents
convicted felons from profiting from their crimes. Iris claimed to
have had other offers to tell her story. "Let me tell you this, we've
been offered over $2 million," she said haughtily. "Now does that
tell you something?"

"Yeah," I replied, not believing her for a second, "you ought
to take it."

• • •

A few minutes later, Marlene called me. "How bad of an ogre am I
up until this point [in the book]?" she asked, laughing. She said
that she hadn't communicated with Debbie in over a year, and
implied that she blamed Debbie for getting her in trouble. "I know
[the police] will have more to tell you about Debbie than what they
will me," she said, laughing again. "You'll find that out if you open
your eyes, all the way through this."

She also talked resentfully about John Wayne Hearn. "I never
knew how much he disliked me until he got arrested," she said.
"No wonder he hated me—anything that would take away Debbie's
attention or throw someone else into the picture." She believes
that Hearn committed other murders besides the three he has
admitted to. "I think three was all he got *caught* for," she said.
"Because it's obvious the man didn't have a conscience. Jesus
Christ, going to a funeral? Taking pictures?" She giggled. "Oh,
no-oo."

Then she talked briefly about Cecil Batie. While she admitted
that she would not have dropped the custody fight if the judge had
awarded split custody of Adam and Brad, she insisted that was not
why Cecil was killed. "Jesus Christ, why in the hell would I have
gone through litigation for three years and turn around and him
get killed?" she said. "He couldn't have died at a worse possible
time, and that's the truth."

At the end, she even tried to sound remorseful about his
death. "I guess you're about the only one that I'll go ahead and say
this to, [but] I'd give anything on earth if the man was still alive,"
she said. "I didn't even have time to mourn. I guess that was one of
the hardest things for me, because it took me six weeks to learn
how to say the word 'murder.' I'd never even had a traffic ticket!"

When I asked her to do a formal interview, she said that she would like to talk to me. I explained, as I had to Iris, that it was unethical and illegal for me to pay her anything. "I'm not worried about that," she replied, and said that her attorney would contact me to arrange the interview.

On November 27, 1989, her attorney wrote me a letter stating that his client was "anxious to tell her side of the story," but felt that it was "only appropriate and fitting that there be some financial compensation to her."

I couldn't help remembering Lloyd Vipperman's description of the Sims family as "a scurrilous bunch of liars."

•   •   •

John Wayne Hearn is serving three life sentences in the Kirkland Correctional Institution in Columbia, South Carolina. In January, 1988, he was transferred from Florida to South Carolina under the Interstate Corrections Compact, under which two states can swap inmates who want to serve their time in their home state.

Hearn's mama got him back. Corrections officials in Florida told Mary Watson that it would most likely take ten years for Hearn to be compacted back to South Carolina. It took Mary less than a year. "I worried those people—my phone bill would be from $150 to $500 a month," she says. "Honey, they knew my name everywhere in Florida and everywhere in South Carolina."

There is no doubt about that. Everywhere I went, the first question people asked me was, "Have you met Hearn's mama?" Wiley Clark, Don Denton, Tom Elwell, Charlie Sanders, and Farnell Cole all asked me. In Texas, Sheriff Ronnie Miller, Chris Kirk, Charlie Owen and Bill Turner asked me. When I interviewed two of Hearn's four wives, they asked me. When I interviewed his sister, Ann, she asked, "Have you talked to my mother?" And when I met Laurie Bessinger, the warden at Kirkland Correctional, just prior to my first interview with Hearn, he asked, "Have you met his mama?"

In June, 1989, I finally did. I spent two full days interviewing Hearn, and the next two days interviewing his mother.

Kirkland Correctional is one of eight prisons located on a huge sprawling complex in Columbia. It sits on a hill and looks like a big high school, except for the double fence topped by brilliant strands of concertina wire. Inside, after my meeting with Bessinger, a deputy warden led me past the security checkpoint, and through a steel-barred door that is electronically controlled.

We turned down a hallway, and there was John Wayne Hearn, sitting on a couch, waiting for me. I was expecting him to be in prison garb and perhaps handcuffed, but he was neither: he was wearing blue jeans, a button-down sport shirt, and white Nikes. He looked smaller than I expected. He stood up, said hello, and shook my hand—the nicest triple murderer you'll ever meet.

We spent the next two days alone in the deputy warden's office. At forty-five, Hearn appears healthy and in fairly good shape. His hair is flecked with gray at the temples. He has deep wrinkles around his eyes, the beginnings of a double chin, and a small roll of fat around the base of his neck. His forearms are fleshy but still powerful. His operation-scarred knees bulge under his jeans.

He talks very quickly, waves his hands a lot, and has a number of nervous tics: He constantly jiggles one foot and twiddles his thumbs. His face is very malleable: While recounting pleasant memories from high school, he laughed heartily and his eyes twinkled, but when he got angry, or sad, his eyes clouded up quickly. He cried often during the two days I was with him, talking about Vietnam or the murders.

He must serve two consecutive mandatory twenty-five-year life sentences—until he is ninety-five years old—before he has a chance of being released. Even if he lives that long, there is no guarantee that he will get out. Florida only established the twenty-five-year mandatory life sentences in 1972, so none have been fully served, and there is no case law on whether an inmate will get out after twenty-five years or not. "A life sentence means life," says Ken Hebert. "The *earliest* you can get out is in twenty-five years, but that doesn't mean you'll get out then."

Hearn expects to die in prison. "This is my home," he told me. "I have to make the best of where I'm at." He is in "B custody," which means that he lives in a six-foot-by-eight-foot room (not a cell), with a toilet, a sink, and a solid steel door, to which *he* has a key. The door is locked at 10 P.M., but otherwise it's up to Hearn whether to keep it open or closed. Inside, he has a color TV, an AM/FM cassette "boom box," and a small desk at which he does leather work. "If you went in my room you'd be shocked," he said. "I have knives and sharp-pointed scissors that I use to cut leather —all kinds of stuff."

Monday through Friday, from 8 A.M. to 3:30 P.M., he works in the prison industries warehouse, which makes and reupholsters furniture. Hearn is the head receiving clerk, and is in charge of seven other men. He has a phone at his desk (to talk to outside suppliers) and can make or receive direct phone calls. "It's just like having a job on the street," he said.

After work, he returns to his room for Kirkland's 4:00 P.M. daily "count," then goes to the library to take college courses on videotape. In June, 1990, he received an associate's degree in religion from the Christian International School of Theology in Point Washington, Florida. In June, 1991, he received an associate of arts degree in religion from Liberty University—founded by Rev. Jerry Falwell. In two years, he hopes to have a bachelor's degree in psychology from Liberty.

"The reason I'm working on a degree, I'd like to be able to talk to some of these young guys and maybe keep a couple of them from coming back to prison," he explained. "There's two things I love talking about: one's the Bible and the other's flying. I'll talk about either one of them all day long."

Several nights a week, he attends church services sponsored by Christian prison ministries. Then he returns to his room and stays up until midnight, studying, doing leather work, or watching TV. His favorite shows are *Tour of Duty* and *China Beach.*

"Sometimes I lay there and watch those shows, bawling, and I wonder why I ever came back from Vietnam," he said. "I have dreams—bad dreams—why didn't I die over there? If I hadn't come back I wouldn't have had my son, but other than that, I wish I hadn't come back. I hurt a lot of people. I killed three, and probably hurt a hundred—my family, the victims' families."

He claims to be a born-again Christian and believes that God has forgiven him and that he is going to heaven, but he still has trouble forgiving himself. "It bothers the hell out of me that I killed Cecil Batie, Joe Banister, and Sandra Black," he said. "I have a hard time dealing with it every day, and if it wasn't for me being able to sit down with God and talk about it, I wouldn't be alive right now—I'd have done myself in."

He is currently up for consideration for "A custody" (minimum security), which would allow him to work outside the prison. That is his biggest goal, and one day he will probably attain it. "Mr. Hearn is a model prisoner," said Tom Wallace, a deputy warden.

Even behind bars, his mother still appears to be running his life. She calls him two or three times a day, visits him on the weekends, and battles with prison officials over his treatment.

In 1988, Hearn was transferred to a new prison next door to Kirkland, which upset him because he had to give up his job in the prison industries warehouse. He was eventually returned to Kirkland, and believes that it was because of his exemplary work record. "[My supervisors] went straight to the prison commissioner and said, 'We need John Hearn back here,' " he said.

Sadly, pathetically, he doesn't realize the real reason—his mother was raising hell behind the scenes. "He thinks that prison industries got him back over there," Mary Watson told me, "but he doesn't know about my bitter battles and everything I did to get him back there."

His mother may be the only person who still doesn't believe that he killed anyone. Although Hearn has testified in three trials and admitted his guilt to anyone who will listen, Mary clings stubbornly—blindly—to her belief in his innocence. "I didn't ever ask him about anything, and I'm not going to," she said doggedly. "Until he tells me, or it comes from someone that I know is telling me the truth, I will not believe he did it. Because I don't believe Johnny did it. Even though he may have given you detail after detail, he might have told you how many ounces of blood that man had flow from his body, I still don't believe it. I believe somebody else did it. I believe Johnny was *told* he did it, or he was *programmed* —or whatever."

His fourth wife, Elaine Hearn, works as a waitress in Columbia. They are still married (because she can't afford to hire a divorce lawyer), but she doesn't visit him in prison. Elaine has accepted the fact that he killed three people, but can't quite believe that he did it for another woman. "How could she get him to do *that*?" she wonders. "I could never get him to do anything."

Although his mother is the only one who doesn't believe that he killed anyone, a whole host of other people don't believe his claims about World Security Group. When he was first arrested in

March, 1985, and interviewed by Chris Kirk, Hearn described his role in World Security Group as no more than a peon: He had delivered some unmarked packages in his truck, had flown two planeloads of guns to Kerrville, Texas, and had flown a plane halfway to "French Guiana," as he mistakenly referred to Guyana, before he got scared and aborted the mission. When two FBI agents interviewed him on May 13, 1985, he told them basically the same story.

By October, 1987, however, when he gave his deposition in the *Soldier of Fortune* case, the story had changed completely. After sitting in prison for two years, knowing that he was going to die there and had nothing else to lose, Hearn had become the *commander* of World Security Group: "I organized the missions, I trained the people, I was in charge." Today, he still maintains that position.

Which version do you believe? Had he downplayed his role in 1985 because he was afraid of being charged with other crimes, or is he lying now—embellishing his own exploits, pumping himself up—as he has done so often in the past?

Most law enforcement people believe that he's lying. They don't doubt that he got the phone calls (the cops monitored his Message World calls after his arrest and confirmed that he was getting ten to twenty calls per day), but they doubt whether he did any missions.

Sheriff Ronnie Miller is the biggest skeptic. "I think it's all bullshit," Miller says. "Hearn was on an ego trip, just like Bob Black. They both wanted to impress everybody with how *bad* they were, but ain't neither one of them got any balls. He'd get the phone calls and go in the closet and jack off, and he was happy, because for the first time in his life he was somebody, and he was bad. But I'm telling you, any guy that slings snot ain't bad."

Wiley Clark, Don Denton, and Tom Elwell are equally skeptical. Others are less certain: Chris Kirk believes that he may have flown the planes to south Texas; Ken Hebert started out believing that it was all fantasy but now doesn't discount that Hearn may have done a few other missions. Farnell Cole didn't believe him either until he recounted Hearn's story to an old friend of his, a former naval intelligence officer. "You're describing the classic CIA operative," the friend told him. "That's exactly who the CIA hires—they're such losers that when they get arrested and spill their guts, nobody believes them." Now Cole isn't so sure.

Two of the men Hearn called frequently have admitted receiving the phone calls but deny ever doing any missions with him. But then, would they admit it if they had?

The cops only believed Hearn when they could corroborate what he said. I was unable to do that with his claims about World Security Group. Only one person knows the real truth: John Wayne Hearn. Can you believe him? I'm not so sure.

In the end, we are left with the three murders that we know he committed. Hearn readily expresses his remorse for those but does so with obvious concern for his public image: He doesn't want to be portrayed as a cold-blooded killer. "Out of Debbie Banister, John Hearn, Marlene Watson, Frank Sims, and Iris Sims, there was only one person that apologized to the families for what happened, and that was me," he said bitterly.

For what it's worth, he has a definite opinion about *Soldier of Fortune* magazine and the personal-services ads. "Do you think that *Soldier of Fortune* magazine knew that there were criminal activities going on?" I asked him.

"From the way the ads were written, they had to," he replied.

He also has a definite opinion about Debbie Banister, the greatest love of his life. Today, he believes that she was using him all along, and never really loved him. However, even knowing that he will die in prison and may never make love to a woman again, the memories of Debbie's sexual powers still live on. Remembering her lovemaking, he shook his head, gave a little smile, and said, "She laid something on me that *nothing* will ever wash off."

•   •   •

Bob Black sits on Death Row in Huntsville, Texas. On May 29, 1991, his conviction and death sentence were affirmed by the Texas Court of Criminal Appeals—the first step in an appeals process that could last for many years. His attorney, James M. Leitner, had argued that Bob should not have been tried in Brazos County and that there wasn't enough evidence of his continuing threat to society to justify the death penalty. His case will now be appealed to the U.S. Supreme Court.

Meanwhile, Bob lives in a five-by-nine-foot cell in Ellis I

Prison Unit in Huntsville, in a wing with approximately fifteen other inmates (there are over 250 altogether on Death Row). Monday through Friday, he works from 7 A.M. to 11 A.M. in the Death Row garment factory, where inmates manufacture sheets, work aprons, napkins, caps, and adult diapers used by the prison system and other state agencies.

In the afternoons, inmates walk or play volleyball in the prison yard, and at night, play dominoes or watch cable TV in the dayroom (HBO and ESPN are popular). Many death row inmates, including Bob Black, make jewelry boxes and picture frames out of matchsticks, which they sell on the outside (Bob has made several for Gary Wayne). On Saturdays, he gets to go to the prison commissary, where he buys ice cream, tortilla chips, and sodas. He is allowed one visitor per week, for two hours.

In his cell is a bunk, a sink, a toilet, a small fan, an electric typewriter that his parents bought him, and a radio with headphones. He spends much of his free time at the typewriter, writing letters to relatives and to several women with whom he corresponds.* He also sketches, reads novels, and studies the Bible. In 1986, he wrote a short autobiography that he sent to John Blackman, his pilot from Vietnam, whose wife was planning to write a book about Vietnam. However, Blackman completely discounted Bob's autobiography. "I didn't think it was truthful," says Blackman. "There were too many things about events in Vietnam that I didn't buy."

During his first two years on Death Row, Bob wrote often to Gary Wayne, but their correspondence has dropped off considerably since then. The letters are the kind that any boy would love to receive from his father—until you realize where they're written from, and why. Bob offered fatherly advice on a variety of subjects: college, dating, cars, hunting, scuba diving, and money. He sent Gary Wayne dozens of religious tracts, newspaper articles on the dangers of crack-cocaine, and a framed copy of the Marine Prayer, which he had handlettered in calligraphy and superimposed over a sketch of two F-4 Phantoms. The prayer reads, in part:

* Teresa Heatherington is *not* one of them. She is now divorced from Ted Heatherington and is married to a deputy sheriff.

Keep me to my best self, guarding me against dishonesty in
purpose and deed and helping me to live so that I can face my
fellow Marines, my loved ones, and Thee without shame or
fear.

In other letters, Bob encouraged Gary Wayne to complete his
Eagle Scout badge (Gary Wayne was one merit badge short when
Bob was arrested but could never face going back to the troop after
that), begged him to send him photos of Sandra, and suggested
that he join the service.

Bob refused my requests for an interview, and has only
granted two interviews since he has been in prison. In April, 1988,
he told a reporter that he had never learned to express his feelings
to Sandra "because she was fat, and I was too proud," and added,
wiping away tears, "I'd take her back if I could, no matter how fat
she was." Ironically, Bob now reportedly weighs nearly 300
pounds.

In August, 1990, using the alias "Jim," he told a reporter for
the Bryan-College Station *Eagle* that he regretted what he had
done but was not in his right mind because of his stint in Vietnam.
"I miss [Sandra] every day," he said. "You're talking about my true
love here." He said that he believed Sandra and his family had
forgiven him and that he is convinced his sentence will be reversed
and he will be free again one day. If that happens, he plans to leave
Texas for good. First, though, he wants to visit Sandra's grave.

David M. Nunnelee, the public information officer at Huntsville, is a former *Eagle* reporter who covered Bob's 1986 trial.
According to him, other than the noticeable weight gain, Bob
Black is "the same as he was during the trial—always smiling,
always polite, always the perfect gentleman." Nunnellee adds,
however, "both Bob and I know that he's an actor. And not a very
good one at that."

• • •

Now that the *Soldier of Fortune* lawsuit is over, the television and
newspaper reporters no longer call on Marjorie Eimann. Although
she was disappointed about the Supreme Court's refusal to hear
the case, she doesn't miss the publicity—and never cared about the
$9.4 million judgment. "We didn't go to court for money," she

insists. "We just wanted the world to know that *Soldier of Fortune* magazine was running ads for hit men."

She is sixty-seven years old, with high blood pressure, periodic dizzy spells, and intestinal problems that forced her to be hospitalized three times in May, 1991. She still lives in fear that Bob Black will one day get out of prison. "I know I'd be the first one he'd have killed," she says. That fear is very real and palpable: she keeps the doors to all of her closets open at all times so that no hit man can hide inside.

One afternoon, recently, she walked into her middle bedroom and saw that the closet door was closed (her daughter-in-law had hung up some clothes and unknowingly closed the door). Marjorie started screaming, ran into the kitchen, and called the police. When three squad cars pulled up in her yard five minutes later, she was crying hysterically on the front porch. It took the officers thirty minutes to calm her down. "I could just see old John Wayne Hearn in that closet," she says mournfully.

In those same closets she still keeps all of the mementos from Sandra's life: boxes of old photos, her school report cards, high school scrapbooks, letters that she wrote from Hawaii, old pay stubs from Happy Face. These are the treasured keepsakes of a mother: Sandra's baby book, showing that her first smile was at seven weeks, that she turned over at eleven weeks, and that she walked at eight months; an IOU on a scrap of paper ("I owe Larry $5.00—SKE"); and her junior-high autograph book—"Good luck running for yell leader," "Always be a sweet girl—Mother," and a message from a classmate:

2 sweet

2 be

4 gotten.

What sustains Marjorie Eimann through her sorrow is her family. Every weekday afternoon, she picks up her nine-year-old grandson, Randy, from school and keeps him until Larry and Mary Eimann get off work. Randy is tow-headed, affectionate, and feisty. Marjorie feeds him an after-school snack (usually one of her homemade brownies and a Dr Pepper), then he plays "Super Mario

Brothers" on his Nintendo set or soccer in the backyard with Aaron Watson, who lives across the street.

Marjorie talks on the phone to at least one of her many brothers and sisters every day, she sees some of them every Sunday at Rock Prairie Baptist Church, and the entire Arnold family gets together four or five times a year—at Thanksgiving, Christmas, Easter, and the Fourth of July.

Every July Fourth they have a family reunion at the old Arnold Homeplace, which is now a city park. Central Park has a sheltered picnic area, a playground, soccer and baseball fields, and a commemorative plaque about the Arnold family's history. During the Christmas season, the park is decorated spectacularly with lights and Christmas ornaments, which people drive from miles around to see.

The Arnolds' July Fourth reunion fills the entire shelter. While the children play on the playground, the women gather around the picnic tables, talking cheerfully as they lay out the big bowls of potato salad and fresh field peas that they cooked that morning. Nearby, the menfolk in their cowboy hats and boots huddle around gas fish cookers, chewing snuff and drinking beer and watching while Larry Eimann and Bill Arnold fry up enormous quantities of catfish, hushpuppies, and another Texas delicacy: squirrel stew.

It is at times like this that Marjorie misses Sandra the most. She took me on a walking tour of the old Homeplace, showing me the pasture where Sandra used to ride "her" horse, the site of Henry Arnold's truck patch, and the tank where he made her "watch the cork."

Central Park was bustling: there were a dozen families picnicking, children fishing in the tank, a pickup softball game going on. It was a beautiful afternoon, with blue skies and brilliant white cumulus clouds rearing up to heaven. A gentle breeze was blowing off the prairie, and rustled Marjorie's curly white hair. She stopped to look at the manifestations of life going on around her, on a piece of land that is filled with memories of what she has gained and lost. "Don't you just know that Daddy is smiling down on all of this," she said.

•   •   •

"How is the son doing?" was the question I heard most often while working on this book. In truth, Gary Wayne Black seems to be doing fine. He is twenty-one years old and a student at Blinn College. He hopes to transfer to Texas A&M next year and graduate with a degree in business. In August, 1990, he moved out of Marjorie's house and rented an apartment about two miles away. Like any twenty-one-year-old, he was ready to be out on his own—but he still feels very close to his grandmother and still feels responsible for her.

He is shy and awkward, particularly around strangers, but fits in well with his friends. He is very much a Texas boy: He drives a pickup truck, keeps its FM radio tuned to the country music station, and loves hunting and fishing. The two places in the world where he seems happiest are at A&M's Kyle Field, whooping it up for his beloved Aggies, and on the Brazos River, where he often goes fishing with his uncle Larry.

I got to see him in both places. In December, 1989, I stood beside him (the A&M student body stands for the entire game) while the Aggies beat the hated Texas Longhorns for the sixth year in a row. I have been going to college football games since I was nine years old, but I have never witnessed such frenzy and excitement. We came home drained and hoarse from screaming.

The night that we talked about his mother's death, we drove to the Brazos and sat on a high bank above the river. It is where Gary Wayne feels most comfortable, most at home. "I guess you could say I've been through a living hell," he said. "There's so much you don't understand when you're fifteen years old."

Even at twenty-one, there is still much that he doesn't understand. He has dealt with Sandra's death fairly well, but his biggest problem is dealing with his father. Bob Black has never admitted his guilt to Gary Wayne, and still tries to act like the same old loving dad he was before. The closest Bob has come to an admission was to tell Gary Wayne that he was "sorry for everything that's happened"—but that could just mean that he's sorry he got caught and is on Death Row. If Bob would admit what he did, then Gary Wayne might have an easier time deciding what kind of relationship, if any, to have with him. But Bob hasn't admitted it, so Gary Wayne is still struggling to understand why his mother was murdered.

"Why do *you* think my dad did it?" he asked me at one point.

"For money," I replied truthfully.

Later, I realized that Gary Wayne's question went much deeper than that. I think what he was really asking was: "How could my dad be that kind of person?" That's one of the questions I set out to answer in this book. And the more I learned about Bob Black—his phoniness and his womanizing and his sick manipulations—the more difficult I knew the answer would be for Gary Wayne. It is a disillusioning experience to learn that your own father has feet of clay. It is also a weighty responsibility to be the one to deliver that news, and I have struggled with that dilemma more than any other. But I finally realized that there is *nothing* I could write about Bob Black that could even approach the horror of what Gary Wayne has already faced about him—that he had his mother killed.

And it is important for Gary Wayne to know the truth, since Bob isn't going to tell him. Bob will be around for many years (his appeal process will take another five or six years at least), still trying to win sympathy from Gary Wayne, still playing with his mind. I hope the lesson Gary Wayne learns most from all of this is that *he* is not to blame. We do not choose our parents, and we do not bear the burdens of their sins.

He seems to be learning that lesson on his own. While he hasn't completely broken with his father, he is weaning himself away. "I guess I'm sort of pulling away," he said. "My dad has this big dream of getting out, and has asked me about the two of us living together. But if he ever does get out, which I doubt he will, I figure I'll be married, and I'm not going to pay all my attention to him. He's the one that messed up his life, he messed up my life, and I'm just trying to go on. It'd be sort of hard to let him in the house."

He is a strong advocate of the death penalty—not just in theory but also for his father. "People ought to get what they did to others," he said. "I'd just as soon they go ahead and get it over with so that I can get on with my life."

He and Kathy Martin are making plans for their future. They became engaged in May, 1991, and are planning a 1992 wedding. Gary Wayne has worked hard to overcome the role model that Bob gave him about how to treat women. "I'm *not* going to be like my dad," he said emphatically. "I see more of my mother's caring and tenderness in me."

One of the hurdles that he knows he will face someday is explaining his life to his own children. "What will I say when my children ask 'Where's your mother and father?' " he wondered out loud, his voice trembling with emotion. "I guess I'll have to sit them down and tell them everything, and let them read the news-paper articles if they want to know more."

One day, he would like to talk to high school students about how he has coped with his tragedy. "There are all these kids who say they've got things so bad, and they go out and drink beer and smoke dope to make themselves feel better, but you don't have to do that to make yourself keep going," he said.

Listening, I wondered what made *him* keep going.

Suddenly, echoing across the river, there came a chorus of high-pitched howls. "Coyotes," Gary Wayne whispered knowingly.

We sat, silently and reverently, listening to the coyotes' lone-some wails. Below us, the Brazos rolled on, churning to the sea. Then the answer hit me: *This* is where Gary Wayne is grounded. When his nightmares come back, or his father's siren songs shake his foundation, this is where he returns—to the constancy of the old Brazos River, and to the deep roots of his mother's family in this valley. The river does not lie or deceive or manipulate. It just rolls on, steadily and forever.

I remembered the English paper that Gary Wayne had shown me earlier that night, which he had written on William Faulkner's *As I Lay Dying*—that wonderful saga of the Bundren family's jour-ney to bury their mother in hallowed ground. He had quoted from Faulkner's Nobel prize acceptance speech, in which the author affirmed his belief that mankind will not just endure but will pre-vail. Gary Wayne saw no analogy to himself, but for me it was striking: like Anse and Darl and Dewey Dell Bundren, like the old muddy Brazos, he will prevail.

AFTERWORD

On December 8, 1990, a federal jury in Montgomery, Alabama, returned a $12.4 million verdict against *Soldier of Fortune* magazine for publishing an ad that led to the 1985 murder of Richard Braun, an Atlanta businessman. The trial was almost an exact replica of the Eimann case, except that the plaintiffs presented even more damaging evidence that *Soldier of Fortune* should have known that crimes were being commissioned from its classified ads.

The most damning testimony was that since 1979, SOF has subscribed to Burrell's Clipping Service, which reviews some 17,000 U.S. newspapers and magazines and clips out any articles that mention its clients. Over the years, Robert K. Brown's personal secretary has collected those clips in four huge scrapbooks. Included are hundreds of articles that mention SOF, sometimes only in passing, from major newspapers, small town dailies, obscure weeklies, even foreign periodicals. Surprisingly absent from the scrapbooks, however, are over thirty articles from the *Denver Post, Rocky Mountain News,* and Boulder *Daily Camera* about the Konitski trial, in 1984, that refer to Konitski's ad in *Soldier of Fortune.* Also missing are articles about many earlier SOF-related crimes that were published in *Time, Newsweek,* the Fort Lauderdale *Sun-Sentinel,* the *Houston Post,* the *Houston Chronicle,* the San Diego *Blade Tribune,* the *Orlando Sentinel,* and the *Daily Oklahoman* (from Oklahoma City), among others.

Following the trial, Judge Truman Hobbs reduced the judgment to $4.37 million. *Soldier of Fortune* is appealing the verdict.